Methods of Teaching Shorthand and Transcription

Doris H. Crank
Northern Illinois University

Ruth I. Anderson
North Texas State University

John C. Peterson
University of North Dakota

Gregg Division / McGraw-Hill Book Company

New York   Atlanta   Dallas   St. Louis   San Francisco   Auckland
Bogotá   Guatemala   Hamburg   Johannesburg   Lisbon   London
Madrid   Mexico   Montreal   New Delhi   Panama   Paris   San Juan
São Paulo   Singapore   Sidney   Tokyo   Toronto

Z53
C7
<

This work is dedicated to John C. Peterson, whose untimely death occurred before the publication of this edition. He taught shorthand students and teachers throughout the United States the meaning of excellence in performance, humanness of person, and curiosity for learning.

Sponsoring Editor: Edward E. Byers
Editing Supervisor: Timothy Perrin
Design Supervisor: Judith Yourman
Production Supervisor: Priscilla Taguer

CREDITS

Pitman Learning, Inc., Belmont, CA. Publisher of Pitman Shorterhand. Shorterhand sample scripted by Roger Landroth, Baruch College, New York City, NY (page 17); South-Western Publishing Company, Cincinnati, OH. Publisher of Century 21 Shorthand (page 18); Employee Development Systems, Silver Springs, MD. Publisher of Quickhand (page 19); Science Research Associates, Inc., Palo Alto, CA. Publisher of Stenospeed (page 19); Educational Research Associates, Portland, OR. Publisher of P.S. or Personal Shorthand (page 20); Forkner Publishing Corporation, Ridgewood, NJ. Publisher of Forkner Shorthand (page 20).

Library of Congress Cataloging in Publication Data

Crank, Doris H.
  Methods of teaching shorthand and

  Includes bibliographical references and
index.
  1. Shorthand—Study and teaching (Higher)
—United States.   I. Anderson, Ruth I.
II. Peterson, John C., date
III. Title.
Z53.C7   653'.07'1073   81-3728
ISBN 0-07-031465-0   AACR2

Methods of Teaching Shorthand and Transcription

 2 3 4 5 6 7 8 9 0   DODO   8 9 8 7 6 5 4

ISBN 0-07-013465-0

PREFACE

Methods of Teaching Shorthand and Transcription is written for prospective shorthand teachers, teachers at present in the classroom, and those contemplating a return to shorthand teaching. The primary purpose of this text is the improvement of the quality of shorthand instruction in the classroom. The authors fervently hope the guidance and direction provided in the eleven chapters of this book will help shorthand teachers simplify the learning process, and will motivate more students to succeed in the study of shorthand.

The authors bring to this work a consensus of teaching/learning judgment, based on years of teaching high school shorthand students, undergraduate shorthand skill-development classes, shorthand and transcription method classes, as well as research evaluation. The methodology discussed is applicable to the teaching of shorthand at the high school, postsecondary, and four-year college levels. It is equally appropriate for teacher trainers.

Methods of Teaching Shorthand and Transcription is an instructional resource for teachers of all shorthand systems—symbol, machine, and abbreviated longhand. Some of the methods discussed may need to be altered slightly to fit the teaching/learning requirements of a particular system. For the most part, however, the methods, procedures, and standards discussed apply to any system of shorthand instruction.

Scope of Presentation

In an effort to preserve the history of shorthand, attention is given in the opening chapter to historical development. The following chapter discusses the shorthand program and presents examples of plans for teaching. Chapters 3 through 9 cover the full scope of learning shorthand and the application of shorthand and transcription competencies.

Recommended grading and standards are discussed in Chapter 10, with the knowledge that the grading and standards suggested will fit neither all teaching situations nor all students. In establishing standards, shorthand teachers will need to consider the system of shorthand taught, the length of the shorthand program, the abilities of students in the classroom, the length of the class period, and the availability of teaching resources. To this extent, the grading and standards provided are intended as guidelines and are based on teaching methodologies presented in preceding chapters.

The final chapter discusses research in shorthand and transcription. It is designed to serve shorthand teachers as a decision-making reference in the areas of teaching procedures, materials, and prognosis.

Acknowledgments

We express our gratitude to the many students and teachers the authors have taught in shorthand classes, methods classes, and improvement of instruction classes. These people have helped us to order our thinking, hone our teaching methods, keep pace with the changing needs of business offices, and keep in perspective the many-faceted process of teaching shorthand and transcription.

Doris H. Crank
Ruth I. Anderson
John C. Peterson

CONTENTS

Chapter 1

Shorthand: Past, Present, and Future

Shorthand is one of the cornerstone subjects of business education. Considered a basic skill for the secretarial occupations, it has provided generations of young people with a means of earning a livelihood. Most people are apt to think of shorthand as a comparatively recent curriculum addition because it meets the current needs of business. However, students were mastering shorthand systems for vocational or personal use before the birth of Christ.

Origins of Shorthand

The roots of shorthand are buried deep in the sands of antiquity, and its origins are shrouded in mystery. Historians have cited biblical passages (Jeremiah, Chapter 10, and Psalm 45) as proof that shorthand was used by the Old Testament tribes of Israel. Others who have researched the subject speculate that Xenophon, the Greek historian and warrior, invented the first shorthand system and used it to record the conversations and speeches of Socrates. There are a few examples of early Greek shorthand in existence, the earliest dating back to the fourth century B.C. Whether these methods of writing more swiftly consisted of abbreviating devices or complete shorthand systems is a matter of conjecture. Certainly there is no evidence that shorthand was widely used.

Roman Shorthand

Credit for the first system of shorthand is often given to Marcus Tullius Tiro, a Roman slave who was freed by his master, Cicero. Tiro's alphabet was based on the capital letters of Latin and supplemented by dots, dashes, and arbitrary marks placed above, below, or alongside the characters. Notice the similarity of Tiro's alphabet to our modern alphabet:

Tiro's system cannot be compared to the high-speed systems of today. For example, when reporting the proceedings of the Roman Senate, 40 writers were stationed in different parts of the Senate. They each recorded portions of the speeches and cooperatively pieced together the speeches afterward. Difficulty in writing rapidly was attributable in part to crude writing materials. Writing was done on clay tablets covered with thin layers of wax. The edges of the tablets were raised to prevent damage to the writing when the tablets were fastened together. Writers used a stylus about the size of an ordinary pencil for making characters in the wax. One end was pointed, and the other end was flattened for smoothing the wax.

Despite its limitations, Tiro's system became widely used during the early days of the Christian era of Rome. Emperors, statesmen, orators, poets, and philosophers were among those who learned the system or used scribes to write in the system. Its use became so widespread that the study of shorthand was introduced in the schools. Stenographers were officially recognized and employed in the legislative and executive branches of government. Father Stovik reports that with the development of the early Christian Church, there was also a demand for a record of the sermons of religious leaders, and the use of shorthand was given an even greater impetus.[1] Trials of the early Christian martyrs were also reported in shorthand by writers employed to make records for the public archives. Historians have expressed the belief that the Sermon on the Mount was recorded in shorthand by St. Luke and that St. Paul dictated the Epistles to the Colossians to two stenographers.

Decline of Shorthand

Shorthand continued to flourish in many walks of Roman life until the decline of the Roman Empire. With the successive invasions of the barbaric tribes from the north, society became turbulent, and the civilization maintained by the Romans began to disintegrate. During the next thousand years, a period often labeled as the Dark Ages and the Middle Ages, only traces of shorthand existed. Society was crude and few persons could even read and write. The arts and sciences, including shorthand, which were so highly developed in earlier civilizations, ceased to flourish. Little progress was made in learning and discoveries that could contribute to an improved way of life.

The countries of Western Europe began to shake themselves out of their doldrums during the 1400s. During the Renaissance, or rebirth of learning, remarkable discoveries and advances were made. The exploration of the New World, the invention of the printing press, and scientific discoveries by Copernicus and Galileo demonstrated the revitalization of society.

Revival of Shorthand

The first step toward the revival of interest in shorthand was made by Timothy Bright in 1588. Bright was an English medical doctor, who later gave up the practice of medicine for service in the church. His system, called *Characterie,* was not an alphabetic system, although it had an alphabet. It was impractical and almost useless, but it stimulated action by other shorthand authors, triggering a flood of systems during the next several hundred years. Butler, in his *Story of British Shorthand,* lists 460 shorthand systems published in the United Kingdom from 1588 to 1950.[2] He cautions that the list, though representative, is not complete, and does not include the multitude of systems published in other countries. The complete history of shorthand since 1588 would require volumes; we will describe only systems that were widely used or of major significance to today's systems.

Individuals interested in the historical development of shorthand will find that a surprisingly large number of sources exist for additional study. However, many of the manuscripts were written in the 1800s and are not available in most libraries. Two of the most readable and readily available sources of historical development are:

John Robert Gregg, "The Story of Gregg Shorthand," *Business Education World.* (A series of articles beginning in September 1933 and concluding in 1941).

E. H. Butler, *The Story of British Shorthand,* Sir Isaac Pitman & Sons, Ltd., London, 1951.

The first system incorporating alphabetic principles dates back to 1602, when John Willis published the *Art of Stenographie.* For the first time, provision was made for representing consonants, vowels, and diphthongs. Gregg, in "The Story of Shorthand," stated that the Willis system determined the trend of shorthand construction for the next three centuries.[3] Willis had evidently studied Tiro's ancient system, because a number of his alphabetic symbols were identical. Although Willis recognized the phonetic principle of shorthand, and his system was alphabetic, it was cumbersome and did not provide for writing fluency. Therefore it was still inadequate for stenography.

Even though Tiro is known as the father of shorthand, Bright is credited for reviving an interest in it, and John Willis is noted for authoring the first system based on alphabetic principles. Edmund Willis is given credit for developing in 1618 the first system that was practical for stenographic use. His alphabet was based primarily on straight lines and simple curves. This system was widely used in England, and there is evidence of its use in the American colonies. The influence of the Willis system is still felt today because part of his original alphabet is used in modern systems.

More than 40 shorthand systems were developed in England in the 1600s.[4] The religious fervor of the Reformation created a desire to record sermons, and many of the systems were developed by the wealthy and influential or by church leaders.

Thomas Shelton's "Shortwriting" was invented in 1626 and is remembered because Samuel Pepys, the famous English diarist, used it to record such events as the Great Fire of London and the Great Plague. Shelton borrowed heavily from the alphabets of John and Edmund Willis, but he introduced the concept of phrasing when he suggested how to make long marks to stand for whole sentences.

The first edition of *Semography* was published in 1642 under the name of William Cartwright and published by his nephew, Jeremiah Rich. In later editions only the name of Rich appeared. Consequently, there is controversy as to whether Rich used Cartwright as a pen name, or whether Cartwright actually invented the system. Semography was an improvement over previous systems, even though 14 of the characters were borrowed from Edmund Willis. As in preceding systems, arbitrary signs were devised and incorporated in his system. Arbitrary signs can probably be best described as word pictures often denoting scriptural terms but having no relationship to a shorthand alphabet. The following are a few examples of arbitrary signs.[5]

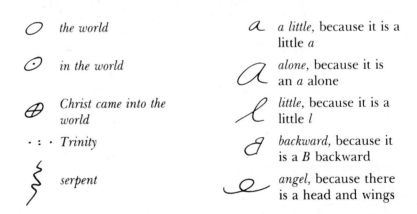

the world	*a little,* because it is a little *a*
in the world	*alone,* because it is an *a* alone
Christ came into the world	*little,* because it is a little *l*
Trinity	*backward,* because it is a *B* backward
serpent	*angel,* because there is a head and wings

William Mason published the first edition of his system, *Pen Pluck'd From an Eagle's Wing,* in 1642. He, too, borrowed much of his alphabet from other authors. However, as time went on, he improved and simplified the system so much that some authorities cite him as the greatest inventor of the seventeenth century. He made two other lasting contributions to shorthand history by reducing the use of the arbitrary signs common to all previous systems, and he sold his books for a comparatively low price.

Thomas Gurney is probably the best known of the eighteenth century shorthand inventors, even though he appropriated most of his alphabet from Mason's 1707 edition. He and his descendants are given credit for popularizing shorthand and expanding it beyond religious uses in England. The House of Gurney supplied official shorthand reporters to the British Parliament, and among writers of the Gurney system was novelist Charles Dickens. Butler states:

> In its beginnings, shorthand was for more than a century largely regarded as a means of bringing the Word of God to the people. Its uses were two: the preservation of pulpit teachings of the day, and the maintenance of secrecy in diaries and confidential papers. Occasionally it was found being used for the report of trials and farewell speeches by those about to die at the hand of the executioner, but in the main it was an academic subject and its transition to present-day uses was slow. Not until the arrival of the Gurneys on the scene was shorthand put to regular professional use, and even then its acceptance was not immediate.[6]

John Byrom's *Universal English Shorthand* was published in 1767. His alphabet was based on the circle and its various segments, and the style was termed *geometric shorthand*. Isaac Pitman, who was to publish one of the world's great systems in the 1800s, may have been influenced by Byrom's geometric principles for forming the alphabet. It is probable, too, that John Robert Gregg secured ideas for a natural flow of writing from Byrom's system. Byrom was also a well-known poet, writer, and composer of hymns. Several of his hymns are still sung. Byrom was a friend of John and Charles Wesley, founders of the Methodist Church, who learned and used his shorthand system.

Other writers who contributed to shorthand history in the 1700s were William Williamson, Samuel Taylor, Simon Bordley, and William Mayer.

Origins of Today's Shorthand

Interest in the construction of shorthand systems reached its height in England during the 1800s. Butler lists 281 different systems published in the United Kingdom during this 100-year span.[7] The intense preoccupation with shorthand resulted in the publication of three systems that are still extensively used. Two of them, Gregg and

Pitman, are synonymous with the word *shorthand* in nearly all parts of the world today.

A cursive system of shorthand was invented by a German, Franz Gabelsburger, in 1834. His shorthand, "Speed-Sign Art," was distinguished from other systems by alphabetic characters similar to strokes used in cursive longhand. The cursive nature of Gabelsburger's shorthand may have influenced John Robert Gregg when he invented his system more than 50 years later. Gabelsburger shorthand, known for its beauty of outlines, is still used in Europe today.

Isaac Pitman was born in England in 1813. As a young schoolmaster, he developed two consuming interests that he maintained until his death in 1897. Butler states: "To the end of his days, he labored for the general adoption of a system of phonetic spelling, but his crusade was as complete a failure as his Phonography was a success."[8]

As a youngster, Pitman learned an adaptation of Taylor shorthand, which encouraged him to publish his first book, *Stenographic Sound-Hand*. The book was primarily an improvement on Taylor's system; but a few years later, in 1840, he published a second edition entitled *Phonography* which bore some resemblance to Taylor shorthand. Throughout his life, Isaac Pitman continued to revise the system, so that today Pitman shorthand has little similarity to the first edition of 1837.

Pitman's brother Benn helped him market the system in England by serving as a traveling teacher and lecturer extolling its virtues. The success of Pitman shorthand in England was rapid, and it soon became the predominant system. Naether states that the system was being taught in 1,260 English schools in 1890.[9] In 1852, Benn Pitman introduced the ninth edition of Pitman Shorthand in the United States. From his headquarters in Cincinnati, he began teaching and lecturing to publicize Pitman shorthand. While Benn Pitman continued to market the ninth edition in America, Isaac Pitman continued to make revisions in succeeding editions. Thus two versions of Pitman continued to be marketed, the ninth edition in America and revised editions in most other parts of the world.

Even though Pitman shorthand reigned supreme in England by 1880, shorthand systems based on entirely different principles were being invented in other countries. Most English systems were patterned after Pitman's geometric principles, but German systems were heavily influenced by Gabelsburger's cursive system. In France, emphasis was on the development of systems that would be simple enough to teach in the elementary schools. Coulon invented a simplified system in 1778, which was widely used; and Emil Duployé, a minister, continued to develop an even more learnable system. In 1861 Duployé published a system consisting of only an alphabet and instructions for writing as words were sounded.

Origins of Gregg Shorthand

The history of Gregg Shorthand is of interest because the system is so predominant in the United States. John Robert Gregg, the youngest of five children, was born in Ireland in 1867. Although not considered a bright scholar when compared to his brothers and sisters, he became interested in shorthand while observing a family friend record a sermon. The experience motivated him to learn an adaptation of Taylor shorthand. Because of his success in mastering shorthand, he developed a consuming interest in it that led him to study other systems. On the basis of his study, probably influenced by a number of different systems, he started as a teenager to develop a new system. Gregg's elimination of position writing and shading prevalent in Pitmanlike systems, may have originated from adaptations of Taylor's system. The idea of inserting vowels within the shorthand outline in their natural order, the use of circles and hooks, and the simplification of the system may have stemmed from his study of French systems. The German systems, which used symbols similar in formation and slope to longhand characters, could have influenced the basic principles of Gregg's shorthand. His study and labor resulted in the publication in 1888 of a 28-page pamphlet outlining the system. Although some of the principles appearing in *Light Line Phonography* had been used in other systems, the little booklet was a revolutionary departure from existing systems.

The early years of Light Line Phonography were difficult. Pitman Shorthand reigned supreme in England, and dozens of other systems were being promoted. Gregg, with unshakable faith in the merits of his new system, expounded it with tireless energy.

Growth of Gregg Shorthand

In 1893, Gregg made a trip to the United States to publish an American copyright edition. Although his stay in America was to be temporary, the eventual success of Gregg Shorthand encouraged him to establish permanent residence. He and a colleague established a school in Boston and began teaching, but their monetary rewards were meager. Two years later he moved to Chicago, and Gregg Shorthand began to prosper.

Even though 313 copyrights had been issued in the United States between 1880 and 1916 for shorthand systems or their revisions, a study by the Bureau of Education in 1910 revealed that Gregg Shorthand was already being taught in twice as many schools as any other single system.[10] Factors that may have contributed to the remarkable success of Gregg Shorthand in America include:

1. The comparative ease of learning the system and the achievements of learners.

2. The growth of public high schools at the time Gregg Shorthand was being introduced.
3. The increasing use of shorthand in business offices, creating a demand for the study of shorthand in high schools and private business colleges.

Changing Applications of Shorthand

During the period when Gregg and Pitman Shorthand were developing into worldwide systems, subtle changes were occurring in the uses of shorthand. During the sixteenth and through most of the nineteenth centuries, the ability to read and write shorthand was highly prized. Not necessarily associated with commercial undertakings, shorthand was considered an integral skill of the educated man. Many early ministers, priests, lawyers, doctors, journalists, and writers used shorthand to promote and supplement their intellectual activities. They often recorded dictation—particularly of interesting sermons—verbatim, but their skill was also used as a method of secret writing; to draft speeches and manuscripts of books, and to summarize speeches and writings. In other words, shorthand had many applications, but few were directly related to commercial undertakings.

When the typewriter became a popular business tool in the 1880s and 1890s, enterprising individuals were quick to see the merit of combining shorthand and typewriting skills into a new skill which would be highly marketable in business. The remarkable success of typewriting-shorthand in business offices opened new career paths for women in stenographic and secretarial occupations. Today's shorthand classrooms are filled with young people who wish to acquire a skill that can be used in business offices. The objectives of shorthand have become vocational, and other applications of shorthand have been ignored or forgotten by most shorthand teachers and students.

Recent Shorthand Systems

Recent efforts of shorthand inventors, with the notable exception of *Century 21 Shorthand*, have focused on the development of alphabetic systems. Although such systems include alphabets based on abbreviations of longhand letters, the concept is not new. Since Andrew Graham published *Brief Longhand* in the 1800s, contemporary authors have been motivated to produce systems that shorten learning time and reduce learning difficulty while achieving the speed potential of symbol systems like Gregg and Pitman shorthand. The following is a partial listing of systems and their publication dates: *Speedwriting* (1923), *HySpeed Longhand* (1932), *Abbreviatrix* (1945), *Zinman* (1950), *Stenoscript* (1950), *Forkner Shorthand* (1952), *Stenospeed* (1953), *Rapid Writing* (1953), *Briefhand* (1957), and *Quickhand* (1974).

Abbreviated longhand systems are commonly taught in proprietary business schools or marketed as self-study courses. They are not taught extensively in public secondary and postsecondary schools, except Forkner Shorthand, which is taught in some areas of the country.

Century 21 Shorthand, a symbol system, was published in 1974. Dr. Edward Christensen of Brigham Young University led a team of authors in developing the system. Using some of the same alphabetic strokes as Gregg Shorthand, Century 21 is characterized by one-direction writing of primary alphabetic symbols.

Future of Shorthand

The demise of shorthand has been predicted since Thomas Edison invented the phonograph, although there is no evidence that shorthand has become or will become obsolete. Two developments have contributed to these mistaken assumptions—the expanded use of dictation-transcription machines and the recent development of sophisticated word processing systems. Impressive statistics are cited that reveal the expanded use of dictation-transcription hardware in business, but the conclusion that shorthand is an archaic subject is fallacious.

Understanding Word Processing

To understand why word processing or other hardware will not eliminate the need for shorthand writers in business and service organizations, it is important to understand the basics behind word processing.

Word processing is a new concept, which originated in Germany during the 1960s after the introduction of the IBM Magnetic Tape Selectric Typewriter. There are essentially three basic components of word processing systems—automatic typewriters, transcription machines, and communication links between dictators and recording machines. The division of labor principle is applied to the duties of the traditional secretary. Responsibility for recording and transcribing communications is transferred to correspondence secretaries, or word processing operators, who, because of specialization and automated typewriters, can produce typed communications more efficiently than traditional secretaries can.

Because many of the shorthand-typing responsibilities are transferred to a word processing department, traditional secretaries are freed to become administrative secretaries. They have the time to assume more responsible duties or to work for more supervisors. Manufacturers of word processing systems can quote impressive productivity gains in firms using the systems, and there is irrefutable evidence that word processing improves efficiency if properly implemented. Thus many people have reached the erroneous conclusion that there will be no need for shorthand; the facts show otherwise.

By 1977, approximately 20 percent of all companies in the United States had established word processing centers and the number will continue to increase.[11] However, word processing will not sweep the country in the way that the typewriter replaced longhand in business. The hardware and implementation is too expensive for some organizations. Word processing systems are designed for high-volume correspondence, and small companies or organizations with low-volume correspondence will not consider such installations economically feasible. Other individuals or organizations will not adopt the equipment because of a preference for face-to-face dictation to a secretary, because of the prestige often associated with having a personal secretary, or because of a need for confidentiality in communications. Secretaries armed with excellent shorthand-transcription skills will continue to find responsible positions and be indispensable to these organizations.

Research on Word Processing and Shorthand Use

Unfortunately, research on the effect of dictating equipment on manual shorthand use has been limited to specific geographic areas of the country. However, a composite of the findings may provide a partial national picture of future job opportunities for office workers with manual shorthand skills and support conjectures on the future of shorthand. The following research bears on the problem:

- Fujii (1971) surveyed businesses in Honolulu, Hawaii, to determine the use of manual shorthand, machine shorthand, and dictating-transcribing equipment.[12] She found that manual shorthand was used more than either machine shorthand or dictating-transcribing machines in the Honolulu area. She concluded that if there was a trend toward the increased use of dictation-transcription machines and a decrease in the use of manual shorthand, it was just beginning.
- Bernstein (1974) surveyed 95 businesses in Cherokee County, South Carolina, to assess the number and kinds of office machines being used.[13] She found that transcribing machines were used in 20 percent of the businesses. However, an increase in the use of dictation hardware was projected.
- Harris (1976) interviewed personnel managers and transcription workers in metropolitan Atlanta, Georgia, to measure the use of manual shorthand, machine shorthand, and dictating-transcribing equipment.[14] Of the 28 personnel managers interviewed, 21, or 75 percent, indicated that manual shorthand was used in their firms; and 25, or 89 percent, also employed workers to operate dictation-

transcription machines. Machine shorthand was not used by the transcription workers in the sample.

- Kennedy (1973) surveyed 42 selected businesses in the San Jose area of California to determine the extent to which word processing had been implemented.[15] She found that 34 percent of the businesses, all of them large, used word processing. However, 61 percent of the businesses favored shorthand, 14 percent required skills in both shorthand and machine transcription, and 24 percent required skill in operating transcribing machines. Eighty-eight percent of the 42 respondents said that shorthand should continue to be offered in the high schools.

- Olson (1973) determined the systems used to record and transcribe business office dictation in Milwaukee, Wisconsin.[16] She found that 89 percent of the firms reported that some office workers used manual shorthand and that 72 percent used dictation-transcribing machines. Of the 1,541 office workers included in the sample, 38 percent used manual shorthand exclusively, 31 percent used transcription machines exclusively, 29 percent used a combination of shorthand and transcribing machines, and 2 percent used machine shorthand only.

- Sain (1972) conducted a survey to determine the number and types of office machines used in York County, South Carolina.[17] She found that transcribing equipment was used in one-third of the offices.

- Williamson (1973), analyzing the responses of 274 Utah businesses, found that dictation-transcribing machines were used in 30.7 percent of the units in her sample, but were not used in 69.3 percent.[18]

- Biggers (1969) determined and compared the status of shorthand and recording machines in representative business firms in Columbus, Ohio.[19] Sixty-three percent of the 97 firms used a combination of media, and 36 percent used a single medium for dictation-recording. She concluded that shorthand was preferred but that there was a trend toward using a combination of media determined by dictator preference and the nature of the work.

- Scammon (1974) completed a dissertation entitled "An Analysis of the Need for and Use of Shorthand by Secretaries in Large Businesses as Indicated by Secretaries, Managers, and Personnel Directors."[20] One of his findings revealed that shorthand was used by 76 percent of the secretaries in the Michigan sample and that 98 percent of those who used shorthand used a symbol system.

- Hornstein (1973) reported a class project that included a telephone survey of personnel officers from some of the largest corporations in New York City.[21] Although the findings may be inconclusive because only 20 corporations participated, all of the companies employed stenographers or secretaries who could take manual shorthand, while few reported the use of dictation-transcription equipment.

- Schmitt (1977) assessed the use of dictating-transcribing equipment in the metropolitan areas of Knoxville and Chattanooga, Tennessee.[22] She found that dictating-transcribing equipment, manual shorthand, machine shorthand, and a combination of these were used for recording dictation. Dictation hardware was used exclusively in 8 of the 30 businesses surveyed; a combination of dictation hardware and manual shorthand was used in 21 of the firms; and one business used a combination of all three.

This research suggests three generalizations regarding the future of shorthand:

1. Shorthand is still and will continue to be a viable skill in the majority of business and service organizations in the United States.
2. Machine transcription and word processing installations will continue to increase.
3. Secretaries often use combinations of manual shorthand and transcription machines to process typed communications.

Shorthand as a Complement to Word Processing

There is even evidence that administrative secretaries in organizations that have adopted word processing find shorthand skills a valuable supplement to their activities. Lewis (1977) surveyed 320 users of word processing facilities and found the origination methods shown in the table on page 13 were used by the respondents before and after word processing was introduced.[23]

The table on page 13 reveals that a variety of origination methods are used, even after the implementation of word processing. Almost 30 percent of the correspondence was originated by personal handwriting or typing. It is probable that more executives would have dictated to secretaries if administrative secretaries had shorthand skills.

Although the secretary is freed from most recording-transcribing responsibilities, there are certain activities that are unsuitable for dictation to a word processing center, and there are other situations in which shorthand skills can be valuable supplements to the secretary's work. The following tasks reflect how shorthand, although not mandatory for initial employment, can be valuable in firms with word processing support systems.

RUSH DICTATION. Although word processing, when measured by total productivity, is probably more efficient, it may not be as effective as a secretary who can record a letter in shorthand and transcribe it in a matter of minutes. There are emergencies when a letter must be

COMPARISON OF BUSINESS LETTER ORIGINATION METHODS USED BEFORE AND AFTER WORD PROCESSING (WP)

ORIGINATION METHOD	MEAN PERCENTAGE OF USE BEFORE WP	RANK	MEAN PERCENTAGE OF USE AFTER WP	RANK
Personal Handwriting	45.92	1	25.75	2
Personal Typing	8.97	4	3.49	6
Dictation to Secretary Writing Shorthand	19.28	2	4.55	5
Dictation to Secretary Using Shorthand Machine	1.44	6	0.27	7
Desk-Top Dictation Machine	15.51	3	14.01	3
Portable Dictation Machine	7.80	5	10.32	4
Direct Telephone Line to Word Processing Center	N/A	N/A	38.51	1

originated, transcribed, and mailed to meet a deadline. A secretary who can record a letter in shorthand has the tools to meet such crucial deadlines.

HIGHLY CONFIDENTIAL DICTATION.   Employers are sometimes reluctant to dictate certain types of confidential correspondence to a central word processing center and would prefer to dictate to secretaries. The close working relationship with secretaries encourages executives to believe that they can maintain greater confidentiality if they originate and prepare confidential communications within their offices.

DICTATION INVOLVING SECRETARIAL RESEARCH.   Often it is convenient to have a secretary who can supply information or data needed by the employer during the dictation-recording process.

ROUGH DRAFT DICTATION.   Not all individuals are effective dictators, and some dictation is so complex that revisions of the first draft are required. A secretary who can record and produce rough draft copies for editing and final dictation to a word processing center has a skill that may be vital to some employers.

JUDGMENTAL DICTATION.   A secretary who can record minutes of meetings is important to some employers. Verbatim transcripts are seldom required, or even desirable, for most meetings; and a secretary who can record, transcribe, and condense the important aspects of meetings can render a valuable service to an employer.

SPECIALIZED FORMAT DICTATION. The preparation of certain forms or tables is often difficult to dictate to a word processing center. If the secretary has shorthand skills, the employer can usually obtain better results from face-to-face dictation.

PERSONAL DICTATION. Most dictation is directly related to the functions of the organization, but some is personal. An employer who might be reluctant to dictate such communications to a centralized word processing center is more apt to dictate them to a secretary because of the confidential relationship between secretary and employer.

DRAFTING FOR DICTATION. Because administrative secretaries are freed for more responsible duties, they may be called upon to originate routine, and even more complex, communications to the word processing center. The ability to quickly outline, or even draft, a letter in shorthand before dictation to the center can save valuable secretarial time and result in more effective communications.

RECORDING MESSAGES. Occasionally it may be necessary to make a verbatim record of or to summarize telephone or face-to-face communications. A secretary who writes shorthand can make a quick documentation for transcription or oral communication of the message.

RECORDING DIRECTIONS. A secretary is often called on to perform complex tasks, and the ability to record directions in shorthand should enable the secretary to perform these tasks more quickly and efficiently.

Occupational Outlook for Shorthand

Three major job classifications that have commonly included shorthand in their job descriptions are described in the 1976 *Occupational Outlook Handbook.* The classifications are secretary, stenographer, and shorthand reporter.

The definition for secretary reveals that shorthand is still considered a secretarial tool, although the effect of word processing systems on some secretarial positions is recognized.

Secretaries (D.O.T. 201.368) relieve their employers of routine duties so that they can work on more important matters. Although most secretaries take shorthand and deal with callers, the time spent on these duties varies in different types of organizations.

In offices where dictation and typing are handled in word processing centers, administrative secretaries handle all other secretarial duties. They often work in clusters of three or four so they can readily help each other. Because they are released from dictation and typing, they can serve several members of the professional staff. Their duties range from filing, routing mail, and answering telephones to more responsible jobs such as answering letters, doing statistical research, and writing reports.[24]

Projected job opportunities for secretaries continue to be excellent, and there is no indication that there will be a decline in the need for secretaries with traditional shorthand skills.

Employment of secretaries is expected to increase faster than the average for all occupations through the mid-1980s as the continued expansion of business and government creates a growing volume of paper work. Several hundred thousand jobs will become available each year due to the growth and the need to replace those who die, retire, or stop working for other reasons.[25]

The job description for stenographers also includes provision for recording dictation.

Stenographers (D.O.T. 202.388) take dictation and then transcribe their notes on a typewriter. They may either take shorthand or use a stenotype machine which prints symbols as certain keys are pressed. General Stenographers, including most beginners, take routine dictation and do other office tasks such as typing, filing, answering telephones, and operating office machines. Experienced and highly skilled stenographers take difficult dictation and do more responsible clerical work. They may sit in on staff meetings and give a summary report or a word-for-word record of the proceedings. They also supervise other stenographers, typists, and clerical workers.[26]

Shorthand reporters are described in the *Occupational Outlook Handbook.*

Shorthand reporters are specialized stenographers who record all statements made in a proceedings. Nearly half of all shorthand reporters work as court reporters attached to courts of law at different levels of government. They take down all statements made at legal proceedings and present their record as the official transcript. Many other shorthand reporters work as free-lance reporters who record out-of-court testimony for attorneys, meetings, and conventions, and other private activities. Still others record the proceedings in the Congress of the United States, in State Legislatures, and in both State and Federal agencies.[27]

Prospects for the employment of shorthand reporters continue to be bright.

Prospects for skilled shorthand reporters, in contrast to the overall outlook for stenographers, appear to be very good as state and federal court systems expand to handle the rising number of criminal court cases and civil lawsuits.[28]

Modern Shorthand Systems

Shorthand systems are often characterized and distinguished by basic principles associated with alphabetic construction. All shorthand systems can be classified as symbol systems, abbreviated longhand systems, or machine shorthand systems.

Symbol Shorthand Systems

Symbol shorthand systems are characterized by the use of symbols, rather than longhand characters, to represent sounds, words, and phrases. The symbols used to represent sounds are written more easily and quickly than longhand characters, allowing students to develop high dictation-recording speeds. The phonetic principles on which such systems are based usually include writing both consonants and dominant vowels. Special symbols are used for word beginnings, word endings, and high-frequency words.

The three predominant symbol shorthand systems in the United States today are Gregg, Pitman, and Century 21.

GREGG SHORTHAND. Today, Gregg Shorthand is taught in an estimated 90 to 95 percent of the secondary and postsecondary schools in the United States that offer shorthand instruction. Since John Robert Gregg published *Light Line Phonography* in 1888, there have been seven system revisions. However, the alphabet and principles fundamental to the system have changed little. Following are some of the basic principles associated with the Gregg system:

1. The shorthand alphabet is based on segments of the elipse, or oval, which represents the natural slope of longhand.
2. Curvilinear motions are used in writing.
3. Obtuse angles (angles of more than 90 degrees) are eliminated by the natural blending of lines.
4. Vowels are joined in words according to the natural order of pronunciation.
5. Shading, or heavy lines, is eliminated, and outlines are written with uniform thickness.
6. Only one writing position—along the line—is used.
7. The continuous flow of the writing along the line is lineal.

Example:

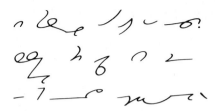

The objectives of the newest edition, *Series 90*, are to teach students to read and write Gregg Shorthand rapidly in the shortest possible time and to develop transcription skills during the first year of instruction. There are four basic textbooks and accompanying supplementary materials for 1- or 2-year programs at both high school and college levels.

PITMAN SHORTHAND. Although Pitman is the prevalent system in all countries comprising the old British Empire, its teaching in the United States is confined primarily to schools in the Northeast. The system has been extensively revised since Sir Isaac Pitman published *Stenographic Sound-Hand* in 1837, but the foundational principles, including those following, have remained unchanged.

1. Consonant symbols are geometrical and derived from segments of the circle.
2. Consonants with similar sounds are paired and distinguished by shading.
3. Vowels are disjoined and indicated by light and heavy dots or dashes.
4. The position of symbols—above, through, or under the line—determines the meaning of words.
5. A contracting principle (writing only the first stroke of the outline) and a halving principle (writing half the outline) are taught for taking dictation under extreme pressure.

Example:

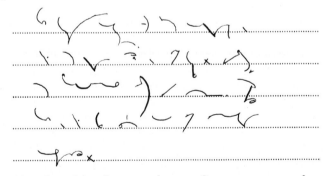

Pitman shorthand is often taught as a 3-year program, but a new version, "Shorterhand," reduces the time required to learn the theory by approximately 50 percent. This new publication is too recent to

17

accurately assess its effect on traditional Pitman Shorthand and its acceptance by teachers.

CENTURY 21 SHORTHAND. Published in 1974, Century 21 Shorthand is now being taught as a 1- or 2-year program at both high school and college levels, but it is probably too early to measure its impact on shorthand instruction. Both series include three basic textbooks, two for the first year and one for the second year, as well as supplemental learning materials. The authors use many of the Gregg alphabetic characters and principles of outline construction, but the following are considered as distinctive characteristics of the system:

1. Primary alphabetic symbols are written in only one direction.
2. Single symbols are used for alphabetic sounds.
3. High-frequency longhand letters and shorthand symbols for the letters have the same dominant direction.

Example:

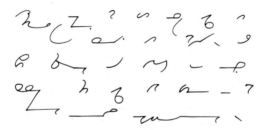

Abbreviated Longhand Systems

Abbreviated longhand systems are generally characterized by the use of simplified longhand letters to represent sounds, words, and phrases. Although longhand letters are used, symbols are also used for word beginnings, word endings, high-frequency words, past tenses, and capitalizations. The systems are based on phonetics, but most involve writing the dominant sounds, usually consonants, and often omitting vowels.

A partial listing of systems that basically meet the above description includes: *Speedwriting, Quickhand, Stenospeed, Stenoscript, P.S.* or *Personal Shorthand,* and *Forkner Shorthand.* A very brief description of these systems illustrates one of the major advantages cited by proponents of abbreviated longhand systems—reducing learning time.

SPEEDWRITING. *Speedwriting* was developed by Emma Dearborn in 1923 and was generally taught in proprietary business schools under franchise agreements. It is also taught as *Landmark* in some public schools. Brevity is achieved through the use of symbols.

QUICKHAND. This system, published in 1974, uses programming techniques to facilitate independent study. Written by Jeremy Grossman, the text is divided into five lessons and designed so students will complete all theory and write from unfamiliar dictation after 3 to 6 weeks.

Example:

STENOSPEED. This system has been marketed since 1953 and was revised in 1973. It includes nine abbreviated longhand characters, ten longhand letters, six symbols, blends, brief forms, and other sounds. Theory is usually presented in 30 to 36 class periods.

Example:

STENOSCRIPT. First published in 1950, *Stenoscript* uses all 26 letters of the alphabet and 3 punctuation marks. The 43 principles or rules are presented in 7 lessons, which take from 30 to 40 hours to cover.

P.S. OR PERSONAL SHORTHAND.   Originally published in 1957 as *Briefhand*, P.S. uses the 26 alphabetic letters but no symbols. Consequently, dictation may be recorded directly at the typewriter or by pencil or pen. P.S. can be taught from a 30- or 70-lesson text, depending on the objectives and the time available for instruction.
Example:

FORKNER SHORTHAND.   This system was developed by Hamden Forkner, Sr., in the late 1940s and published in 1952. It is designed as a 1-year program, with the 37 theory chapters presented in the first semester and the second semester reserved for continued speed development and transcription refinement.
Example:

Advantages of Abbreviated Longhand Systems

Proponents of the dozens of abbreviated longhand systems marketed today often cite one or more of the following advantages that longhand systems have over symbol systems:

1. The familiarity of the longhand alphabet reduces learning difficulty and learning time.
2. Reading and transcription of notes is apt to be more accurate because the notes are derivatives of already familiar longhand.
3. Above-average students can usually write at double their

longhand speed in from 20 to 30 hours of instruction and at triple their longhand speed after the first semester of study.

4. No special training is required to teach the systems because teachers can learn the systems as they teach them.
5. The simplicity of alphabetic systems makes self-teaching possible.
6. Because these systems are easy to learn, they can be taught to students of all ability levels.
7. The systems are ideal for teaching in adult education classes where students cannot meet daily and must achieve a skill within a relatively short time.

Disadvantages of Abbreviated Longhand Systems

Proponents of symbol systems are apt to counter with one or more of the following arguments against abbreviated longhand systems:

1. The systems do not provide the speed potential necessary to meet the heavy dictation needs of the typical office.
2. Abbreviated longhand notes are not necessarily more legible than symbol notes. It is difficult to read and transcribe notes when only the consonants or a small portion of each word is written.
3. It takes time to learn an abbreviation, even if the abbreviation is based on longhand letters.
4. The teaching or systematic review of the mechanics for successful transcription cannot be reduced to a very short time.
5. It is difficult to write high speed dictation for extended periods.
6. Supplementary learning materials are often limited.
7. With increased simplification and brevity of theory, there is a corresponding decrease in speed potential.

Machine Shorthand

Like other shorthand systems, machine shorthand is phonetically based. The 23 keys on the machine allow the operator to print letters, syllables, words, phrases, and numbers on a paper tape by depressing individual keys, or combinations of keys simultaneously. Each stroke automatically advances the paper tape in readiness for the next stroke. The keyboard is arranged to take advantage of the uniqueness of the English language. Most English words begin with one or more consonant sounds followed by a vowel sound and end with one or more consonant sounds. Therefore, the keyboard is arranged so that initial consonants are made with the fingers of the left hand; the vowel keys, located in the center, are struck with the thumbs; and final consonants are struck with the fingers of the right hand. The upper bank of keys, when depressed simultaneously with the numeral shift bar, prints numbers.

The two leading shorthand machines are Stenograph and Stenoprint. Both are compact and weigh approximately 4 pounds. Manual operation ensures complete portability, and they are designed for noiseless operation of the keys with minimum pressure.

Machine shorthand has been used primarily for high-speed court reporting since Miles Bartholomew (1879) and Ward Stone Ireland (1910) patented their machines, but manufacturers have recently promoted it as a secretarial tool. Machine shorthand is taught at both the secondary and postsecondary levels.

The length of programs depends largely on the career goals of the students enrolled. The most common goals of students in these programs are preparation for stenographic or general secretarial positions; specialization in conference, convention, and/or court reporting; and preparation for medical, legal, or technical secretarial careers.

The following is a keyboard illustration.

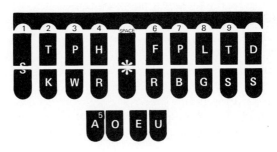

Notice, in the following illustration of a machine tape, how combinations of letters are used for the formation of words, phrases, and punctuation.

			W		E			
ST				O		P		D
				A			T	
		T	H		E			
ST				O	R			
				A				
	K		R	O				S
	T		H		E			
ST			R		E		T	
	T			O				
S					E			
		P			E		G	

Personal-Use Systems

Abbreviated longhand systems often have stated vocational as well as personal-use objectives. However, several publications are limited to personal-use applications. *Notetaking & Study Skills,* published by the Forkner Publishing Corporation, and *Gregg Notehand* are designed for students who wish to improve their study habits and become effective notemakers.

The two major objectives of *Gregg Notehand* are:

1. To provide instruction in notemaking processes and procedures.
2. To develop a writing facility with which to make notes rapidly and easily.

The objectives of Forkner's *Notetaking & Study Skills* are similar and include:

1. Teaching techniques for making notes from lectures, reading, and observations.
2. Teaching the skills associated with organizing and developing term papers, research studies, and related academic assignments.

Gregg Notehand is designed as a one-semester course for college-bound high school students; business and professional people who need to make notes from reading and listening; and individuals who must draft reports, speeches, articles, and research papers. The Forkner publication is designed as a quarter or semester course for high school students who need to improve their study skills and for college-bound students. It is also suggested as a worthwhile course for community college students who plan to continue their education.

Because the objectives of these publications differ from those of vocational learning materials, there are philosophical and methodological differences. For example, *Gregg Notehand* differs from Gregg Shorthand in the following ways:

1. Students are trained to record key ideas, and there is no emphasis on recording dictation verbatim.
2. Students are encouraged to write words in longhand when they encounter difficulty in formulating shorthand outlines.
3. There is no emphasis on words-a-minute dictation.
4. There is a heavy emphasis on developing study skills—including outlining, making notes from reading, recording relevant facts, listening, drafting original essays, developing research papers, reviewing, summarizing meetings, and so on. **23**

Selecting a System

Publishers of symbol systems, abbreviated longhand systems, and machine shorthand systems can emphatically express the merits of their particular system, but the shorthand teacher must intelligently select a system that will meet the students' needs. Determining whether a system meets the objectives of the course should be a major consideration in system selection. The following illustration provides a rough guideline for comparing systems with objectives:

Comparative Shorthand Systems

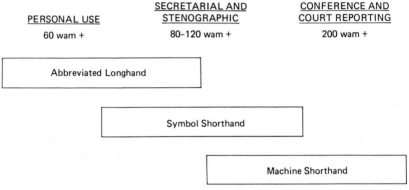

Courtesy Bulletin 27, Department of Public Instruction, Commonwealth of Pennsylvania, Harrisburg, 1968, p. 20.

Other considerations in system selection include the following:

1. Studying the learning materials to determine whether they conform to their stated objectives.
2. Analyzing the system theory to estimate ease of learning, logical presentation, and adherence to principles of outline construction.
3. Reviewing all learning materials to estimate quality and comprehensiveness of supplementary materials.
4. Weighing the reputation of the publisher for providing high-quality materials in business education.
5. Studying the literature pertaining to the system and talking with individuals who have taught the system to gain impressions of its strengths and weaknesses.

Shorthand Students

Approximately 274,000 high school students enroll in shorthand each year.[29] Although generalizations are subject to error, there are more similarities than differences in the characteristics of high school shorthand enrollees. The typical shorthand student:

1. Will enroll in a Gregg shorthand class.
2. Plans to complete one year of shorthand study.
3. Is a young woman between the ages of 16 and 17 and is in the eleventh or twelfth grade.
4. Wants to develop a skill for recording and transcribing oral communications and apply that skill in business situations.
5. Has completed a typing class before enrolling in shorthand.
6. Does not think of shorthand as a particularly useful tool for personal or academic applications.
7. Does not consider shorthand as a subject that will significantly improve language arts skills.
8. Has at least "average" academic potential, although the total shorthand population is subject to wide ranges of ability.

Generalizations 6 and 7 should be a major cause of concern to shorthand teachers. Students need to know of the shorthand-related job opportunities available to college students to help pay college expenses. Also, some college students frequently use shorthand for notetaking in their classes.

Students and teachers need to be aware of the language arts skill development that occurs in shorthand classes. Johnson found that high school shorthand students performed significantly better than nonshorthand students in the language arts skills of punctuation, spelling, and vocabulary.[30]

Postsecondary shorthand students cannot be so easily categorized. Although the majority are women enrolled in Gregg classes, their objectives for electing shorthand are more diverse. Students elect shorthand as preparation for business teaching and for careers in court or conference reporting as well as for secretarial careers. Although postsecondary institutions attract mature individuals seeking second careers as well as recent high school graduates, shorthand students are most apt to be from 18 to 20 years old. The mean age of postsecondary shorthand classes is increasing, however.

Recruiting Shorthand Students

The projected decline in total school population, emphasis on nontraditional careers, and mistaken assumptions that shorthand is no longer used in business will create new challenges for shorthand teachers. Already, some teachers are noticing a gradual decline in shorthand enrollments. If enrollments are to stabilize or increase, teachers must do more than merely register students for first-year shorthand. They must implement a campaign to inform students of the advantages associated with shorthand study.

Shorthand teachers who had successfully increased their enrollments participated in a series of panel discussions at the *Gregg*

25

Shorthand, Series 90, workshops held in February 1978. Among the techniques suggested by these teachers were the following:[31]

Recruiting Junior High School Students

Ninth graders should learn about the potential benefits of shorthand before they register for the tenth grade so that they can properly sequence courses. Ideally, they should elect typing in the tenth grade and complete two years of shorthand during the junior and senior years.

Junior and senior high school counselors should understand the ideal sequence of typing-shorthand courses. A meeting of counselors and business teachers should be held to discuss the curriculum and the types of students who could benefit from the study of shorthand and to make the counseling staff more knowledgeable about business education. Many counselors have the mistaken idea that shorthand is only for students who intend to terminate their education with the completion of high school. They should understand that shorthand can be a valuable source of income through part-time employment and an entry-level tool for college students who intend to pursue careers in business.

Communicating With Parents

Parents of ninth grade students should understand the values of shorthand. They are apt to influence what courses their children elect; therefore a mailing to parents may be fruitful. It could include a brochure describing the program and an invitation to an orientation session before registration. A short orientation session will give teachers an opportunity to explain the personal and business advantages of learning shorthand.

Visiting Classes

Shorthand teachers should visit as many junior and senior high school classes as possible. Typing classes in particular are important sources of potential enrollees. A short talk on the values of shorthand and a demonstration by a senior shorthand student are apt to create favorable responses from students.

Teaching Orientation Classes

Students often have a mistaken impression of shorthand or lack any knowledge about it. Shorthand teachers have been successful in exchanging classes with typing, social studies, or English teachers. During such days, shorthand teachers present a modified version of the first lesson so that students will be able to read and write simple sentences in shorthand by the end of the period. Teachers who have tried teaching such classes report generating a high degree of student interest. Even though shorthand is offered primarily for those who aspire to secretarial occupations, it is important to stress that shorthand has other uses. The ability to record lecture notes and messages and to draft compositions are but a few applications of shorthand for both nonacademic and college-bound students.

Developing Slide/Tape Presentations

A slide/tape presentation can be prepared to illustrate the applications of shorthand. The pictures and narration can dramatize shorthand's value for positions in business and its potential for improving academic study skills.

Conducting Shorthand Seminars

Other teachers have increased interest and enrollments in shorthand by conducting shorthand seminars, which give an opportunity to provide information to prospective students and answer questions about shorthand. Of course, advance publicity is required if seminars are to be successful. Teachers who have used this technique have enlisted their present shorthand classes to attract potential shorthand students to seminars. The content of seminars might include short talks by the shorthand teacher, a senior shorthand student, a practicing secretary, and a member of the personnel department of a local company. The slide/tape presentation may also be used if the majority of the students have not already seen it. To encourage attendance, prizes might be given or refreshments served.

Publicizing Your Products

It is important that the shorthand program be made as visible as possible to all potential enrollees. A series of articles in school or local newspapers might feature students in the cooperative program who use their shorthand skills, students who are using shorthand while working part-time, or graduates or students who have been particularly successful in using shorthand. Publicize shorthand contests sponsored for youth groups at the local, state, and national levels.

Contacting Every Prospect

Personal contact with individual students is perhaps the most effective of all techniques. After teachers have sent mailings to parents, visited classes, held orientation sessions, presented slide/tape programs, and hosted shorthand seminars, individual contact is the final and most important step. It allows teachers to discuss individual needs and concerns with the student. If teachers let students know that they are interested in their futures and are willing to help them reach career goals, students are more apt to enroll in shorthand.

Counseling Shorthand Students

To achieve the goals of shorthand instruction, the student must exercise self-discipline, apply sound study habits, and devote daily practice time to the study of shorthand. As a result, dropout rates are higher than for other secondary school business subjects. Researchers recognized the problems of shorthand failures and dropouts in the early 1900s, and the problem of predicting shorthand achievement has continued to be a highly popular topic for master's and doctoral research.

Dropout and Failure Rates

Despite the body of knowledge that has been developed about achievement in shorthand, the dropout and failure rate continues to be a concern of shorthand educators.

Tonne (1962) secured shorthand enrollments from 32 of the 50 states and the District of Columbia.[34] A comparison of enrollments in first- and second-year shorthand revealed that about 23 percent of the students who enrolled in first-year shorthand continued study in the second year. The remaining 77 percent failed or terminated study after one year. Cwierz (1968) stated that "Shorthand presents the greatest problem of prognosis and has a mortality of more than 50 percent; that is, less than half of the pupils who start first-year shorthand will complete second-year shorthand."[35]

Ryals (1970) wrote, "The number of failures among first-year shorthand students is appalling."[36] Other writers on the subject have expressed similar concerns during the last 40 years. Fortunately, the situation may not be as dismal as writers have portrayed. The inability to separate failure from dropout has probably inflated the mortality rate out of proportion. Many students who are successful in first-year shorthand do not elect another year of study for the following reasons.

1. Not all secondary schools offer a second year of shorthand instruction.
2. Students sometimes enroll in first-year shorthand when they are high school seniors.
3. Students who originally intended to become secretaries change their career objectives.

4. Students encounter scheduling conflicts and cannot elect a second year of study.
5. Students may not be highly motivated to elect a second year because of the homework and study pressures associated with mastering a motor skill.
6. Students may mistakenly assume that they have developed enough shorthand skill after one year of study and elect other courses.

It is evident, however, that a substantial number of students have difficulty in learning shorthand and never develop enough skill for use in business. These individuals may lack the innate abilities and attitudes to be successful in shorthand and to become proficient stenographers or secretaries. To encourage them to enroll in shorthand is doing them a disservice and results in a discouraging waste of student and teacher time. In addition, being the lowest-ranking student in a shorthand class is frustrating and does little for character development. Teachers with failing students in their classes have tried to provide for individual differences and to meet the needs of all students. However, the end result is often an overall lowering of class performance and a group of learners who are still frustrated by their lack of success.

If the failure rate is to be reduced significantly, the body of research knowledge which has been developed must be applied in counseling so that students can begin to make realistic choices about the study of shorthand.

Factors Associated with Performance

The following have been found to be significantly related to achievement in shorthand:

INTELLIGENCE. IQ has been a common criterion for forecasting success or failure in shorthand, and most research has revealed a positive relationship between intelligence and shorthand achievement. Seldon (1961) reported that between 80 and 90 percent of the students with IQs below 100 drop out of shorthand during the two-year instructional period.[35] Other research studies place the lower limits of IQ at 90 and indicate that the higher the intelligence the greater the probability of success in shorthand. Van Kirk's (1960) analysis of IQ and achievement reveals the importance of intelligence to performance in shorthand.[36]

Van Kirk's table illustrates the danger of using IQ as the only measurement for predicting shorthand success. Intelligence, as measured by paper and pencil tests, is subject to error. In the table, one out of five students with IQs below 99 were able to attain above-average success. Interest, desire, and dedication may have contributed greatly to this success.

COMPARISON OF IQ AND SHORTHAND I GRADES

NUMBER OF STUDENTS	RATIO	IQ	SHORTHAND I GRADES
31 out of 46	2 out of 3	110+	A or B
24 out of 51	1 out of 2	100–109	A or B
10 out of 51	1 out of 5	99 or below	A or B

MOTIVATION AND INTEREST. Motivation plays a key role in short-hand achievement, and it is the one factor which has confounded researchers when predicting performance. For example, students may enroll in shorthand for reasons such as parental pressure, peer pressure, fondness for typing, or because shorthand fits conveniently into a class schedule. Although none of these reasons are very relevant, some of the students will become motivated because they find that they enjoy and are successful at shorthand.

Other students who want to become secretaries enroll in the class with a high degree of motivation but quickly lose interest because of the work involved or their lack of success. Other students, with all the abilities for success in shorthand, fail miserably because of a lack of drive and zeal for attaining skill. Few research studies have been conducted to determine the relationship between motivation and success in shorthand. However, Varah (1967) found that academic motivation, as measured by the Michigan M-Scales, was a learning factor in first-semester Gregg Shorthand.[37]

All shorthand teachers and researchers agree that motivation is directly related to shorthand achievement, but there are no ready formulas to forecast the degree of motivation that an individual student must maintain during the period of shorthand study.

SCHOLASTIC ACHIEVEMENT. Research during the last 15 years indicates that overall grade point average (GPA) is one of the best predictors of shorthand performance. In general, the higher the GPA the greater the probability for success. Shorthand teachers have found, to their sorrow, that it is virtually impossible for a C or D student to achieve A or B levels in shorthand. A high cumulative GPA seems to roughly reflect a combination of factors or traits associated with successful achievement in shorthand. These may include intelligence, general attitude toward school, study habits, motivation, interest, and so on.

ENGLISH ACHIEVEMENT. English grades are sometimes used to forecast shorthand performance, and research reveals a relationship between English ability and shorthand success. English grades usually reflect reading ability, vocabulary development, English usage, and ability to punctuate and spell—all factors associated with transcription performance, the ultimate goal of all shorthand instruction. Considering English achievement predictively is particularly important if students have completed classes emphasizing grammar, vocabulary building, and writing, and not so important if English grades reflect achievement in literature only.

PROGNOSTIC TESTS. Researchers have attempted to isolate segments of the total shorthand-transcription skill and develop non-shorthand tests to predict shorthand performance. Four of these tests will be described briefly.

The Turse Shorthand Aptitude Test was developed in 1940.[38] It consists of seven parts, and approximately 45 minutes are consumed in administering the test to student groups.

SUBTESTS	TASKS
Part I: Stroking	Students write lines inside boxes for measurement of manual dexterity.
Part II: Spelling	Students select the correct spelling of words from a choice of three.
Part III: Phonetic Association	Students correctly spell words written phonetically.
Part IV: Symbol Transcription	Students transcribe six sentences from symbols by using a symbol key.
Part V: Word Discrimination	Students select the word that best completes meanings of sentences.
Part VI: Dictation	Students write in longhand from dictation to measure word-carrying ability and writing speed.
Part VII: Word Sense	Students correctly spell contracted, abbreviated, or incomplete words.

To reduce the administration and correction time for the Turse test, researchers have experimented with eliminating some of the seven subtests. Pauk (1963) used the four subtests measuring verbal ability—spelling, phonetic association, word discrimination, and word sense—and found that the four subtests predicted success as effectively as the whole test.[39] Davis (1966) concluded that the four verbal subtests of the Turse test could predict success better than all seven subtests.[40]

The ERC Stenographic Aptitude Test was developed in 1944 by Walter Deemer.[41] Published by Science Research Associates, it is comprised of five subtests and takes approximately 45 minutes to administer.

SUBTESTS	TASKS
Part I: Speed of Writing	Student copies the Gettysburg Address in longhand under time pressure.
Part II: Word Discrimination	Student selects the best word from a choice of two or three.
Part III: Phonetic Spelling	Student correctly spells phonetically spelled words.
Part IV: Vocabulary	Student selects from five words the one that corresponds in meaning to the key word.
Part V: Sentence Dictation	Student writes dictated sentences in longhand.

The Byers' First-Year Shorthand Aptitude Test was developed in 1959 by Edward Byers.[42] Consisting of five subtests, it takes approximately 35 minutes to administer each part of the two-part test battery.

SUBTESTS	ABILITIES MEASURED
Test I: Phonetic Perception	Detection of phonetic sounds.
Test II: Retention Ability	Remembering in sequence, transliteration, and reproducing accurately.
Test III: Observation Aptitude	Observation of distinctions in symbols.
Test IV: Patterns from Parts	Visualization of complete words from partial words in context.
Test V: Hand Dexterity	Recording symbols automatically.

The First-Semester Aptitude Test was developed by Lorrine Skaff in 1972 and is the most recent effort to develop a test to predict performance.[43] Divided into five parts, it can be administered in 45 minutes.

SUBTESTS	TASKS
Test I: Phonetic Understanding and Spelling	Students translate words phonetically spelled.
Test II: Symbol Retention	Students translate symbols to alphabetic letters using their memories and a key.
Test III: Manual Dexterity	Students write selected Gregg Shorthand outlines after practice.

SUBTESTS	TASKS
Test IV: Proofreading and Punctuation	Students locate misspelled words, misused words, and punctuation errors.
Test V: Sentence Retention and Writing Speed	Students write in longhand from dictation to test word-carrying ability and writing speed.

Since the development of these and other prognostic tests, researchers have assessed their value in predicting shorthand achievement. Although research results differ regarding their precision, it can be concluded that the tests have predictive value. However, none of the tests account for the most important variable for success or failure in shorthand—the attitude and motivation of the student.

Even though prognostic tests have been well researched, there are practical considerations operating against their widespread use for guidance in the secondary schools. These often include one or more of the following: the cost of purchasing the tests, the time necessary for their administration, and the time necessary to correct the tests and interpret the scores.

FOREIGN LANGUAGE ACHIEVEMENT. The relationship between achievement in foreign language classes and shorthand achievement has been assessed by several researchers. Although the results of the research are somewhat conflicting, there appears to be a moderate relationship between success in foreign language study and the learning of shorthand. Although such a relationship may exist, foreign language achievement is seldom used for prediction, because only a limited number of students elect foreign language study before shorthand instruction.

TYPING ACHIEVEMENT. Although there is no evidence that typing achievement can be used as an accurate predictor of shorthand performance, some teachers consider prior typing performance when counseling students about shorthand. Their rationale is that typing ability is important to the ultimate transcription goal of shorthand instruction. If the student is a mediocre typist, there is limited opportunity for developing vocational transcription skills even though shorthand skills can be achieved.

ATTENDANCE RECORD. There is little research to indicate that attendance is related to shorthand achievement, but the importance of the student attending classes during the presentation of theory is considered paramount by most shorthand teachers. A student with a history of chronic absenteeism will probably be a high-risk shorthand student.

OTHER FACTORS. Some researchers have investigated the relationship between scores on existing standardized tests and shorthand achievement. In general, the results have been disappointing and most of the tests do not lend themselves to preciseness of prediction. Among these tests are:

Differential Aptitude Test
Iowa Test of Educational Development
Gates Visual Perception Test
Revised Minnesota Paper Form Board Test
Iowa Silent Reading Test
Brown-Carlson Listening Comprehension Test
American Council of Education Psychological Examination

Limitations of Prediction

Despite all the research that has been conducted, there are still aspects of prognosis that need further investigation before shorthand teachers and counselors can apply it reliably to guidance. Below are some aspects of prognosis that need additional study:

1. There are no precise answers about the most appropriate combinations of factors to use and their degree of contribution to performance.
2. There are no precise answers concerning the extent to which motivation and purpose contribute to performance.
3. There are no precise cutoff scores derived for factors that would be indicative of failure or success.
4. There may be other factors not yet investigated that have a significant relationship to shorthand performance.

Yet there is enough evidence available to begin to apply prognosis, but teachers must remember that the tools for shorthand prediction are subject to error. In the area of prognosis, a correlation coefficient of approximately .60, with a forecasting efficiency of 20 percent, is considered to be significant and to have considerable value for predicting shorthand accomplishment for guidance purposes.

Using Prediction Knowledge

When applying predictive evidence, teachers need to remember the following principles, which have been substantiated by research:

1. It is difficult to predict shorthand success with any degree of accuracy, but it is possible to predict failure with greater precision.
2. There is no single element in the student's background that can be used to make accurate predictions about performance. Shorthand performance can be predicted with greater accuracy when combinations of factors are considered.

3. Intelligence, grade point average, English achievement, foreign

language achievement, and scores on prognostic tests have a relationship to first-year shorthand achievement.

4. Prognostic testing can improve classroom instruction as an indicator of subject mastery potential and of required learning time for employable skill development.

A plan that considers research evidence has been developed and is recommended for use in Pennsylvania Schools.

SUGGESTED CRITERIA TO USE IN SELECTING PUPILS WHO WILL BE ENCOURAGED TO TAKE SHORTHAND[44]

I. Subject Matter Achievement

Grade Average or Class Rank	Suggested Scores
A Upper 10 percent	7
B Next 29 percent	5
C Middle 40 percent	3
D Lower 20 percent	1
E Last 10 percent	0

II. English

This score should be based on grades in English mechanics and vocabulary or on an English achievement test.	4 to 0 (the highest score would be 4)

III. Aptitude Tests

Use norms established for the particular aptitude test being used as the basis for rating	4 to 0 (the highest score would be 4)

IV. Intelligence Quotient

IQ	Suggested Scores
120 or above	4
110–119	3
100–109	2
90– 99	1
89 or below	0

V. Other Factors

Teacher's subjective ratings of pupil interest, work habits, self-discipline, concentration, and attendance record should be included.	4 to 0 (the highest score would be 4)

The following cut-off points are recommended when counseling students: (1) Anyone with a score of 15 or more should be encouraged to elect shorthand; (2) Students with scores between 11 and 14 should be counseled carefully before deciding to elect shorthand; and (3) Students with scores of 10 or less should be discouraged from taking shorthand.

Numerous factors associated with potential shorthand performance have been used in other similar plans. However, none of the plans has been used extensively in the nation's schools because of three factors:

1. The time required to collect and interpret the data for each student expressing an interest in shorthand has discouraged most teachers from attempting prognosis.
2. Shorthand teachers' concern about small enrollments has led to the encouragement of all students, no matter what their potential, to take shorthand.
3. The prevailing attitude in American public education that students have the right to self-determination of career goals has contributed to a lack of proper guidance.

It is true that most shorthand teachers and guidance counselors lack the time to collect and analyze all the data required to successfully implement a sound shorthand counseling program. Yet if the small proportion of students without innate abilities for shorthand success is not identified and counseled against enrolling, shorthand teachers will probably spend a disproportionate amount of time working with students who lack the ability to learn shorthand effectively.

Perhaps teachers and/or guidance counselors should consider an alternative approach to prognosis which does not require collecting multiple data for each potential shorthand enrollee. Although not scientifically tested, the plan is certainly more effective than no plan at all. It is based on the premise that only a few students actually need to be counseled about their chances for success in shorthand, and it consists of the following procedures:

1. Compile cumulative GPAs for all students who pre-register for shorthand. Students who meet or exceed the average GPA for the school need no further investigation or counseling. Only those with GPAs below the school's average would require additional assessment of potential performance.
2. If IQ scores are available, collect them only for students with below-average GPAs. Those with average or above-average IQ scores would need no further investigation or counseling. They might not be highly successful students because of a lack of motivation, but they have the basic intellectual ability to be successful at shorthand.

3. Administer shorthand prognostic tests only to those students with below-average grades and IQs to determine whether they have an aptitude for shorthand. These students should be talked with individually to assess their chances for success in shorthand. After individual discussions about their career goals and chances of success, students can make more realistic decisions about whether or not to study shorthand. The results of prognostic tests might also suggest diagnoses helpful in prescribing remedial techniques for students with potential learning difficulties who decide to enroll in shorthand.

Probably not more than 5 to 10 percent of all students who pre-register for shorthand would need counseling, but it is imperative that this group make intelligent career choices. No interested student can, or should, be denied admission to a shorthand class on the basis of anticipated performance; but students should be made aware of prognostic evidence indicating potential failure.

Motivating Shorthand Students

Students enroll in shorthand with differing objectives, values, self-images, and study habits. These differences are evident to shorthand teachers during the early days of instruction, and they become even more pronounced as the year progresses. Teachers frequently try to influence achievement and attitude with large doses of "motivation"—often, however, with little effect other than making the shorthand class temporarily more enjoyable. As a result, shorthand teachers sometimes express a great deal of concern about how students can be motivated to learn shorthand.

There is no one way to motivate all students within a group. Easy prescriptions, including games, puzzles, bulletin boards, and so on, may bring short-term improvement, but they do not cure the ailments of lack of interest, apathy, and low achievement.

The following includes a review of principles appropriate to instilling long-term interest in and enthusiasm for shorthand, as well as selected short-term remedies to enhance shorthand learning:

Teacher Image Has a Direct Influence on Student Motivation

Shorthand teachers, like all other instructors, are models for students. The teacher who can demonstrate shorthand skills effectively and enthusiastically may, at least indirectly, arouse student desire to become proficient.

The ability of the teacher to direct learning in a positive way is also a factor. Recognizing individual student improvement, showing concern about lack of progress, and expressing interest in the student as a person all have definite positive influences on attitudes.

37

Conversely, if teachers show little enthusiasm for shorthand, fail to give the impression of recognizing individual worth in students, and are often negative, they may multiply negative attitudes.

Success Is a Motivational Factor

The old axiom that "success breeds success" is important to remember in all teaching. Thus, it is important for shorthand teachers to use the best methodologies, materials, and strategies to help students achieve the greatest success of which each is capable. The ideas explained and illustrated in this book will help shorthand students and teachers experience this success.

Students often are not aware that they are doing as well as they actually are in the shorthand classroom. Shorthand teaching and learning involve various kinds of testing and frequent testing. Sometimes students remember only the poorer results and forget about the good results. Teachers can help to avoid this self-defeating assessment by keeping in front of the student the short-term goals, by identifying strongly the individual's successes, by recommending effective remedial procedures, and by individual encouragement. Developing a "midpoint of grading period" reporting system and actually showing the students where each stands on every aspect of learning can be very motivational. If a teacher uses the grading system of cancelling out some of the poorest grades for reading, transcription rates, and mailable letter attempts, students will be motivated to try harder to achieve and will not be so quickly "swallowed up" in the depths of defeat and failure.

Classroom Experiences Must Be Related to Future Jobs

High school sophomores and juniors taking beginning shorthand cannot be expected to know automatically what jobs will be available to them on completion of their shorthand study. In fact, those in advanced classes and at postsecondary levels may need to have job opportunities vividly pointed out to them.

A few ways of making the shorthand classroom come alive with its relationship to the "real world" follow:

1. Teachers with recent work experience can relate experiences and opportunities.
2. Arrange talks by enthusiastic office workers, including recent graduates.
3. Post bulletin board displays of secretarial workers on the job, want-ad sections of the newspapers with shorthand positions highlighted, reports of salary surveys, and current newspaper articles discussing secretarial positions and shortages.

4. Give a slide/tape presentation of past graduates working in positions using shorthand skills.
5. Seek the assistance of members of the local chapter of the National Secretaries Association to let students "shadow" them at work or work with them for part of a day.

Intrinsic Motivation is More Effective Than Extrinsic Motivation

Intrinsic motivation can be defined as the inherent desire to learn, and extrinsic motivation can be classified as the desire to learn because of the direct or indirect rewards associated with learning. For example, competitive games can be classified as extrinsic motivation devices. Students are often more concerned with achievement and tangible rewards than with the intangible rewards associated with learning shorthand. The effective teacher realizes that long-term motivation is built on intrinsic motivation, and not on extrinsic-motivation devices. Generally, students will develop an intrinsic motivation for learning shorthand if they (1) experience success, (2) see progress toward teacher and/or personal goals, (3) receive recognition for success, and (4) perceive a positive relationship between themselves and the teacher.

Wise Use of Competition Should Prevail

Competitive games, wall charts, grades, and other devices that stimulate competition within the group will certainly be effective for individuals who are potentially high achievers in shorthand. However, competition has a tendency to destroy interest and motivation in students who have been previously pegged as low or average achievers. Wall charts, awards, and grades based on competition are not absolutely necessary to efficient shorthand learning. Students who are usually rewarded for high achievement are the type of individuals who would be self-motivated by their natural success. There is no surer way of "turning off" low achievers than by having them constantly participate in competitive games or strive for grades based on competition. Experience tells them that such rewards are not for them but are reserved for individuals who are already motivated by their talent.

A Variety of Motivational Devices Should Be Used

Motivational devices and procedures are basically extrinsic. Therefore the continual use of any single motivational device will reduce its effectiveness, and once the newness has worn off, it ceases to inspire interest. Charts of shorthand progress are a good example. Students may be highly interested in these charts during the initial stages of

39

learning; but, as the year progresses, the charts may lose their motivational impact.

Bulletin boards are another example. An attractive bulletin board may create a great deal of interest during the first week, but student interest in it may wane. For these reasons, the timing of the use of the device is important. Removing it for a time and bringing it back later can be effective. A device used in one format may be used again later in another format to remotivate student learning.

Learning Should Be Associated with Motivational Devices

Motivational devices should be related to learning shorthand skill. If the device cannot directly contribute to more efficient shorthand learning, it is probably merely a source of entertainment. Entertainment devices are potentially dangerous because they steal valuable time from necessary learning activities. A motivational device should provide a pleasant experience for students, but it should also contribute to the development of theory knowledge, recording speed, transcription ability, or other aspects of shorthand skill.

The Sequence of Learning Activities Has a Direct Influence on Motivation

Repetition and classroom routines are necessary to shorthand learning, but passiveness and boredom can be by-products if care is not exercised. As soon as human beings are required to perform the same sequence of activities in the same way over an extended period, they begin to perform these activities passively. Passive learning is inefficient; the more active the involvement, the greater the tendency to learn.

Wise shorthand teachers develop daily lesson plans that include a variety of activities, and they are careful to avoid undue repetition within each class period. Shorthand students have a right to expect that each class period will be somewhat different from previous periods.

Clearly Stated Goals and Objectives Have a Positive Relationship to Motivation

If students know exactly what they must do to achieve, they are apt to work with greater intensity and purpose. It is imperative that teachers establish realistic standards for the many aspects of shorthand skill, and all students must be fully aware of these standards. Setting end-of-the-year goals will not suffice. Intermediate goals realistic to their stages of learning must also be developed. A few examples of where short-term performance standards need to be established are in reading sections of brief forms, writing brief forms, reading rates using part of the homework lesson, reading rates using homework notes, recording dictation for varying lengths of time and speeds, and transcribing from homework notes at prescribed rates.

All Levels of Shorthand Progress Should Be Recognized and Rewarded

Learners need feedback about progress toward teacher-imposed goals. Informal teacher recognition of improvement in any phase of shorthand skill encourages the student to establish new and higher self-imposed goals. The almost daily "pat on the back" for individual progress in reading, writing, and transcription lends new vigor to all students, no matter what their ability.

Formal recognition of progress must of necessity include the use of extrinsic-motivation devices. Devices such as certificates of achievement should be used primarily to encourage higher achievement, not exclusively to honor high achievement. Awards should be given for the various components of shorthand skill as well as for levels of skill. The Gregg Awards Program meets this criterion because recognition is given for recording speed, transcription ability, penmanship ability, and shorthand vocabulary proficiency—all elements of total shorthand skill. The receipt of a certificate honoring achievement of 60 words a minute probably is just as satisfying to some students as a certificate for 120 words a minute would be to others.

Notes

1. Father Raphael Stovik, "A Short History of Stenography Through the Fifth Century," master's thesis, University of North Dakota, Grand Forks, 1960.
2. E. H. Butler, *The Story of British Shorthand*, Sir Isaac Pitman and Sons, Ltd., London, 1951, pp. 231–242.
3. John Robert Gregg, "The Story of Shorthand," *The Business Education World*, Vol. XV, No. 1, p. 9, September 1934.
4. Butler, pp. 231–232
5. John Robert Gregg, "The Story of Shorthand," *The Business Education World*, Vol. XV, No. 8, pp. 603–607, April 1935.
6. Butler, p. 117.
7. Ibid., pp. 234–240.
8. Ibid., p. 90.
9. Carl Naether, "Beginnings of Shorthand," *Journal of Business Education*, Vol. VIII, No. 10, p. 33, June 1933.
10. Edwin G. Knepper, *History of Business Education in the United States*, Edward Brothers, Inc., Ann Arbor, MI, 1941, pp. 142–145.

11. Ronald D. Hahn, "Characteristics of Office Administration Personnel and Requirements for Future Employees with Curriculum Implications for a Four-Year Degree Program in Office Administration . . .," doctoral dissertation, Northern Illinois University, DeKalb, 1977.

12. Amy T. Fujii, "A Survey to Determine the Need for Shorthand Skills and the Extent to which Shorthand is Used in Selected Business Firms in Honolulu, Hawaii," master's thesis, University of Montana, Missoula, 1971.

13. Ethel Kassler Bernstein, "A Survey to Determine the Types of Office Machines Needed in the Office Practice Curricula in the Cherokee County Secondary Schools Based on the Number and Types of Office Machines Being Used by Selected Business Firms of the Cherokee County Area," master's thesis, Winthrop College, Rock Hill, SC, 1974.

14. Benita Lynn Harris, "The Use of Manual Shorthand, Dictating-Transcribing Machines, and Machine Shorthand in Selected Businesses in the Metropolitan Atlanta, Georgia, Area, in 1976," master's thesis, University of Tennessee, Knoxville, 1976.

15. Vivian Mary Kennedy, "The Development of the Word Processing Concept and Its Implications on the Teaching of Shorthand in the High School," master's thesis, San Jose State University, San Jose, CA, 1973.

16. Judith Ann Olson, "A Study to Determine the Systems Used to Record and Transcribe Business Office Dictation in the Milwaukee, Wisconsin, Area," master's thesis, University of Wisconsin, Madison, 1973.

17. Jean Corum Sain, "A Survey to Determine the Number and Types of Office Machines Used in the York County, South Carolina, Area by Business Firms that Employed York Technical Education Center Graduates," master's thesis, Winthrop College, Rock Hill, SC, 1972.

18. Doris Williamson, "Office Machines Used in Student Training Programs in Post Secondary Schools as Compared with Business Usage," master's thesis, Utah State University, Logan, 1973.

19. Beverly A. Biggers, "The Status of Shorthand and Recording Machines Used for Dictation in Representative Business Firms in Columbus, Ohio, in 1969," master's thesis, The Ohio State University, Columbus, 1969.

20. Samuel M. Scammon, "An Analysis of the Need for and Use of Shorthand by Secretaries, Managers, and Personnel Directors," doctoral dissertation, Michigan State University, East Lansing, 1974.

21. Brenda Hornstein, "Is Stenography Still Relevant in the

Business Office?," *Business Education Forum*, Vol. 27, No. 6, pp. 47–48, April 1973.

22. Gail Marie Schmitt, "The Use of Dictating-Transcribing Equipment in Selected Businesses in Metropolitan Knoxville and Chattanooga, Tennessee," master's thesis, The University of Tennessee, Knoxville, 1977.

23. Stephen Lewis, "The Effect of Word Processing on Business Letter Writing," doctoral dissertation, University of North Dakota, Grand Forks, 1977, p. 51.

24. *Occupational Outlook Handbook, 1976–77 Edition*, Bulletin 1875, U.S. Department of Labor, Bureau of Labor Statistics, Superintendent of Public Documents, U.S. Government Printing Office, 1976, p. 94.

25. Ibid., p. 96.

26. Ibid., pp. 94–95.

27. Ibid., p. 95.

28. Ibid., p. 96.

29. Based on 1982 estimated school population of 13,690,000 in grades 9 through 12 and an assumed 2 percent of the population enrolling in shorthand.

30. Jack E. Johnson, "The Effect of Beginning Shorthand on Learning in Selected Language Arts Skills," doctoral dissertation, University of North Dakota, Grand Forks, 1975.

31. Ideas for recruiting students were summarized by Sharon Bouchard from presentations made by: Nancy Wagner, Hutchinson Senior High School, MN; Scharlott Walstedt, Richfield Senior High School, MN; Diane Kolstad, Woodbury Senior High School, MN; Jan Weaver, Arlington High School, IN; Shirley Hall, Richard High School, IL; Lorene Gottschalk, South High School, OH; Evelyn Finley, Polaris Joint Vocational School, OH; and Linda Sietz, Andover High School, MI.

32. Herbert A. Tonne, "A Report on National Enrollment," *The Delta Pi Epsilon Journal*, Vol. 4, No. 3, p. 3, May 1962.

33. Helen A. Cwierz, "The Relationship of the Turse Shorthand Aptitude Test, I.Q., and English Grades to Success in Beginning Shorthand," master's thesis, Indiana University of Pennsylvania, PA, 1968.

34. Timothy V. Ryals, "A Second Look at the Teaching of First-Year Shorthand," *The Balance Sheet*, Vol. 51, No. 6, p. 256, February 1970.

35. William Selden, "Criteria for Selection of Stenographic Student . . .," *Journal of Business Education*, Vol. XXXVII, No. 3, p. 105, December 1961.

36. Mary Virginia VanKirk, "The Relationship Between First-Semester Shorthand Success and Five Predictive Factors,"

master's thesis, University of Southern California, Los Angeles, 1960.

37. Leonard J. Varah, "Effect of Academic Motivation and Other Selected Criteria on Achievement of First- and Second-Semester Students," *The Delta Pi Epsilon Journal*, Vol. X, No. 1, p. 27, November 1967.

38. Paul L. Turse, *Turse Shorthand Aptitude Test*, Harcourt, Brace & World, Inc., New York, 1940, pp. 1–8.

39. Walter Pauk, "What's the Best Way to Predict Success in Shorthand," *Business Education World*, Vol. 43, No. 8, pp. 7–8, April 1963.

40. Rose Anne Davis, "Will Half a Turse Do Just as Well," *Business Education World*, Vol. 45, No. 5, pp. 11–12, January 1966.

41. Walter L. Deemer, Jr., *E.R.C. Stenographic Aptitude Test*, Science Research Associates, Chicago, IL, 1947, pp. 1–15.

42. Edward E. Byers, *Byers' First-Year Shorthand Aptitude Tests, Parts 1 and 2*, Allied Publishers, Inc., Portland, OR, 1959, pp. 1–5, pp. 1–13.

43. Lorrine Skaff, "The Development and Validation of a Predictive Instrument to Measure Student Success in the First Semester of Gregg Shorthand," doctoral dissertation, Oregon State University, Corvallis, 1972.

44. Department of Public Instruction, *Shorthand for Business Education Departments in Pennsylvania's Public Schools*, Bulletin 27, Commonwealth of Pennsylvania, 1968, p. 30.

Chapter 2

The Shorthand Program

The value of the shorthand program is judged by the ability of the shorthand user to produce mailable letters and other usable materials in an office position. One of the major components of effective shorthand use is the correct application of the rules for spelling, punctuation, number expression, sentence structure, possessives, vocabulary, and other transcription elements. This proficiency is cumulative from the first association with the rules at the elementary school level. The shorthand program devotes intensive efforts to improving this ability, culminating in its application to mailable letter production. Thus, a major goal of the shorthand program is to refine the knowledge of transcription elements.

The second major component of effective shorthand use is the ability to respond quickly to the spoken word. This component is the one that deteriorates over time if shorthand is not written regularly. Authors writing about the sequence of shorthand in the curriculum usually recommend that it be scheduled closest to the time of use on the job. Since shorthand is taught at the secondary, postsecondary (community college, vocational technical institute, private business school), and four-year college levels, curriculum specialists, shorthand teachers, and department heads need to decide on the most effective placement of shorthand courses within the program. The length of the program is an important factor to consider in this decision.

The Secondary School

Placement in the Curriculum

The following recommendations are made for placement of the shorthand courses in both three-year and four-year high schools:

1. The beginning course should be offered during the sophomore year, or the tenth grade, for those students planning to enter a cooperative education program in their junior or senior year. For these students, an advanced course can then be provided in the junior year, or the eleventh grade. However, it is also possible for cooperative education students to enroll in the

advanced shorthand course during the senior year if it can be offered during the time they are on campus.

2. The beginning course should be offered during the junior year, or the eleventh grade, for those students not planning to enter a cooperative education program and in secondary schools where the cooperative education program is not offered. For these students an advanced course in the senior year, or the twelfth grade, is recommended.

Length of Program

Many of the average-size and large comprehensive secondary schools will have a two-year shorthand program. Some of them will have a three-semester program with a fourth semester devoted to a "capstone course" entitled *Secretarial Procedures, Clerical Precedures,* or *Office Procedures.* Such a fourth-semester capstone course may have units of shorthand and transcription instruction for those students who are shorthand writers. However, some capstone or procedures courses do not include further study of shorthand, and shorthand teachers in such schools will need to plan their shorthand instruction for a three-semester program.

Shorthand teachers in secondary schools with only one-year programs should encourage their students to continue their shorthand education at the community college, technical school, private business school, or four-year college level.

The Postsecondary School

Placement in the Curriculum

Following the same considerations as for the secondary school, shorthand study in the postsecondary school should be scheduled closest to the point of use in a business situation. The following recommendations are made for placement of the shorthand courses:

ONE-YEAR INTENSIVE STUDY.   For students who will be entering the job market after a one-year postsecondary program, shorthand study will take the form of a year of intensive study from beginning through advanced work. For students with prior instruction, shorthand study will be a continuation of study started in secondary school, culminating with the advanced course by the end of the one-year postsecondary program.

TWO-YEAR PROGRAMS.   For students who will be entering the job market after two years of postsecondary study, their shorthand program may be spread over the two years if they are beginners. For other students, it may be a continuation of study begun in secondary school and completed during the second year of postsecondary work.

FOUR-YEAR PROGRAMS. For students planning to transfer to four-year colleges to complete a business teacher education degree or an office administration degree, the beginning and intermediate courses could be taken at the two-year institution. The advanced course should be taken at the four-year college to conform to the idea of completing the shorthand program closest to the time of use—at the completion of the four-year degree program.

Articulation with the Secondary School

The postsecondary schools and feeder high schools will need to maintain a close working relationship so that shorthand teachers in both will teach the classes with similar content, goals and objectives, and standards and evaluation procedures. If the postsecondary school plans to accept high school shorthand as a prerequisite to placement in its intermediate and/or advanced shorthand classes, skills and learning developed in high school should be equivalent to those developed at the postsecondary level.

Articulation with the Four-Year College

A close working relationship between the postsecondary school and the four-year college, in which both educational institutions are pursuing similar content, goals and objectives, and standards and evaluation procedures, is also important. Students will benefit from this articulation by being able to move easily from the postsecondary shorthand program to the program at the four-year college.

Length of Program

The majority of community colleges, technical schools, and private business schools have three or four semesters or five or six quarters of shorthand instruction for general business correspondence. Schools with specialized-vocabulary shorthand courses have additional semesters or quarters to learn the specialized terminology.

The Four-Year College

Placement in the Curriculum

The same curricular considerations described for the postsecondary school are needed at the four-year college level. Students pursuing the office administration degree should complete their shorthand education near the end of their four-year program. For office administration majors, shorthand study may be started in the soph-

47

omore or junior year, followed by the intermediate course, and completed with advanced shorthand instruction during their senior year. For the student in a teacher-education program, shorthand study should be completed during the semester or quarter preceding the methods course and student teaching. In some business teacher-education programs, the advanced shorthand course is a prerequisite to the shorthand methods course. Other teacher-training institutions allow the advanced shorthand course to be taken concurrently with the methods course. When planning the shorthand course sequences, such requirements must be considered.

Articulation with the Secondary and Postsecondary Schools

Four-year colleges must maintain a close working relationship with the feeder secondary and postsecondary schools to see that content, goals and objectives, standards and evaluation procedures are similar enough to allow students to enter the shorthand program at a level determined by their previous instruction without repetition of course work already completed.

Length of Program

Most four-year colleges will have three or four semesters or five or six quarters of shorthand instruction at the beginning, intermediate, and advanced levels for general business correspondence. Some four-year colleges, however, do not offer beginning and intermediate courses; so students pursuing the office administration or business teacher education degrees must take these courses at a postsecondary or secondary school before entering the college.

Advantages of offering all levels of shorthand instruction at the four-year college are:

1. An opportunity for the four-year institution to fulfill a commitment to research by using the beginning and intermediate classes in research studies.
2. An opportunity for the shorthand students in business teacher education to use the beginning and intermediate classes for laboratory observation and/or teaching experience.
3. An opportunity for the shorthand methods teachers to teach at the beginning and intermediate levels, thus keeping beginning and intermediate learning strategies and methods in acute focus for use with methods students.
4. An opportunity to provide a teaching-internship program for graduate students to teach under the supervision of a master teacher at the very important instructional levels of beginning and intermediate shorthand.

Previous Shorthand Instruction and Placement Procedures

Postsecondary institutions and four-year colleges will need to evaluate the shorthand competencies of students entering their programs with previous shorthand instruction.

Some schools have devised placement tests to determine competency in shorthand vocabulary, dictation, typewritten transcription, spelling, grammar, punctuation, transcription element use, and so on. Other schools place students with one year of high school shorthand into an intermediate class and students with two years of high school shorthand into an advanced class, without the use of formal placement testing.

Four-year college shorthand teachers who follow the latter procedure probably will need to be flexible about allowing students to repeat courses previously taken in postsecondary or secondary schools if the students feel deficient in the beginning or intermediate levels. If such deficiences (for example, in shorthand vocabulary, reading, writing, typewritten transcription, mailable letter production, or transcription element use) are real, it is probably wise for students to retake the courses necessary to fulfill the prerequisites for successful completion of the next highest course.

Prerequisites

The philosophy of the shorthand teacher and the business education department probably will govern the prerequisites for each of the particular shorthand courses. If the shorthand teachers and the departments believe that typewritten transcription should be started in the first semester of shorthand instruction, it will be necessary to require one semester or one year of typing as a prerequisite to the beginning shorthand course. In such situations it is logically assumed that this commitment to typewritten transcription would continue into the advanced shorthand course; therefore, advanced typing would be a prerequisite to advanced shorthand.

In some secondary schools such a prerequisite arrangement would mean that students would take beginning typing as sophomores, beginning shorthand and advanced typing as juniors, and advanced shorthand as seniors. In still other secondary schools it would mean that students would take beginning typing as freshmen, beginning shorthand and advanced typing as sophomores, advanced shorthand as juniors, and the cooperative office education program as seniors.

In the two-year community college, private business school, technical school, and four-year college, there might be variations in program planning, but the same prerequisite arrangement would exist. Beginning typing would be a prerequisite for beginning shorthand (thus intermediate typing and beginning shorthand could be taken during the same semester or quarter), intermediate typing would be a prerequisite for intermediate shorthand, advanced typing would be a prerequisite for advanced shorthand (thus advanced typing and intermediate shorthand could be taken during the same semester or quarter).

Types of Shorthand Courses

Because of the time limitation imposed on course offerings, the vocational goals of high school students, and the relatively low numbers of students desiring highly specialized course work, most comprehensive secondary schools teach shorthand for general business correspondence. The technical schools, two-year postsecondary schools, and private business schools, however, because of their philosophy of purpose and the maturity and goal-orientation of their students, are able to provide more technical shorthand education including medical, legal, and technical terminology.

Most four-year colleges are not designed for such highly specialized education; but, for the most part, teach shorthand for general business correspondence to office administration and business teacher education majors.

Length of Shorthand Period and Class Meetings Per Week

In most schools, the beginning and intermediate classes of shorthand, or the first two semesters or three quarters, have class periods of 40 to 60 minutes. The class periods in the advanced or second-year course in most schools are of similar length; however, some schools have double-period advanced classes. In still other situations, the advanced shorthand class may be part of a secretarial office block, and the shorthand instruction may be a single period in the block or may be integrated with other learning activities of the secretarial office block to more nearly simulate an office situation.

In the secondary school, the shorthand classes usually meet five days a week, while at the postsecondary and four-year college levels, classes may meet three, four, or five days a week.

A Basis for Curriculum Development—Competencies and Emphases

Important elements to consider in determining the length of a shorthand program (number of semesters or quarters, length of class periods, number of class meetings a week) are (1) content, (2) goals or objectives, (3) emphases to be applied, and (4) standards of evaluation. Standards for a vocational course can be based on national and local employment requirements, normative data from studies of student achievement, current writings in the field, data obtained from job studies, and the achievement that can be expected of students.

Most job studies will point out the following competencies as employment requirements related to shorthand writing and transcribing on the job:

1. The ability to take dictation at the rate given by the employer.
2. The ability to transcribe dictation into mailable letters or other types of communication media.
3. The ability to apply transcription elements (grammar, punctuation, capitalization, possessives, spelling, number usage, word usage, and so on) correctly.
4. The ability to make correct decisions regarding the transcription activities of use of stationery, letter placement, letter style, application of special lines, application of special directions, proofreading, and the correction of errors.

To relate the shorthand writing and transcribing functions of the secretarial or stenographic job to the shorthand classroom requires a more detailed breakdown, which involves identifying the competencies to be acquired.

The following competencies, listed by semesters and learning activities, are meant only to provide guidance to shorthand teachers and curriculum directors at the secondary, postsecondary, and college levels. In identifying competencies and learning activities, several factors need to be considered, including the following:

1. Length of program (length of class periods, number of class meetings a week, number of semesters or quarters)
2. Philosophies of teachers
3. Evaluation methods
4. Student attendance patterns
5. Student population
6. Availability of equipment (tape laboratories, typewriters, and so on)
7. Previous typing instruction

In using the following competencies, teachers at all levels will need to consider raising or lowering the standards, excluding some types of instruction indicated and including others, and substituting tried and true learning activities.

First Semester Competencies

1. Learning Activity—*Reading Development*
   a. During the first six weeks, students can be expected to read from shorthand *plates* at a range of 40 to 100 words a minute (*wam*).
   b. During the second six weeks, students can be expected to read from shorthand *homework notes* at a range of 40 to 100 wam.

    c. During the third six weeks, students can be expected to read from shorthand *homework notes* at a range of 60 to 120 wam.

2. Learning Activity—*Shorthand Vocabulary Development*

    a. Students will write sample shorthand vocabulary words from textbook lessons with correct symbol use, theory application, joining of symbols, proportion, and line of writing at the *minimum* level of 70 percent accuracy.

    b. Students will write brief forms and frequently used phrases with correct symbol use, joining of symbols, proportion, and line of writing at a *minimum* level of 80 percent accuracy.

3. Learning Activity—*Dictation Recording Development*

    a. By the end of the first five to six weeks, students will write homework material using a 30-second speed-building dictation plan, with textbooks open for reference, at rates of 60, 70, and 80 wam for a block of time of about 20 minutes.

    b. By the end of the twelfth week, students will attempt dictation recording tests on practiced material at the minimum rate of 60 wam and transcribe two or three minutes of dictation on the typewriter with 95 percent accuracy. Some students will be able to attain 70 wam for two or three minutes on dictation recording tests on practiced material.

    c. By the end of the first semester, students will attempt unpreviewed new-material dictation recording tests at the rate of 60 wam, transcribe on the typewriter with an attempt to pass two or three minutes of dictation with 95 percent accuracy. Some students will be able to attain 70 wam for two or three minutes on dictation recording tests on new material.

4. Learning Activity—*Typewritten Transcription Development*

    a. During the first three to six weeks, students will transcribe on the typewriter (using plate material first and then homework notes) to learn the transcription-transliteration process with the accuracy, speed, and transcription element usage appropriate to this period of development.

    b. By the end of the twelfth week, students will transcribe on the typewriter from homework notes for three minutes, errors corrected, at transcription rates ranging from 10 to 20 wam.

    c. By the end of the first semester, students will transcribe on the typewriter from homework notes for three minutes, errors corrected, at transcription rates ranging from 13 to 25 wam.

    d. Students will study the Student Transcript as part of each day's lesson to observe and study spelling problems, hyphenated words, number expression, capitalization rules, and so on.

5. Learning Activity—*Transcription Element Application*
   a. Beginning with Lesson 19, students will study the marginal reminders to review the correct spelling of shorthand words.
   b. Beginning with Lesson 31, students will (1) study the punctuation and reasons for punctuation within the letters and (2) continue the study of the marginal reminders to learn the spelling of problem words and other transcription element use.
   c. Beginning with Lesson 31, students will place the punctuation and coded reasons for the punctuation in the writing of each homework lesson. Example:

   par ap nc
   ⊙ ⊙ ⊙

   d. Beginning with Lesson 31, students will attempt to pass, at a minimum of 70 percent accuracy, chapter tests comprised of spelling words, sentences containing punctuation and other transcription elements, and vocabulary words.

Second Semester Competencies

1. Learning Activity—*Reading Development*
   a. Students will continue to maintain accurate and rapid reading ability by reading from homework notes as part of the three-minute transcription rate work, by reading back from controlled writing of dictation practice, and by reading from self-written notes of three-minute dictation tests and mailable letter production sets.
2. Learning Activity—*Shorthand Vocabulary Development*
   a. Students will write sample shorthand vocabulary words from chapters studied, with correct symbol use, theory application, joining of symbols, proportion, and line of writing at a *minimum* of 70 percent accuracy.
   b. Students will write all brief forms and frequently used phrases from dictation at the rate of 15 to 17 wam at a *minimum* level of 88 percent accuracy.
3. Learning Activity—*Dictation Recording Development*
   a. By the midpoint of the second semester, students will pass unpreviewed, new-material three-minute dictation tests at the rates of 80, 70, or 60 wam, transcribed on the typewriter, with 95 percent accuracy.
   b. By the end of the second semester, students will pass unpreviewed new-material three-minute dictation tests at

the rates of 90, 80, 70, or 60 wam*, transcribed on the typewriter, with 95 percent accuracy.

4. Learning Activity—*Typewritten Transcription Development*
   a. Throughout the second semester, students will increase speed and improve accuracy on typewritten transcription drill work by a series of short weekly drills.
   b. During the second semester, students will transcribe on the typewriter from homework notes for three minutes, errors corrected, at transcription rates ranging from 15 to 29 wam by the midpoint of the semester and at transcription rates ranging from 18 to 32 wam by the end of the semester.
   c. Students will continue to use the Student Transcript as a resource manual as part of each day's lesson to learn the transcription elements of spelling, number usage, capitalization usage, hyphenation, compound words, possessives, and punctuation.
   d. By the midpoint of the second semester students will attempt to transcribe into mailable form heavily previewed short letters dictated at the rate of 60 wam.
   e. By the end of the second semester students will attempt to transcribe into mailable form, at the production rate of 15 to 20 wam, three short letters dictated at the rates of 70 and/or 60 wam.

5. Learning Activity—*Transcription Element Application*
   a. Throughout the second semester, students will continue to study the spelling lists, vocabulary words, and explanations of transcription elements and punctuation usages.
   b. Throughout the second semester, students will use a reference manual during transcription of three-minute dictation tests and during mailable letter production.
   c. Throughout the second semester, students will study the marginal reminders and insert punctuation and coded reasons in the homework writing assignment.
   d. Throughout the second semester, students will attempt to pass, at a minimum of 70 percent accuracy, chapter tests comprised of spelling words, sentences containing punctuation and other transcription elements, and vocabulary words.
   e. From the point of mailable letter introduction, students will attempt to apply to mailable letter production all transcription-element information practiced during transcription drills, three-minute transcription rates, and classroom discussions from transparencies and workbook sheets.

* Rates are given as examples and may need to be altered to fit class situations.

Third Semester Competencies—Speed-Building Emphasis Semester*

1. Learning Activity—*Reading Development*
   a. Students will continue to maintain accurate and rapid reading ability by reading from homework notes as part of the three-minute transcription rate work, by reading back from controlled writing of dictation practice, and by reading from self-written notes of three-minute dictation tests and mailable letter production sets.

2. Learning Activity—*Shorthand Vocabulary Development*
   a. Students will write sample shorthand vocabulary words from chapters studied, with correct symbol use, theory application, joining of symbols, proportion, and line of writing at a *minimum* of 70 percent accuracy.
   b. Students will write all brief forms and frequently used phrases from dictation at the rate of 15 to 17 wam at a *minimum* level of 92 percent accuracy.

3. Learning Activity—*Dictation Recording Development*
   a. By the midpoint of the third semester, students will pass unpreviewed, new-material three-minute dictation tests at the rates of 100, 90, or 80 wam**, transcribed on the typewriter, with 95 percent accuracy.
   b. By the end of the third semester, students will pass unpreviewed, new-material three-minute dictation tests at the rates of 110, 100, or 90 wam**, transcribed on the typewriter, with 95 percent accuracy.

4. Learning Activity—*Typewritten Transcription Development*
   a. Throughout the third semester, students will increase speed and accuracy on typewritten transcription drill work by a series of short weekly drills.
   b. During the third semester, students will transcribe on the typewriter from homework notes for three minutes, errors corrected, at transcription rates ranging from 21 to 36 wam by the midpoint and at transcription rates ranging from 25 to 40 wam by the end of the semester.
   c. Throughout the semester, students will increase speed and accuracy of typewritten transcription of mailable letter production work, with an attempt by the end of the semester to transcribe consistently into mailable form three- and four-letter sets of medium-length letters (dictated at a minimum of 80 wam as well as letters dictated office-style) at a production rate of 17 to 20 wam.

   * Some teachers prefer to use the third semester for dictation speed-building emphasis, and others prefer to use it for transcription emphasis.

   ** Rates may need to be altered to fit class situations.

    d. Throughout the third semester, students will perform mailable letter tasks using carbons, envelopes, special notation lines, interoffice memorandums, letters of varying lengths, and various other office correspondence tasks.

    e. Throughout the third semester, students will practice making decisions regarding lengths of letters, transcription element usage, allocation of time, and various office procedures.

5. Learning Activity—*Transcription Element Application*

    a. Throughout the third semester, students will continue to study the spelling lists, vocabulary words, and explanations of transcription elements and punctuation usages.

    b. Throughout the third semester, students will continue to use a reference manual during transcription of three-minute dictation tests and during mailable letter production.

    c. Throughout the third semester, students will study the marginal reminders and insert punctuation and coded reasons in the homework writing assignment.

    d. Throughout the third semester, students will attempt to pass, at a minimum of 70 percent accuracy, chapter tests comprised of spelling words, sentences containing punctuation and other transcription elements, and vocabulary words at a *minimum* of 70 percent accuracy.

    e. Throughout the third semester, students will attempt to apply to mailable-letter production all transcription-element information practiced during transcription drills, three-minute transcription rates, and classroom discussions from transparencies and workbook sheets.

Fourth-Semester Competencies

Basically, the learning activities for the fourth semester will be similar to those for the third. Differences will center around whether the shorthand teachers prefer to consider the major emphasis of the fourth semester to be typewritten transcription development or dictation speed development. If the secondary school does not offer a fourth semester of shorthand instruction, the third semester probably will emphasize transcription, in recognition of the fact that the ability to transcribe materials into usable form is of paramount importance in the business office.

Assuming that the third semester of the advanced shorthand program has emphasized dictation speed development and that the fourth semester of instruction will place major emphasis on typewritten transcription development, the following suggested, but not all-inclusive, list should be considered in curriculum planning, instruction, and evaluation of the fourth semester of instruction:

1. Shorthand vocabulary development will still be a part of teaching and testing, with the refinement of shorthand vocabulary knowledge and the development of a more advanced shorthand vocabulary base being important considerations.
2. Dictation writing ability will continue to be developed but, if typewritten transcription is the major emphasis of the semester, most of the time will be spent on typewritten transcription activities; therefore, higher dictation speeds might not necessarily be developed. The emphasis for dictation recording may be on maintaining the speeds developed in the third semester and refining the dictation recording process to the point of 97 percent accuracy on dictation tests rather than the previous 95 percent. An additional emphasis of dictation recording will be to refine the ability to write from office-style dictation that includes changes, additions, deletions, and directions.
3. Typewritten transcription rate and accuracy will continue to be improved by drills and three-minute transcription rates with the transcription rate within the range of 40 to 55 wam by the end of the fourth semester.
4. Transcription element usage will continue to be improved by studying more demanding usages in the workbook, reference manual, and the information from the textbook and Student Transcript.
5. Mailable-letter production will continue to be improved by increasing dictation speed, lengthening letters, adding variety to the special lines in letters, varying the sizes of stationery, and using a variety of letter styles and a variety of correspondence forms (messages, reports, interoffice memos, manuscripts, news releases, telephone messages).
6. Decision-making abilities will be sharpened by including mini-simulations, in-basket exercises, and office-related assignments.
7. Knowledge of career opportunities will be expanded by cooperative work arrangements with businesses, "shadowing" experiences in offices, field trips, professional affiliations with student organizations, and reading professional literature.
8. Emphasis on oral and written communication skills, listening skills, dress and grooming habits, attitudes and work habits will become an integral and integrated part of the day-to-day classroom activities.

Allocation of Emphases

As a summarizing statement about competencies for four semesters of shorthand instruction, the competencies listed above must be translated into emphases for particular semesters or quarters of instruction. In addition, it is necessary to set priorities for time allotment to each emphasis. For purposes of discussion, these priorities will be called *major* and *minor* emphases. It is obvious that all learning activities within a particular class period cannot be major; otherwise, for example, a 60-minute class period with three learning activities— shorthand vocabulary development, reading development, and dictation recording development—would be divided equally among the three activities. Most shorthand teachers, in their own minds at least, have decided that certain learning activities require greater emphasis than others and that the amount of time devoted to each should change from time to time throughout the shorthand program. The following diagram attempts to allocate the emphases according to the competencies which appear on pages 50–58 of this chapter and according to the standards and grading designated in Chapter 10, pages 343–356.

ALLOCATION OF EMPHASES FOR SHORTHAND INSTRUCTION TO DEVELOP GENERAL BUSINESS CORRESPONDENCE USAGE

COMPONENTS OF LEARNING AND SKILL DEVELOPMENT	1ST SEMES- TER	2D SEMES- TER	3D SEMES- TER**	4TH SEMES- TER**
Reading Development	Major first 6 weeks; minor thereafter	Minor	Minor	Minor
Shorthand Vocabulary Development	Major	Minor	Minor	Minor
Dictation Recording Development	Major	Major	Major	Minor
Typewritten Transcription Development	Minor	Major	Major	Major
Transcription-Element* Development	Minor	Minor	Minor	Minor

*Transcription Element: punctuation, spelling, hyphenation, possessives, number expression, capitalization, and so on.
**Emphases may be reversed according to teacher philosophy and preferences. In three-semester programs, the fourth-semester emphases shown may become the third-semester emphases.

The emphases allocated in the preceding diagram and the competencies identified by semester in the preceding pages can be easily altered to fit a quarter structure or the three-semester postsecondary or college situations.

Planning for Teaching

The competencies and emphases identified in the preceding pages become the basis for developing yearly plans; semester, six-week or quarter plans; and finally weekly and daily plans. The long-term goals identified in the competencies can provide the necessary ingredients to develop the yearly and semester and/or quarter plans. Somewhat more difficult is the task of placing these competencies into weekly and daily plans. As stated earlier, the degree of emphasis given to an area of learning will determine the amount of time during the week and during the day that will be devoted to it.

The following weekly plans are bare skeletons. The flesh to be added would be the methodology, the allocation of time based upon emphases, and the rearrangement of the activities to provide variety and motivation. The recommended methodology for each area of learning is explained in detail in various sections of this book.

SKELETON WEEKLY PLAN FOR THE FIRST HALF OF THE FIRST SEMESTER

MONDAY	TUESDAY WEDNESDAY THURSDAY FRIDAY
a. Review of homework	a. Review of homework
b. Timed reading of homework lesson*	b. Timed reading of homework lesson
c. Dictation speed building of parts of the homework lesson**	c. Dictation speed building of parts of the homework lesson
d. Teaching new lesson	d. Teaching new lesson
e. Sight reading part of new lesson***	e. Sight reading part of new lesson
	f. Typewritten transcription drills and/or typewritten transcription rates from homework lesson

*Starting about the third week of the first semester
**Starting about the fifth or sixth day of the first semester
***In early stages of semester

Other learning activities that can be included throughout the four semesters are workbook exercises, motivational games, and testing.

SKELETON WEEKLY PLAN FOR THE SECOND HALF OF THE FIRST SEMESTER

MONDAY	TUESDAY WEDNESDAY THURSDAY	FRIDAY
a. Review of homework	a. Typewritten transcription drills and/or typewritten transcription rates from homework lesson	a. Review of homework
b. Dictation speed building of parts of homework and some new related material*	b. Review of homework	b. Teaching new lesson
c. Teaching new lesson	c. Dictation speed building of parts of homework and some new related material	c. Dictation warmup
	d. Teaching new lesson	d. Dictation testing
		e. Transcription of dictation tests

*Dictation speed-building material would change to new material entirely when the introduction of new theory has been completed.

The basic design for the first half of the second semester would be similar to the design for the second half of the first semester, with new material used for the dictation speed building. This weekly plan could be in effect until the introduction of mailable-letter work. The suggested weekly plan after the three-day recommended introduction to mailable letters, described in Chapter 9, might be:

SKELETON WEEKLY PLAN FOR THE SECOND SEMESTER

MONDAY TUESDAY	WEDNESDAY THURSDAY	FRIDAY
a. Review of homework	a. Typewritten transcription drills and/or typewritten transcription rates from homework lesson	a. Review of homework
b. Teaching new lesson	b. Review of homework	b. Teaching new lesson
c. Mailable letter production	c. Teaching new lesson	c. Dictation warmup
	d. Dictation speed building	d. Dictation testing
		e. Transcription of dictation tests

SKELETON WEEKLY PLAN FOR THE THIRD SEMESTER—DICTATION SPEED BUILDING IS THE EMPHASIS

MONDAY	TUESDAY	WEDNESDAY
a. Typewritten transcription drills and/or typewritten transcription rates from homework lesson **b.** Review of homework **c.** Teaching new lesson **d.** Dictation speed building	**a.** Review of homework **b.** Teaching new lesson **c.** Mailable letter production	**a.** Typewritten transcription drills and/or typewritten transcription rates from homework lesson **b.** Review of homework **c.** Teaching new lesson **d.** Dictation speed building

THURSDAY	FRIDAY
a. Typewritten transcription drills and/or typewritten transcription rates from homework lesson **b.** Review of homework **c.** Teaching new lesson **d.** Dictation speed building	**a.** Review of homework **b.** Teaching new lesson **c.** Dictation warmup **d.** Dictation testing **e.** Transcription of dictation tests

OR:

MONDAY TUESDAY	WEDNESDAY THURSDAY	FRIDAY
a. Review of homework **b.** Teaching new lesson **c.** Mailable letter production	**a.** Typewritten transcription drills and/or typewritten transcription rates from homework lesson **b.** Teaching new lesson **c.** Dictation speed building	**a.** Review of homework **b.** Teaching new lesson **c.** Dictation warmup **d.** Dictation testing **e.** Transcription of dictation tests

SKELETON WEEKLY PLAN FOR THE FOURTH SEMESTER*— TRANSCRIPTION IS THE EMPHASIS

MONDAY TUESDAY WEDNESDAY	THURSDAY	FRIDAY
a. Review of homework b. Teaching new lesson c. Mailable letter production	a. Typewritten transcription drills and/or typewritten transcription rates from homework lesson b. Review of homework c. Teaching new lesson d. Dictation speed building	a. Review of homework b. Teaching new lesson c. Dictation speed building and/or dictation testing (recommended that testing be on alternate weeks rather than every week)

*Time should be allocated within this semester for in-basket exercises, minisimulations, and so on.

Planning Daily for Effective Teaching and Learning

Planning for teaching involves organizing the long-term competencies into the short-term competencies developed into a weekly schedule and, finally, planning the details of each day's teaching. Following are sample daily lessons for each of the four semesters. These represent only one day of the semester but are intended to suggest the minimum planning recommended for each day. The time intervals in the plans are given for guidance. Because readers may be using various editions of textbooks or various systems of shorthand, no effort has been made to be precise in matching words to paragraphs indicated, and so on.

Sample First Semester Daily Lesson Plan

Situation:

A lesson during Week 5 of the first semester: The class period is approximately 55 minutes.

Today's Lesson: 25
Tomorrow's Lesson: 26

Performance Objectives

Students will:

1. Spell and pronounce quickly the review words of Lesson 25 as teacher writes words on the board.

2. Drypen (write over shorthand outlines in the textbook with the nonwriting end of the pen) and read from Lesson 25 for individual 30-second reading rates.
3. Take dictation at rates of 70, 80, and 90 wam using the 30-second speed-forcing plan; books open to homework lesson during first part of practice, closed during latter part.
4. Spell and pronounce quickly the new shorthand vocabulary of Lesson 26 as teacher writes words on the board.
5. Attempt to do typewritten transcription 30-second goal-setting drills from homework notes at 40 wam.

Materials:

Gregg Shorthand, Series 90, Leslie and Zoubek
Student Transcript
Stopwatch
Interval Dictation Chart

Activities:

1. (6 min.) Review of Lesson 25.
   a. Write the following shorthand outlines on the chalkboard; students spell and pronounce quickly as teacher points and directs.

   Brief Forms

   Cities and States

   Business Phrases

   b. Write the following business vocabulary words on the chalkboard, and ask individual students to give the definitions and spellings:

   (1)

   (2)

(3)

2. (6 min.) Students drypen and read from homework notes of Lesson 25, letters 232, 233, 234 on pages 123–124. Ask individual students to read for 30-second periods. Post rates on bulletin board by student number or inform students of rates upon completion of individual's reading.

3. (20 min.) Dictate at rates of 70, 80, and 90 wam using the 30-second speed-forcing plan. Students have books open for first three dictations, but dictation at controlled rates is conducted without reference to textbooks.

30-Second Speed-Forcing Plan: Lesson 25, letters 235 and 236

First 30 Seconds	Second 30 Seconds	Third 30 Seconds
70	70	70
80	80	80
90	90	90
Control at 80	Control at 80	Control at 80

Control all three pieces at 80

Repeat procedure for letter 236

PREVIEW WORDS. (Since books are open, only the shorthand vocabulary that might create the greatest problems in writing are placed on the board and drilled before dictation and between dictations.)

Letter 235   Letter 236

4. (6 min.) Preview of Lesson 26. Write the following shorthand outlines on the chalkboard; students spell and pronounce each quickly as teacher points and directs. *iah*—a vowel following

long *i* is represented by a small circle within a larger circle. Spell it *iah*.
Compare:

en-, un- word beginnings are represented by *n* before a consonant.

en-

un-

in-, en-, un- followed by a vowel are written in full.

in- ; en- ; un-

Useful Business Phrases

5. (15 min.) Students will do typewritten transcription drills using the 30-second goal-setting plan, with homework notes as the source. Ask students to get typewriter ready as follows:
a. Set margins for a five-inch line.
b. Set machine on single spacing.

Procedure:
1. Find letter 232 in the homework notes.
2. Drypen and read in unison.
3. Write on board in longhand and discuss the following transcription elements:
spelling of *Overman, ice-making, cooperation, warranty.*
4. Have students mark superior figures 1, 2, 3, 4 at each 20-word interval. (Indicate where these are by referring to Student Transcript.)
5. Remind students to assume correct typing position, use snap stroking, keep eyes on copy.
6. Transcribe for 30 seconds, with the goal of being at the first superior figure at the end of 30 seconds.
7. Transcribe same material again. Ask students reaching first goal to try to increase goal by two or three words.

       8. Start at superior figure 1 and do two more drills to transcribe to superior figure 2 in 30 seconds.

       9. Continue through letter this way as far as time permits.

     10. Finish by having students transcribe all or part of letter, with accuracy of transcription as the goal.

6. (2 min.) Instructions to students for doing homework.

  a. Drypen, spell, and pronounce the shorthand vocabulary at the beginning of Lesson 26. Write the shorthand outlines in groups of three, each group three times.

  b. Drypen and read Lesson 26 until you can read it fluently.

  c. Self-dictate Lesson 26 as rapidly as you can read. Read a phrase and then write a phrase. As problem shorthand vocabulary arises, practice these outlines rapidly, spelling as you write, and taking difficult outlines apart and building them back up until you attain writing fluency.

  d. Self-dictate the first three letters a second time concentrating on controlled, well-written notes.

Sample Second Semester Daily Lesson Plan

Situation:

A lesson during the last nine weeks of the second semester. The class period in this plan is approximately 55 minutes.

Today's Lesson: 58
Tomorrow's Lesson: 59

Performance Objectives

The student will attempt to:

1. Spell and pronounce rapidly the shorthand vocabulary words reviewed from Lesson 58.
2. Understand the shorthand vocabulary principles of the new Lesson 59 by spelling, pronouncing, and writing sample shorthand outlines.
3. Transcribe one set (three letters*) of mailable letters that are related to Lessons 56, 57, and 58 of the homework practice, at the standard of:

      3 letters mailable   = A
      2 letters mailable   = B
      1 letter mailable   = C
      1 letter correctable = D

Production time is based on a 15 to 20 wam production rate.

*If a class period is less than 55 minutes, the length of the letters could be reduced, or two letters rather than three could be dictated.

Materials:

Interval Chart
Stopwatch
Student Transcript
Gregg Dictation and Introductory Transcription, Series 90
Instructor's Handbook for Gregg Dictation and Introductory Transcription and Series 90, letters 56, 57, and 58.

Activities:

1. (5 min.) Review Lesson 58 by explaining the word family and placing selected shorthand vocabulary on the chalkboard. Students will sound/spell and pronounce outlines as teacher points to each. After each family is sound/spelled, students write the shorthand outlines from teacher dictation in their notebooks as many times as possible. The teacher dictates and points to the appropriate shorthand outline on the chalkboard so students can look quickly if necessary. After all families are completed, briefly re-explain each family and have students sound/spell and pronounce selected shorthand vocabulary. Write on the chalkboard:

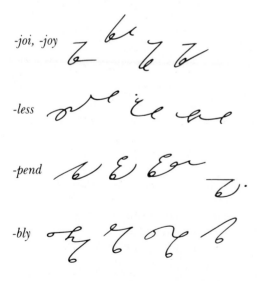

Ask students to quickly spell the following *common prefixes* words: *immeasurable, improbable, impolite, impatient.* Write each word on the board in longhand as the student spells it.

For a review of the business vocabulary words in Lesson 58, **67** place the shorthand outline on the chalkboard and ask a student to spell and define it. Write on the chalkboard:

Place the longhand for the words on the chalkboard as the student spells them.

2. (5 min.) Preview Lesson 59 by placing the word beginnings and endings on the board. Students will sound/spell and pronounce shorthand vocabulary as teacher directs. After each group, go back to selected shorthand outlines and ask students to sound/spell, pronounce, and write. After previewing all groups, quickly recap each group. Ask the students to sound/spell and pronounce sample shorthand vocabulary. Write on chalkboard:

re-

sub-

-lity, -lty

-ther

Discuss briefly the *similar-word drill* of *choose, chose.* Preview the business vocabulary outlines. Write *intervals* on the chalkboard and ask a student for a definition, then use in a sentence such as, "Bill timed the intervals of the game." Write the shorthand outline and have the students sound/spell and pronounce. Then preview the word *apportioned*, write the longhand on the board, ask for volunteers for the definition, and write the shorthand outline . Use a similar procedure with *technicians*. Use it in a sentence: "The technicians received special training." Write longhand and shorthand outline on the board:

technicians

3. (2 min.) Instructions to students for doing homework.
   In Lesson 59, write the shorthand vocabulary words in groups of three, each three times. Self-check from the key to see if you know all the words and how to write them correctly. Study similar-word drill and be able to use words correctly. Study the business vocabulary on page 319 and know the spelling, definition, and shorthand outline; and be able to use the words in a business sentence. Drypen and read the letters on pages 319–322. Self-dictate as rapidly as you can, and repeatedly write problem words in the second column. Self-dictate a second time, and write with controlled outlines, inserting punctuation and reasons.

4. (2 min.) Warmup for mailable-letter dictation. Dictate at 80 wam half of letter 491 from Lesson 56, which relates to one of the mailable letters. Postview on the board:

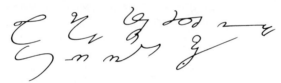

   Ask students if they would like to see any other words written on the chalkboard, then dictate this letter at 90 wam.

5. (3 min.) Preview the following words on the board, having students write as the words are written on the board:

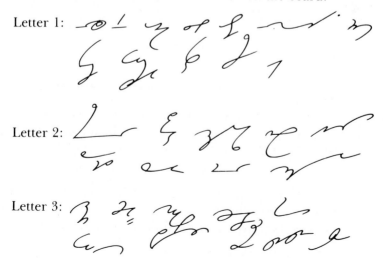

Letter 1:

Letter 2:

Letter 3:

69

6. (6 min.) Dictate letters.

Letter 1: 56 of Instructor's Handbook—105 words
Letter 2: 57 of Instructor's Handbook—108 words
Letter 3: 58 of Instructor's Handbook—<u>110</u> words
323 words

Note: Letters can be cut to fit time available.

7. (6 min.) Allow six minutes for students to read through and refine outlines, determine lengths, make decisions about punctuation and transcription elements, and look up materials in reference manuals. During this time, write the following grid on the board. Students use information in columns 4 and 5 to help make transcription decisions.

Column 1	Column 2	Column 3	Column 4	Column 5
LETTER	LENGTH	INCH-LINE	REQUIRED PUNCTUATION	OTHER TRANSCRIPTION ELEMENTS
1	(105 medium)	(5)	conj ⊙ intro ⊙ intro ⊙ intro ⊙	100 ⟋ 30
2	(108 medium)	(5)	conj ⊙ intro ⊙ par ⊙	5 percent
3	(110 medium)	(5)	ap ⊙ if ⊙ nc ⊙ par ⊙ when ⊙	

8. (4 min.) Discuss the transcription decisions in the grid by asking for volunteers to supply length of letters and inch line to be used, punctuation, and correct application of transcription elements. (Material in parentheses is added during discussion.) Discuss briefly the rules involved in the transcription of these elements.

9. (20 min.) Give students 20 minutes to transcribe the mailable letters.

323 words: bodies of letters
+ 45 words: inside addresses and endings
Total words: 368

Based on 20 transcription words a minute, approximately 18 minutes would need to be allocated for transcription time. However, because these students are beginners at mailable letter production, rounding up to 20 minutes would provide more successful results.

If teachers wish to allow more time, items 1, 2 and 3 of the plan can be shortened.

Sample Third Semester Daily Lesson Plan

Situation:

A lesson during the last half of the third semester. The class period in this plan is approximately 50 minutes.

Today's Lesson: 56
Tomorrow's Lesson: 57

Performance Objectives

The student will attempt to:

1. Transcribe short drills from homework notes at the rate of 50 wam.
2. Transcribe for three minutes from homework notes at the A level of 40 wam.
3. Achieve the A level of 95 percent accuracy on a practice shorthand vocabulary quiz of the day's lesson.
4. Understand the theory of Lesson 57 by spelling, pronouncing, and writing sample shorthand vocabulary.
5. Write new material for dictation speed building at the rates of 100, 110, 120, and 130 wam in an effort to pass dictation test rates for the week of 90, 100, and 110 wam.

Materials:

Gregg Speedbuilding, Series 90, Leslie, Zoubek, Mendenhall
Student Transcript
Interval Chart
Stopwatch
Dictation Motivation Chart (a chart displaying the dictation plan and rates to be used)

71

Activities:

1. (6 min.) Typewritten transcription accuracy development.
   a. As the students come into the room, the following instructions will be on the board:
      (1) Get ready for typewritten transcription.
      (2) Set machine for a 5-inch line, single spacing, no paragraph indentation.
      (3) Adjust chair height and/or typewriter height and distance from the machine.
   b. Using homework notes of Lesson 56, students will place superior figures 1, 2, 3, 4, 5, and 6 in letter 512 of the day's homework notes by the teacher indicating location or by students using Student Transcript to determine locations.
   c. Remind students how to achieve transcription accuracy:
      (1) Have notes in well-written form.
      (2) Know the transcription element usage by having studied the Student Transcript as a reference source.
      (3) Take the correct position at the typewriter.
      (4) Stroke at a controlled rate.
      (5) Focus attention on each shorthand outline and transliterate at the level of total word, syllables, or letters.
      (6) Have a mind-set for accurate typing.
   d. Give a series of one-minute timings to try to achieve accurate transcription at 50 wam. Call the superior figures 1, 2, and 3 at 24-second intervals. The same interval chart used for dictation can be used for goal calling because the superior figure is still the base of timing. Check after each attempt to see if students are achieving 50 wam and if they are attaining accuracy of not more than one error per timing. After starting twice at the beginning of the letter, start the next timings at superior figure 2 and call figures 3, 4, and 5.
   e. (6 min.) Have students insert a clean sheet of paper and set typewriter for double spacing. Type name, date, and rate in the upper right corner. Give a three-minute transcription rate on another letter, or other letters, from the day's homework notes. See Chapter 8, pages 246–247, for the administration and scoring of the three-minute transcription rate.
   f. Collect papers at the completion of the scoring.

2. (5 min.) Students will number a shorthand notebook page from 1 through 20. Pronounce the following words, selected from the shorthand vocabulary drill at the beginning of Lesson 56 and the letters in Lesson 56, at ten words per minute. Students should attempt to write with correct proportion, theory application, and line of writing.

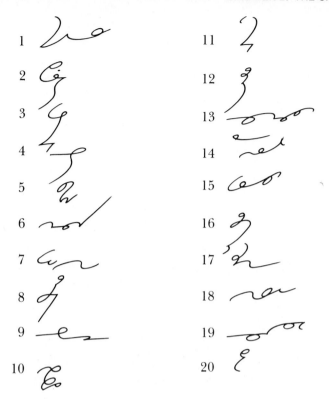

1

2

3

4

5

6

7

8

9

10

11

12

13

14

15

16

17

18

19

20

After the words are pronounced, give students about a minute to look over the words and cancel out and rewrite outlines. Then place the shorthand outlines on the board, explaining rule application, joinings, and sounds, while students check their own papers. They will then deduct five points for each incorrect outline and subtract from 100 to determine the degree of accuracy of their writing. Shorthand vocabulary incorrectly written will be part of the homework for tomorrow. (Papers are not always collected; the purpose of the activity is to help students see how thorough the day's preparation has been. At times the papers are collected to see how accurately the student is judging the work.)

3. (6 min.) Previewing new Lesson 57. Place the following shorthand vocabulary on the board and ask students to sound/spell and pronounce and then write the shorthand outlines for those which are circled. (Words are circled in this plan to suggest that only selected words would be written).

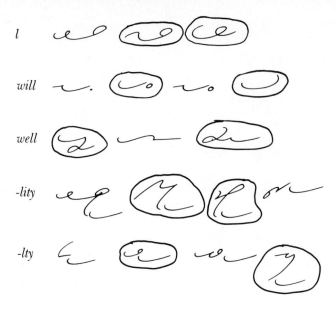

4. Instructions to students for doing homework.
   a. Write the shorthand vocabulary from the key on page 315, check with the word list on page 314, and practice the shorthand outlines for those words written incorrectly.
   b. Do the accuracy practice giving attention to accurately writing each outline.
   c. Write the preview shorthand vocabulary of paragraph 517, spelling each word as it is written. Practice groups of three words, three times.
   d. Write the letters 518, 519, 520 in shorthand, inserting punctuation and reason.
   e. Drypen and read letters 521–524. Self-dictate and write as rapidly as you can read the material. Then self-dictate again, writing with control, inserting punctuation and reason.
5. (27 min.) Dictation speed building on new material. (The source could be—to mention a few—related letters from the Instructor's Handbook; letters from the next day's lesson, which provide a good refinement of the vocabulary when it is studied for homework on the succeeding day; short letters in the transcription tests of the *Gregg Tests and Awards* booklet; or short letters from the *Short Business Letters for Dictation and Transcription.*) This chapter's subject matter is Automation and Data Processing. If possible, choose letters related to this topic. For this lesson plan, four letters from Lesson 57 will be used, with the stair-step plan for the dictation speed building and the postview procedure. The plan is as follows:

			100 Letter 4
		100 Letter 3	110 Letter 3
	100 Letter 2	110 Letter 2	120 Letter 2
100 Letter 1	110 Letter 1	120 Letter 1	130 Letter 1
Step 1	**Step 2**	**Step 3**	**Step 4**

Procedure:

1. Dictate letter 1 (518) at 100 wam.
2. Check on achievement.
3. Students write quickly the following shorthand vocabulary of letter 1 as the teacher writes the shorthand outlines on the chalkboard.

4. Set goal and dictate letter 1 at 110 and letter 2 (519) at 100.
5. Check on achievement of letter 1 at 110 and letter 2 at 100.
6. Students write quickly the following shorthand vocabulary of letter 2 as the teacher writes the shorthand outlines on the chalkboard.

7. Ask if there is additional letter 1 shorthand vocabulary which the student needs to practice. To provide additional motivation for learning shorthand vocabulary in letter 1, add the following shorthand outlines. (Students write as these are placed on the chalkboard.)

Then review the words of letter 1 previously placed on the chalkboard by having students say these shorthand outlines as the teacher points to them selectively.

8. Set goal and dictate letter 1 at 120, letter 2 at 110, and letter 3 (520) at 100 wam.

9. Check achievement on letter 1 at 120, letter 2 at 110, and letter 3 at 100.

10. Since the students may be getting tired from writing, place the postview of letter 3 on the chalkboard, asking students to say each outline. After the shorthand vocabulary is placed on the chalkboard, ask the students to write rapidly each outline as the teacher points to it.

Ask if additional shorthand vocabulary is needed for letters 2 and 1, and add a few words and phrases if necessary.

Letter 2:

Letter 1:

As a final review before the last step of dictation, have the students read quickly selected shorthand vocabulary from the postviews of letters 1, 2, and 3.

11. Set the goal and dictate letter 1 at 130 wam, letter 2 at 120 wam, letter 3 at 110 wam, and letter 4 (521) at 100 wam.

12. Check on achievement for each letter individually.

13. Since the students may need to rest, ask them to look, think, and silently sound/spell the postview shorthand vocabulary of letter 4 as the teacher writes the outlines on the chalkboard.

After the shorthand outlines are on the chalkboard, have students write each outline rapidly and then say selected outlines from the postviews of letters 3, 2, and 1.

14. The final step is to control the writing on all four letters at 110 or 120, depending on the responses of the students when the teacher checks achievements. If time is running out, the letters can be shortened and only part of each letter dictated.
15. As a further check on achievement, ask students to read back and insert punctuation and reason for the punctuation choices.

Daily Lesson Planning for Fourth Semester

The daily lesson planning for fourth semester would include activities similar to those described for semesters 2 and 3. Alterations that would need to be considered are:

1. Expected transcription rates would be increased.
2. Rates for dictation speed building would be increased.
3. Mailable letters would be longer, rates of dictation recording would be higher, carbon copies and envelopes would be a part of both third and fourth semesters, office style and alertness dictation would be frequently used, decision-making opportunities would be numerous, and office simulation and in-basket activities would be employed.

The daily lesson plans described are presented as guides for developing some of the competencies identified for each semester of shorthand. Similar plans need to be developed on a daily basis. Time allotments are given to indicate the degree of emphasis recommended and to provide adequate time for the major learning activity of the class session. Such time considerations are important in each day's planning, but they are especially important when planning for mailable letter production and dictation testing in order to be sure that adequate time is given for transcription of the material. In planning, therefore, teachers should determine the total amount of time needed for the learning activities and the time in the class period when the activity must begin in order to allow adequate transcription time.

As stated earlier in this discussion, weekly plans are the skeletons; and daily plans include the learning activities to be performed, combined with the appropriate methodology to apply to bring about the development of the desired competencies.

Chapter 3

Introducing the Student to Shorthand

Shorthand performance at the conclusion of instruction is directly related to achievement during the first semester. Students who encounter extreme learning difficulties during theory presentation have meager prospects for success. Likewise, early shorthand success is an indicator of probable continued successful performance. That is why teachers must give thoughtful consideration to the "hows" of introducing students to shorthand. This chapter is devoted to three introductory aspects of teaching shorthand: approaches to teaching shorthand, teaching the first lesson, and effective use of the chalkboard and/or overhead projector.

Teaching Approaches—First Semester High School

The methodology for first semester or first quarter high school teaching has evolved from two distinct philosophies of teaching shorthand. Science-type approaches were used almost exclusively up to 1934, when the language arts approach was introduced for teaching shorthand. Controversy over the revolutionary new approach continued throughout the 1930s and 1940s, but the dispute has subsided. Today's teachers almost unanimously select methodology from both approaches. Leslie states:

> In the 20,000 shorthand classrooms of the United States there are hundreds of variations in teaching procedures as each teacher gives more emphasis to one procedure and less to another.[1]

Even though there has been a trend to combine the methodologies of both approaches, there are marked differences in the basic principles of language arts and science-type teaching. To meet the preference of teachers, two books are published for the first semester of high school instruction. *Gregg Shorthand* is designed for teachers who prefer science-type methodology, and *Gregg Shorthand, Functional Method* for those who favor language arts approaches.[2,3]

A review of the characteristics associated with science-type and language arts teaching follows. The two approaches discussed represent the pure, or extreme, philosophies of teaching shorthand and are seldom used in their entireties in today's classrooms. It is important to emphasize that shorthand teachers have modified and combined the characteristics of both approaches.

Language Arts Teaching

The language arts approach, commonly labeled the functional method, is also known as the direct method. Formulated and popularized by Louis Leslie, it is most clearly distinguished from science-type approaches by the elimination of rules for outline construction. Students learn to read and write shorthand through the repeated sound/spelling, reading, and writing of a wide variety of contextual shorthand material. They intuitively learn to formulate correct outlines without consciously learning the rules of outline construction.

The following characteristics are associated with the use of the language arts, or functional, method.

RULES FOR OUTLINE FORMATION AND JOININGS ARE NEVER TAUGHT OR DISCUSSED.   Teachers who use the functional method believe that shorthand students learn to write transcribable outlines through extensive reading and writing of contextual material. They believe that memorization of rules (for example, circles are written inside curves and outside angles) introduces another learning difficulty without improving ultimate shorthand performance.

Functional methodology includes rapid, concerted sound/spelling and reading of isolated outlines from the chalkboard to learn new theory principles; reading and copying of connected material in which there are many examples of new theory principles; and repetitive recording of practiced dictation material. These three basic activities ultimately develop the skills necessary to record new dictation and to transcribe it with mailable accuracy.

Questions regarding the "whys" of outline construction are discouraged, and rules of outline formation are never mentioned. Students taught by the functional method meet course objectives unaware that rules exist, and rules for outline construction are omitted completely from *Gregg Shorthand, Functional Method.*

The functional method is based on incidental learning. Shorthand skill is considered a developmental process, and students ultimately write usable outlines under pressure of dictation because they intuitively develop reading and writing skills through practice on a wide variety of contextual material.

THEORETICALLY CORRECT OUTLINES ARE CONSIDERED SECONDARY TO OUTLINE UTILITY.   Readability or transcribability of shorthand outlines is the major goal of instruction. Although hoping that students will eventually write theoretically correct outlines, teachers do not evaluate performance on the basis of outline correctness. The sole criterion for evaluation is usability. Turning a circle incorrectly, adding or omitting a vowel, or improperly joining alphabetic strokes when writing under pressure of dictation are considered of little consequence. The ability to record an outline under pressure of dictation and to transcribe it accurately are considered the criteria for satisfactory performance.

Teachers believe that students eventually learn to write correct outlines and that undue emphasis on correct outlines during the developmental stages of shorthand results in a hesitant writing style.

WRITING IS DELAYED UNTIL BASIC READING SKILLS HAVE BEEN DEVELOPED. Students are given an opportunity to develop reading skills before writing from dictation is introduced. Proponents suggest that learning difficulty is reduced when teachers concentrate on developing ability to read shorthand for approximately 20 class periods. Since the major emphasis of classroom instruction is on learning theory and on increasing reading speed and accuracy, students will naturally make significant progress in reading shorthand.

The use of the reading approach for about 20 class periods also eases the initial difficulty of writing shorthand from dictation. As students read, they continue to master the shorthand alphabet; they begin to intuitively recognize the proper joinings in outlines; and they begin to form mental images of commonly occurring words. Proponents believe that skills developed during the reading stage have a positive effect on writing and that students will write quickly, accurately, and easily when writing is introduced.

PERCEIVED OBSTACLES TO LEARNING ARE REDUCED DURING THE INITIAL STAGES OF SKILL DEVELOPMENT. If learning can be simplified, frustrations associated with mastering a psychomotor skill like shorthand will be reduced. The result should be a higher degree of motivation and a reduction in failures during the initial stages of learning. Four examples are cited to illustrate how learning difficulty is reduced by the functional method.

Students are encouraged to keep their books open and to refer to difficult or unfamiliar outlines when recording practiced-matter dictation. They do not have the expertise to formulate theoretically correct outlines, or even incorrect outlines, under pressure of dictation during the early stages of learning. Teachers using the functional approach believe that allowing students to glance in their books for assistance in forming outlines allows faster dictation and greater progress toward the ultimate objective of rapidly recording dictation. As skills develop, students become less dependent on, and finally totally independent of, the text. Thus, the transition to writing new-matter dictation is relatively easy.

Students are encouraged to refer to the printed key when they are unable to read an outline in the homework lesson. If an outline cannot be read after sound/spelling it, the student should quickly consult the key. Time is not to be wasted in trying to decipher the outline. By using the key while studying, students can quickly read the homework lesson and use the saved time for rereading it.

Delaying writing from dictation until reading skills have been developed and eliminating rules are other ways to reduce learning obstacles during the initial stages of skill development.

FREQUENCY AND TYPE OF FORMAL TESTS ARE LIMITED. Since teachers are not concerned with the memorization and application of shorthand rules, the number and types of tests are reduced. When tests are administered, they are evaluated on the transcription of shorthand rather than on accuracy of shorthand notes.

Teachers who use the functional method realize that there is little need for formal testing because of the daily opportunity for informal evaluation of student performance. As a result, the number of tests is limited and generally confined to evaluating shorthand reading ability or the transcribing of contextual material.

FORMAL PENMANSHIP DRILLS ARE NOT INCLUDED IN INSTRUCTIONAL PLANNING. Advocates of the functional method believe that penmanship skills are developmental and that improvement will come about through incidental learning. They believe that system mastery resulting from reading and writing shorthand contributes to writing legibility. Because penmanship skills develop as an indirect result of improvements in other facets of shorthand skill, formal penmanship drills are not used in the functional approach.

The functional shorthand teacher is not overconcerned with proportion, size, slant, beauty, or position on the writing line. A well-written outline is one that can be correctly transcribed. Utility of outlines is the sole criterion used for the assessment of penmanship style.

FORMAL REVIEWS OF THEORY PRINCIPLES ARE ELIMINATED. Teachers who use the functional method believe that reading and writing homework lessons and the daily classroom activities provide built-in reviews for each theory principle. By the time students have completed the shorthand program, the repetition of theory principles in contextual material will develop a comprehensive shorthand vocabulary. Formal theory reviews are considered unnecessary and highly undesirable if they include repetitive reading and writing of isolated outlines in word lists or verbalizing rules for outline construction. No time is set aside for formal theory review in the functional classroom because there is continual informal review of theory principles throughout the program.

SHORTHAND HOMEWORK IS COPIED FROM PLATE OUTLINES RATHER THAN FROM TYPESCRIPT COPY. Advocates of the functional method believe that copying from typescript into shorthand is harmful to the potential writing speed of students. They believe that requiring students to write shorthand from typescript copy contributes to a hesitant writing style. Leslie states that students should not stop and think about the various alternatives for writing the outline while writing homework assignments.[4] He believes that nothing can be more harmful and more opposed to correct shorthand learning. Thus the plate outlines, rather than the typescript, should be the source for student homework.

Proponents of the functional method require students, as part of their homework, to copy shorthand plates from self-dictation to encourage the development of a fluent, rapid writing style.

DICTATION SPEEDS ARE FORCED THROUGHOUT THE LEARNING CYCLE. Repetitive dictation is usually given at speeds beyond students' normal writing ability; to record the dictation, quality of penmanship and outline accuracy must be sacrificed. In the language arts approach, dictation is considered too slow if well-formed outlines can be written with a high degree of theoretical accuracy.

After students have recorded dictation at speeds beyond their normal writing rates, dictation is repeated at controlled rates so students can concentrate on penmanship and apply their theory knowledge. The constant prodding for speed and dropping back for control enables students to maximize speed potential while still writing legible shorthand outlines.

SHORTHAND LEARNING IS CONSIDERED A DEVELOPMENTAL PROCESS, AND ERRORS ARE REGARDED AS NORMAL SYMPTOMS OF GROWTH. Advocates of the functional method realize that errors will occur as students strive for new levels of reading and writing skill. However, such errors are regarded as temporary symptoms that will decrease as each new level of skill is attained. Patience and proper practice will ultimately have positive effects on penmanship, reading speed and accuracy, and dictation recording speed and accuracy. Leslie compares the teaching of science-type and of language arts subjects by writing:

> In teaching algebra, the teacher must insist on correctness of understanding, of reasoning, of application, of result. In teaching shorthand or a language, the teacher does harm to the learner's development by insisting on these same things. In shorthand or a language, the learner achieves better eventual success if he is allowed to muddle along for a time until everything clears up and good skill performance is achieved.[5]

SKILLS ARE DEVELOPED FROM READING AND WRITING CONTEXTUAL MATERIAL, NOT ISOLATED OUTLINES OR WORD LISTS. In the functional method, word lists are used to introduce new theory principles, but repetitive reading and writing of word lists is discouraged. The use of word lists for repetitive practice probably resulted from scarcity of connected matter in early textbooks. However, since today's texts contain ample amounts of shorthand copy, connected material is used for skill development. Connected matter is used for homework practice, developing reading skills, and attaining dictation recording skill, but word lists are primarily used to illustrate new theory principles.

Science-Type Teaching

A wide variety of terminology has been used to describe science-type shorthand teaching. Two of the most common names are the traditional method and the manual method, but such names as the rule method, indirect method, logical method, and grammatical method have been used over the years. For consistency of terminology, the manual method will be used to describe science-type teaching and learning in this section.

Nearly all shorthand teachers used variations of the manual method before the introduction of the functional method. After the functional approach was introduced, teachers tended to liberalize manual teaching procedures. Teachers who had used pure science-type approaches realized that strict adherence to the principles of science-type teaching increased the difficulty of learning. As a result, modifications to ease learning have been made in the teaching procedures of the manual method. Elements of the functional method have become part of today's manual approach and elements of the manual method have become part of today's functional approach.

Lamb contrasts the two approaches by writing, "Learning shorthand by this indirect method is similar to learning a language through the rules of grammar rather than by the direct conversational method."[6] Rules of grammar are analogous to rules of shorthand outline construction, and teaching by rule is the major distinguishing feature of the manual method for teaching shorthand.

The following are characteristics of manual methodology, but it is important to remember that teaching practices range from strict adherence to principles of science-type teaching to very liberal interpretations.

RULES FOR OUTLINE CONSTRUCTION ARE LEARNED AND CONSCIOUSLY APPLIED. Advocates of the manual approach believe that students must consciously learn the rules of outline construction to write theoretically correct outlines under pressure of dictation. Accordingly, a rule such as "Circles are written inside curves and outside angles" is taught to students, and they consciously apply the rule through directed practice.

Rules are presented by either deductive or inductive methods. In the deductive method, the teacher verbalizes the rule and illustrates it by writing word examples on the chalkboard. Practice is given in reading and writing the words containing the principle being taught. Sentences containing examples of the new rule are dictated. Outline formation is periodically checked to determine if students are applying the rule correctly. If rules are presented by the inductive method, the teacher merely writes on the chalkboard a list of words illustrating the principle to be taught. After the words are read, the teacher asks students to verbalize the principle being illustrated. Thus, members of the class formulate the rule or principle through illustrations that have been provided by the teacher. The teacher then reinforces the rule with reading and writing practice of word illustrations and dictation of sentences including words to which the rule applies.

The degree of emphasis given to rule mastery varies in the manual approach. Few teachers would require students to memorize and recite rules, some would expect them to verbalize the general intent of rules, and others would call attention to rules so that students become aware of the scientific construction of shorthand outlines.

There are also differences of opinion about when to present rules. Some teachers may delay the discussion of rules until Lesson 6 in *Gregg Shorthand;* others, with firm convictions about using the basic principles of science-type teaching, may introduce rules during the first day of instruction.

READING AND WRITING SKILLS ARE INTRODUCED CONCURRENTLY. At one time, students began writing from dictation during the first lesson. The emphasis varied from dictation of alphabetic symbols to dictation of individual words or even short, simple sentences. Thus students in manual-instruction classrooms were exposed to both the reading and writing of shorthand during the first day of instruction. Some teachers still prefer to begin writing the first day, but others prefer to introduce it sometime between the second and seventh class periods.

WORD LISTS ARE CONSIDERED INSTRUCTIONAL TOOLS FOR DEVEL- OPING READING AND WRITING SKILLS.   Manual-method teachers believe that repetitive reading and writing of word lists ensures learning of theory principles, ultimately leading to improved performance. Perhaps in part because early shorthand textbooks had little connected matter, teachers relied heavily on the practicing of word lists as a learning activity. The abundance of connected matter in modern texts has encouraged teachers to modify emphasis on the use of word lists. Some manual-method teachers ask students to repetitively copy the word lists as well as the connected matter as part of homework assignments. Dictation of word lists and administration of shorthand vocabulary tests are frequent class activities.

FORMAL PENMANSHIP DRILLS ARE CONSIDERED AN INTEGRAL PART OF CLASS ACTIVITIES.   Years ago manual-method teachers were apt to include penmanship drills in their daily lesson plans. Lessons of the manual-approach first-semester high school textbook emphasized the proportion and correctness of writing similar strokes. Students were instructed to concentrate on and emphasize penmanship basics.

Believers in the manual method are concerned with outline appearance and take formal steps to improve penmanship.

FORMAL REVIEW IS GIVEN TO REINFORCE THEORY KNOWLEDGE AND APPLICATION. The manual-method teacher does not depend entirely on the reading and writing of contextual material for perfecting theory knowledge, but systematically provides drills for the periodic review of theory principles.

Although a strong advocate of the functional method, Leslie describes how rule drills can be administered.[7] For example, the teacher selects a list of about ten words, each containing the same theory principle. The first word, *cave,* is dictated, and the teacher immediately asks, "the circle?" to obtain the answer, "inside the curve," from members of the class. As the next word, *bear,* is dictated, students write it in their notebooks and respond, "inside the curve." After each word is dictated and recorded and a partial rule is verbalized by students, the teacher writes the correct outline on the chalkboard for student reference.

A drill of this nature consumes approximately 3 minutes, and proponents of the manual method consider the time spent in theory drills highly valuable for achieving ultimate objectives.

HOMEWORK ASSIGNMENTS MAY INCLUDE WRITING SHORTHAND FROM TYPESCRIPT. Although writing shorthand from typescript was once a common homework practice, most manual-method teachers now ask students to self-dictate homework assignments from shorthand plates. However, writing shorthand from typescript is sometimes used as a supplement to regular assignments to determine need for theory review or to focus student attention on the importance of writing theoretically correct outlines. Most first-semester students need to see the outlines in their correct form; therefore, using the typescript as a writing source is not recommended for beginners.

DICTATION SPEEDS ARE CONTROLLED THROUGHOUT THE LEARNING CYCLE. Teachers favoring manual methods believe that dictation rates should not cause students to sacrifice penmanship and outline accuracy. Speed improvement is encouraged, but not forced, by the rate of dictation. They are apt to believe that speed will develop as a by-product of theory mastery and the use of carefully controlled dictation rates within the students' writing abilities. Speed forcing, so characteristic of the functional method, is tempered in favor of mild pressure which allows maintenance of accuracy standards.

SHORTHAND SKILLS ARE APT TO BE DEVELOPED THROUGH A STEP-BY-STEP MASTERY OF THEORY PRINCIPLES. Manual method advocates are concerned with accuracy and correct performance throughout the shorthand program, whereas teachers who use the functional method believe that accuracy improves as reading and writing skills increase. Teachers using manual approaches are concerned not only with reading and dictation speed, but they are vitally interested in reading and writing accuracy, correctly written outlines, rules, and penmanship at every stage of shorthand development. Because accuracy is considered important at all levels of learning, science-type teachers are apt to slow the presentation of theory until they are reasonably satisfied with student performance. Accordingly, some teachers who use manual methods may spend more class periods in presenting and teaching shorthand theory.

Summary of Differences Between the Two Approaches

Lamb summarizes the manual or traditional method by writing:

> The traditional method is a "parts method" because words are learned not as whole words but as combinations of shorthand characters joined according to rules of word construction learned in relation to reading and writing practice. It is an indirect method because pupils learn "through rules" to read and write rather than by imitation involving word-recognition and word-writing ... The method is a logical one, proceeding from the simple to the complex and from the rule to the application of the rule or, as the case may be, from the application of the rule to the statement of the rule.[8]

Lamb also summarizes selected characteristics of the functional method by stating:

> In functional-method learning, students learn to read shorthand by spelling and reading the outlines for words in the word lists illustrating various rules of word construction; they learn to write by reading and writing contextual shorthand. In brief, they learn shorthand by spelling classified shorthand outlines and by practicing the reading and writing of contextual shorthand without reference to the rules of word construction and without penmanship drills. The principle involved is that through repeated spelling, reading, and writing of a wide vocabulary of high-frequency words, students automatize not only the outlines, but also the ways of constructing the outlines.[9]

Leslie uses a two-column list of characteristics to distinguish between the two approaches for teaching shorthand.[10]

Science-Type	Language Arts
part method	whole method
conscious control	subconscious control
physical skill	mental organization
accuracy and refinement of shorthand characters	fluency and correctness in taking dictation
correction of shorthand outline	correction of transcripts only

Science-Type	Language Arts
end in itself—conformity with textbook	means to an end—transcription
verbalized generalization	unverbalized generalization
problem solving	habit forming
intensive repetitive home practice	extensive nonrepetitive home practice
emphasis on word lists	emphasis on connected matter
vocabulary building	constructional ability

Combination Approaches

Pure manual and functional approaches represent extreme opposites in teaching philosophy and methodology. There are advantages and disadvantages associated with each approach, but both are important because they include basic learning theories on the basis of which new methodology can be formulated and judged.

Throughout the years teachers and researchers have attempted to combine the most positive elements of both approaches into workable plans for developing shorthand skills. Some of these plans involved only minor modifications, while others have made significant changes.

Two of the most interesting combination approaches were developed and published by Brewington and Soutter in 1937 and by Odell and Stewart in 1944.[11,12] Although the approaches are not used today, they provide insight into ways in which language arts and science-type methodology have been combined.

Both approaches introduced shorthand by direct methods, or modifications of language arts approaches. In the Brewington-Soutter method, students were initially taught to read and write shorthand in thought units. In the Odell-Stewart method, they initially learned to write high-frequency vocabulary in word wholes. After students gained reading and writing skills through direct approaches, emphasis shifted to indirect methods, or science-type methodology. Rules for outline construction, penmanship, and accuracy were stressed throughout the remainder of the shorthand program. Thus, both approaches used direct methods during the initial stages of learning but changed to indirect, or science-type instruction, after initial reading and writing fluency had been developed.

These authors believed that reading and writing fluency was enhanced by emphasis on word wholes and lack of emphasis on rules, penmanship, and techniques during the initial stages of learning. However, they believed that science-type methodology was important for developing the ability to construct unfamiliar words under pressure of dictation and for improving penmanship skills.

Russon's Combination Approach

A combination approach advocated by Russon illustrates how methodologies from functional and manual approaches have been combined.[13]

Students sound/spell and read all homework assignments during the first two weeks of instruction. At the beginning of the third week, they read contextual material without sound/spelling, unless they encounter a word that they cannot read immediately. A printed key is used to assist in preparing homework lessons.

Every sixth lesson is used for speed reading practice. Students are asked to reread these lessons until they can do it rapidly. One-minute timings are administered on these lessons to determine reading rates. There is no emphasis on memorizing rules, but they are presented and explained to students.

Writing from dictation is introduced on the third day of class and continued each day thereafter. During dictation, students are allowed to refer to their written homework notes for difficult outlines.

New-matter dictation practice is introduced the day after the first two groups of brief forms are presented. Sentences dictated are heavily loaded with brief forms, and all other words are previewed before the dictation. A new letter, loaded with previously automatized brief forms, is dictated each day.

New-matter dictation tests are administered during the fourth week of instruction, and continued throughout the theory presentation. The source of the dictation is *Dictation ABC's*.[14]

Formal reviews are also provided in the plan. When the class is assigned Lesson 21 for homework, students are instructed to review Lesson 1. This procedure is used for the duration of the semester, with review lessons always those 20 lessons before the new lessons. Students prepare the new lessons in the conventional manner, but are instructed to use the following homework procedure for the review lessons: Write word lists that illustrate theory principles several times; use the line-skip method to write the last page of each review lesson. In the line-skip method, students write contextual material on every third line of their notebooks. After the material has been written once, they close their texts and write on the blank line under their notes while reading aloud from their shorthand notes. The same procedure is used for writing on the third blank line.

There is heavy emphasis on brief-form mastery from the outset, because of introduction to new-matter dictation which is loaded with brief forms. Consequently, Russon suggests a folded-paper technique for the brief-form practice.

As the second list of brief forms is presented (in Lesson 5), the students are instructed to fold a piece of typing paper into eight folds by folding it from the bottom to the top three times. The paper is then unfolded, and they write the two groups of brief forms in a column down the first fold, copying from their books, as the teacher dictates the brief forms slowly. After writing the two groups of brief forms, one below the other, in the first space, they write the longhand transcription of each shorthand outline in a column on the second fold.

Next, the first column is folded back, leaving the column of longhand words visible. The students now write the shorthand for the brief forms as they read the longhand, checking with the book if necessary. Now the second column is folded back leaving the short-hand column uppermost. Again, they transcribe from shorthand to longhand as before. This procedure is continued until all eight spaces are filled. The paper is left folded, with the student's name on the outside, and submitted as part of the homework assignment.

The table on page 90 provides a summary of the procedures recommended by Russon.[15]

The following list describes modifications that have been made in the methodology basic to the functional method during the first semester. The extent of modification ranges from one minor adap-tation to incorporating all the variations appearing in the list.

Modifications Made by Teachers Using the Functional Approach

Teachers of the functional method sometimes:

1. Check student ability to construct theoretically correct outlines by using short tests from daily homework or chapter tests. The purpose of these tests is to encourage better homework prepa-ration and promote accurately written outlines.
2. Require repetitive writing of word lists as part of homework assignments or for in-class practice. These teachers believe repetition will encourage greater facility in writing theoretically correct outlines.
3. Require students to occasionally write shorthand from type-script as part of the homework assignment. Usually, this type of assignment is reserved for semesters after the first. It is used to supplement and add variety to regular homework procedures.
4. Require students to write homework assignments more than once. Although functional methodology stresses that once is enough, there are functional teachers who believe that more practice leads to greater achievement.
5. Introduce writing before the twentieth class period. These teachers introduce writing when they feel that students are beginning to read and sound/spell with fluency.
6. Stress penmanship drills occasionally. Usually, the emphasis of

these drills is on proportion and proper position on the line. There is little demand for conformity to slant or size of writing.

7. Review shorthand vocabulary by reading, sound/spelling, and

TABLE I
AN OUTLINE OF THE FIRST FOUR WEEKS SHOWING THE APPLICATION OF THE EARLY-NEW-MATTER APPROACH

WEEK	DAY	LESSON	PRESENTATION OF NEW MATERIAL	HOMEWORK*
First	1	1	Introduce Lesson 1	No homework assigned
	2	1	Repeat Lesson 1	Read and spell Lesson 1 twice
	3	2	Present Lesson 2	
	4	3	Explain tracing	Trace lesson once
	5	4	Introduce writing	
Second	1	5	Explain speed reading Folded paper (brief forms)	Folded paper for brief forms Reading for speed
	2	6	Reading for speed New-matter dictation	
	3	7		
	4	8		
	5	9		
Third	1	10		Omit spelling from reading
	2	11		
	3	12	Reading for speed	
	4	13		
	5	14		
Fourth	1	15		
	2	16		
	3	17	Introduce transcription	
	4	18	Reading for speed	
	5	19	Transcribe 3-minute takes	
Fifth	1	20	Introduce formal review	Review Lesson 1
	2	21		Review Lesson 2

* Each new homework assignment is in addition to other homework.

writing word lists. Although rules of outline formation are not taught, these teachers believe that formal reviews encourage mastery of theory principles.

8. Introduce new-matter dictation during the first semester. Although functional methodology suggests that new-matter dictation be delayed until the second semester, there are teachers who introduce it relatively early in the first semester.

9. Encourage students to close their books when recording practiced-matter dictation after the first five or six weeks of the first semester. They believe that students will develop dictation skills more rapidly if the book is not used as a crutch.

The following list illustrates how teachers modify and adapt elements of manual methodology. Most of the changes involve reducing initial learning difficulty during the presentation of theory, but the extent of modification depends on teacher opinion. Some teachers who use manual approaches make no modifications, while others make wholesale methodology changes. Sometimes the only distinguishable difference between functional and science-type teaching is in the emphasis on rules for outline construction.

Modifications Made by Teachers Using the Manual Approach

Teachers using the manual method sometimes:

1. Encourage students to use a printed key in preparing homework assignments. These teachers believe that initial learning difficulty should be reduced and that students will develop reading skills more rapidly if they have a reference for homework.

2. Require students to self-dictate their shorthand from connected material as part of the homework assignment and limit the writing of shorthand from typescript. They agree that skills are best learned through extensive reading and writing of well-written contextual material.

3. Rely more heavily on connected material than on word lists for homework and in-class practice. They recognize that word lists are valuable for teaching theory principles but believe skill is ultimately developed from recording connected material.

4. Use functional textbooks, but supplement them with rule illustrations. These teachers prefer to use a textbook in which the key is bound in the book.

5. Pace theory presentations at a lesson a day even though students have not thoroughly mastered all theory principles within the preceding lessons. These teachers prefer to move to the next lesson, realizing that further theory mastery will result from practice. They believe that learning theory is

cumulative because theory principles are constantly used in succeeding lessons.

6. Correct transcripts only and ignore written shorthand notes when evaluating the ability to record dictation. They realize that transcription effectiveness is the ultimate objective of all shorthand instruction.

7. Force speed during dictation speed building even though students must sacrifice outline accuracy and penmanship style.

8. Allow students to refer to textbooks when taking practiced-matter dictation during the first five to six weeks of the first semester. These teachers believe that obstacles to learning should be minimized during the initial stages of instruction.

Even though there are great differences in philosophy between the functional and traditional approaches, there are teaching procedures that are basic to all shorthand instruction. In fact, it may be difficult to determine whether a teacher is using functional or manual methodology on the basis of casual classroom observation. The following list illustrates methodology common to both approaches during the first semester of shorthand instruction.

Commonalities of Manual and Functional Methodology

Teachers who use either approach usually:

1. Use the chalkboard or overhead projector for intensive drill on new theory principles. Students learn new theory by rapid, repetitive, and concerted sound/spelling and reading of outlines as the teacher points randomly.

2. Emphasize sound/spelling of shorthand outlines for teaching new theory principles and for reviewing previously presented principles. Teachers realize that sound/spelling provides the basic building blocks for all aspects of shorthand reading and writing skill.

3. Depend heavily on repetition for teaching theory principles, developing reading skills, and improving dictation-recording abilities. Although the extent of repetition in the two approaches may differ, all teachers use repetition as a basis for skill building.

4. Require the completion of daily homework assignments. Although the type of assignments may vary with the approach, teachers require reading and/or writing of connected material.

5. Ask individual students to read from the daily homework lesson. Depending on the stage of learning, students read daily from connected material in the textbook or from written homework notes.

6. Prompt students who have difficulty reading homework as-

signments. Teachers help students with reading difficulty in order to save class time, reduce student embarrassment, keep the pace of the class moving quickly, and motivate all class members.

7. Use homework material for developing initial writing skills. Teachers realize that developing high speeds on practiced material will make the transition to recording new-matter dictation easier.

8. Give daily dictation practice after writing has been introduced. Although the preferred amount of time devoted to dictation varies, teachers realize that dictation skills must be developed through extensive practice.

9. Use repetitive-dictation plans to develop dictation-recording skills. Teachers realize that each repetition develops speed because difficulty of recording is lessened. They hope that the artificial speed gained through repetition will have a positive effect on ultimate dictation-recording speed.

10. Pace classes to economize on time and motivate students. Emphasis is on speed of sound/spelling, reading, and writing shorthand, and teachers develop lesson plans that provide for maximum reading and writing practice time.

11. Alternate classroom activities to relieve boredom and to develop skill in short, intensive bursts of effort.

12. Teach such language arts fundamentals as word usage, punctuation, and English usage. Teachers realize that language skills are fundamental to transcription success, and they begin reviewing and teaching these skills during the first semester.

Micromolar Approach Applied to Shorthand

The micromolar theory (dictation procedure in which all dictation is heard at one speed) includes a premise that speed is a learned response; that is, a fast response is essentially different from a slow response. For example, responses to shorthand dictation at 100 wam are not 80-wam responses performed at a greater speed; they are new responses. As students learn to write shorthand at various speeds from low to high, they must relearn speed responses at each level of skill. The micromolar approach applies the idea "input equals output." If student response or speed output is to be 80 wam, dictation input must always be at 80 wam.

Eiken theorizes the implications for shorthand teachers by writing:

At present we seem largely concerned with advancing from slow to fast speeds as a method of providing for the easy-to-difficult progression of learning. This is logical since slow responses are generally considered to be easier than fast responses . . . Could students develop greater

93

performance speed in the long run by taking dictation initially at 100 or 110 words a minute if the difficulty of this speed were compensated for by using extremely easy material and exceedingly short periods of dictation.[16]

Sloan's micromolar approach research demonstrated no long-term ill effects in student ability to record dictation when micromolar speedbuilding was used during the first 12 weeks of instruction.[17] Boss stated that a constant rate of 100 wam was feasible for students of medium and high ability if the procedures outlined in her research were followed.[18]

On the basis of these studies, micromolar approaches do not seem to offer student achievement advantages over more traditional speed building plans. However, further experimentation will undoubtedly be done which may shed new light on the advantages or disadvantages of the micromolar theory.

Grubbs' "Explore the New; Build Skill on the Old" Approach

In 1960 Robert Grubbs presented a plan based on a cycle of emphasis.[19] The cycle is effected by using a 6-day reading approach that continues throughout the first semester. The learners explore each new shorthand principle through reading it in the lesson in which it is presented and reading it in each of the following five lessons before they are expected to write it. Grubbs explains that the cycle interval of 6 days was chosen because there are six lessons in each chapter of the first semester book. After the first 6-day reading approach and after the class presentation introducing writing in Lesson 6, students are building skill in class using the material presented in the lesson one chapter (six lessons) preceding the one they are reading.

The 54-day calendar on pages 96–97 gives a daily schedule for in-class and out-of-class activities using the 6-day six-lesson approach of cycling the learning. Teachers throughout the United States have found this approach effective for teaching the first semester of shorthand.

Summary of Approaches

Although experiments have been conducted to compare manual, functional, and combination approaches, overall findings have not been conclusive. Many of the early experiments comparing manual and functional approaches were limited by sample size, statistical treatment, and variable control. Controlling the teacher variable in research comparing teaching approaches is particularly difficult because no teacher is likely to be equally effective in using the methodologies of both manual and functional approaches.

Shorthand has been taught effectively by manual, functional, and combination approaches, and the question of which approach to use is best answered by the individual teacher. The ability of the teacher to establish rapport with students and to enthusiastically use an approach and its associated methodology is a prime consideration. Approaches or methods, no matter how psychologically sound, will not be effective if teachers do not enthusiastically endorse and believe in them.

Today's teachers have a tendency to select methodology from both the manual and functional approaches. Information gained from professional literature as well as personal experience often determines the methods used. The authors of this book, through research and classroom experience, have also developed a "hybrid" approach, aspects of which will be seen in the remainder of this chapter and the following chapters.

Using the Chalkboard Effectively

A piece of chalk can be a powerful teaching instrument in the hand of a skillful shorthand teacher who understands the importance of chalkboard drill. Students learn shorthand by rapid, intensive, and repetitive in-class practice; and the chalkboard is an ideal instructional medium because teachers can control the speed, intensity, and repetitiveness of drill practice.

The old adage, "a picture is worth a thousand words," could be used to refer to the teaching of shorthand, because shorthand teachers have relied heavily on the chalkboard for at least 75 years. Gregg recognized the value of the chalkboard early in his career and in 1928 wrote a still timely book, *The Use of the Blackboard in Teaching Shorthand*.[20] A review of the text reveals that basic principles of chalkboard writing have not changed and that the chalkboard must be a focal point of instruction at all levels of shorthand learning. The chalkboard should be used for presenting or reinforcing new theory principles and brief forms as well as for previewing and postviewing unfamiliar or difficult-to-construct outlines.

Beginning shorthand teachers sometimes lack confidence in using the chalkboard, but they should remember that their own chalkboard writing ability will improve through practice and attention to correctness of writing. Continued practice will polish the skills of chalkboard presentation.

Principles of Chalkboard Presentation

Basic shorthand skills essential to influence effective chalkboard writing include ability to write theoretically correct outlines; to sound/spell outlines as they are written; and to write legible, well-propor-

60-DAY CALENDAR FOR THE GREGG SHORTHAND MANUAL SIMPLIFIED
(ADAPTED TO SERIES 90—A 54-DAY CALENDAR)

Theory period	CLASS DRILL (SKILLBUILDING ON THE OLD)		TEACH (EXPLORING THE NEW)	HOMEWORK ASSIGNMENTS	
	Spelling and reading drills on:	Dictating and writing drills on:		Read lesson:	Write lesson:
1	Lesson 1	no writing	Lesson 1	1	none
2	Lesson 1 and 2	no writing	Lesson 2	2	none
3	Lesson 1, 2, and 3	no writing	Lesson 3	3	none
4	Lesson 3 and 4	no writing	Lesson 4	4	none
5	Lesson 4 and 5	no writing	Lesson 5	5	none
6	Lesson (6)	(limited writing of brief form sentences)	Lesson 6	6	none
7	Lesson (7)		Lesson 7	7	none
8	Lesson (8)		Lesson 8	8	none
9	Lesson 9	Lesson 3	Lesson 9	9	none
10	Lesson 10	Lesson 4	Lesson 10	10	5
11	Lesson 11	Lesson 5	Lesson 11	11	6
12	Lesson 12	Lesson 6	Lesson 12	12	7
13	Lesson 13	Lesson 7	Lesson 13	13	8
14	Lesson 14	Lesson 8	Lesson 14	14	9
15	Lesson 15	Lesson 9	Lesson 15	15	10
16	Lesson 16	Lesson 10	Lesson 16	16	11
17	Lesson 17	Lesson 11	Lesson 17	17	12
18		(Review)	Lesson 18 (Test)	18	
19	Lesson 18	Lesson 12	Lesson 19	19	13
20	Lesson 19	Lesson 13	Lesson 20	20	14
21	Lesson 20	Lesson 14	Lesson 21	21	15
22	Lesson 21	Lesson 15	Lesson 22	22	16
23	Lesson 22	Lesson 16	Lesson 23	23	17
24	Lesson 23	Lesson 17	Lesson 24	24	18

25	Lesson 24	Lesson 18	Lesson 25	25	19
26	Lesson 25	Lesson 19	Lesson 26	26	20
27	Lesson 26	Lesson 20	Lesson 27	27	21
28	Lesson 27	Lesson 21	Lesson 28	28	22
29	Lesson 28	Lesson 22	Lesson 29	29	23
30	Lesson 29	Lesson 23	Lesson 30	30	24
	—— (Review) ——	—— (Review) ——	—— (Test) ——		
31	Lesson 30	Lesson 24	Lesson 31	31	25
32	Lesson 31	Lesson 25	Lesson 32	32	26
33	Lesson 32	Lesson 26	Lesson 33	33	27
34	Lesson 33	Lesson 27	Lesson 34	34	28
35	Lesson 34	Lesson 28	Lesson 35	35	29
36	Lesson 35	Lesson 29	Lesson 36	36	30
37	Lesson 36	Lesson 30	Lesson 37	37	31
38	Lesson 37	Lesson 31	Lesson 38	38	32
39	Lesson 38	Lesson 32	Lesson 39	39	33
40	Lesson 39	Lesson 33	Lesson 40	40	34
41	Lesson 40	Lesson 34	Lesson 41	41	35
42	Lesson 41	Lesson 35	Lesson 42	42	36
	—— (Review) ——	—— (Test) ——	—— (Test) ——		
43	Lesson 42	Lesson 36	Lesson 43	43	37
44	Lesson 43	Lesson 37	Lesson 44	44	38
45	Lesson 44	Lesson 38	Lesson 45	45	39
46	Lesson 45	Lesson 39	Lesson 46	46	40
47	Lesson 46	Lesson 40	Lesson 47	47	41
48	Lesson 47	Lesson 41	Lesson 48	48	42
49	Lesson 48	Lesson 42	Lesson 49, 50, 51	49–50–51	43
50	Lesson 49, 50, 51	Lesson 43	Lesson 52, 53, 54	52–53–54	44
51	Lesson 52, 53, 54	Lesson 44	Lesson 55, 56, 57	55–56–57	45
52	Lesson 55, 56, 57	Lesson 45	Lesson 58, 59, 60	58–59–60	46
53	Lesson 58, 59, 60	Lesson 46	Lesson 61, 62, 63	61–62–63	47
54	Lesson 61, 62, 63	Lesson 47	Lesson 64, 65, 66	64–65–66	48
	—— (Review) ——	—— (Review) ——	—— (Test) ——		

Lessons 49 to 70 are short review and integrating lessons. Because they are quite easy, three lessons have been scheduled for each day. They may be assigned on another basis, or not assigned at all, with no harmful results.

tioned outlines. These skills are intrinsic to effective presentations, and novice teachers who lack them should adopt self-improvement programs.

The following are principles to be considered by all teachers of shorthand.

OUTLINES SHOULD BE CLEARLY OBSERVABLE TO STUDENT. All students should have an opportunity to see outlines being written on the chalkboard. Yet the teacher's writing position and the positioning of outlines on the board sometimes make this impossible. Gregg states why it is important for students to observe outlines being written by stating:

> Blackboard illustration, being intensely graphic, focuses attention and impresses forms and principles so vividly that the student carries them away with him permanently. Textbook illustrations go much farther in real teaching than any amount of printed description. But they cannot go so far as the teacher goes in his illustrations on the board. The teacher can demonstrate movement, which is just as important as form, because form is the result of movement. This the textbook illustration cannot give.[21]

Accordingly, shorthand teachers must use a writing position that allows students to see the outline formation. There are two writing positions that may be adopted. For maximum utilization of chalkboard space and maximum opportunity for students to see the teacher writing, teachers need to become proficient in both.

Teachers may write on the left half of the chalkboard (as students face it). As shown in the first of two illustrations that follow, the teacher almost faces the chalkboard, assuming a position to the left of the writing block, with body and head turned slightly out toward the students, in order to establish eye contact after writing the word or words on the chalkboard. This position may be a disadvantage for right-handed teachers. As outlines are written in a left-to-right motion, the teacher may be moving in front of the shorthand outlines previously written. To alleviate the problem, experiment with writing the isolated outlines used for previewing, postviewing, or shorthand vocabulary word lists in a right-to-left sequence. As the outlines are written on the chalkboard, move the body to the left slightly. The simple technique of adding an outline just to the left of those previously written gives the observing students an unobstructed view of each outline.

In the second illustration on page 100, the teacher is writing on the right half of the chalkboard (as students face it). When first used, this position may feel unnatural and awkward. With practice, however, most teachers find it effective. Notice that in the illustration, the teacher faces the class with back to the chalkboard at approximately a 45-degree angle. The teacher stands close to the chalkboard with

Ken Karp

writing arm almost parallel to it while writing, thus maintaining good eye contact, with less possibility of obstructing the view of outlines.

In writing from either position, it is important to keep the block of writing within an arm's length. Using the full length of the arm will enable the teacher to stand beside the block of writing and point to the outlines for student response. When one arm's-length block is completed, the teacher will step to the left or the right to write words in another block. Depending on the size of the chalkboard, the teacher may be able to have six or seven blocks of previews or postviews for dictation speed building or of sample shorthand vocabulary words for reviewing today's homework lesson and previewing tomorrow's.

The positioning of outlines on the chalkboard also influences visibility. Generally, the upper two-thirds of the board should be used for shorthand, and the lower third considered "dead space." It is virtually impossible for students seated in the rear of the classroom to see outlines written in the dead space. Additionally, writing outlines near the bottom of the chalkboard is not conducive to good penmanship, particularly if the teacher must bend or crouch to form outlines.

Other factors associated with visibility include outline size, heaviness of outlines, the light reflection. Extremely large outlines can be used to demonstrate special theory points. They should be of a size that

99

Ken Karp

will provide for easy reading and clear illustration of joining principles. Lightly written outlines may illustrate desired fluency, but if they are too light, students have difficulty seeing them. Using softer chalk and grasping it more firmly, with the butt end toward the palm (*not* as a pen is held), should encourage writing firm, strong-looking outlines that will create desired visual effects. Although probably not a major factor in most shorthand classrooms, light reflecting off the chalkboard can cause excessive glare. All teachers need to make periodic checks to determine if chalkboard glare is reducing visibility.

OUTLINES SHOULD BE SOUND/SPELLED AS THEY ARE WRITTEN ON THE CHALKBOARD. Hearing the sound/spelling of outlines as they are written is almost as important as seeing their formation. Students have a greater opportunity for learning and reinforcement because two senses, seeing and hearing, are involved. If an outline is important enough to write on the board, it is important for the teacher to sound/spell. During the theory presentation stage, teacher sound/spelling is crucial, but it is still important during the advanced levels of shorthand because is provides continual sound-symbol relationship and informal theory review.

Some teachers believe that sound/spelling inhibits the fluency of their chalkboard writing. They would find, however, that they can combine fluent writing and sound/spelling if they realized that the writing and spelling do not have to be perfectly synchronized. As outlines are written and sound/spelled by the teacher over a period of time, improvements in synchronization and fluency will occur naturally.

There are no firm rules for pronouncing shorthand strokes. Using the sounds that are easiest for students and using them consistently are the most important considerations. A list of suggested spelling sounds from the *Instructor's Handbook for Gregg Shorthand, Series 90* is included on pages 101–105 for reference:[22]

SUGGESTED NAMES FOR SERIES 90 SHORTHAND SYMBOLS (IN ORDER OF PRESENTATION)

	STROKE	SHORTHAND NAME	ILLUSTRATION	SHORTHAND SPELLING
Lesson 1	s	ĕs		s-ā
	a	ā	say	s-ā
	f	ĕf	safe	s-ā-f
	v	vē	save	s-ā-v
	e	ē	fee	f-ē
	n	ĕn	knee	n-ē
	m	ĕm	may	m-ā
	t	tē	tea	t-ē
	d	dē	day	d-ā
Lesson 2	o	oh	no	n-ō
	r	är	ray	r-ā
	l	ĕl	ail	ā-l
	h	ātch	he	h-ē
	-ing	ing	heating	h-ē-t-ing
	ī	eye	my	m-ī
Lesson 3	s	ĕs	eats	ē-t-s
	p	pē	pay	p-ā
	b	bē	bay	b-ā
Lesson 4	o͞o	o͞o	who	h-o͞o
	w	o͞o	we	o͞o-ē
	sw	s-o͞o	sweet	s-o͞o-ē-t
	wh	o͞o	white	o͞o-ī-t
	k	kā	take	t-ā-k
	g	gay	gain	gay-ā-n
Lesson 5	ă	ā	has	h-ā-s
	ä	ā	mark	m-ā-r-k
	ĕ	ē	let	l-ē-t
	ĭ	ē	trim	t-r-ē-m

	STROKE	SHORTHAND NAME	ILLUSTRATION	SHORTHAND SPELLING
Lesson 5 (Continued)	obscure vowel	ē	her	h-ē-r
	th	ĭth	these	ith-ē-s
	th	ĭth	though	ith-ō
Lesson 7	sh	ĭsh	she	ĭsh-e
	ch	chay	each	ē-chay
	j	jay	age	ā-j
	ŏ	ō	hot	h-ō-t
	aw	ō	law	l-ō
Lesson 8	be-	bē	became	bē-k-ā-m
	-ly	lē	briefly	b-r-ē-f-lē
Lesson 9	-tion	shun	nation	n-ā-shun
	-cient	shun-t	efficient	ē-f-ē-shun-t
	-ciency	shun-s-ē	efficiency	ē-f-ē-shun-s-ē
Lesson 10	nd	end	trained	t-r-ā-end
	nt	ent	sent	s-ē-ent
	ses	sez	passes	p-ā-sez
			basis	b-ā-sez
			versus	v-ē-r-sez
			sister	sez-t-r
Lesson 11	rd	ärd	hard	h-ā-ard
			heard	h-ē-ard
			tired	t-ī-ard
	ld	ĕld	failed	f-ā-eld
			told	t-ō-eld
Lesson 13	ŭ	$\overline{oo}$	does	d-$\overline{oo}$-s
			just	j-$\overline{oo}$-s-t
	oo	oo	foot	f-oo-t
Lesson 14	w dash	$\overline{oo}$	twin	t-$\overline{oo}$-ē-n
	ted	ted	acted	ā-k-ted
			today	ted-ā
			steady	s-ted-ē
	ded	ded	needed	n-ē-ded
	det	det	detail	det-ā-l
			credit	k-r-ē-det
Lesson 15	-ble	bul	payable	p-ā-bul
			troubled	t-r-bul-d
	re-	rē	revise	rē-v-ī-s
Lesson 16	oi	oi	toy	t-oi
	men	men	mental	men-t-l
			minute	men-ē-t
			month	men-ith

	STROKE	SHORTHAND NAME	ILLUSTRATION	SHORTHAND SPELLING
Lesson 16 (Continued)	ye ya	ē ā	manner year yarn	men-r ē-r ā-r-n
Lesson 17	per- pur- de- dĭ	pur pur de de	permit purple decide direct	pur-m-ē-t pur-p-l de-s-ī-d de-r-ē-k-t
Lesson 19	ū -ment -cial, -tial	ū ment shul	few payment official	f-ū p-ā-ment ō-f-ē-shul
Lesson 20	ow -ther con- com-	ow -ther con com	now other concern compose	n-ow o͞o-ther con-s-ē-r-n com-p-ō-s
Lesson 21	den ten -tain	den ten tain	sudden danger dinner attend cotton stand tonight obtain	s-o͞o-den den-j-ē-r den-r ā-ten-d k-ō-ten s-ten-d ten-ī-t ō-b-tain
Lesson 22	dem tem	dem tem	condemn random medium damage temper estimate	con-dem r-ā-n-dem m-ē-dem dem-j tem-p-r ē-s-tem-ā-t
Lesson 23	over def div ĭa, ēa	over def dīv ēah	overdo defeat differ divide devise area	over-d-o͞o def-ē-t def-r div-ī-d div-ī-s ā-r-ēah
Lesson 25	under	under	underneath	under-n-ē-ith
Lesson 26	īa un- en-	īah un en	trial unfair enjoy	t-r-īah-l un-f-ā-r en-j-oi
Lesson 27	ng	ing	sing strong angle	s-ē-ing s-t-r-ō-ing ā-ing-l

	STROKE	SHORTHAND NAME	ILLUSTRATION	SHORTHAND SPELLING
Lesson 27 (Continued)	ngk	ink	link bank uncle	l-ē-ink b-ā-ink ōō-ink-l
Lesson 28	ah aw x xes	ā-ātch ā-ōō ex exes	ahead aware tax taxes	ā-h-ē-d ā-ōō-ā-r t-ā-ex t-ā-exes
Lesson 29	ex- -ful -cal, -cle	ex full īkal	extra careful chemical article	ex-t-r-ā k-ā-r-ful k-ē-m-īkle ā-r-t-īkle
Lesson 31	-ure -ual	är ĕl	feature actual	f-ē-t-r ā-k-t-l
Lesson 32	-ily al- dis- des-	īly all dis dis	easily also dispose despite	ē-s-ily all-s-ō dis-p-ō-s dis-p-ī-t
Lesson 33	for-, fore- fur-	for fur	forget furnace	for-gay-ē-t fur-n-ā-s
Lesson 34	ort -ern -erm md mt	ō-t ē-r-n ē-r-m emd emt	report turn term seemed empty	re-p-ō-t t-ē-n t-ē-m s-ē-emd emt-ē
Lesson 35	inter- intr- enter- entr- -ings	inter intro enter enter ings	interest introduce entertain entrance openings	inter-s-t intro-d-ōō-s enter-tain enter-n-s ō-p-n-ings
Lesson 37	-ingly im- em-	ingly im em	knowingly improve embrace	n-ō-ingly im-p-r-ōō-v em-b-r-ā-s
Lesson 38	-ship sub- -ulate -ulation -rity	ship sub ulate ulation rity	steamship submit circulate circulation majority minority security	s-t-ē-m-ship sub-m-ē-t s-ē-r-k-ulate s-ē-r-k-ulation m-ā-j-rity men-rity s-ē-k-rity
Lesson 39	-lity	lity	ability	ā-b-lity

	STROKE	SHORTHAND NAME	ILLUSTRATION	SHORTHAND SPELLING
Lesson 39 (Continued)	-lty	ulty	faculty penalty	f-ā-k-ulty p-n-ulty
	-self	self	herself	h-ē-r-self
	-selves	selves	yourselves	your-selves
Lesson 41	trans-	trans	transfer	trans-f-ē-r
Lesson 43	mis-	miss	mistake	mis-t-ā-k
	super-	super	supervise	super-v-ī-s
	ē omitted in ū	o͞o	music	m-o͞o-s-ē-k
			continue	con-ten-o͞o
Lesson 44	self-	self	selfish	self-ish
	circum-	circum	circumstance	circum-s-ten-s
	-ification	-ification	classification	k-l-ā-s-ification
Lesson 45	-hood	hood	neighborhood	n-ā-b-r-hood
	-ward	ward	backward	b-ā-k-ward
	ul	ŭl	result	rē-s-ŭl-t
Lesson 46	-gram	gram	telegram	t-ē-l-gram
	electric-	electric	electrical	electric-l
	electr-	electro	electronic	electro-n-ē-k
Lesson 47	-burg	berg	Harrisburg	h-ā-r-ē-s-berg
	-ingham	ingham	Buckingham	b-o͞o-k-ingham
	-ington	ington	Lexington	l-ē-ex-ington
	-ville	ville	Nashville	n-ā-ish-ville

Note: Brief forms, phrases, salutations and closings, days of the week, months of the year, intersections, and geographical expressions (other than those presented in Lesson 47) should not be spelled out by the students.

Outlines Should Be Fluently Written and Well Formed. When the teacher places a shorthand outline on the chalkboard, students instinctively imitate the manner of writing. If a teacher consistently *draws* outlines, there are apt to be an unusual number of students with a tendency to draw outlines. Likewise, habitually writing sloppy, ill-formed outlines on the chalkboard is apt to have a negative effect on class penmanship. With practice, teachers will find it easy to observe an imaginary line of writing. Following an imaginary line of writing will help develop accurate proportion, which is necessary for the student to read one symbol in comparison to another. After writing the first word of a line, try to align the following words with it.

Since shorthand is in part an imitative skill acquired through

105

hearing, seeing, reading, and copying, shorthand teachers have an obligation to provide the best models for students to imitate.

Chalkboard Presentations Should Be Paced. Outlines should be sound/spelled and written on the chalkboard at a measured, but brisk, pace. Lengthy pauses between presentations of outlines divert attention from what the teacher is doing, and the chalkboard ceases to be the focal point of learning.

Additionally, a brisk presentation implies teacher confidence, which is important in establishing proper classroom atmosphere. All student activities are paced in shorthand classes, and teachers need to convey that pace in all their activities.

Chalkboard Presentations Should Be Organized. Teachers should remember that outlines illustrating similar theory principles should be grouped, or blocked, and arranged for convenient review throughout the class period.

If nine outlines are used in a block to illustrate theory principles being previewed or reviewed, the outlines can be easily grouped into two or three lines. If 12 outlines are used, a convenient arrangement might be three lines with four outlines in each. There are no absolutes for grouping outlines; however, outline grouping should facilitate drill. For example, the teacher should be able to point quickly to any outline in the block without undue body movement. Because student sound/spelling and reading should be repetitive, random, and in unison, a compact group or block of outlines is suggested.

Blocks of outlines illustrating new theory principles or brief forms, and reviews of the previous theory assignment, should be retained on the chalkboard for short, quick reviews throughout the class period. Because these reviews are vitally important to learning, teachers need to organize chalkboard presentations within the limitations of available chalkboard space.

Writing the longhand for the sound on the board helps students hear and see the sound being used. Sample theory-principle presentations, showing blocking, longhand, imaginary lines of writing, and suggested number of outlines per line and lines per block are illustrated on page 107.

Chalkboard Presentations Should Be Used for Drill. The following is suggested as a general pattern for chalkboard drill on new theory principles, brief forms, and reviews of previous theory assignments, or for previewing unfamiliar words that are identified in dictation:

1. The teacher sound/spells and writes each outline on the board while students observe writing motions and hear spelling sounds.
2. The teacher points under each outline while loudly sound/spelling and pronouncing it in unison with students. Each new word should be sound/spelled and said about three times in

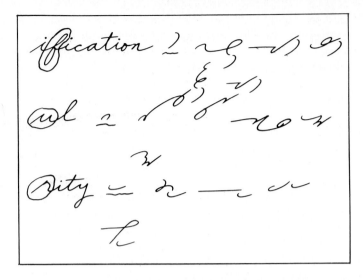

succession, while review words may need to be sound/spelled and pronounced only twice. Brief forms are not sound/spelled after being written on the board because students are taught to recognize them as whole words. However, many teachers find that showing the longhand and the derivation of the symbols used to develop the brief form, helps the student associate the strong sounds used in brief forms with the words represented.

3. After repetitive practice of words in order listed, the teacher points to outlines in random order within the theory grouping as students sound/spell and pronounce the words in unison.

4. The teacher calls on students and points to outlines as individual students sound/spell and pronounce the outlines within theory groupings to assess how much additional drill is necessary. It is not recommended that students be directed to jump back and forth from one theory grouping to another, a procedure which is difficult for the beginner. Also, students need the reinforcement of sound/spelling and pronouncing review words twice in succession.

5. The teacher dictates the words and students write them, referring to the chalkboard list if they are unsure of outline construction. The teacher points to the words so the students can locate the outline quickly. The practice of writing outlines is used only after students have been introduced to writing from dictation and after the teacher is satisfied with the repetitive reading and sound/spelling performance of the class.

6. The teacher retains the outlines on the chalkboard for periodic review throughout the class period. As outlines are reviewed, theory principles being emphasized should be quickly restated

and sounded by the teacher. Example: "The *ification* ending is expressed by a disjoined *f* sound/spelled *ification*. Please sound/spell and pronounce . . ." (Teacher points, sound/spelling and pronouncing with students.) The introduction of word lists and this type of periodic review should provide the necessary in-class learning to help students prepare the next day's lesson. Through repeated saying, seeing, hearing, and feeling how an outline is written, learning is maximized.

Using Overhead Projectors

Although chalkboards are still used as an instructional medium by the majority of shorthand teachers, some prefer overhead projectors. A few of these teachers depend entirely on overhead projection for theory presentation, previewing and postviewing for dictation speed building, teaching basic language arts, and all other learning activities formerly associated with the chalkboard.

There is no evidence that either the chalkboard or the overhead projector has inherent instructional superiority. Teacher preference is probably the sole criterion for determining the most appropriate medium of shorthand instruction. However, teachers who have never used overhead projectors may wish to consider trying them to determine their merits. By the same token, teachers who do not ordinarily use the chalkboard should try to develop effective chalkboard writing techniques as an alternative teaching procedure.

Advantages

Putney cites five advantages associated with using overhead projectors in preference to chalkboards for shorthand instruction:[23]

1. Instructors can face their classes while writing outlines.
2. Students are able to observe hand movements as instructors write.
3. Projections more clearly resemble stenographers' notebooks.
4. Outlines more clearly resemble students' notes.
5. Transparencies can be used for review throughout the class period or retained for review later in the course.

Another commonly given advantage for using overhead projectors with prepared transparencies is that class time is saved which would otherwise be used in writing at the chalkboard.

Miller lists nine uses of the overhead projector for shorthand instruction: theory presentation and review; brief form presentation and recall; business vocabulary building; reading practice; dictation previews and postviews; teaching or reviewing spelling, punctuation, and letter styles; and demonstrating writing from dictation.[24]

Disadvantages

The medium should never be a hindrance to learning. If previously written word lists, previews, and postviews cannot be found and placed on the equipment quickly, valuable time is lost. Sometimes shorthand classrooms do not lend themselves to convenient location of the projector in terms of the instructor's mobility and opportunity to observe students writing. Some teachers believe the use of the overhead limits quick reviews of materials.

Formats

Three basic transparency formats are available for teachers who wish to use overhead projectors: single sheet transparencies, transparency rolls, and transparency packages. Lemaster believes there are advantages associated with each.[25] Single sheets are easy to prepare, require no special attachment for using on projectors. Transparency rolls are useful for writing in class because they do not require erasing during the class period. When the teacher finishes writing on one section, the roll can be quickly advanced to another section. Transparency packages are bound so they are always properly sequenced. These packages are apt to be commercially prepared, so transparencies are well organized and arranged, appealing to the eye, and contain well-written outline models for students to read and copy.

Using Transparencies

All the principles for effective chalkboard presentation previously discussed apply to teaching shorthand with projectors. When transparencies are used, students should be able to see outlines and the proper writing motions while hearing outlines sound/spelled. Presentations from transparencies should be organized to facilitate paced drill, which may include student sound/spelling, reading, and writing.

Single and roll transparencies are commonly prepared during class periods so that overhead projections function identically to the chalkboard. Transparencies commercially prepared or prepared by the teacher before class have the advantage of being well planned and organized, but students will be unable to observe proper writing motions unless teachers drypen over the outlines as they sound/spell them.

The smooth surface of all transparencies encourages fluent writing motions while allowing the projection of dark, easy-to-read outlines. However, clarity of outlines depends on the type of writing instrument used. Grease pencils make dark lines that tend to flake and smudge, and they are not particularly conducive to fluent writing. Water-base pens make lighter, more translucent lines, and transparencies can be easily cleaned with water. Permanent-ink pens make

109

dark, almost nonsmudgeable lines, but the lines cannot be easily erased. Teachers should experiment to determine the writing instrument most suitable for them.

Commercially prepared transparencies are available for teaching shorthand vocabulary, brief forms, phrases, punctuation, typing style, and spelling. Because the methodology for teaching transcription fundamentals differs somewhat from that for teaching shorthand vocabulary and developing writing skills, not all of the basic principles for chalkboard presentation apply.

LESSON 42

Brief Forms and Derivatives

A	B	C	D	E	F

Words

The methodology used will, in large measure, depend upon the organization and format of the transparencies. Therefore, teachers should consider using recommended methodology accompanying the transparency packages.

The question of whether to use the overhead projector or the chalkboard is moot. Either medium is effective if used properly by a skillful, enthusiastic teacher.

The First Few Days

The first several days of shorthand instruction are crucial to ultimate success. First impressions count, and student attitudes are shaped by what occurs during this time. Additionally, almost all of the basic shorthand alphabet is presented in the first three lessons. If students do not learn these lessons, progress on succeeding lessons will be limited.

Students should have a positive attitude about shorthand and their teacher. After the first several days of instruction, they should feel that they are making good progress and experiencing success. They should consider the teacher as friendly, approachable, and enthusiastic about their progress; and they should consider shorthand a skill that can be developed. The objectives for the first few days have not been met if these attitudinal ingredients are missing.

Planning for the First Day

Presentation of the first lesson includes some special problems for teachers. Class periods are sometimes shortened, administrative chores may have to be completed, and the composition of the class often changes during the first few days. As a result, two class periods are normally consumed in teaching the first lesson.

Ideally, there should be sufficient class time to present all the principles in the first lesson on the first day so that a duplicate presentation can be made on the second day. On the first day, the first lesson is presented entirely on the chalkboard. On the second day, the first lesson is repeated. The chalkboard is used for presentation and drill, and textbooks are used for sound/spelling, drypenning, and reading practice.

Many teachers will not have time to present the entire lesson during the first day but shorthand instruction should begin even if only a few minutes are available. Partial coverage of a lesson will reduce the difficulty when the lesson is presented again on the second day. Talking about the history or importance of shorthand may seem interesting to teachers, but students are more curious about learning to write shorthand. Pep talks and lectures to arouse interest are more effective after students have begun to learn shorthand.

Objectives for the First Lesson

Seven objectives are associated with teaching the first lesson. Some of the objectives relate to shorthand learning while others are more attitudinal. All of them are important to the successful completion of the first lesson, however.

TO DEVELOP AN UNDERSTANDING OF THE PRINCIPLES OF FORMULATING SHORTHAND OUTLINES. The class can be introduced to the first lesson by a short elaboration of the three reasons why shorthand is written more rapidly than longhand. (1) *We write only what we hear in shorthand.* The teacher writes words on the chalkboard to illustrate that silent letters are not written in shorthand and asks the class what sounds are heard and what letters are silent. Such words as "main, same, save, snow, knee, and right" can be used to illustrate that shorthand is a "sound" language. (2) *We use symbols instead of longhand letters for writing shorthand. Many of these symbols are merely abbreviations of the longhand alphabet.* The teacher shows how the shorthand symbols for *a* and *s* are derived from longhand symbols. (3) *We abbreviate commonly used words, just as we do in longhand, and call them brief forms.* The teacher uses the longhand examples of words like *Mr.* and *Mister* to illustrate brief forms.

TO DEVELOP THE ATTITUDE THAT SHORTHAND IS COMPARATIVELY EASY TO LEARN. Showing the many options for writing longhand letters (for example, $F, f, f, \mathcal{F}$) and informing students that there is only one way to write *f* in shorthand is a first step toward achievement of this objective.

Illustrating how shorthand symbols can be derived from a longhand letter may interest some students. However, symbol associations should not be overused, and students should be told that only the basic symbols are derived from the longhand alphabet. Some teachers prefer not to use this type of illustration at any time. The following are examples of longhand derivations which can be used as each shorthand symbol is introduced.

The response of the teacher to student sound/spelling and reading is the most important factor in influencing student attitude about the difficulty of learning shorthand. Expressions of satisfaction and praise for concerted and individual sound/spelling and reading is of paramount importance. Each student should leave the classroom with the attitude that "I can do it; I did well today."

TO LEARN A PORTION OF THE BASIC SHORTHAND ALPHABET. Students will be able to sound/spell and read shorthand outlines only to the extent that they know the shorthand alphabet. That is why alphabetic symbols must be reviewed throughout the first lesson and in succeeding lessons. As alphabetic strokes and their accompanying word illustrations are introduced, they are written on the chalkboard for repetitive student sound/spelling and reading. However, outline grouping is essential for efficiency in review. Basic shorthand strokes should be grouped, and additions made to the list as new strokes are introduced. Words illustrating alphabetic strokes should also be grouped and retained on the board for periodic review throughout the class period.

The teacher points rapidly, randomly, and repetitively to the basic alphabetic characters or word lists, and students are expected to respond orally. The inclusion of 15- to 30-second review drills on alphabetic characters and word lists throughout the class period should enable most students to recognize the basic alphabet after the first two periods of instruction.

TO DEVELOP RAPID, CONCERTED READING AND SOUND/SPELLING SKILLS.   Recognition of basic alphabetic strokes is essential, but not sufficient. Recognition must become an automatic response. Paced repetitive practice is introduced the first day, and recognition skills are refined through chalkboard drills orchestrated by the teacher. The habit of responding orally as the teacher points to outlines on the chalkboard must be established during the first class period because this methodology is intrinsic to teaching shorthand theory. Usually, the following drill pattern is used:

1. The teacher sound/spells and writes each outline on the board as students observe writing motions and hear spelling sounds.
2. The teacher points to outlines in random order while sound/spelling and pronouncing the outlines in unison with the students.
3. The teacher points to outlines randomly and repetitively as students sound/spell and pronounce words in unison without the teacher's aid.
4. The teacher calls on individuals or volunteers to sound/spell and read outlines to assess the degree of mastery.
5. The teacher retains the outlines on the chalkboard and uses them for periodic review drills throughout the class period.

TO CREATE A CLASSROOM RAPPORT CONDUCIVE TO ACTIVE PARTICIPATION.   Students may initially be reluctant to participate in unison drills. Fear of making mistakes, shyness, inability to anticipate teacher reactions, and new surroundings all contribute to nonparticipation. The attitude and actions of the teacher will have a profound effect on the degree of participation.

Students must be made to realize that everyone makes occasional errors and that the teacher will either ignore them or pass them off with a smile. When an error is made, the teacher merely keeps drilling until the error disappears. Individuals are not singled out or embarrassed.

Students must learn during the first class period to sound/spell loudly when the teacher points to an outline on the chalkboard. To maximize the degree of participation, teachers may have to resort to

113

a few gimmicks. Repeated or pronounced pointing of the finger under an outline, mouthing the word "louder" to the class, using facial expressions of disappointment or pleasure, or any other device that conveys the message to students should be used. When inhibitions and self-consciousness are removed, students are free to focus their full attention on learning shorthand.

TO CREATE A SPIRIT OF FRIENDLY COMPETITION. Greater participation can be obtained if students are encouraged to compete with themselves and with their classmates. For example, they can be exhorted to read louder and faster than the person sitting next to them or to strive for self-improvement with each repetition of the material. Dividing the class into informal competitive groups sometimes encourages louder and faster sound/spelling and reading. For example, each row may be asked to read from the chalkboard and unofficial speed and volume champions can be declared.

TO DEVELOP PERFORMANCE GUIDELINES FOR HOMEWORK PREPARATION. Whether to give a homework assignment on the first day or to wait until the first lesson has been repeated before giving an assignment, is a matter of individual teacher preference. The first homework assignment generally includes sound/spelling, drypenning, and reading word lists and spelling, drypenning, and reading the connected material of the lesson. Most of the reading during the next class period will be in unison, with everyone drypenning, spelling, and saying each word. The teacher should be an active speller and reader and be setting the example of drypenning. Within a few days individual students who volunteer are asked to spell and read the assignment. Students need guidelines for homework preparation during this early stage of learning. The teacher can give these guidelines by a reading demonstration of what is expected for A, B, and C performance of the reading of plate material.

Suggested Lesson Plans

FIRST LESSON, FIRST DAY

ACTIVITY	ESTIMATED TIME
Preliminaries	4 minutes
Discussion and illustration of why shorthand is written faster than longhand:	
a. Write only what is heard.	
b. Use symbols for longhand letters.	
c. Abbreviate common words (brief forms).	4 minutes
Introduction of *S–Z* and *A*, showing longhand derivation, followed by unison chalkboard drill on words	2 minutes

ACTIVITY	ESTIMATED TIME
Introduction of *F* and *V* showing longhand derivation, followed by unison chalkboard drill on words	4 minutes
Unison chalkboard drill on alphabetic strokes	30 seconds
Introduction of *E* showing longhand derivation, followed by unison chalkboard drill on words	2 minutes
Rest period	30 seconds
Unison chalkboard drill on alphabetic strokes and all words written on the board	1 minute
Introduction of *N* and *M* showing longhand derivation, followed by unison chalkboard drill on words	4 minutes
Unison sound/spelling and reading of outlines on the chalkboard	3 minutes
Unison chalkboard drill on alphabetic strokes	30 seconds
Rest period	30 seconds
Introduction of *T* and *D,* showing longhand derivation, followed by unison chalkboard drill on words	4 minutes
Unison chalkboard drill on alphabetic strokes	30 seconds
Introduction and drill on punctuation and capitalization marks	3 minutes
Unison chalkboard drill on all words	1½ minutes
Rest period	30 seconds
Unison sound/spelling and reading of words on chalkboard	2 minutes
Distribution of textbooks	5 minutes
Unison sound/spelling and reading of connected material in first lesson of textbooks	4 minutes
Unison drill on all chalkboard words	1½ minutes
Homework assignment including demonstrations of *A, B,* and *C* performance	2 minutes

The lesson plan on pages 114–115 provides suggested activities and time allocations for the first day. The plan on page 116 outlines activities and time frames for repeating the lesson on the second day. Both plans are based on a 50-minute class period; adjustments must be made in time allocations and class activities for longer or shorter periods. All time allocations should be considered as approximate. It is virtually impossible to follow a rigid time schedule in shorthand unless each activity is subjected to a stop watch. Attempting to adhere to exact time frames is dangerous because student learning rates are ignored. The time devoted to each activity must be determined by how quickly students grasp each principle.

FIRST LESSON, SECOND DAY

ACTIVITY	ESTIMATED TIME
Preliminaries	4 minutes
Individual sound/spelling and reading of word lists in homework	4 minutes
Unison chalkboard drill on alphabetic strokes	1 minute
Individual sound/spelling and reading of connected matter in homework	3 minutes
Unison chalkboard drill on S–Z, A, E, F, and V words	5 minutes
Rest period	30 seconds
Unison chalkboard drill on alphabetic characters and S–Z, A, E, F, and V words	2 minutes
Individual or unison sound/spelling and reading of connected matter in homework	2 minutes
Unison chalkboard drill on N, M, T, and D words	5 minutes
Rest period	30 seconds
Review of punctuation and capitalization marks	2 minutes
Unison chalkboard drill on alphabetic strokes	30 seconds
Unison chalkboard drill on all words on chalkboard	2 minutes
Individual or unison sound/spelling and reading of connected matter in homework	2 minutes
Sound/spelling and reading of all shorthand on chalkboard by individual students to the person next to them	3 minutes
Unison chalkboard drill on alphabetic strokes	30 seconds
Rest period	30 seconds
Sound/spelling and reading of all shorthand on chalkboard by individual students to person next to them	3 minutes
One-minute timings to determine silent reading and sound/spelling skills on connected material in textbook	4 minutes
Unison chalkboard drill on alphabetic strokes	30 seconds
Unison sound/spelling and reading of word lists in homework	1 minute
Unison chalkboard drill on all words on chalkboard	2 minutes
Homework assignment including demonstrations of A, B, and C performance	1 minute

Students are introduced to shorthand by the reading approach in these lesson plans. Many teachers successfully use the writing approach or make adaptations in the reading approach. There is no one best lesson plan for teaching the first day of shorthand, but the following are essential ingredients for all first-day plans: teacher chalkboard demonstrations, student drill on alphabetic symbols and shorthand outlines incorporating the symbols, and frequent changes in activity.

The Instructor's Handbook for Gregg Shorthand, Series 90 provides additional ideas for teachers who wish to use the reading approach for the first shorthand lesson.[26] Following is a partial narration of teacher and student activities when the reading approach is used to teach the first session in shorthand. Notice that there are more similarities than differences between this plan and the one previously outlined.

Methods and procedures for using the writing approach, a component of the manual method, on the first day are also included in the *Instructor's Handbook for Gregg Shorthand, Series 90.*[27] Page 119 contains a partial outline of teacher and student activities when the writing approach is used from the very beginning.

First Lesson, Reading Approach (Series 90)

Teacher: The first letter you will learn in Gregg Shorthand is *s*. Tell me what this little mark means in longhand.

[Teacher writes *comma s* on the blackboard.]

Class: The comma.

Teacher: That's right. The stroke that resembles the comma is the shorthand *s*. Notice how the shorthand *s* comes from the small longhand *s* or from the small printed *s*.

[Teacher writes ↗ and ∫ on the chalkboard—rather lightly— and then goes over and strengthens those parts of the letters that represent the shorthand *s* and finally writes the shorthand *s*.]

Teacher: Notice that the *s* is written downward, just like the longhand comma.

[Teacher again writes shorthand *s* once or twice, saying "down" each time.]

Teacher: Many of the shorthand characters are taken right out of the longhand characters for the same sound—as you have seen with the letter *s*. Now watch how we get the shorthand *a* from the longhand letter. What letter is this in longhand?

[Teacher writes ⟳ on the chalkboard.]

Class: *A.*

Teacher: We will now take off the connecting stroke. This is the shorthand *a*.

[Teacher either marks through the connecting stroke or erases it and then writes the shorthand *a*.]

[Teacher then points alternately to *s* and *a* several times as students read in concert.]

Teacher: You have seen one device that enables us to write faster— we write only enough of a longhand letter to be able to recognize it. Another way that we can write faster is to omit any letters that are not pronounced. In the word *say*, for example,

[Teacher writes ___ on the chalkboard.]

what letter is not pronounced?

Class: *Y*.

[Teacher strikes out the *y* in the longhand— ___ .]

Teacher: With the shorthand letters *s* and *a*, we can write the word *say*. Watch me write it.

[Teacher writes ___ on the chalkboard, saying *s-a, say* aloud.]

Teacher: Spell and read it a few times.

Class: *S-a, say; s-a, say; s-a, say.*

Teacher: The next letter we will take up is *f*. *F* is a larger comma— about three times as big as *s*. It is also written downward.

[Teacher writes the shorthand *f* and points alternately to *s* and *f* as the students respond in unison.]

Teacher: With the shorthand strokes for *f*, *s*, and *a*, we can write a number of words.

[Teacher writes the word *face* on the board in longhand.]

Teacher: What letter would not be written in shorthand in *face*?

Class: *E*.

[Teacher strikes through the *e*.]

Teacher: What shorthand letters would be written?

[Note: Some students will respond *f-a-s;* some, *f-a-c*. This will give the teacher an opportunity to stress that the sound heard is *s*, not *c*.]

[Teacher writes ___ on the board, saying *f-a-s, face*.]

Class: *F-a-s, face; f-a-s, face.*

The same procedure may be followed in presenting *safe, safes, save, vase.* The word *saves* may be used to present the letter *z*, thus:

[Teacher writes *saves* in longhand on the chalkboard.]

Teacher: What sounds do you hear in *saves?*

[Note: Class will probably respond *s-a-v-s.*]

Teacher: No. In the word *saves* you hear *s-a-v-Z*—the *s* is pronounced *z*. Because *s* often is pronounced *z*, we express *z* with the same stroke that we use for *s*.

The procedures just discussed may be used to present the remaining letters in Lesson 1, except that the longhand spellings may be omitted.

First Lesson, Writing Approach (Series 90)

Teachers who wish to have the class write from the very beginning will find the following procedures effective:

Teacher: The first letter you will learn in Gregg Shorthand is *s*. Tell me what this little mark means in longhand.

[Teacher writes *comma s* on the chalkboard.]

Class: The comma.

Teacher: That's right. This stroke that resembles the comma is the shorthand *s*. Let us see how fast you can write the comma. I will time you for 5 seconds. Write just as many commas as you can in 5 seconds. Ready, go!

[Class writes commas for 5 seconds.]

Teacher: How many commas did you write in 5 seconds?

[Students count commas they have written and call out the number. The teacher multiplies the figure by 12 to arrive at "words a minute."]

Teacher: That's fine. That means you wrote the shorthand stroke for *s* at the rate of about 200 words per minute (or whatever the actual figure may be). Notice how the shorthand for *s* comes from the small longhand *s* or from the small printed *s*.

[Teacher writes ⟋ and ∫ on the chalkboard—rather lightly— and then goes over and strengthens that part of the longhand character that represents the shorthand *s* and finally writes the shorthand *s*.]

Teacher: Now let's repeat the 5-second drill once again. This time say *s* to yourself each time you write the comma.

[Class writes *comma s* for 5 seconds.]

Teacher: Many of the shorthand characters are taken right out of the longhand characters for the same sound. Now watch how we get the shorthand *a* from the longhand letter. What letter is this in longhand?

[Teacher writes a on the chalkboard.]

Class: *A*.

Teacher: We will now take off the connecting stroke. This is the shorthand *a*.

[Teacher then points alternately to *s* and *a* several times as students read in concert.]

Teacher: Now write the shorthand *a* for 5 seconds. Remember, the *a* is just like the longhand zero.

[Students write shorthand *a* for 5 seconds.]

Teacher: You have seen one device that enables us to write faster— we write only enough of a longhand letter to be able to recognize it. Another way that we write faster is to omit any letters that are not pronounced. In the word *say*, for example,

[Teacher writes pay on the chalkboard.]

what letter is not pronounced?

Class: *Y*.

[Teacher strikes out the *y* in the longhand— pay.]

Teacher: We are now ready to write the word. We have just learned that this is *s*.

[Teacher writes the shorthand *s* on the chalkboard.]

Teacher: And this is *a* in shorthand.

[Teacher writes *a* on the chalkboard.]

Teacher: We join them like this.

[Teacher writes ∂ on the board, saying *s-a, say*.]

Teacher: Now spell the word.

[Teacher points to the word several times, as the class spells and reads in concert.]

Teacher: Watch me write *say* again.

[Teacher writes *say* in shorthand, slowly and large.]

Teacher: Now you write it.

[Class writes *say* several times.]

Teacher: The next letter we will take up is *f*. *F* is a larger comma—about three times as big as *s*. It is also written downward.

[Teacher writes shorthand *f* and points alternately to *s* and *f* as students respond in unison.]

Teacher: Now try *s, f*. Make the *s* tiny; the *f* about three times as large—or about half the height of the line space.

[Students write *s, f, s, f*.]

Teacher: With the shorthand strokes for *f, s,* and *a,* we can write a number of words.

[Teacher writes the word *face* on the chalkboard in longhand.]

Teacher: What letter would not be written in *face*?

Class: *E*.

Teacher: What letters would be written?

[Note: some students will say *f-a-s;* others will say *f-a-c*. Take this opportunity to stress that in shorthand we write only the sounds that we hear and that the sound heard is *s*, not *c*. Teacher then writes *ợ* on the chalkboard, saying *f-a-s, face*.]

Teacher: Now spell and read the word a few times as I point.

Class: *F-a-s, face; f-a-s, face*.

Teacher: Now write *face* several times.

[Class writes *face* two or three times as the teacher dictates.]

The same procedure may be used for *safe, safes, save,* and *vase*. The word *saves* can be used to present the letter *z*, thus:

[Teacher writes *saves* in longhand.]

Teacher: What sounds do you hear in *saves*?

[Note: Class will probably respond *s-a-v-s*.]

Teacher: No. In *saves* you hear *s-a-s-Z*—the *s* is pronounced *z*. Because *s* is often pronounced *z*, we express *z* with the same stroke that we use for *s*.

Notes

1. Louis Leslie, *Methods of Teaching Gregg Shorthand*, Gregg Division, McGraw-Hill Book Company, New York, 1953, p. 26.

2. John R. Gregg, Louis A. Leslie, and Charles E. Zoubek, *Gregg Shorthand, Series 90,* Gregg Division, McGraw-Hill Book Company, New York, 1978.
3. John R. Gregg, Louis A. Leslie, and Charles E. Zoubek, *Gregg Shorthand, Series 90, Functional Method,* Gregg Division, McGraw-Hill Book Company, New York, 1978.
4. Leslie, pp. 7–8.
5. Ibid., p. 11.
6. Marion M. Lamb, *Your First Year of Teaching Shorthand and Transcription,* South-Western Publishing Co., Cincinnati, OH, 1961, p. 42.
7. Leslie, p. 59.
8. Lamb, pp. 42–43.
9. Ibid., p. 50.
10. Leslie, p. 4.
11. Ann Brewington and Helen Soutter, *Direct-Method Materials for Gregg Shorthand, Teacher's Manual,* The Gregg Publishing Company, New York, 1937.
12. William Odell and Esta Ross Stewart, *Gregg Shorthand, Direct Approach Method,* The Gregg Publishing Company, New York, 1944.
13. Allien R. Russon, *Methods of Teaching Shorthand,* Monograph No. 119, South-Western Publishing Company, Cincinnati, OH, April 1968, pp. 13–16.
14. ———, *Dictation ABC's,* University Book Store, University of Utah, Salt Lake City, 1962.
15. ———, *Methods of Teaching Shorthand,* p. 17.
16. Shirley Eiken, "Consider the Micromolar Behavior Theory in Speed Development," *The Delta Pi Epsilon Journal,* Vol. VII, No. 4, p. 111, July 1965.
17. Rita Sloan, "An Application of the Micromolar Behavior Theory to the Instruction of Beginning Shorthand," *The Delta Pi Epsilon Journal,* Vol. XI, No. 1, pp. 22–26, November 1968.
18. Marion L. Boss, "The Micromolar Behavior Theory and Its Application to Beginning Shorthand," *Business Education Forum,* Vol. 25, No. 5, pp. 29–31, February 1971.
19. Robert L. Grubbs, "Rx for Effective Shorthand Teaching," *Business Education World,* Vol. 41, No. 1, pp. 15–18, September, 1960.
20. John Robert Gregg, *The Use of the Blackboard in Teaching Shorthand,* The Gregg Publishing Company, New York, 1928.
21. Ibid., p. 4.
22. John R. Gregg, Louis A. Leslie, and Charles E. Zoubek, *Instructor's Handbook for Gregg Shorthand, Series 90,* Gregg Division, McGraw-Hill Book Company, New York, 1978, pp. 31–34.

23. Agnes Putney, "Using an Overhead Projector in Beginning Shorthand," *Journal of Business Education,* Vol. XXXX, No. 1, p. 20, October 1964.
24. Ernest E. Miller, "Using the Overhead Projector in Selected Shorthand Classroom Activities," *Business Education World,* Vol. 55, No. 3, p. 14, January–February, 1975.
25. A. James Lemaster, "Transparencies: A Valuable Aid in Teaching Transcription," *Business Education World,* Vol. 53, No. 3, p. 18, January–February 1973.
26. Gregg, Leslie, and Zoubek, *Instructor's Handbook,* pp. 12–13.
27. Ibid., pp. 14–15.

Chapter 4

Teaching Shorthand Vocabulary Competency

The first 60 to 90 days of the first semester of instruction are crucial to meeting the objectives of the second, third, and fourth semesters of shorthand. If students do not learn the theory and associated reading and writing applications, they are apt to encounter severe learning difficulties at more advanced levels. In other words, the first semester is considered the foundation for all later instruction.

Theory skill, defined as the ability to construct accurate outlines or demonstrate shorthand vocabulary competency, should be a major teaching goal during the first and subsequent semesters. Research studies by Pullis, Goetz, and others indicate that there is a positive relationship between outline accuracy and speed of recording dictation.[1,2,3] Generally, the students who write the highest proportion of outlines correctly are faster writers than those with lower outline accuracy scores. What is more, theory skill has a direct bearing on transcription ability. Cook, Klaseus, Gallenberg, and others found in their research that students who write the highest percentages of theoretically correct outlines are the most accurate transcribers.[4,5,6]

Because theory skill, or shorthand vocabulary competency, is important to the terminal objectives of all shorthand instruction, teachers must be constantly alert for ways and methods of improving written outline accuracy. Yet, there is danger in isolating the teaching of shorthand vocabulary from other commonly taught skills during the first semester. Reading, writing, and transcription skills are developed concurrently with shorthand vocabulary skill, and each contributes to the improvement and refinement of written outline accuracy. Ignoring shorthand vocabulary refinement while developing reading, writing, and transcription skills in subsequent semesters is likewise an error in judgment. Successful shorthand teachers find the proper balance between shorthand vocabulary emphasis, reading activities, writing practice, and transcription development.

Learning Material Option for Teaching Shorthand

Teachers of first semester high school shorthand have a choice of two textbooks, depending on their philosophy of teaching. (See Chapter 3 on teaching approaches for a discussion of science-type teaching and the functional method.) There are, essentially, two major differences between the Gregg texts. *Gregg Shorthand, Functional Method*[7] does not include rules for outline construction, and a printed key or transcript for all shorthand outlines is located at the end of the text. *Gregg Shorthand,*[8] includes an explanation of the rules for outline construction in every sixth lesson, and a printed key is not included in the book. However, teachers who use this textbook usually recommend that all students should be supplied with a transcript of the Reading and Writing Practice exercises in preparing homework assignments.

The organization of the two textbooks is very similar, and they have the following commonalities:

1. Texts are organized so that students can study a lesson a day after the initial introduction to shorthand.
2. Shorthand vocabulary principles are presented in the same sequence.
3. Texts include 70 lessons that can be normally completed in one semester of 15 or more weeks.
4. All shorthand vocabulary principles are completed by Lesson 47, and the remaining lessons are designed to systematically review the principles presented in earlier lessons.
5. Every sixth lesson includes a review of shorthand vocabulary principles presented in the five previous lessons. No new symbols are introduced in the review lessons.
6. Shorthand phrasing principles are introduced in Lesson 3.
7. Brief forms are introduced in Lesson 3, and the last group of brief forms is presented in Lesson 37.
8. Marginal reminders are used for teaching spelling and punctuation, and selected language arts skills are included for review in many lessons.
9. Student reading and writing practice material is provided in all lessons.

Effective Learning Activities During the Presentation of Shorthand Theory Principles

Research has determined no one proper method for teaching shorthand theory principles and developing basic reading, writing, and transcribing skills. Teachers have been successful in teaching by a variety of methods. However, there are basic student activities common to all methods. Teachers can be reasonably sure of teaching-learning success if students conscientiously engage in the following activities during the first semester:

1. Observing correct, well-formed outlines being written on the chalkboard.
2. Sound/spelling and reading outlines from the chalkboard individually and/or in unison.
3. Reading shorthand contextual material individually and/or in unison.
4. Reading brief forms individually and/or in unison.
5. Reviewing previously presented theory principles.
6. Writing from dictation of homework material and occasionally reading notes individually and/or in unison.
7. Transcribing from homework plate material and from self-written homework notes.
8. Writing brief forms from dictation.
9. Reviewing basic punctuation rules, spelling, and business vocabulary.
10. Reading shorthand homework assignments until they can be read smoothly and rapidly and then writing the lessons at least once from self-dictation.

Analysis of the above list reveals that nearly all activities include reading and writing shorthand. Classroom lesson plans must be developed so students are provided with maximum reading and writing time. Therefore, lessons must be well planned and organized, and all activities should be paced to economize on time and to acclimate students to the time pressures commonly associated with recording shorthand from dictation.

First Five Lessons of Shorthand Principles Presentation

Normally, a lesson a day is covered during the first semester of shorthand; however, there are advantages to spending from 6 to 10 days in teaching the first five lessons. Almost the entire basic shorthand alphabet is presented in these lessons (*a, b, d, e, f, gay, h, i, k, l, m, n, o, p, r, s, t, v, w, z*), and students must learn these strokes if they are to experience success during the remainder of theory presentation. Theoretically, students should be able to read and write thousands of English words in shorthand after learning the first five lessons, because most of the remaining theory consists of word beginnings and endings, blends, and other abbreviations for writing faster.

Considerations for presenting the first lesson were given in Chapter 3, Introducing the Student to Shorthand. Basically, the same teaching pattern is used for each of the first five lessons. The most important difference is that after the first lesson has been presented, the teacher and students always work with at least two lessons during each class period. For example, the teacher reviews the principles previously presented in Lesson 3 through intensive, repetitive chalkboard drill and introduces the shorthand vocabulary principles in Lesson 4.

The following are prime considerations for presenting the first five lessons:

1. The teacher writes all alphabetic strokes previously presented on the chalkboard and provides periodic drill on them throughout the class periods.
2. The teacher requires students to sound/spell and read individual outlines as well as the Reading Practice sections until fluency in sound/spelling and reading is attained.
3. The teacher always works with at least two lessons during a class period; for example, the new lesson being introduced and the old lesson assigned as homework.
4. The teacher uses rapid, repetitive oral drill from outlines written on the chalkboard or appearing in the textbook. (See drill procedures described in Chapter 3, Introducing the Student to Shorthand.)

Lesson Plan Example for Teaching Shorthand Vocabulary Principles

The following is a sample lesson plan for presenting shorthand vocabulary principles in Lesson 4 and determining the degree of student mastery for Lesson 3. The plan is developed for a 45-minute class period; note that there are frequent opportunities for vocabulary reinforcement and changes in activities.

LESSON	ACTIVITY	TIME
1, 2, 3	Chalkboard review of all alphabetic strokes in previous lessons	2 minutes
3	Sound/spelling and reading of shorthand vocabulary illustrated on the chalkboard	5 minutes
—	Rest Period	30 seconds
3	Unison sound/spelling and reading of Reading Practice sentences	3 minutes
4	Chalkboard presentation and drill on paragraphs 21, ($\overline{oo}$ sound), 22 and 23 (w, sw, and wh)	6 minutes
3	Unison sound/spelling and reading of Reading Practice sentences	3 minutes
1, 2, 3, 4	Chalkboard review of alphabetic strokes previously presented	2 minutes

LESSON	ACTIVITY	TIME
—	Rest period	30 seconds
4	Chalkboard presentation and drill on paragraphs 24 (useful phrases) and 25 *(k,* and *gay* sounds)	6 minutes
3	Individual sound/spelling, and reading of Reading Practice sentences	3 minutes
—	Rest period	30 seconds
4	Chalkboard drill on all outlines on board	2 minutes
4	Unison sight reading of Reading Practice in new lesson	3 minutes
4	Directions for homework assignment	2 minutes
4	Chalkboard drill on outlines on board	3 minutes
—	Rest period	30 seconds
1, 2, 3	Unison or individual reading of selections from Reading Practice sections	3 minutes
		45 minutes

Remaining Lessons of Shorthand Vocabulary Principles Presentation

The remaining lessons of the first semester textbooks are organized so students should progress at the rate of about one lesson a day during the remainder of the semester. Intensive chalkboard drills on new shorthand vocabulary principles, review of previous lessons through chalkboard drill, reading from homework assignments, writing from dictation, and performing typewritten transcription drills must be essential activities of daily lesson planning during the first semester. However, provision must be made for an increasing amount of dictation practice as the course progresses; therefore, the emphasis on reading activity will no doubt be decreased.

Every sixth lesson in first semester textbooks is designed for student review; new symbols are not presented in these lessons. The sixth lesson contains a review of shorthand vocabulary principles presented in the previous five lessons plus a cumulative review of theory previously introduced. The word lists and reading and writing practice incorporate these principles. Teachers need to take the time for a review of vocabulary by selecting outlines illustrating principles in each of the previous five lessons and providing extensive spelling, reading, and writing practice.

Lesson plans during the first shorthand vocabulary and reading lessons will not differ significantly from the plan appearing on pages 127 and 128. However, plans such as those illustrated in Chapter 2 will need to be developed to provide for an increasing amount of dictation and transcription practice.

Relationship of Theory Knowledge to Reading Skill Development

Although there has been no research to determine the process by which students learn to read shorthand outlines, it is probable that reading shorthand involves a variety of skills. Initially, students probably learn to think, verbalize, and recognize individual symbols and then learn to combine the symbol sounds into words. Through repetitive spelling and reading practice, they begin to develop a sight vocabulary of outlines and to recognize combinations of symbols used in words and phrases. As sight vocabulary increases and symbol recognition improves, students begin to depend on contextual cues, which aid significantly in improving reading speed. Thus reading shorthand involves a combination of sound/spelling, sight vocabulary, and contextual cues.

The sound/spelling of symbols is an initial building block for sounding out words as well as a way for students to begin to develop sight vocabulary. Accordingly, a major emphasis on sound/spelling outlines applying new shorthand vocabulary principles and sound/spelling outlines during the review of vocabulary principles should have a positive effect on shorthand reading skills. Just how important are reading skills to the ultimate objectives of recording and transcribing dictation?

Obviously, reading skills must be used in transcription. Less obvious, but just as important, is the relationship between shorthand reading ability and ability to record dictation. Both Beringson and Pullis found a positive relationship between ability to record dictation and oral shorthand reading skill.[9,10] Consequently, competency in reading shorthand appears to be a factor in meeting the ultimate objectives of shorthand.

Relationship of Shorthand Vocabulary Competency to Dictation and Transcription Development

As stated earlier in this chapter and to be reported completely in Chapter 11, research supports a positive relationship between outline accuracy and speed of recording dictation on one hand and outline accuracy and speed and accuracy of transcription on the other. For these reasons, shorthand teachers will want to help students write as correctly as possible during dictation recording.

Not all words will be written correctly during all dictation speed-building attempts, and outlines will deteriorate as speeds are forced higher and higher. However, there are several benefits from students knowing how words are correctly written and attempting to write as correctly as possible:

1. Students are less apt to hesitate during writing.
2. A problem-solving situation will not occur—"Is it written this way, or is it written that way?"
3. Through repeatedly writing the words correctly, the students will more likely automatize writing correctly under speed.
4. If only one form of an outline is used, rather than "chance multiple" forms, the recording of the correct form will come more quickly.

The following suggestions will help to develop the automatization of correct responses for a large vocabulary of words:

1. During the early days, when the book is still open during dictation, work with the students from the chalkboard or the overhead projector, showing the correct writing of words that may be causing difficulty, showing the joining of strokes, and indicating the rule application whenever appropriate.
2. After the books are closed for dictation, heavily preview before dictating the material, and point out quickly the vocabulary principle base for writing certain words. Review frequently between dictations to develop automatization for many of the words in the material. Vary the method of previewing and reviewing in order to keep interest high and students actively involved in learning how to write words correctly.
3. In the second, third, and fourth semesters, use the postview as a method of helping students to be somewhat independent on the first dictation of the material, but reinforce the correctness of writing after the dictation has been given by postviewing selected words. Continuing to do this during the advanced work will help students maintain a healthy respect for the need to write outlines correctly.
4. In dictation for mailable letter work, students need to know that recording correctly written outlines will help them to transcribe more rapidly and accurately. Therefore, in the early stages of dictation of mailable letters, preview words that may be difficult to write or unfamiliar to the students, again explaining the rule base for writing the word correctly.

Teaching Brief Forms, Brief Form Derivatives, and Frequently Used Phrases

Brief forms, some brief form derivatives, and the frequently used phrases should be learned to the point of automatic response and use. Consequently, periodic reading and writing reviews of these words should be provided throughout all semesters of instruction.

Usually six to nine brief forms are presented in a lesson, and the following procedure can be used for teaching them:

1. Sound/spell and write a brief form on the chalkboard.
2. Students pronounce the brief form, without spelling, as the teacher points.
3. Sound/spell and write a second brief form on the chalkboard and provide intensive chalkboard drill on the two brief forms.
4. Sound/spell and write a third brief form on the chalkboard and provide intensive chalkboard drill on the three brief forms.
5. Continue to sound/spell and write brief forms on the board and provide repetitive, intensive drill until all the brief forms of the lesson have been presented.
6. Retain all brief forms on the chalkboard for periodic drill throughout the remainder of the class period.

When introducing a group of brief forms, some teachers like to put the longhand word on the board and show how the brief form is derived. This helps students learn that the strong sounds of words are usually used. For example:

advertise a v t i s ; envelope n v l

The brief-form charts in the back of all Gregg texts show all brief forms in order of presentation. Teachers can use the charts for quick reading and writing reviews throughout every semester. To ensure further brief-form mastery, teachers can use flash cards, window shade charts, commercially published charts, games, and/or audio tapes that include brief forms, brief-form derivatives, and frequently used phrases.

The presentation procedures previously recommended for brief forms are effective for teaching brief-form derivatives and frequently used phrases. In addition, intensive drilling from the chalkboard while previewing and postviewing dictation will help to develop automatization of brief forms, brief form derivatives, and frequently used phrases.

Objective of the Homework Assignment

The primary objective of homework assignments is the reinforcement and review of new outline symbols and shorthand vocabulary principles. Students initially learn outline symbols and principles during the class period from chalkboard presentations and drills, reading activities, and writing practice. However, homework assignments provide timely opportunities for meaningful review and reinforcement. Therefore, daily homework assignments that include a study of the shorthand vocabulary principles of the lesson are considered an integral part of shorthand instruction.

During the lessons prior to the introduction of writing, students are generally expected to sound/spell and read the outlines illustrating shorthand vocabulary principles at the beginning of each lesson as well as sound/spell and/or read the connected material of each lesson. Students sound/spell and read repetitively until the material can be read accurately and fluently. However, they do not write these homework assignments.

After homework writing is begun, it is recommended that students study the shorthand vocabulary words by sound/spelling the sample words and then write the word lists in groups of three words, repeating each group three times. This type of repetitive writing practice increases writing fluency and requires mental alertness.

Some teachers ask students to select words from the letters in the homework lesson and practice writing these words with either a whole or piecemeal-whole practice pattern. Students will attempt to observe the joining of strokes, the order of sounds, and the rule application of the word during the practice.

Suggestions for Shorthand Vocabulary Presentation and Reinforcement

The importance of shorthand vocabulary mastery should not be underestimated. Emphasis on shorthand vocabulary development, during the first and all semesters of instruction will have a bearing on dictation and transcription skill. Therefore, teachers must consider shorthand vocabulary presentation and review a major objective of all stages of shorthand learning.

During First Semester of Shorthand Instruction

Provide intensive chalkboard drill, including sound/spelling, when new symbols or shorthand vocabulary principles are introduced. Sound/spelling during chalkboard drills forces learners to break down the structure of outlines into their component parts. Thus they practice recognizing the symbol being introduced, review previously presented symbols, and make mental notations of how shorthand symbols are joined to form correctly written outlines. Without chalkboard shorthand vocabulary/spelling drills, students may learn shorthand outlines as word wholes through memorization and never obtain the tools for forming outlines that are new to their shorthand vocabulary. However, every word listed in the word list does not have to be previewed on the chalkboard. In the next day's class period, review those words that were not placed on the board during the previewing the previous day. When reviewing word lists that have been placed on the board (word lists are grouped according to shorthand vocabulary principles being introduced), recap the rule and remind the students what sound should be said. Example: *ul*

"Let us review the $\overline{oo}$ which stands for the sound of *ul* before an upward stroke or before a forward stroke. Please spell and call this stroke *ul . . .*"

Provide extensive chalkboard drill, including sound/spelling of previously presented symbols of shorthand vocabulary principles. Chalkboard sound/spelling drills are crucial for supplying a systematic review of shorthand vocabulary principles. Although students may learn a shorthand symbol when it is initially introduced through chalkboard drill, refinement will not be obtained until they have opportunities to read and write the symbol in a wide variety of contexts. Short, daily chalkboard drills on selected principles and symbols from the five previous lessons are apt to provide the necessary reinforcement for refinement. Once is never enough in shorthand because reading and writing responses must become almost reflexive.

Use longhand liberally on the chalkboard in the beginning stages to show the derivation of sounds. Example: *d o ugh* ; *al t er a tion* ;

com pe ten t . Continue to show longhand derivations whenever students experience difficulty understanding sound derivation.

Use short sound/symbol relationship tests early in the first semester. During the first two weeks, short duplicated tests giving the shorthand word and asking the students to indicate the sounds and the transcription of the word are a method of determining if they understand the sounds. Examples:

Shorthand Outline	Student Response	
	n o t	note
	b o l	bowl
	gay o l	goal

Use short, unannounced shorthand vocabulary tests, as described in Chapter 10, to ensure better homework preparation and to focus attention on the importance of correctly written outlines. Brief, unannounced shorthand vocabulary tests consisting of about ten words from the homework assignment can be administered two or three times weekly. The dictation of ten words takes only a minute or two of the class period and focuses student attention on the importance of correctly written outlines while encouraging more thorough homework preparation. In addition, brief shorthand vocabulary tests give quick feedback to the students on their shorthand vocabulary competency, rather than waiting until a chapter test is given and then finding that misunderstandings exist. Some teachers prefer to consider these tests as diagnostic and remedial exercises and do not count the scores for course grades.

Use every sixth lesson to systematically review shorthand theory principles presented in the previous five lessons. New shorthand symbols are not introduced in Lessons 6, 12, 18, 24, 30, 36, and 42. These lessons are ideal for a systematic review of symbols and shorthand vocabulary principles presented in the previous five lessons. Included in the day's class activities should be an explanation and recapping of the vocabulary principles involved, sound/spelling and reading associated words, and writing selected words from the lesson as well as from the previous five lessons.

Help students learn to use "piecemeal" practice as an effective means of learning to write rather involved words. During previews and reviews for dictation speed building, illustrate on the chalkboard how to take difficult words apart, practice them piecemeal, and build them back to the original form. Examples:

Students should be encouraged to apply this technique during the writing of homework to words that cause hesitation in writing.

Use chapter shorthand vocabulary tests, as described in Chapter 10, to assess student competency levels and to determine the need for additional review. Six lessons comprise a chapter and shorthand teachers often select 25 to 50 words as the theory section of the chapter test. The primary purpose of such tests is to help students review the shorthand vocabulary principles presented in the last five lessons and to highlight those that may need additional review. A secondary purpose is to encourage better homework preparation and to focus attention on the ability to write accurate shorthand outlines. One-chapter tests are recommended in the first semester. In succeeding semesters, tests may cover two or three chapters.

Provide alternative homework assignments for students encountering severe difficulty in writing outlines correctly. Prompt remedial measures need to be taken to help students experiencing difficulty in applying shorthand vocabulary principles to develop an understanding of the symbol-sound relationship, the proportion of writing, the joining of strokes for ease and correctness of writing, and other related short-hand vocabulary problems. If the class is being taught by traditional methods, teachers can use the Presentation Book and the accompanying tapes from *Gregg Shorthand, Individual Progress Method* as remedial homework assignments.[11] These materials provide students with ample reinforcement practice by prescription.

Other teachers, without access to IPM materials, may move the homework assignment back to where the individual student first began to have difficulty. For example, a student who first encountered severe difficulty in Lesson 13 would be assigned that lesson for homework, but the remainder of the class would do the reading and writing practice for the regular lesson. The same lesson-a-day pattern is continued throughout the presentation of theory, but the individual who needs an alternative assignment is always reading and writing lessons which the other class members have completed previously.

Place special emphasis on shorthand vocabulary principles that are commonly considered difficult to learn. Experienced shorthand teachers sometimes discover that certain shorthand vocabulary principles cause learning difficulties for students. They usually develop special teaching strategies to deal with them. Often causing student concern are the $\overline{oo}$ and $\bar{o}$ hooks; the *w, sw, w within a word;* the abbreviating principles; the application of the *left* and *right s;* the *al* and *ul* word beginnings; and the *ng* and *nk* endings. Following are some ideas on how to present potentially difficult shorthand vocabulary principles:

The $\overline{oo}$ and $\bar{o}$ hooks. Fortunately these symbols are introduced in separate lessons, and only the long sounds are initially presented. With the $\bar{o}$ hook, show the shorthand form for $\bar{o}$ and have students practice writing the form while pronouncing it (never misspeak and call it $\overline{oo}$). Place on the board sample longhand words containing the $\bar{o}$: *no, so, toe, row, Joe* (words with simple sounds and a dominant $\bar{o}$). Under each of the longhand words write the shorthand outline and sound/spell rapidly in unison, followed by the students, who practice writing the words with a strong sound/spelling emphasis on the sound of $\bar{o}$ as they write. Between this time and the time the $\overline{oo}$ is introduced, give students much direction as to what they should call the $\bar{o}$. When the $\overline{oo}$ is introduced, a similar drill procedure can be used.

Soon the short and medium sounds of *o* and *oo* will be taught. Start with the sound of the long $\bar{o}$ which students know, and show long $\bar{o}$ words on the chalkboard; for example *Joan, home, lone.* Then move to the *short o* and *medium o* drill by pointing out that students are to sound/spell $\bar{o}$ but sound $\breve{o}$ in words such as *hot, top, lot,* and *hop.* After drilling on sound/spelling and writing these words, introduce the *medium o* (aw), and have students practice by sound/spelling $\bar{o}$ but sounding *aw* in such words as *saw, law, caught,* and *coffee.* Finally, provide a review of the three sounds by having students sound/spell and pronounce selected words on the chalkboard. Interspersed

135

between presentations of outline groups would be an explanation of how the *o* is sound/spelled and pronounced. After an introduction of the *short* and *medium oo*, a comparison of how the three *o*'s are pronounced and how the three *oo*'s are pronounced and formed within the mouth helps students understand the two distinctly different sounds, because the sound formation within the mouth is similar for all *o* sounds and similar for all *oo* sounds. Later, when words such as *to* and *together* are used in chalkboard work, point out that the sound is $\overline{oo}$.

The above explanation for these sounds has taken much longer than the actual "doing," but a similar detailed explanation can be made for any shorthand vocabulary principle that seems to cause learning difficulty.

Use word drills to help students learn to distinguish word sounds. Unfortunately, many students who enroll in shorthand have difficulty in distinguishing word sounds, possibly because of a weakness in their phonics background. For example, some students have difficulty distinguishing between the *o* and *oo* and the *nt* and *mt* sounds. Short, dictated word-list drills such as the following provide remedial training in word-sound recognition.

Dictate the following words at the rate of about one pair every 10 seconds, and instruct students to write the shorthand outlines:

(so—sue) (to—toe) (rule—roll) (do—dough) (tone—tune) (jewel—Joel) (grew—grow) (knew—know) (nut—note) (booth—both) (crew—crow) (house—host) (Boone—bone)

After all words in the list are dictated, write the correct outlines on the chalkboard, and have students correct their outlines. The drill is repeated after a discussion of the *o* and *oo* sounds.

Prepare shorthand vocabulary review tapes for difficult-to-learn symbols or principles. Teachers can develop review tapes focusing on a particular principle or symbol that is consistently difficult for students to master. The tapes and accompanying preview sheets contain words illustrating the principle as well as letters loaded with words containing the principle. For example, if students consistently encounter difficulty in correctly writing words containing the symbol *x* or the *ex* beginning, a preview sheet could be prepared containing the following words in shorthand: *Rex, extremely, relaxing, Lexington, maximum, excitement, mixing, mixer, extra, fixing, exceptional, extraordinary, Cox.*

Instruct students to repetitively sound/spell the words on the preview sheet and to self-dictate and write each word several times. After they complete the preview sheet, instruct them to turn on the tape player. Again, students write the isolated words from recorded dictation then record the following letter from dictation taped at a relatively low rate of speed, about 60 wam:

Dear Rex: It was extremely relaxing in Lexington last week. However, there was maximum excitement when we opened the box containing the new mixing machine. It is nice to own an extra mixer because our old one needs fixing. I believe the new mixer is of exceptional quality. Thank you for your extraordinary kindness. Alice Cox.

After completing the dictation, students read their notes as the letter is repeated, and they are instructed to circle all "x-words" and "ex words" that they were unable to write correctly. After a minute or two of word practice, students record the letter again at a slightly higher speed.

Loaded letters are easy to compose, provided teachers remember that quality of communication is relatively unimportant. The following letter was composed by Klein for reviewing the *ses* blend.[12] Note how many times students are required to write *ses* words in the dictation.

Dear Cecil: I have finished the analysis of the finances of the Lane Home for Nurses. John Moses, the man in charge of the nurses' home, is facing criticism since heavy losses are occurring.

If my analysis is taken as a basis, it will be seen Moses is not at fault. The main causes for these losses are the higher prices being paid for services. My analysis shows the necessity for raising the fees as a means of offsetting these advances in prices. If the fees are not raised, the chances are the Lane Home for Nurses will close its doors before May 30, even if Moses is relieved of his post. Sam.

Review shorthand vocabulary principles by using word family and outline expansion drills. Short dictation drills focusing on word families or expansions of words are helpful for improving writing accuracy throughout all semesters of shorthand instruction. For example, when reviewing the word ending *cial*, the teacher could dictate the following words: special, financial, beneficial, commercial, commercials, substantial, confidential, artificial, potential, and so on. Or the teacher might use an outline expansion drill for the word *come* and dictate the following: *come, comes, become, becoming, welcome, outcome, outcomes, income, incoming, overcome, overcomes, coming,* and so on.

After students have recorded the outlines, they read them back, and the teacher writes the outlines on the board as students check their own accuracy. After individual practice, the dictation is repeated until students are able to write all outlines quickly and accurately.

Reduce the rate of dictation for controlled writing practice and focus student attention on outline correctness after speed forcing during dictation speed building. Sometimes students are unable to write correct outlines because the dictation is too rapid. To give them an opportunity to write correct outlines and concentrate on controlled writing, teachers should finish a dictation-speed-building block of time with dictation

137

at a rate students can write with correct outlines. Glancing over students' dictation notes may reveal the need for a review of shorthand vocabulary principles that they are unable to apply correctly.

Use the homework assignment plan advocated by Grubbs and described in Chapter 3. Provision for reading new lessons and writing review lessons, as described in the Grubbs plan, should improve shorthand vocabulary mastery. The coverage of two lessons in the homework assignment, including writing familiar shorthand vocabulary in review lessons, should improve students' competency level, provided they write from self-dictation. The idea of "exploring the new and building skill on the old" should result in beneficial learning reinforcement, inasmuch as shorthand vocabulary is read for six lessons before it is written.

During Second, Third, and Fourth Semesters of Shorthand Instruction

Provide chalkboard drill on the new day's lesson by sampling the shorthand vocabulary. Spell and pronounce shorthand vocabulary as long as students need to think of the separate sounds of the word and be especially conscious of the joining of the sounds in particular words. For some shorthand vocabulary, this form of emphasis may be helpful to some students throughout the four semesters of instruction. For review of the day's lesson completed for homework, sample the shorthand vocabulary by choosing for chalkboard drill those words omitted from the drill the previous day during the presentation of the new lesson.

Use longhand on the chalkboard to show the derivation of sounds to develop the shorthand outline. Students should continue to use sound as a base to develop new vocabulary in each subsequent lesson. As the vocabulary becomes more difficult, the benefit derived from writing new words according to sound and correct shorthand vocabulary principle increases. When using the chalkboard, the teacher may illustrate the derivation of the word from longhand into the shorthand outline.

Example:

dissemination—dis / right *s* before *men; mination* —— drop vowel before *tion.*

Help and encourage second semester and advanced students to take pride in correctness of writing shorthand outlines. Tell students that research supports the position that writing correct shorthand outlines increases the speed of writing and the speed and accuracy of transcription. Review the homework assignment theory and preview the new theory lesson daily by using the chalkboard or the overhead projector. Help students in the second semester and advanced courses to understand that shorthand outlines will deteriorate as they push for higher speeds. To offset this tendency, students need to demonstrate the ability to write accurate outlines.

Encourage students to expand their shorthand vocabulary. Introduce unpracticed vocabulary in class, and show students how the shorthand outlines are derived. Encourage students to bring additional words to share with the class. Whenever school events are attended, suggest that students take the proceedings in shorthand, and present in class new words that were heard.

Devote a part of each chapter or two-chapter test to the shorthand vocabulary principles of the lessons studied. Give unannounced shorthand vocabulary tests on the day's lesson (for grading or for teaching/learning feed-back). At the end of a chapter or at the end of each two chapters, select 40 to 50 words to be dictated at the rate of ten words a minute. Evaluate each student's shorthand outlines for outline-construction correctness. The words may be chosen entirely from the word lists at the beginning of the lessons, or may include words from the letters within the lessons.

Encourage students to practice all problem words that cause hesitation in writing either in homework practice or in dictation speed-building work. Encourage students to take involved words apart and practice them in piecemeal fashion during homework practice or while taking dictation with records, tapes, or in class. A word such as *generosity* should be practiced in parts by some students and then written as a complete shorthand outline.

Ask students to concentrate on learning all the words of the paragraph-connected material. Ask the students to keep the second column of the notebook free when self-dictating the homework material from the textbook, in order to have a place to practice individual words that cannot be written quickly or words they think would cause writing difficulty when taking speed dictation. These words could be practiced piecemeal when they are very involved, or repetitively practiced to gain writing speed.

When previewing new lessons in *Gregg Transcription* (theory word lists are omitted after Lesson 20), the teacher may choose some words from the connected material as a preview of shorthand vocabulary knowledge. The following day, certain words of the same type could be chosen as a review of the day's lesson. This procedure helps to keep the students aware of the need to learn all words in the day's lesson.

Vary the chalkboard activity for theory preview and reviews to fit the level of the instruction. Second-semester students need to be able to relate shorthand vocabulary principles to the writing of the shorthand word lists. Therefore, as the new lesson is previewed and the day's lesson reviewed, shorthand outlines need to be drilled, that is: Briefly state the rule as word family groups and other outlines are placed on the chalkboard. As reviews are completed, recap the rule for each grouping and remind the students of the sound used in the sound/ spelling. In the third and fourth semesters, somewhat less detailed explanation may be necessary for most of the rules. An example of a situation in which little explanation is necessary might be *tern words:*

Examples of situations in which greater explanation may be necessary are:

w within words:

short *u* omitted before *n, m,* or a form of *n* or *m:*

As an occasional method of previewing the new lesson and reviewing the old lesson during the third and fourth semesters, the teacher may wish to dictate a few of the shorthand vocabulary review words for the day's lesson and have students write as correctly as possible. After eight to ten words are dictated, ask students to read them, or at times to sound/spell and pronounce the words from their notes. As they read, write the outlines on the chalkboard for a quick check and a brief explanation of the rule involved. Then dictate eight to ten more words until a sample of the shorthand vocabulary has been reviewed. As a preview of the new lesson, the same technique may be used, with the rule being explained before dictating the words, after which the students write and then sound/spell and/or read the words back as the teacher writes the shorthand outlines on the chalkboard. Such a pretest procedure helps students see the amount of study needed to master the shorthand vocabulary principles presented in the new lesson.

Notes

1. Joe M. Pullis, "The Relationship Between Shorthand Vocabulary Outline Errors and Dictation/Recording Transcription Errors With the Effects of IQ Partialed Out," independent study, Louisiana Tech University, Ruston, 1979.

2. Joe M. Pullis, "The Relationship Between Competency in

Shorthand Accuracy and Achievement in Shorthand Dictation," doctoral dissertation, North Texas State University, Denton, 1966.

3. Leo G. Goetz, "The Relationship Between Symbol Mastery of Selected Dictation Achievements in Gregg Shorthand," doctoral dissertation, University of North Dakota, Grand Forks, 1966.

4. Romayne Reed Cook, "Transcription Achievement of Eight Shorthand Classes in Milwaukee, Wisconsin," master's thesis, University of Wisconsin, Madison, 1966.

5. Richard C. Klaseus, "An Analysis of Some of the Factors that Contribute to the Difficulty of Transcription Materials in Gregg Shorthand—Diamond Jubilee Series," master's thesis, Mankato State College, Mankato, MN, 1964.

6. Barbara Gallenberg, "A Study Showing the Relationship Between the Writing of Theoretically Correct Shorthand Outlines to the Transcription Process," master's thesis, University of Wisconsin, Madison, 1975.

7. John Robert Gregg, Louis Leslie, and Charles Zoubek, *Gregg Shorthand, Functional Method, Series 90,* Gregg Division, McGraw-Hill Book Company, New York, 1978.

8. John Robert Gregg, Louis Leslie, and Charles Zoubek, *Gregg Shorthand, Series 90,* Gregg Division, McGraw-Hill Book Company, New York, 1978.

9. Donald L. Beringson, "The Relationship Between Oral Reading Ability From Shorthand Plate Material and the Ability to Take Dictation," doctoral dissertation, University of North Dakota, Grand Forks, 1971.

10. Joe M. Pullis, "The Relationship Between Fluency in Reading Shorthand Plates and Achievement in Shorthand Dictation," independent study, Louisiana Tech University, Ruston, 1972.

11. Louis A. Leslie, Charles E. Zoubek, Aleen M. Henson, *Gregg Shorthand, Individual Progress Method,* Gregg Division, McGraw-Hill Book Company, New York, 1972.

12. A. E. Klein, *Graded Drills in Gregg Shorthand Simplified,* Gregg Division, McGraw-Hill Book Company, New York, 1951.

Chapter 5

Reading and Writing in Shorthand

Shorthand authorities have frequently said that time devoted to classroom activities other than reading and writing shorthand represents a potential loss in shorthand learning or skill development. While the statement may be a slight exaggeration, it does emphasize the importance of focusing on these particular skills during shorthand instruction.

The students are introduced to shorthand reading when the first symbol is placed on the chalkboard. Beginning with the first period, as they spell and pronounce the words, the emphasis is on rapid reading and sound/spelling. While the instructor is presenting new theory to the class, the students are reading shorthand outlines from the chalkboard or from transparencies. They may or may not write the outlines in their notebooks. The instructor may review the previous day's theory lesson, again having students read. Students may be asked to read from their homework before taking dictation on certain letters practiced as part of the homework. Even when students reach the more advanced stages of mailable letter transcription, they are still reading and writing shorthand. Since their future progress may well depend upon their early shorthand reading and writing techniques, the shorthand instructor should consider carefully the procedures to be used in building these two basic skills.

Reading

Relationship Between Students' Reading Ability and Shorthand Achievement

Shorthand teachers have often been led to believe that the fluency with which their students read shorthand notes was unimportant since reading fluency was not necessary for the completion of a mailable transcript. It was theorized that if students could transcribe at only 20 to 25 wam, there was little need for them to be able to read shorthand at 150 to 200 wam or more. However, Pullis (1972) found, when correlating shorthand reading rates with dictation achievement in first- and second-semester shorthand, that fluency in writing shorthand appeared to be fostered by fluency in reading shorthand. He indicated the belief that reading shorthand apparently served as an effective mediator in writing shorthand as well as an effective motivation for homework preparation.[1]

While there are exceptional cases, most students who are proficient in reading shorthand also become proficient in taking dictation. Knowing this, every effort should be made to help the student acquire skill in reading shorthand plates and notes.

Difficulties of Students in Reading Shorthand Outlines

RECOGNITION OF ALPHABETIC CHARACTERS. If students are to develop good shorthand reading skills, they must quickly recognize the strokes for the shorthand alphabet. During the first two or three weeks, chalkboard drill on the characters that have been introduced helps to ensure mastery of each character before additional ones are added. Special drills may be needed on opposite motion curve strokes, o and $\overline{oo}$, and pairs causing confusion. Students should be encouraged to review these basic alphabetic characters again before attempting to read the shorthand plate in the text. Students who complain that reading shorthand plates requires an inordinate amount of time are often confusing strokes because they have not mastered them thoroughly. Teachers may sometimes assume that presentation and drill on alphabetic characters results in mastery when this is not the case. Howard (1968) reported in his study that a significantly large number of students did not know the basic shorthand alphabet.[2]

CONFUSION OF SHORTHAND CHARACTERS, BRIEF FORMS, AND PHRASES. When students have difficulty reading the shorthand plates in class, the instructor should try to determine the cause. If students are taught to sound/spell the outlines as soon as they hesitate, the instructor will know whether the problem is confusion of related strokes, confusion of characters of similar length, or simply lack of mastery of the basic shorthand alphabet. The sound/spelling of outlines will also indicate whether phrases or brief forms are causing problems and, if so, which need additional drill. The confusion of basic alphabetic characters, brief forms, and phrases is ordinarily a problem only in the early stages of shorthand learning, and with drill on these brief forms and phrases, together with daily reading of shorthand plates, the problem soon disappears.

Prompting

A student who has difficulty reading a shorthand outline should follow the rule, "When in doubt, spell it out." If sound/spelling does not result in recognition of the word, the teacher should prompt the student at once. This practice saves valuable class time, keeps the class from becoming bored, and helps retain the meaning of what is being read. Another aspect of prompting involves giving cues to the student. If a student who is reading pauses, the teacher should say, "brief form," "brief-form derivative," "phrase," or "spell it," whichever cue applies. If the student still cannot say the word, the teacher can say, "class," thus eliciting a response from the class. Such a practice helps maintain interest in the material being read.

Individual or Unison Reading

While most reading in the classroom should be by individuals, there is some merit to occasional unison reading in the early weeks of the first semester. During this period, it is often desirable to assist the students with their homework by sight reading part of the next day's lesson in class. Since the class has not read the material previously, unison reading is recommended. The better students will have little difficulty reading the plates, and the other students will be able to follow along with them. Likewise, during the early stages, occasional group reading enables all students to participate without undue embarrassment for those who may be having difficulty keeping up with the reading pace when the reading is done individually. Unison reading, however, is ordinarily not continued as a regular practice for more than two or three weeks, as it tends to make some students dependent on the rest of the class.

Reading for Meaning

For most students the first step in learning to read shorthand is learning to read on the individual-character level. As they gain skill in recognizing these individual characters, their recognition unit should increase to words, phrases, and short thought units.

During the first two or three weeks, some students find it difficult to read for meaning since they must spell out many of the outlines. If, as soon as they have completed a sentence, they will try to reread it in short thought units, they will be able to grasp the meaning much more rapidly on the second reading. Students must eventually progress to this level, or they will have difficulty transcribing their shorthand notes. Students who cannot read shorthand in thought units may produce transcripts of meaningless words and phrases. Thus the final stage in the development of shorthand reading skill is the ability to grasp the thought unit rapidly and accurately on the first reading with no unnecessary hesitations or regressions.

Intensive Versus Extensive Reading Practice

Over the years extensive rather than intensive reading practice has been advocated by most people. However, research studies on homework in recent years have varied so widely in procedures that no generalizations are possible.

Teachers might do well to consider the possibility that for some shorthand students intensive practice is highly desirable but that for others, extensive practice is superior. For instance, students who continue to have difficulty distinguishing shorthand characters and symbols may need to read fewer shorthand plates but read those assigned until they can read them fluently. In this way they would begin to recognize certain symbols and characters that they see repeatedly in the same setting and, at the same time, experience a degree of success in reading that they were never able to achieve when attempting to read the entire lesson. However, sudents who are having no difficulties may benefit far more from extensive reading practice where they have the opportunity to see shorthand symbols, brief forms, and phrases presented in many different settings. For these students, constantly changing patterns present no problems.

The shorthand teacher who follows the progress of the members of the class can quickly tell which students should be asked to read certain portions of the next day's plates several times and which should be asked to read the entire lesson once or twice. Thus, homework assignments for the class may vary. It should be emphasized, however, that this procedure is to be followed only during the initial learning period and that after the first few weeks all students should be expected to complete the entire reading assignment.

Reading as a Diagnostic Tool

Since reading is one of the main classroom activities used early in the first semester, it can serve as a diagnostic tool to alert the teacher to those students needing extra help. Students who have difficulty reading fluently, saying the correct sounds of the symbols, recognizing the direction of strokes, or spelling sounds in the order written are giving signals to the teacher that help is needed quickly. The teacher should immediately help them to work on the sounds that are causing the difficulty; give them extra sound/spelling practice; and help them to understand the order of writing sounds of certain words and to recognize that certain strokes are always written upward, others downward, others forward, and so on.

Reading as a Motivational Factor

Most students are able to read fairly well early in the shorthand course because reading is not a particularly difficult skill to master.

145

So for most students, succeeding in reading will prove to be highly motivational. This is important for several reasons: (1) If students can be successful early, they will more likely remain in the course; (2) when they are successful early in the course, they will be more willing to do the homework and studying necessary as the course proceeds; and (3) if they can be successful in reading, perhaps they will be more patient with dictation, which may present a greater challenge to them.

Developing Fast Reading Rates

TEACHING STUDENTS TO READ SHORTHAND PLATES. Many students develop a slow, hesitant style of shorthand reading because they were never given specific instructions about the correct procedures to follow in reading shorthand plates. Instructions may vary, but they should all have the objective of developing reading fluency.

For example, when the students are first beginning to read plates, the instructor might give them the following instructions designed to develop fluent reading:

1. Review the shorthand alphabet thoroughly.
2. Sound/spell and read each word in the word lists illustrating the new shorthand vocabulary principles. Check the key immediately if sound/spelling the outline does not give you the word. (At this point, some teachers ask the students to repetitively practice writing the shorthand vocabulary lists.)
3. Turn to the first letter in the reading assignment. Place the forefinger of the left hand under the shorthand characters being read and the forefinger of the right hand under the corresponding words in the transcript in the key in the back of the text. Sound/spell any outline you cannot recognize immediately. Refer to the key if sound/spelling does not reveal the word.
4. Reread the sentence, trying to read in thought units for its meaning.
5. Read the second sentence in the same manner.
6. After the complete letter has been read in thought units, read it straight through, referring to the key only when necessary.
7. Following the same procedure, read the remaining letters in the assignment.

Teachers who prefer not to use the key or transcript will need to modify these instructions slightly.

SHORTHAND READING RATE GOALS. Shorthand reading-rate goals are an excellent method for developing shorthand reading fluency. The reading rates are gradually increased throughout the first semester. Considering the positive correlation between reading rates and dictation skills, the practice of setting such goals can be easily justified. In addition, because students are able to check their own progress, these goals are excellent motivators for developing fluency in reading.

HOMEWORK READING-RATE GOALS. The teacher may distribute to the students early in the course reading-rate goals they should reach every two weeks or perhaps each grading period. An illustration of such reading-rate goals is given below:

	Grade		
Week	C	B	A
4	60	70	80
6	80	90	100
8	90	100	110
10	100	110	120
12	110	120	130
14	120	130	140
16	130	140	150
18	140	150	160

With the use of this chart and the transcript when the students are reading their homework plates, they can compute both their one-minute reading rates and their reading-rate grade at any point in the semester. Thus they can determine before class whether their reading rates are satisfactory. (Reading-rate standards are also discussed in Chapter 10.)

Some teachers suggest that students should be able to read all the plates in the lesson within a certain time, depending on the total number of words in the lesson. Suppose the plates in the day's lesson total 480 words and are to be read in four to six minutes. Students completing the reading of the lesson in four to six minutes would be reading between 80 and 120 wam ($480 \div 6 = 80$ wam; $480 \div 5 = 96$ wam; $480 \div 4 = 120$ wam).

Other teachers set reading goals for selected letters in the plates. The number of words in each letter is divided by the desired reading rate goals. Assume that a letter contains 120 words; using the reading-rate goals shown in the chart for Week 4, if the student reads the letter in two minutes, the reading rate is 60, and a grade of C would be received. To earn a B, the letter must be read in 1.7 minutes; and for an A, in 1.5 minutes. Teachers may find it advisable to use a somewhat lower reading rate for long letters and a higher rate for short letters.

If the students are given a set time to finish reading certain letters or the entire lesson, the teacher should perform all arithmetical calculations. While this requires a little time, giving the students definite reading-rate goals they should be able to reach can be very effective in causing them to try to complete the assignment within the specified time.

It should be noted that reading-rate goals for the completion of daily lessons are far more difficult to attain than are goals set by the other two methods. If not used with caution, many students could become discouraged when they find they are unable to complete the lesson within the specified time. Many students who can read rapidly for short periods cannot continue this pace throughout the entire lesson. Before using this technique with students, the teacher should be able to read the lesson in not more than half the allotted time. Reading-rate goals must be realistic or students will make little effort to attain them.

Some teachers prefer to use more informal procedures for home-work goals. They may ask their students to time themselves to determine how long they require to read through all the plates in the lesson. They will then have the students read through the plates once again, this time trying to reduce the length of time needed to complete the reading.

Students may try to "beat the clock" when reading shorthand plates at home. In this case the student records the number of minutes required to read the first plate in the lesson. The next step is to decide by how many seconds or minutes to try to reduce the reading time on a second reading of the plate. The student again reads the plate, trying to reach the new goal. Since the goals are set by the students themselves, they are expected to try to beat the clock on every plate in the lesson.

Teachers should make clear from the beginning of the course that the students can always determine exactly how well they are progressing toward their reading goals. Students should be taught early the meaning of the superior figures in the keys in the back of the text or in the separate transcript. They can then determine their reading rates any time they wish to check their progress. The fact that each figure represents 20 standard words should be just as helpful to the student as it is to the teacher.

CHECKING READING RATES OR GOALS IN CLASS. The easiest reading-rate goal for the teacher to use is to figure reading rates on the basis of 30-second or one-minute readings by individual students. As the student reads from the plate, the teacher follows in the transcript in which the material is counted in 20 standard-word groups. Thus if a student reads through 6½ word groups in a minute, the reading rate would be 130 wam (6 superior figures × 20 standard words = 120; plus ½ a group = 10 words; 120 + 10 = 130). When the student's time expires within a standard word group, the teacher should estimate the number of words in that group rather than taking time for an exact count.

If reading rates are recorded as a part of the grade, at least three or four reading rates should be recorded for each student during each grading period. Because of the short reading period, it is important that the instructor have several reading rates for each student to be sure the rates recorded accurately reflect the student's reading ability. Only a few reading rates should be recorded in any one class period.

READING TAPES FOR OUTSIDE-OF-CLASS USE. Teacher-made reading tapes, as described in Chapter 7, can be very effective for helping students develop fluent and accurate reading. Students experiencing reading difficulty might use tapes at home for paced-reading practice.

Varying Reading Activities in Class

If the same procedures are followed every day in reading the shorthand plates in class, the students may soon lose interest in this activity, especially if the teacher has delayed the introduction of writing. The following additional procedures for varying the reading of shorthand plates are suggested.

GROUP READING. Occasionally have students read the plate aloud together. The teacher reads with the group only at the beginning to set the pace or again joins in if students hesitate over difficult words and are no longer reading in unison.

NONPACED UNISON READING. The students read the plates aloud at their own pace without regard for the reading rate of the other members of the class.

READING IN PAIRS. The class is arranged so that students of approximately equal ability are seated next to each other. During the reading of the plates, one member of each pair reads to the other, who prompts the reader whenever necessary. Then on the next letter the reading is reversed, with the second person reading and the first prompting. The fact that several persons may be reading aloud at one time does not seem to cause any difficulty. To encourage students to read rapidly, allow a set time to complete the reading of each letter, the time limit depending on the reading-rate goals of the class at that point in the course.

SILENT READING. Ask the students to read silently a specified letter from the homework and stand when they have finished. Time is called when about half the class has finished reading the letter.

READING FOR ERRORS. Ask one student to begin the reading. If the student misreads an outline or hesitates, the first one to catch the error or say the word continues with the reading until he or she misreads, or pauses on, an outline. This keeps the reading moving rapidly with each student trying to be the first to correct any reading errors others may make.

RELAY READING. Make sure there are the same number of students in each row. Then assign a letter, which all rows are to read. The first student in the row reads one sentence, the next student immediately reads the next sentence, and so on until the entire letter has been completed. Each row tries to read the letter in less time than the other rows.

BEAT-THE-CLOCK. Still another way to emphasize fluency in reading is to ask students to beat the clock. For instance, give the students one minute to read a letter silently in class. If most of the class meets the goal, give 50 seconds to read it silently the second time and possibly 40 seconds on a third attempt.

Reading From Plates Versus Homework Notes

Most of the reading practice is from the chalkboard and the shorthand plates during the early phases of shorthand; but after writing has been introduced, at least part of the timed reading should be from the homework notes. The quality of such notes often is far superior to notes written for homework that are never used in class. Reading from these notes in class also helps to ensure that they are complete and that the homework instructions have been followed. After punctuation review has been introduced, the students will be inserting punctuation in their homework notes, circling the punctuation mark, and writing in code the reason for it above the punctuation. When reading is from homework notes, the punctuation and reason would be given.

Writing

Much controversy exists about when writing should be introduced. Some advocate a delayed approach, emphasizing reading for the first month of instruction; others introduce writing the first day; others wait until the third or fourth day. Still others prefer a conservative approach, waiting until shortly after the first two weeks of shorthand instruction. It appears that the proper time to introduce writing depends on such factors as the caliber of the students, their objectives, the duration of the class period, the length of the course, and the skill of the instructor. In some classes, introducing writing the first day might lead to serious problems. In others, such as adult evening classes, time is so limited and the students' objectives so definite, the instructor must introduce writing immediately.

Introduction of Writing

EARLY INTRODUCTION OF WRITING. If writing is introduced the first day of shorthand, the teacher needs to be sure the students do not develop a hesitant, fumbling style of writing. The manner in which they learn to write the shorthand alphabet characters the first day will depend largely on the way these characters are presented by the teacher. If the characters are written with fluency on the board a number of times, students will tend to imitate the teacher's example. If, however, the teacher is unduly concerned about the appearance of the chalkboard outlines, if the outlines are patched or written slowly, then the students might adopt these undesirable writing patterns. Therefore, it is imperative that the teacher write with fluency and ease on the chalkboard so that when the students are asked to write the same outlines, they will try to write them fluently. When students are practicing an alphabetic stroke, such as *t* or *n*, if the stroke is called several times, the tendency will be to write the stroke rapidly, trying to keep up with the dictation. When it is called only once, with a pause, the beginning student may draw the stroke, trying to form it perfectly.

It is beneficial for the student to see the teacher construct the outlines on the board that they are to write in their notebooks. In this way there should be no confusion about the direction strokes are written or the joinings of the strokes. Even though students have perfect outlines in their texts, they need to see the outlines being written, observe the joinings of the strokes, and note the fluency with which they are written. These are skills even the best text cannot convey.

Students should not be asked to write the plates as part of their homework until they have written at least two or three days in class. Some students will write earlier outside class, but writing should not be part of the homework assignment until they have been shown how to write shorthand characters and the direction in which the strokes are written.

Students should be required to use a pen and a shorthand notebook from the first day of writing. Use of a pencil often results in cramped fingers and excessive tension. A beginner permitted to use a pencil tends to grip it tightly, pushing down heavily on the page instead of writing lightly across it. This excess tension quickly causes fatigue.

LATER INTRODUCTION OF WRITING. When writing is introduced during the second week or thereafter, it is recommended that the instructor select an early lesson in the text plates consisting of paragraphs or letters. Since the students have been reading these outlines for a number of days, the material should be fairly easy for them to write; and they will be able to record the outlines with much greater fluency than those in the current assignment. Some teachers may prefer, however, to select an easy letter from the day's assignment. A number of different procedures such as those described in the following paragraphs may be used to develop writing of contextual material.

DRYPENNING METHOD. Students are asked to drypen over the outlines in the text as the material is being read by an individual member of the class or by the group in unison. This procedure helps students write through the pattern of the word, focusing attention on the order in which the sounds are written, the joinings of the strokes, the size of the strokes, and the direction of writing. The student is experiencing the use of several senses in hearing the word, seeing the word, and writing the word. The effectiveness of the drypenning method depends largely on the mental effort of the students during the process. Drypenning outlines may or may not be beneficial to the students, depending on the thought process that occurs.

Students may also be taught to use this procedure in doing their homework. In this case, they drypen the shorthand outlines as they read the plates. They reread the plates at a faster pace, again drypenning the outlines as they read.

AIR WRITING. Students are asked to write the shorthand outlines in the air for the material being read by a member of the class. Here they must be able to think of the correct outlines without assistance since they are not following the outlines in the book. When writing is being introduced, this procedure may not be highly desirable because emphasis should be on correctly written outlines.

SCRIBBLE WRITING. Students are instructed to write the dictated material on a single line of the notebook, writing over and over the same spot. When the line becomes worn, they drop down to the next line and follow the same procedure. Proponents of the scribble technique claim students write more rapidly because they cannot see their outlines and are not tempted to try to make them appear like those in the text. Students can also be taught to use this procedure in doing their homework. In this case, they read the shorthand paragraph several times until they can read it fluently. Then they self-dictate the material at a normal reading rate, writing the sentence on one line of their notebook while keeping their eyes focused on the textbook and reading from the shorthand plates. The process is repeated three or four times, self-dictating at a higher rate each time.

SENTENCE REPETITIVE METHOD. The students first read a sentence from the plate in the text. The teacher may have an individual read the sentence again while the rest of the class observes the teacher writing it on the chalkboard. The sentence is then read by the entire group. The teacher next dictates the sentence. Following this, the students practice the outlines with which they had difficulty. Then the sentence is dictated two more times, each time slightly faster. The sentence is written one final time at a lower rate to enable the students to write fluently but with precision. The same procedure is followed for all the sentences in the paragraph or letter.

WHOLE SENTENCE METHOD. The whole sentence method is probably the most widely used procedure for introducing writing. The students read the first sentence in the plate. The teacher then dictates the sentence. The class next reads the second sentence, which is then dictated by the teacher. This procedure is continued until the entire paragraph or letter has been written. Then the paragraph or letter is repeated once or twice.

WHOLE SENTENCE BUILD-UP METHOD. This is a variation of the whole sentence method. The first sentence is read by the class and then dictated by the teacher. The second sentence is read then dictated. At this point the teacher dictates sentences one and two without pausing. The third sentence is read and dictated. Then the first three sentences are dictated without a pause. The procedure is continued throughout the paragraph or letter.

Note: Some teachers use a "phrase build-up method" in introducing writing. Instead of dictating an entire sentence, they dictate the first phrase several times, then add the next phrase several times, then the next phrase, and continue in this manner.

TWENTY-WORD PLAN. The first 20 standard-word group is dictated at 60 wam (in 20 seconds). These 20 words are redictated, first at 70 and then at 80 wam. The second 20 standard-word group is dictated in the same manner. Then the two 20 standard-word groups are combined. Finally the third 20 word group is practiced in this manner and combined with the first two groups.

TEN-SECOND INTERVAL PLAN. This plan is especially well suited to the introduction of writing. The teacher gives 10 seconds of dictation at a predetermined rate, such as 60 wam. If most of the class is able to record the material, the teacher again dictates this 10 seconds of material and adds the next 10 seconds of dictation, again checking to determine whether the students were able to keep up with the dictation rate. This procedure is continued until they are able to take 30 seconds to 1 minute of dictation without pausing.

BROKEN RECORD DICTATION METHOD. Students first read the paragraph from the shorthand plate. Then the instructor writes the paragraph on the board while the class observes. The class reads the paragraph once again, this time from the board, stopping to sound/spell any outline the instructor believes may cause hesitation in writing.

The instructor then starts dictating the paragraph, forcing the students to try to write the outlines as many times as they are dictated. The dictation might sound like this: Dear Mr. Dear Mr. Dear Mr. Dear Mr. Gray Gray Gray Thank you for Thank you for Thank you for writing writing writing writing us us us us about about about about your your your your last last last last order order order order. Dear Mr. Gray: Thank you for writing us about your last order. We want We want We want We want to know to know to know to know immediately immediately immediately immediately whenever whenever whenever whenever goods goods goods goods are are are are received received received received in in in in a a a a damaged damaged damaged damaged condition condition condition condition. We want to know immediately whenever goods are received in a damaged condition.

LINE SKIP METHOD. When students begin to write the day's lesson, they are asked to skip three or four lines between each line of writing. They then read from their own shorthand notes as they write the material a second time on the first blank line beneath the material written from the text. They may repeat this self-dictation, using an additional blank line, or they may be instructed to bring their homework to class after writing the material twice. In class they first read the material from their own shorthand notes. Then they take the material from dictation, writing on the blank line immediately below their homework. Should they have difficulty with any outline, they can locate the correct form on the line directly above the one on which they are writing.

Some teachers prefer to have their students write the shorthand plate in the left column of the shorthand notebook, leaving the right column blank. Then students are told to write the same material in the right column from the key and to compare their notes in the two columns. Or they may be directed to write the material a second time in the right column, reading from their notes in the left column.

DOUBLE TAKE. When introducing writing in classes with a wide range of ability, the teacher may instruct the students who can do so to write everything twice. Some students may have difficulty recording the outlines once, while others will be able to "double take" the dictation and need this kind of challenge to hold their interest.

Regardless of the method the teacher may choose to introduce writing, easy material should be selected for the first writing practice. Material that is too difficult will result in a hesitant writing style and the drawing of outlines.

Amount of Writing in Introductory Lessons

During the first few days of writing, teachers will find that their students tire after only 10 to 15 minutes of dictation. The degree of concentration required to develop a new skill is often underestimated by persons who have thoroughly mastered that skill over a period of years. Seldom should more than 10 to 15 minutes be devoted to writing in any one period during the first week of writing practice. Teachers who observe the students during their writing can quickly detect signs of excessive tension and fatigue. Students who grasp the pen too tightly or who are pushing against the pen point heavily instead of writing fluently across the page will tire rapidly because of the tension under which they are working.

Writing With Text Open

The length of time students should be permitted to take dictation with their shorthand texts open depends on the use being made of the text. Students who use the text merely to copy the shorthand are not taking dictation and are deriving little or no benefit from the dictation practice in class. If, however, the students are using the text to check the accuracy of an outline or to recall how to construct an occasional outline, that may be an acceptable procedure. Students should be able to take dictation with their texts closed certainly by the fifth, sixth, or seventh week of the first semester. If the teacher is following a sound speed-building plan, the problem of the open text frequently takes care of itself. At 60 wam students may be able to follow along in the book closely; at 70, it becomes somewhat more difficult; and at 80 wam, it is nearly impossible to copy from the text and keep up with the dictation. Consequently, students soon find, without any comment from the teacher, that as the speed increases, if they are to get the dictation, they cannot depend upon copying from the text.

Some teachers recommend the use of the open textbook in a three-step program. In the beginning stages of dictation development, the first step is employed as the students are urged to keep their eyes on the textbook and write in the notebook at the rate of 60 wam. The notes will not be written on the line of writing—students will need to be convinced that this does not make any difference; the purpose of the activity is to respond to the dictation at the rate given. The teacher dictates the first 20 words of the letter. On the next dictation of the same piece of material at 70, the student may again completely watch the textbook and write in the notebook; or this time the student may be ready for the second step, which is to look at the textbook, see the shorthand outlines dictated, and look quickly to the notebook and write what was dictated. On the next dictation of the same piece of material at 80, the students probably would again be at the second-step stage, where they look at the textbook first and then look quickly to the notebook and write the material. At this point the teacher would move to the next 20 words of material, and the same procedure would be repeated. After these 20 words have been practiced at 60, 70, and 80, the third step is to combine the two pieces and dictate at 60 or 70 wam, with controlled writing and looking only at the notebook as the goals.

Teachers who use this program recommend that students continue to look at the book when necessary rather than stop writing or "doodle" excessive pen motions in attempts to recall outlines. The major point of such a practice is that students are hearing, seeing, and writing the material at the rates dictated; they are responding to each word dictated without dropping words or developing habits of false writing starts; and they are motivated to keep trying because

155

their progression throughout the three-step program is individual. The teacher will need to intervene whenever a student is not moving to step three after an appropriate number of repetitions and try to detect the reasons for the problem and prescribe remedial homework procedures, practice with taped material, and the like.

SAMPLE LESSON PLAN FOR INTRODUCTION OF WRITING
(Lesson 5, Gregg Shorthand, Series 90)

Today's Homework Assignment:	Review the shorthand alphabet thoroughly. Sound/spell and read through the words in paragraphs 27, 28, and 29 at least twice. Read paragraphs 30 and 31 twice. Read paragraphs 33, 34, and 35 once. If time permits, reread these three paragraphs.
Check Roll and Make Announcements:	(During this time students may be responding to brief-form flash cards or phrase flash cards held by another student, or they may be performing paired reading.)　　　(3 min.)
Warmup:	Students sound/spell and read in concert and/or individually as teacher points to the characters and words written on the chalkboard. Books closed.

Alphabet (Students say):

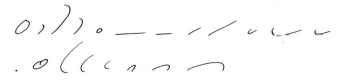

Theory (Students sound/spell and say the word—before each group of words teacher indicates the sound that is to be said.)

Brief forms (Students say):

Phrases (Students say):

(10 min.)

Introduction of writing, books open:

1. Dictate alphabet, writing strokes on board and dictating. Students write each stroke as many times as possible before the next is dictated. (Briefly indicate line of writing and proportion when appropriate or when students might be doubtful.)

2. Students sound/spell, read, and write outlines in paragraph 27, p. 32. Write selected words on the board to illustrate rules:

3. Continue sound/spelling, reading, and writing outlines, paragraphs 28 and 29, pp. 32–33, continuing to place on the board selected words to illustrate theory principles:

(10 min.)

Theory: Review principles of joinings in paragraphs 37 to 42, pp. 36 and 37.

Presentation: Lesson 6 (review lesson)

Students sound/spell and say each group of words as the teacher explains the rules.

Circles with curves:

Circles with straight lines:

Circles between opposite curves:

ō hook before *n* and *m:*

ō hook following downward strokes:

$\overline{oo}$ hook after *n, m:*

th with *o, r, l:*

th in all other cases:

Students read together brief forms and phrases, paragraph 43, p. 38,
Lesson 6.   (10 min.)

Reading and Writing:

1. Students read together the brief-form letter 32, p. 34.
2. Write first sentence on board as students observe.
3. Dictate first sentence. Afterwards, students practice any outline giving them difficulty. Dictate first sentence once more.
4. Dictate next sentence in letter in same manner.
5. Dictate first two sentences.
6. Dictate the third sentence in the same manner as the two previous sentences.
7. Dictate the first three sentences together.
                                                            (12 min.)

Reading: Class begins sight reading letters in Lesson 6 to give them a start on their homework. Read in unison.

Assignment: See duplicated Homework Assignment Sheet

Shorthand Penmanship

The penmanship of the students in the shorthand class will be as varied as their longhand writing style. Before criticizing a student for being a "backhand" writer or for other peculiarities of penmanship, the teacher needs to look at the student's longhand writing. The shorthand penmanship will invariably reflect the same writing qualities as the longhand. The slant of the outlines may not be similar to those in the book, but if they are consistent, the student will be able to read them. The shorthand teacher who thinks writing patterns established throughout 10 or 11 years of schooling can be changed in the shorthand course is indeed optimistic.

However, dictation practice in class may at times cause penmanship problems for some students. Those whose shorthand recording speed is below that of most of the other students frequently must make great effort to get the dictation when the teacher increases the speed. A few students may find that the dictation is so far beyond their writing ability that the legibility of their shorthand breaks down completely. Good penmanship—the ability to write legible shorthand that can be read quickly and accurately—is essential, and provision must be made for it in such ways as the following:

- Dictating at the beginning and end of the dictation-speed-development block in a class period at a rate that every student can record easily with good control. This practice will counteract to some extent the illegible notes that result from pushing the entire class for high speeds during most of the dictation-speed-development block.
- Dropping back to the control level after pushing shorthand speeds to high levels.
- Giving sustained dictation for control of material used for speed forcing.
- Dictating material containing strokes of similar lengths, opposite motion strokes or strokes commonly confused ($\bar{o}$ and $\overline{oo}$, r and l, e and a, and so on).
- Encouraging students who find the dictation too rapid in class to write their shorthand homework at least once for control.
- Encouraging students to try to earn penmanship awards.
- Frequently changing activities to avoid excessive fatigue.

Every class period should include dictation that each student can

159

record at a control rate, legibly, without pressure. Failure to provide such practice often results in illegible outlines and careless writing habits.

Use of the Shorthand Notebook and Pen

All students should be taught to use their shorthand notebooks and pens correctly early in the course. The shorthand notebook should be opened flat on the desk if space permits. The choice of pen may be left to the student as long as the ink flows evenly and freely. Some will prefer a fine point and others a broader one. Students should be cautioned to always have at least two pens or a pen and a pencil in case their pens should go dry during dictation.

Students should be taught to write to the vertical line in the middle of the page of the shorthand notebook, completing the first column before continuing to the second. Left-handed writers may find it more satisfactory to write in the right column first so the hand will not smear the ink.

Notes should be recorded on one side of the page only. When the last page is filled, the notebook is turned over and the backs of the pages used. Students should not flip the pages from front to back while taking dictation. They should keep a rubber band around the used portion of the notebook to enable them to turn to a clean page immediately.

One skill many students do not learn properly is that of turning pages in the shorthand notebook. To save time, the student should hold down the notebook with the left hand, moving the pages up with the thumb while recording the dictation. (Left-handed students would hold down the notebook with the right hand and move the pages up with the right thumb). Upon completing the last line of the second column, the thumb of the left hand flips the page quickly and quietly.

The desk top should have adequate space for the notebook to be opened flat, front and back covers on the desk. The completely open notebook, rather than with the front cover tucked under, has less edge at the bottom for the student to move over, and the cover provides a place to hold down and stabilize the book while writing. Teachers will need to encourage the students to sit close to the desk, supporting both arms on it, and to keep pushing the book upward on the desk as they write so the large arm muscle is supporting the writing arm—the elbow is not off the desk.

The Shorthand Homework Assignment

Most teachers will agree that students have written thousands of pages of homework that contributed little or nothing to the development of their shorthand writing skills. Perhaps in no area of shorthand instruction has there been so little creativity as in homework. Students have been given standard assignments—read and write the next day's lesson once or twice—with no change whatever for an entire year. The standard assignment required no effort on the part of the teacher. If students were absent, they still knew exactly what the assignment was. They could, if they chose—and they sometimes did—do the assignments for an entire week on the preceding weekend. Many more did not take time to read the plate material before copying the plates for their homework, with the result that they could neither read nor take dictation the following day in class. Writing from shorthand plates has never guaranteed that learning was taking place.

Recently a number of shorthand authorities have begun to question the value of the standard shorthand assignment and to suggest that variable assignments might prove far more productive.

STANDARD HOMEWORK ASSIGNMENT. Those teachers who prefer the standard assignment need to tell their students more than "read and write the lesson." They need to carefully go through the procedures that they wish their students to follow and give specific instructions for studying both word lists and contextual material. The instructions might be similar to the following:

- Do your homework in a quiet place. Do not try to watch television or talk with others while you are studying.
- Have a large flat surface on which you can place your shorthand notebook and on which your arms can be supported. Do not try to practice shorthand with your notebook on your lap.
- When studying word lists, cover the key to the words with a card or paper. Sound/spell the word aloud. If you do not recognize the word, consult the key. Do not sound/spell brief forms and phrases. When you have finished, sound/spell and read the word list a second time.
- If you are using a textbook with the key to the shorthand plate in the back of the book, place your left index finger under the shorthand outlines you are reading and your right index finger under the words in the key. Read the words aloud, sound/spelling each word you cannot read. If sound/spelling the outline does not give you the word, refer to the key immediately.
- After reading the letter, self-dictate it.
- When you are self-dictating, read the first group of outlines or thought unit; then write that group of outlines as you say each word. Continue in this manner throughout the letter. Do not copy the shorthand outlines one at a time from the text; write in groups of outlines.
- If you have difficulty with an outline, practice it several times at the

point where it occurs in the writing practice. As you practice individual words, sound/spell the word and notice particularly the sequence of the sounds. Some words may need to be practiced in a piecemeal fashion.

Example:

- Check to see if you can read your shorthand notes.
- Continue practicing the next letter in the same manner.

If teachers using the standard homework assignment will give this kind of detailed instructions to their students, modifying them somewhat occasionally, the time students spend doing homework will be beneficial. Unless students think about the shorthand outlines as they read and write, the homework assignment all too frequently becomes merely a copying exercise, which benefits no one.

When students are taught to self-dictate the material they write from the shorthand plates in the text, the result should be meaningful practice. During the first two or three weeks they may read and copy the plates, but they should soon learn to read in thought units, then look up from the text and repeat the same phrase aloud as they write it in their shorthand notebooks, checking back only if they are unable to recall an outline. With practice, students should be able to self-dictate their homework assignment at approximately 20 wam.

THE VARIABLE ASSIGNMENT. Teachers using the variable homework assignment are attempting to make homework more attractive to the students and the time spent doing the homework more beneficial. In this case, the students may be given a homework sheet each week showing the daily assignment with each assignment being different; or they may be given the assignment each day in class. The latter procedure is more time consuming, but does ensure that students do their homework on the day it is assigned.

All types of variations may be made in the weekly assignments. For example, students may be instructed to read and write twice a letter or letters the teacher wishes to use for speed building the following day in class. Students may be asked to check their reading rates on certain letters. Some letters may be read but not written. At times students may be instructed to write a letter once from the plate and a second time from the key. They may be asked to write shorthand outlines for words illustrating the theory principles in the day's lesson, but which were not included in the text, or to compose sentences using these new theory words. An illustration of variable assignments is shown on pages 163 and 164.

Other types of homework assignments designed to stimulate student interest include ideas such as the following:

- Write the words you see on the billboards when you are riding the bus to and from school.
- Write a letter to your pen pal. (Shorthand teachers in different cities or states can arrange for pen pal letters between their classes.)
- Record the words to a popular song from the radio or TV.
- Record the TV news in shorthand.
- Take the Sunday sermon in shorthand.
- Record the assembly speaker's talk in shorthand.
- Write an article appearing on the front page of the newspaper in shorthand.
- Record a conversation in shorthand.
- Write a paragraph in shorthand, describing your problems in the course.
- Write the first page of one of your textbooks in shorthand.
- Transcribe a letter from the textbook.
- Practice the previews and then write the typescript material in shorthand from the sheet given to you in class.
- After reading and writing the plate material from the text, practice the same lesson from taped dictation in the shorthand laboratory.

Many of these suggestions are, of course, designed for advanced students, but some of the assignments can be undertaken by first-year students.

VARIABLE HOMEWORK ASSIGNMENT
(Gregg Shorthand, Series 90)

Lesson 31

> Sound/spell, read, and write through the word lists in paragraphs 282, 283, and 284 three times.
> Read paragraph 285.
> Read paragraphs 287, 288, 289, 290, and 292.
> Write paragraph 287 twice. Write paragraphs 288 and 289 once.
> Compose three sentences in shorthand in which you use words or principles in paragraphs 282–284.

Lesson 32

> Sound/spell, read, and write through the word lists twice in paragraphs 293, 294, and 295.
> Read paragraph 298, trying to read it in no more than two minutes.
> Read paragraphs 299, 300, and 302 twice.
> See how many of your friends' names you can write in shorthand.

163

Lesson 33

Sound/spell and read through the word lists in paragraphs 304, 305, and 306 three times.

Read and then write paragraph 309 in the left column of your notebook. Then, reading from your shorthand notes, rewrite the paragraph in the right column of your notebook.

Read paragraph 310, trying to read it in two minutes.

Read and then write paragraphs 311, 312, and 314 once.

See how many names of foods you can write in shorthand.

Lesson 34

Read and write through the word lists in paragraphs 315, 316, 317, and 318 twice.

Then go back and read through the lists once again.

Read and write paragraph 321 twice.

Read paragraphs 322 through 325. Your goal is to read these letters in no more than ten minutes.

Try to read paragraph 324 in one minute. (112 words)

Lesson 35

Sound/spell, read, and write the words listed in paragraph 326 and 327 twice.

Read and then write paragraph 330 in the left column of your notebook. Then, reading from your shorthand notes, rewrite the paragraph in the right column of your notebook.

Read paragraphs 331, 332, 333, and 334. Write paragraphs 331 and 333.

Write in shorthand the names of as many objects as you can in the room where you are studying.

AMOUNT OF HOMEWORK. The amount of homework that can and should be assigned must be determined by each shorthand teacher based on the particular school situation. Years ago teachers often required students to write a given number of lines or complete a specific number of pages of homework. While many students dutifully completed these assignments, sometimes they were careless. Students soon realized that the larger they wrote their shorthand notes, the faster they would be able to fill the required pages.

Today teachers recognize that the student who achieves proficiency on the assigned lesson after reading and writing it once should not be required to do the lesson three times. On the other hand, the student who is still reading and writing hesitantly after completing the lesson once certainly needs additional practice. Teachers should check with students having difficulty reading shorthand plates or taking dictation in class to see whether they are performing their homework in the right manner. It is also possible that the assignment for individuals should be adjusted to meet their particular needs. The basic assignment usually consists of one lesson a day.

Teachers need to use wise judgment in making homework assignments and realize that (1) students have academic obligations other than shorthand, (2) excessive daily assignments may lead to student frustration and increase the dropout rate, and (3) large assignments do not necessarily ensure better learning but may encourage improper techniques for completing lessons.

Students may find completing shorthand homework, especially in the beginning weeks, a very time-consuming task. A prudent teacher will try to recommend time-saving techniques to the student, will teach theory in class so that homework is a relatively easy extension of the class learning, will reassure the student that soon homework will take less time, and will be alert to students' frustrations about homework and take steps to remedy problems before the students withdraw from the situation.

USE OF HOMEWORK IN CLASS. By using the homework notes in class for reading rates, typewritten transcription drills, and typewritten transcription rates, the student soon realizes the importance of accuracy in writing, of fluency and correctness in reading the notes, and of knowing the transcription-element usage that applies.

EVALUATION OF HOMEWORK. While the teacher should check to see that the homework has been done, it does not need to be corrected or graded. Occasionally the homework should be checked to determine whether the written assignment is being completed according to the directions on the assignment sheet. Seldom, however, does a teacher need to do more than check to see that the homework is completed each day.

A common practice associated with the mechanics of homework assignments is to ask students to use two shorthand notebooks. They prepare the homework assignment in one notebook, writing their name, lesson number, and date at the bottom of the page. Some teachers ask students to hand in the notebook, while others ask them to write on both sides of the page, tear out the pages, and staple them together to hand in. The second notebook is used for dictation practice in class.

Notes

1. Joe M. Pullis, "The Relationship Between Fluency in Reading Shorthand Plates and Achievement in Shorthand Dictation," independent study, Louisiana Tech University, Ruston, 1972.
2. Milton Earle Howard, "The Relationship Between Knowledge of Principles and Transcription Errors in Writing Diamond Jubilee Shorthand as Compared with Gregg Shorthand Simplified at the Two-Year College Level," doctoral dissertation, New York University, NY, 1968.

Chapter 6

Dictation Speed Building

As soon as students begin to write shorthand vocabulary, they receive dictation practice in some form—words, phrases, sentences, or paragraphs and letters. After the first few days of instruction, dictation should be timed. The building of shorthand writing speed is not an extraneous aspect of the students' shorthand skill development. It begins when dictation is introduced and continues as long as the students remain in the shorthand program. The impression that the first semester is devoted exclusively to the mastery of shorthand theory, the second to dictation practice, and the third and fourth to transcription and speed development is very misleading. Although shorthand vocabulary is emphasized in the first semester, it must be studied and mastered in every subsequent period of instruction. Dictation for speed building is introduced during the first semester. It, too, continues to be emphasized every semester thereafter. It is the degree of emphasis or the amount of time devoted to speed development that changes.

Relationship Between Shorthand Vocabulary Mastery and Shorthand Speed Development

One of the most serious roadblocks to speed development in the past has been the failure to recognize the relationship between mastery of shorthand vocabulary and development of shorthand speed. Students are sometimes told it does not matter how they write a shorthand outline as long as they can read it when they transcribe their notes. However, research has shown the opposite to be true. Students who write accurate outlines can expect to develop their shorthand writing speed more rapidly than students who do not write correct outlines.[1] Research has also shown that it is the hesitations in writing that cause problems in the development of shorthand speed—the more hesitations, the more difficulty the student has in advancing from one speed level to another.[2] It seems logical that the students who cannot recall or construct correct shorthand outlines but who must make up their own—and not necessarily according to sound—will have more hesitations in writing than those students who know the correct outlines and can recall or construct them automatically. Therefore, the first requisite for the development of speed is the thorough mastery of shorthand vocabulary. The student who writes accurate shorthand notes has a base on which to build and will ordinarily progress much faster than the one who has been permitted to write with little regard for accuracy.

Speed Building, A Mental, Not Physical, Problem

Problems related to the forcing of shorthand speed are mental rather than physical hurdles. Students who say that their hand will simply not move as fast as the dictation is given are in effect saying that they cannot think that fast. They have not automatized the commonly used words and phrases or developed competency in constructing short-hand outlines by sound to the point that they can write them without hesitation. If they could recall these outlines and/or automatically write them by sound/spelling, they would have time to construct the outlines with which they were not thoroughly familiar. They may, in fact, be writing the words that they have automatized at exceedingly high rates of speed. Considering the number of pauses and hesitations of most students when recording shorthand dictation, it is obvious that much of the dictation they do record is written far above the rate at which the teacher is dictating. Students who are taking dictation at 60 wam may be writing some words and phrases at speeds of 80, 100, and even 120 to offset the hesitations and pauses when they encounter unfamiliar outlines.

Dictation Materials

Difficulty of Dictation Material

PREDICTING THE DIFFICULTY LEVEL. Experienced teachers know that the ability of students to record material dictated for speed building varies considerably from day to day. While part of this variation may be due to such factors as physical condition, interest, emotional health, personal problems, and degree of concentration, frequently the difference is because of the varying difficulty of the material being dictated.

It has long been recognized that syllabic intensity is not a precise indicator of the difficulty of a shorthand take. A "word" in shorthand is considered to consist of 1.40 syllables; the number of actual words in dictation material may be either greater or smaller than the number of 1.40 syllable words.

Teachers who use dictation books regularly can tell which "takes" few of their students will pass at a given dictation speed. They can also pick out three or four takes most of the class will pass when dictated at the same rate of speed. They probably cannot explain why, but experience has shown certain takes to be much more difficult than others.

Hillestad (1960) and Uthe (1966) were among the first researchers to study the factors that might be used to predict shorthand outline errors.[3,4] Other investigators have also isolated factors that could be used to predict shorthand transcription errors. Henrie, in a 1971 comparative analysis of four prediction formulas, reported that the Hillestad shorthand difficulty prediction formula was the most valid and most reliable of the four for predicting difficulty of shorthand dictation materials when transcription errors rather than shorthand outline errors were used as the criterion.[5] Henrie also found that the two most valid prediction formulas contained more than one variable and both included the number of words beyond the first 1,500 most frequently used words in the Silverthorn-Perry List.

The factors most often considered by researchers include syllabic intensity, stroke intensity, word frequency (percentage of high-frequency words, usually within the first 1,500 of the Silverthorn list, and percentage of low-frequency words), average word length, number of brief forms, and number of word beginnings and endings. It is now generally recognized that the use of the single factor of syllabic intensity alone does not adequately control the difficulty of the dictation material. However, the formulas that have been developed for preparing or analyzing material for dictation are too time-consuming and difficult for classroom teachers to apply.

CONTROLLED AND UNCONTROLLED MATERIALS. Shorthand authorities have strongly disagreed about the relative merits of controlled and uncontrolled shorthand dictation material. One form of controlled material is considered to be that in which the vocabulary is limited to a specified word frequency, such as the first 1,500 words of the Silverthorn, Perry, Mellinger or similar lists. Uncontrolled dictation material makes no attempt to limit the vocabulary to words of high frequency or to cycle certain words throughout the textual matter. Advocates of controlled material point out that students should build vocabulary on high-frequency words, expanding the frequency as they develop their shorthand skill. They argue that high-frequency words are those that students will most likely encounter on the job. Those favoring uncontrolled dictation point out that words of high frequency will occur with sufficient repetition in the dictation materials without exercising artificial control. They also stress the point that the very fact that the low-frequency words occur far less often makes it all the more important that such words be retained or incorporated in the uncontrolled dictation. They believe that students have much less difficulty recording high-frequency words than they do words of low frequency and that speed-development materials should not be contrived in such a way that low-frequency words are eliminated. The true issue, of course, is the effect that the use of controlled versus uncontrolled shorthand materials has on the students' skill development.

Research findings are not conclusive on this issue. Gallion (1968) found that students using vocabulary-controlled dictation material received slightly but not significantly higher mean transcription-accuracy scores than did students receiving dictation from textbook materials.[6] Prince (1967) reported that students who used vocabulary-controlled dictation material (limited to the first 1,500 most-used words in business correspondence and correlated with textbooks) received slightly higher mean transcription accuracy scores than did those receiving dictation from textbook material.[7] Larsen (1970), however, found that intermediate and advanced students given dictation composed of the 2,800 most frequently occurring words in business correspondence attained approximately the same terminal achievement as students exposed to a larger textbook vocabulary.[8]

Few shorthand teachers quarrel with the purpose of controlled shorthand vocabulary material: to give the student intensive practice in writing high-frequency words. The debatable question is just how much practice students need on such material and how many high-frequency words they can master while in the shorthand program. According to some authorities, if students could automatize the first 5,000 most frequently used words, they would be able to write approximately 95 percent of the words they would encounter in taking dictation. But most teachers find few students who automatize more than 1,000 of the most-used words, or at best 1,500, regardless of the amount and type of dictation given. Since 15 to 20 percent of the words these students will later encounter on the job will not be among the first 1,500 in frequency, some provision must be made to assist students in writing these words. Teachers concerned with this problem will give their students numerous opportunities to construct shorthand outlines for new and unfamiliar words, emphasizing sound/spelling and the word-building principles for each new outline.

Few shorthand authorities would want to limit the vocabulary of shorthand materials used throughout the program to the first 1,500 to 2,000 most-used words. Some might elect to use the first 5,000 words. In any event, there are numerous teachers who are more concerned with sensible content and the writing of new words than with the percentage of high-frequency words used in the early lessons. However, they do not want those lessons to include an unrealistic number of difficult or unusual vocabulary words. Regardless of the material the teacher elects to use, the speed-building program should provide for writing new and unfamiliar words. If the shorthand sound/spelling principles are mastered, that knowledge can then be transferred to constructing any new words students may later encounter in the business world.

Types of Material for Dictation Speed Building

EASY, REPETITIVE MATERIAL. In the early stages of speed development, easy material should be selected. Such material will enable the students to master quickly a high-frequency vocabulary. Remember, in business the first 500 most frequently occurring words account for 70 percent of all words used in correspondence, and the first 1,500 words account for approximately 85 percent of all words in business and office correspondence.[9] Gradually, the materials selected for dictation should increase in difficulty, thus enlarging the students' shorthand vocabulary. During the first semester, if the material dictated is selected from the text, students will constantly be provided with an automatic review of many frequently used words in a context that is also saturated with the current day's shorthand vocabulary principles. This form of repetitive dictation practice should result in the automatization of many of those high-frequency words that make up such a large portion of business dictation. In other semesters, however, unfamiliar material is ordinarily used to give the students an opportunity to practice these words in new settings and to expand and broaden their shorthand vocabulary. While most teachers prefer to begin speed building with easy dictation material and gradually increase the difficulty as their students build their recording skill, Boggess (1970) found that it made no difference in student achievement whether the material used for speed building was consistently easy, average, or difficult. Students performed the same when they were evaluated on the basis of shorthand dictation tests.[10]

NEW-MATTER DICTATION. In the past, shorthand authorities have generally recommended that new-matter dictation be deferred until the second semester of shorthand. However, recent research studies do not indicate that the point at which new-matter dictation is introduced has any significant effect on the students' achievement at the end of the course. McKenna (1965) and Pershing (1966) both reported that classes in which new-matter dictation was introduced early in the first semester performed as well at the end of the year as did classes in which new-matter dictation was delayed until later in the program.[11,12]

Introducing new-matter dictation early does have the distinct advantage of giving students additional opportunity to become accustomed to writing unfamiliar words by sound. Since shorthand teachers who follow the reading approach have repeatedly stated that their students' most serious problem was inability to construct new words, it is apparent that such new-matter dictation could be helpful. On the other hand, introducing an extensive amount of new-matter dictation too early could easily result in a hesitant style of recording outlines because the students' shorthand vocabulary may be too limited to permit fluent writing of unfamiliar material.

170   The manner in which the teacher introduces new-matter dictation

may have as much to do with the students' success in recording it as does the specific time in the program when new matter is introduced. For example, a teacher could, in the early lessons, add words not in the text to give students practice in writing by sound. The teacher who dictates a few new words illustrating the shorthand principles in the day's lesson or who dictates two or three sentences incorporating these word-building principles as part of the regular classroom routine may often avert much of the concern some students develop about new-matter dictation. However, the new words should be common, high-frequency words, and the time given to such practice should be strictly limited. At this point students need to be reading hundreds of accurate shorthand outlines from their text. Those who wish to try this procedure can, within the first two weeks, give their students practice in writing four or five sentences of new material which incorporate the shorthand principles of the day. Teachers who introduce writing from the beginning of the shorthand program and follow the procedure of giving new-matter dictation early should remember that little time should be used for this. Such practice has two purposes—to provide additional opportunities for constructing new outlines and to further emphasize the shorthand principles in the current assignment. Other teachers who introduce new-matter dictation early prefer to wait until the midpoint of the first semester.

Another easy procedure for introducing students to new-matter dictation is to use the chalkboard preview, which they practice before taking the dictation on which the preview was based. After they finish the preview practice, the teacher may ask the students to record whatever they hear. The teacher then composes a short letter loaded with the words and phrases of the preview just practiced. Because they are so familiar with these words and phrases, students often do not realize that they have had their first introduction to new-matter dictation.

Teachers who wish to introduce new-matter dictation early in the first semester will find the reinforcement lessons starting with Lesson 49 excellent sources of new-matter dictation material. Lesson 49, for example, concentrates on the shorthand vocabulary principles studied in Chapter 1 (Lessons 1 through 6) and Lesson 50 on the principles in Chapter 2 (Lessons 7 through 12). The material through Lesson 56 can be used then for new-matter dictation while the theory of the first 48 lessons is being introduced.

Another source of new-matter dictation that teachers have found helpful is the new lesson, the homework lesson. After the shorthand vocabulary for the new homework lesson has been previewed, students are familiar with the new principles and their applications within a variety of words. Using this new lesson for new-matter dictation gives the students a headstart on learning the material in the homework lesson, in addition to the experience of taking new-matter dictation. **171**

New-matter dictation is composed, for the most part, simply of words that the students have written many times while taking dictation for speed building, arranged in a new setting. Thus the gap between practiced and new-matter dictation is not nearly so wide as many teachers unintentionally lead their students to believe.

The time when new matter is introduced will necessarily be influenced by the shorthand standards. Teachers requiring students to pass three-minute, new-matter dictation tests the first semester must obviously introduce new-matter dictation practice some time before the first three-minute test takes. Teachers who evaluate the shorthand students' progress only on practiced material the first semester may defer new-matter dictation until the second semester or until all shorthand vocabulary principles have been introduced.

Considerations in Speed Building

Emphasis on Shorthand Vocabulary During Dictation Speed Building

Because the ability to construct correct outlines instantly is vitally important in speed building, the instructor should find opportunities for incidental review and/or word-building expansion of shorthand vocabulary. For example, if the word *impart* appears in the dictation, the teacher might write on the board the shorthand outline for *part, partly, party, partner, partisan, partnership, depart*. The class then reads from the board and the words are dictated rapidly again.

Following the same procedure, if the word *oracle* appears in the dictation, the teacher might dictate rapidly *radical, chemical, physical, logical, medical, surgical, musical, miracle, whimsical, pinnacle*. This type of drill takes no more than two minutes and provides intensive practice on derivatives and word beginnings and endings that are frequently not mastered as thoroughly as they should be.

Developing Word-Carrying Ability

When taking dictation for speed building, students are faced with the problem of recording what has been dictated, remembering what has not yet been recorded, and hearing still other dictation being given by the teacher. In effect, they record one thought phrase, remember another, and hear yet another. To be able to record the dictation, students must develop word-carrying ability. Most speed-building plans, if used correctly, will automatically force them to develop the ability to remember and record what has been dictated. The amount students must remember will vary with the degree of skill in recording the dictation and the rate at which the dictation is given. If the dictation is given at a speed-forcing rate for every member of the class at some point during the dictation period, then all should develop word-carrying ability.

Word-carrying ability can also be developed through special drills. The teacher may dictate a sentence of 10 words, asking the student to begin writing when the dictation is finished. The next sentence dictated may contain 15 words and so on. Gradually the students are able to remember more and more as the length of the sentences increases. While this technique might be an acceptable alternative, the same objective can be accomplished through speed-forcing dictation without loss of class time.

Emphasis on Phrases in Dictation Speed Building

While it is possible to write shorthand rapidly without phrasing, commonly used phrases can contribute to the ease with which students build their speed. The amount of phrasing will vary considerably from student to student. Some will begin to write phrases much sooner than others. They have reached the point in their skill development where they are no longer recording each word individually, stroke by stroke, but are listening to the phrases as the teacher dictates. Others, who are still on the word level, will not hear the phrases and will record each word as a separate outline. No attempt should be made to force all students to phrase the same way or the same amount. At the end of the year some students will be phrasing only the most commonly used expressions, while others will be phrasing to a much greater extent.

Perry (1975) emphasized that there are three factors to consider in phrasing—frequency, facility, and sound.[13] A phrase must be of high frequency, it must be one that can be written easily, and it must sound like a phrase to the shorthand writer.

Size of Notes

Just as longhand writing size varies, so does the size of shorthand notes. The person whose longhand writing is especially petite will probably write small shorthand notes, while the person with large longhand will write large shorthand notes.

Under speed-forcing pressures, however, nearly everyone writes larger shorthand notes than when recording dictation at a controlled rate. As the pressure increases, the writer's shorthand notes increase in size and begin to spread across the page. This tendency should not be discouraged; students should be encouraged to write shorthand notes as large as may be necessary to keep up with the pace of dictation. Permitting them to write shorthand notes naturally will enable them to build higher recording skill while producing notes that are proportionately written and legible.

173

Using Previews, Reviews, and Postviews in Dictation Speed Building

Previewing is fundamental to dictation speed building. By previewing material to be dictated, shorthand teachers decrease the difficulty of the dictation material so that students can achieve speed beyond their usual writing rates.

Several procedures are recommended when previewing, reviewing, and postviewing:

- During the first five weeks of the first semester, with the textbook open, introduce piecemeal practice when previewing problem words on the chalkboard or screen before a dictation speed-building practice. When presenting the preview, call the students' attention to the order of sounds within certain words and the joining of sounds. For example, when previewing the outline ⟨shorthand outline⟩ , write the ⟨shorthand outline⟩ segment of the word, emphasizing the sound of *o*, and then the ⟨shorthand outline⟩ segment of the word, emphasizing the short *oo*, and have the students write the word in piecemeal fashion, writing each segment several times before combining the two segments into a complete outline.

  Piecemeal preview practice is recommended any time difficult-to-write words are encountered. The practice focuses the students' attention on the sounds and their order and the particular joinings of one sound or symbol to another. Following a dictation speed-building practice, additional problem words identified in the dictation material may be postviewed in a similar manner.
- After the first five weeks, when students are taking dictation with their books closed, heavier previewing is recommended.
- Shorthand vocabulary should be reviewed on the chalkboard or screen between most dictation speed-building attempts. Such reviews give students an opportunity to see correctly written words and also encourage automatization of a wider shorthand vocabulary.
- Previewing is recommended throughout the first semester; later, postviewing may be used.

  The postview is similar to the preview. In postviewing, shorthand outlines are placed on the chalkboard or transparency after the material has been dictated the first time. Advocates of the postview believe this procedure better prepares students for new-material dictation and ultimately for the type of dictation given on the job.

VALUES OF PREVIEWING, REVIEWING, AND POSTVIEWING.   Research has shown that the more accurately students write shorthand, the more rapidly they write and the more accurately they transcribe their shorthand notes. By previewing, reviewing, and postviewing as recommended, students learn to construct correctly a wide vocabulary of words, develop an automatic response to those words, and through their responses more ably write new words as they hear them in dictation.

Soellers (1973) found that intermediate shorthand students who had practiced 10 percent of the words as previewed material made significantly fewer errors in outlines and in transcription than did students who had not practiced a group of preview words. The previews were found to be more beneficial to students taking dictation at 60 wam than to students taking dictation at 80 wam.[14]

VARIETY IN PREVIEWING, REVIEWING, AND POSTVIEWING. Previewing, reviewing, and postviewing procedures need to be varied if they are to help students to write shorthand outlines most effectively. Using a variety of techniques will help to keep students motivated and mentally alert—ready to automatize shorthand outlines and to write them without hesitation.

Here are some ways teachers can consider varying the use of previews, reviews, and postviews, making use of either the chalkboard or transparency and screen.

- Place selected words on the chalkboard or screen, pointing, sound/ spelling, and saying as the students write the shorthand outlines repeatedly in their notebooks. This writing approach should be used before any of the following nonwriting options are used. As students become hand-weary, the nonwriting approaches to previewing, reviewing, or postviewing are beneficial, inasmuch as they keep students involved mentally with learning the shorthand vocabulary but allow an opportunity to rest the hand.
- While viewing the outlines displayed on the chalkboard or screen, students silently say those words that have caused executional difficulties.
- Point to and sound/spell each shorthand outline as the students orally say it.
- Students sound/spell and pronounce as teacher points rapidly and at random to selected outlines. Some teachers encourage students to sound/spell very difficult words during all semesters of instruction.
- Students observe the chalkboard or screen as the teacher points, sound/spells, and/or pronounces the outlines.
- Students silently sound/spell, write the shorthand outlines, and mentally pronounce the outlines appearing on the chalkboard or screen.
- Students scribble-write words by looking at the chalkboard or screen as the teacher points, sound/spells, and pronounces each outline. They continue to look at the chalkboard or screen and write in their notebooks. The emphasis is on seeing the correctly written outline and quickly writing through the patterns of the word fluently.

- Pronounce a group of words, repeatedly pointing to the shorthand outlines on the chalkboard or screen that are included in the grouping. The students look to the chalkboard or screen for necessary help and write the group of words quickly and repetitively. Continue with additional word groups selected from troublesome sections of the dictation material. This procedure is referred to as the "multiple outline" or "multiple phrase" drill.
- Students write from the chalkboard or screen shorthand phrases that need to be automatized. Periodic drills can focus attention on these phrases. By selecting a phrase letter for dictation speed building and employing a variety of the drill procedures recommended in this section, automatization of the commonly used phrases can be accomplished.
- Before dictation, the students read silently or aloud the material from the shorthand plate. Reading can be in unison, by individuals, or by groups. By reading the material before dictation, the students have an opportunity to review the content of the dictation and mentally note difficult-to-construct shorthand outlines.
- The students copy the letter or part of a letter from the shorthand plate immediately before it is dictated. The teacher may set a time limit for copying the letter. This provides practice in writing contextual material under pressure of time.
- The students read a letter from homework notes prior to its dictation. Direct them to write one outline over another as the letter is dictated at a speed considerably higher than they normally write.
- The students mentally construct the shorthand outlines of the letter as the teacher reads it slowly before writing it from dictation.
- The students select and practice their own previews from the plate before the letter is dictated.
- As a corrective preview, the students write shorthand outlines rapidly as the teacher dictates a list of words selected from the material to be dictated. The primary objective is to construct readable outlines. The secondary objective is to construct theoretically correct outlines. Write the correct outlines on the chalkboard or transparency while dictating the list and as the students write. Following the dictation, the students check their lists against the words on the chalkboard or transparency, identifying outlines written incorrectly or with difficulty.

The Dictation Process

Amount of Dictation

The amount of dictation appropriate in a class period depends on the length of time the students have been writing in class and the time requirements of other activities that must be completed during the period. When timed dictation is first introduced, it should be limited to 10 to 15 minutes. The time allotment should be increased over a six-week period until 20 to 25 minutes are being spent on the dictation speed-building block each day. By the time the theory lessons are completed (Lesson 47) and a greater emphasis is placed on dictation, about 30 minutes of a 50-minute period should be devoted to speed-building dictation.

Teachers often wonder why their students do not achieve higher rates of speed. Frequently the answer is simple—they do not receive enough dictation practice. Teachers often overestimate the number of minutes actually spent giving dictation. Only a few dictate more than 10 to 12 minutes in any one period. To illustrate, a teacher using the one-minute speed-building plan may dictate each of three one-minute dictations three times, making a total of nine minutes of dictation. Then, if the three minutes of dictation are combined for sustained dictation, the total dictation during the period would be 12 minutes. Yet when working for speed development, the goal should be at least 20 to 30 minutes of dictation. In the illustration of a speed building lesson on page 190 and 191, 24 minutes are devoted to dictation.

Speed of Dictation

Dictation for speed building should be forced to a point that it is 20 to 30 wam above the speed the students are attempting to pass on new-matter dictation takes. If all students had the same speed objective, the dictation could be given at exactly the right pace for everyone in the class. That is seldom the case. In a first-year shorthand class, the dictation competency rates may range from 60 to 90 or 100 wam.

During each class period, dictation should be given at a rate that will challenge every student in the class. With a class dictation-competency range of 60 to 100 wam, some of the dictation must be given at 80 or 90 wam. But the teacher must remember that those students who fall outside the 80 to 90 range must be challenged also. This means those writing at 100 wam require dictation practice at 110 to 120 wam. And dictation at an appropriate rate must be given to those students who have not yet passed a 60 wam test. In this way, all students can get all the dictation some of the time, but not necessarily all the dictation all the time.

Students who have the most difficulty with class dictation are those who cannot manage dictation at the 60-wam rate. Except for the controlled dictation given at the beginning and end of the shorthand period, these students may never be able to write shorthand outlines for all the dictation. Their penmanship will always be extremely poor under these circumstances, as it will be with any student when forced dictation speeds are being used.

What instructions are appropriate for students who cannot record all the dictation? Some teachers suggest that these students be instructed to write something on the paper for every word dictated, even if it is only a scribble or scrawl. Other teachers suggest that when students find they cannot keep up with the dictation, they be told to skip and begin with the material currently being dictated. There are good reasons for these latter instructions.

During speed-building dictation, some students fall behind and are unable to record all the dictation. When they fall behind, they should be told to skip and start with the dictation currently being given. Students who try to remember a great deal of the dictation while at the same time writing other material and hearing still other words, are going to write more and more slowly as they struggle to pace themselves with the dictation. The result is just the opposite of the desired outcome. Instead of writing shorthand faster, the student is writing more slowly because of the memory burden. Had these students dropped that portion of the dictation they were trying to remember and started anew with the words being dictated, they could have continued to write rapidly for some time before again losing the dictation. There is little benefit in telling the student to write a "wiggle" for words lost. Such wiggles are not shorthand.

Teachers may hesitate to tell students to skip portions of the material when they fall behind in a speed-building practice. With respect to transcription ability, dropping dictation does not have a greater adverse effect on transcription competence than does writing scribbles. In fact, as previously stated, by dropping portions of the dictation that are a memory burden, students have more opportunities to write rapidly the words being dictated before falling behind again and losing more dictation. Remember, too, that the purpose of speed-building practice is to force students to write shorthand outlines at rates that exceed controlled writing capability. When the purpose of the dictation is for transcription, students are given dictation at rates within their recording-competency range.

During speed-building practice, teachers should encourage their students to start writing the first sounds of a troublesome outline rather than attempting to visualize the whole word before writing. A benefit derived from this procedure is that often students can complete the word once it is started but may not record any of it if they wait to visualize the entire word. In addition, students continue writing; they do not develop a habit of stopping.

Number of Repetitions

Most teachers use some type of speed-building plan that includes repeating short spurts of dictation a number of times at ever-increasing rates. The number of times the dictation should be repeated depends on the difficulty of the material, the speed at which it is dictated, and the ease with which the students are able to record it. If at least half the students are getting the dictation, then the teacher may safely repeat the material at a faster rate. However, it should be noted that repeating the dictation at a faster rate does not necessarily increase the students' writing skill. The teacher needs to observe the students as they write to determine those outlines causing hesitation. Outlines causing difficulty should be reviewed on the chalkboard or screen before the dictation is repeated; otherwise students will continue to hesitate or write incorrect outlines each time the dictation is repeated.

Teachers may fear that their students are memorizing the dictation when it is repeated several times, rather than concentrating on what is being dictated. By changing a word here and there in the dictation as it is repeated, the teacher can quickly determine whether the students are actually taking the dictation. If students read back the original wording rather than what was dictated in the last repetition, it is obvious they need to concentrate more on the material. Changing an occasional word in repeated dictation will help to develop concentration and a meaningful response to what is dictated.

Reading Back Dictation

One way to increase the amount of time available for dictation is to limit the time devoted to reading it back. Reading back one fourth of the dictation gives an adequate indication of whether students are able to keep up with the dictation rate and still write legible notes. When asking students to read back from their notes, however, remember that those students who are working to pass lower rates of speed should not be expected to read back notes taken at the fastest rates dictated. It is enough that they attempt to record the material. Shorthand notes are not likely to be legible when the dictation rate is well beyond a student's speed-building objective.

Sustained Dictation

In every speed-building session, students should receive not only short spurts of speed-building dictation but also some sustained dictation. For students just beginning to write shorthand, sustained dictation may be 30 seconds of uninterrupted dictation. With a few days' writing practice, one minute of dictation may represent sustained dictation. Later in the shorthand program, as the students develop writing skill, one minute becomes simply a "speed spurt," with three to five minutes representing sustained dictation. During the second year of the shorthand program the teacher may dictate speeches, minutes, articles for publication, or a series of business memorandums and letters for a period of 20 to 30 minutes and instruct the students to transcribe the material dictated. In this case, the dictation may be timed or it may be dictated "office-style." The main objective is to prepare the students for the type of sustained dictation encountered in the office.

What constitutes sustained dictation depends on the writing skill of the students. Early in the shorthand course, it may be 30 seconds, while near the end of the two-year program, 30 minutes may be sustained dictation. Three- or five-minute timed dictation takes, however, are always considered tests of sustained writing ability since they measure the students' maximum recording rate.

Three- or Five-Minute Takes

Should three-minute or five-minute dictation tests be used to measure the speed development of shorthand students? Some teachers contend that the two tests measure exactly the same degree of skill and that therefore to use a five-minute test is a waste of time and effort for both teacher and students. Others argue that tests of different lengths cannot possibly measure the same skill.

In 1970 Pullis reported the results of an experimental study to determine whether three- and five-minute shorthand takes did indeed provide the same measure of skill. He reported for takes dictated at 60 and 80 wam a median average difference of 20 wam between the two lengths of dictation takes and a mean average difference of 16 wam. Students who could pass a three-minute dictation take at 80 wam could be expected to pass only a 60-wam take dictated for five minutes.[15]

Each shorthand teacher must decide whether to use three-minute or five-minute dictation tests or both. The five-minute test does require more class time to administer and to grade. Regardless of the length of test used, the significant point is to understand the difference in what the two tests measure. A student who passes a three-minute dictation test at 60 wam does not have the same degree of recording skill as the student who passes a five-minute test at 60 wam.

Timing the Dictation

DICTATION IN 20 STANDARD-WORD GROUPS. Much of the material for shorthand dictation is counted in groups of 20 standard words, and each group of 20 standard words is marked with a superior figure. Thus to dictate at 60 wam, the teacher must dictate up to the third superior figure in one minute; to dictate at 80, to the fourth superior figure; at 100, to the fifth; and so on. The chart on page 181 is designed to assist teachers in dictating at a given rate of speed, using a stop watch or a watch with a second hand.

DICTATION IN QUARTER MINUTES. Some dictation material, especially material designed for three- or five-minute dictation takes,

CONVERSION TABLE FOR DICTATION SPEEDS

						WORDS A MINUTE							
Groups of 20:	40	50	60	70	80	90	100	110	120	130	140	150	160
						TIME INTERVALS IN SECONDS							
	30	24	20	17	15	13	12	11	10	9	8	8	7
	60	48	40	34	30	26	24	22	20	18	17	16	15
	30	12	60	51	45	40	36	33	30	27	25	24	22
	60	36	20	08	60	53	48	44	40	37	34	32	30
		60	40	25	15	06	60	55	50	46	42	40	37
			60	42	30	20	12	06	60	55	51	48	45
				60	45	33	24	17	10	04	60	56	52
					60	47	36	28	20	14	08	04	60
						60	48	39	30	23	17	12	07
							60	50	40	32	25	20	15
								60	50	41	34	28	22
									60	51	42	36	30
										60	51	44	37
											60	52	45
												60	52
													60

Example: To dictate at 70 wam material counted in groups of 20 standard words, place your finger on the line that reads "Groups of 20." Run your finger along that line until you reach 70. Drop down to the first figure below the rule, which is 17. To dictate at 70 wam material counted in groups of 20 words, dictate each group in 17 seconds. The figures below 17 indicate the points on the watch where the second hand should be at the end of each group of 20 words. These time indications have been carried through the first 2 minutes.

is marked in quarter minutes rather than in 20 standard-word groups. Each piece of material to be dictated in 15 seconds is marked with a diagonal or a slash. Such designated-rate material is easy to dictate since it is marked for a specific dictation speed. The dictator need only be sure to dictate each group of words within a quarter minute. Unlike the 20 standard-word group, which always contains 20 standard words, in the designated-rate material the number of standard words in the quarter minute of dictation varies according to the speed for which the dictation is designed.

Such material is easy to dictate at the designated rates, but it is also easy to use for dictation at other rates. If a teacher wishes to use designated-rate material marked at 90 wam for dictation speed building, how can the quarter minutes be converted to the number of seconds required to dictate at 100 or 110 wam? The conversion formula developed by Grubbs enables the teacher to determine the number of seconds to use for dictating each slash- or diagonal-marked group of words at a speed other than that designated.[16] The Grubbs formula has been applied to the designated rates of 120, 100, 80, and 60 to provide for dictation ranging from 60 to 140 wam. To use the table on pages 184 and 185, locate the speed at which the take is designated, and the rate at which the dictation is to be given.

The figures in the column under the conversion speed represent the number of seconds in which each slash-marked piece should be dictated.

The number of seconds in which each marked group of words (standard word group) should be dictated can be calculated by using the formula described by Grubbs:

$$\frac{\text{Standard Word Count}}{\text{Desired Rate}} \times 60 \text{ seconds} = \frac{\text{seconds per diagonal-marked}}{\text{group of words}}$$

To determine the standard word count, always divide the designated rate by 4, because designated-rate material is marked in quarter minutes. (At the designated rate, each standard word group is dictated in 15 seconds, and four of these groups are dictated in one minute.) Example: The designated rate for the material to be used is 100 wam. Divide the 100 by 4 to obtain the standard word count for each diagonal- or slash-marked group of words in this 100-wam material. The standard word count then is 25. If one wishes to use the material for dictation speed building at 110, 120, or 130 wam, the application of the formula would be:

$\frac{25}{110} \times 60 = 13+$ seconds per slash-marked group, or per standard group, of words for dictation at 110 wam.

$\frac{25}{120} \times 60 = 12.5$ seconds per slash-marked group, or per standard group, of words for dictation at 120 wam.

$\frac{25}{130} \times 60 = 11+$ seconds per slash-marked group, or per standard group, of words for dictation at 130 wam.

Marking Material for Dictation

Occasionally a teacher may wish to dictate material that has not been marked for dictation. Syllable counting and marking material for dictation is a simple process every teacher should understand.

TWENTY STANDARD-WORD GROUPS. A standard word, as designated by the authors of Gregg shorthand, consists of 1.4 syllables. Thus, a 20 standard-word group always contains 28 syllables, (20 × 1.4 = 28). Simply count 28 syllables in the unmarked material and place a superior figure 1 above the word. Continue counting 28-syllable groups and marking superior figures 2, 3, and so on for each consecutive group.

When the twenty-eighth syllable occurs in the middle of a word, the superior figure for the word group is placed either before or after the word, whichever point is closest to the actual count. However, when continuing to count the next 28 syllables, the count begins exactly where it stopped, in the middle of the word, not where the superior figure was placed.

In counting figures, every syllable is counted. Thus $1,285,662.98 would be counted as a total of 24 syllables (one million two hundred eighty-five thousand six hundred sixty-two dollars and ninety-eight cents).

QUARTER MINUTES. To mark material in quarter minutes for designated-speed dictation, multiply the desired speed by 1.4 (the number of syllables in a standard word) and divide the result by 4. For example, if you wish to dictate some material at 90 wam, multiply 90 by 1.4 and divide this product by 4; i.e., $90 \times 1.4 \div 4 = 31.5$ syllables to be dictated in each quarter minute. Since it is impossible to divide a syllable, you mark off 31 syllables in the first word group, 32 in the second, 31 in the third, 32 in the fourth and so on throughout the rest of the material.

Dictation Techniques for the Teacher

DICTATE SKILLFULLY. The way a teacher dictates appreciably affects the students' ability to record the dictation. Dictation at 60 wam can sound like 80 when some teachers dictate, yet others may dictate at 60 and it sounds slow and easy. Teachers who dictate in a high-pitched voice create hurdles for their students. A low-pitched voice sounds quieter and calmer, but students should not have to strain to hear the dictation. Dictation in which each word is evenly spaced throughout the dictation intervals causes problems. Students will miss common phrases and will devote as much time to the writing of simple words such as *the, a, at, of,* and *and* as they do to more difficult or longer outlines for which they need additional time. The dictation should be given as naturally as possible. Even at extremely slow rates, short phrases should not be broken and the dictation should be as smooth and natural as the dictator can make it.

When conducting a dictation speed-building exercise, pause at the end of the step of the plan without saying anything, to give students who are still writing an opportunity to finish what is being retained in memory. Such a procedure encourages the student to work on retention and to write every word that can be retained.

TIME THE DICTATION. Teachers who dictate without using a stop watch or a watch with a second hand are seldom able to demonstrate this skill accurately. When asked to dictate at a given rate, they may miss by 20 to 30 wam. They may misjudge the dictation rate by at least 10 to 20 wam when asked to indicate how fast dictation was given. If students are to build their writing skill systematically

TIMING INTERVALS FOR CONVERTED DICTATION
TAKES ALREADY MARKED OFF AT 15-SECOND INTERVALS

120-wam Take Converted to:

60	70	80	90	100	110	130	140
30	26	23	20	18	16	14	13
60	51	45	40	36	33	28	26
30	17	8	60	54	49	42	39
60	43	30	20	12	6	55	51
30	9	53	40	30	23	9	4
*60	34	15	60	48	39	23	17
	60	38	20	6	56	37	30
		60	40	24	12	51	43
			60	42	28	5	56
				60	45	19	9
					60	32	21
						46	34
						60	47
							60

100-wam Take Converted to:

60	70	80	90	110	120	130	140
25	19	19	17	14	13	12	11
50	38	37	33	27	25	23	21
15	57	56	50	41	38	35	32
40	16	15	7	55	50	46	43
5	35	34	23	8	3	58	54
30	54	53	40	22	15	9	4
55	13	11	57	35	28	21	14
	32	30	13	49	40	32	25
	51	49	30	3	53	44	35
			47	17	5	55	46
				30	18	7	56
				44	30	18	7
				58	43	30	17
					55	41	28
						53	38
							49
							59

*Underscore indicates 3 minutes of dictation if figure is 60; if not, stop dictating at 60 seconds immediately after the underscored figure. For example, if underscored figure is 55 (as a 100-wam take dictated at 60 wam), this indicates dictation for 2 minutes and 55 seconds; continue to dictate for another 5 seconds.

80-wam Take Converted to:

60	70	90	100	110	120	130	140
20	17	13	12	11	10	9	9
40	34	27	24	22	20	18	17
60	51	40	36	33	30	28	26
20	9	53	48	44	40	37	34
40	26	7	60	55	50	46	43
60	43	20	12	6	60	55	51
20	60	33	24	17	10	5	60
40	17	47	36	28	20	14	9
60	34	60	48	39	30	23	17
	51	13	60	50	40	32	26
		27		1	50	42	34
		40		12	60	51	43
		53		23		60	51
				34		9	
				45		18	
				56		28	
						37	
						46	
						55	

60-wam Take Converted to:

70	80	90	100	110	120	130	140
13	11	10	9	8	8	7	6
26	22	20	18	16	15	14	13
39	33	30	27	24	23	21	19
51	45	40	36	33	30	28	25
4	56	50	45	41	38	35	32
17	7	60	54	49	45	42	38
30	18	10	3	57	53	49	45
43	30	20	12	5	60	56	51
56	41	30	21	14	8	3	58
9	52	40	30	22	15	10	4
21	3	50	39	30	23	17	11
34	15	60	48	38	30	24	17
47	26		57	46	38	31	24
60	37		6	55	45	38	30
	48		15	3	53	45	37
	60		24	11	60	52	43
			33	19	8	59	50
			42	27	15	6	56
			51	35	23	13	3
			60	44	30	20	9

Many teachers prefer to "sweep back" the second hand and start timing at 0 rather than to continue with new seconds for the second minute, etc. Example: In dictating at 70 wam from material designated to be dictated at 100 wam, dictate to the first slash in 19 seconds, to the second slash in 38 seconds, to the third slash in 57 seconds, sweep back to 0 and continue dictating, using the intervals of 19, 38, 57 again.

throughout the shorthand program, dictation practice must be accurately timed. Students should not be told they received dictation at a given rate unless it was carefully timed.

ADJUSTING INACCURATE DICTATION RATES. If a teacher's dictation rate is only a few words too fast or too slow, an adjustment can be made for it through the remainder of the dictation. For example, if the teacher is using the one-minute speed-builder plan and discovers at the end of the first standard word group the dictation is a few words a minute too slow, then these words can be made up while dictating the other word groups in the minute take. However, if instead of 100 wam as announced, the actual dictation rate is only 80 wam at the end of 30 seconds, the teacher should simply stop and say the rate was too slow and repeat the dictation.

DICTATING AT A RATE THAT PRECLUDES DRAWING OUTLINES. The rate of dictation should not encourage students to draw their shorthand outlines. Dictation rates of 40 and 50 wam, which are slower than most students' longhand writing rates, make drawing shorthand outlines possible. For this reason, dictation at rates less than 60 wam is rarely justified.

ANNOUNCING THE DICTATION RATE. Teachers generally announce the dictation rate immediately preceding the dictation. This gives the students a definite speed objective toward which to work throughout the speed-building period. However, announcing the rate after the dictation has been given is also acceptable. When students become discouraged or feel unable to achieve certain dictation rates, less tension is generated if they are not aware of the rate until after the take is completed. Once they have demonstrated that they can write shorthand outlines at a given rate, the teacher may resume the practice of announcing the dictation rate in advance.

DICTATE AT RATES THAT BUILD MAXIMUM SKILL. When the minimum dictation-competency standard for the first semester has been achieved by one or more students, faster dictation tests should be administered to these students. For example, if the minimum dictation-competency level is 60 wam, 70- or 80-wam takes are essential for those who have satisfied the minimum competency standard. The rate of dictation, both for speed building and for dictation testing, should permit all students to develop their shorthand speed as rapidly as possible.

OBSERVE STUDENTS DURING DICTATION SPEED-BUILDING PRACTICE. A skillful dictator keeps one eye on the dictation copy and the stop watch and the other on the students. In some cases, the teacher may assist students at their desks when the dictation is finished. At other times, outlines may be written on the chalkboard or transparency for the benefit of the entire class. While moving about the room during dictation speed-building practice, the teacher can determine whether the students are keeping up with the dictation and writing the outlines fluently or are encountering problems in recording the dictation.

TEACH THE STUDENTS TO DICTATE. Students should be taught the meaning of the superior figures in their transcripts so that they can time their reading rates and determine typewritten transcription rates. They can also use these figures to dictate to each other. After the first semester of instruction, encourage students to do their homework in pairs, first reading the assignment and then dictating the material to one another. This procedure supplements the dictation practice they receive in class. It is especially beneficial when dictation tapes are not available for the students to check out for homework practice. Teach them the simple one-minute speed-forcing and one-minute speed-builder plans for use during homework practice.

Speed-Building Plans

Shorthand teachers need to be familiar with the various speed-building plans and to know when they can be used most effectively. Most speed-building plans and their objectives can be explained to students in sufficient detail in two or three minutes. This is recommended, as it enables them to understand the purpose of the plan being used and to relate it to their speed-building goals. Withholding an explanation of the plan to be used or its objective can result in frustration and discouragement when the rate of dictation increases and students find they are unable to keep up. When they understand the strategy of speed-building plans, they know that at some point they may not be able to record all that was dictated.

Among the speed-building plans described in the following paragraphs, some start at low rates of speed and build to higher levels, while others start fast, then decrease to lower dictation rates. Pawelski (1966) reports that there is no evidence to support either of these approaches as better than the other in developing competency in recording shorthand outlines at faster rates.[17]

USING THE ONE-MINUTE DICTATION SPEED-DEVELOPMENT PLAN. The one-minute plan is frequently used for building shorthand writing speed. While there are variations, basically the plan involves dictating the same material several times at increasing rates of speed, with pauses between repetitions for checks on achievement, adding additional words to the chalkboard or screen, and reviewing the words on the chalkboard or screen.

ONE-MINUTE SPEED BUILDER. One of the easiest dictation speed-building plans to execute is the one-minute speed builder. Time remains constant; but with each repetition of a letter fragment, the rate is stepped up.

An example of the plan in action should clarify its use with shorthand students. Suppose most members of the class have passed a three-minute, new-matter take at 60 wam. The goal is to help them push their shorthand outline-writing competency to three minutes at 70 wam. Using the one-minute speed-builder plan, proceed in the following manner:

Step 1. Select easy, new-matter dictation containing approximately 270 words. Three letters of about 90 words each will suffice, or choose one long letter of 270 words.

Step 2. Preview at the chalkboard or overhead projector the first 90-word letter, or the first 90-word fragment if one long letter has been selected. Dictate the first 60 words of the letter in one minute. Check on student achievement, add additional troublesome words to the preview, and read/write the preview again. Now dictate the first 70 words of the letter; i.e., the first 60 words plus an additional 10 words in the minute. Practice the preview words again and dictate the first 80 words in a minute. Repeat the dictation at this rate until one-half or more of the students get the take at 80 wam. Then dictate the entire 90-word letter in one-minute. Repeat this step until half or more of the class get the take at 90 wam.

Step 3. Follow exactly the procedure just outlined with the second 90-word letter (or letter fragment). Remember to preview the second take and to proceed to the third letter or letter fragment when at least half of the class can get the second letter.

Step 4. Use the same procedure outlined for the two previous letters or letter fragments with the third 90-word letter or letter fragment. Be sure to preview the third take and to proceed to the final step in the plan when approximately half of the students can record the third letter or letter fragment of 90 words.

Step 5. Ask the students to rapidly read and then write the shorthand outlines in all three preview lists. Then dictate all three 90-word letters or the single 270-word letter without pause at the rates of 70 or 80 wam. Remind the students to write only as fast as they must and to give maximum thought to outline accuracy. Repeat the final take if necessary. Teachers sometimes elect to have the final take read back in concert.

The value of the one-minute speed builder rests in the repetitions and in pushing each student's rates for the one-minute takes to 20 wam above the rate set as the goal. Thus, if the goal is three minutes at 80 wam, choose three letters of 100 words each (or one letter of 300 words) to provide sufficient material for three one-minute takes at the rate of 100 wam.

The diagram on page 189 summarizes the organization of the one-minute speed-builder plan when the goal is 90 wam for three minutes.

ONE-MINUTE SPEED-FORCING PLAN. The one-minute speed-forcing plan is a variation of the one-minute speed-builder plan. With this plan, the dictation rates increase three times rather than four, and the controlled writing is done at the end of each minute rather

ONE-MINUTE SPEED-BUILDER PLAN

Letter material: 330 words
Goal: 90 wam

Four 1-minute takes; first 110-word letter or fragment:	1. Rate: 80 wam 2. Rate: 90 wam 3. Rate: 100 wam 4. Rate: 110 wam	
	Four 1-minute takes; second 110-word letter or fragment:	5. Rate: 80 wam 6. Rate: 90 wam 7. Rate: 100 wam 8. Rate: 110 wam
		Four 1-minute takes; third 110-word letter or fragment: 9. Rate: 80 wam 10. Rate: 90 wam 11. Rate: 100 wam 12. Rate: 110 wam
Finally, dictate all material:	13. Control rate: 90 wam	

than at the end of the three minutes. The procedure for previewing, checking on achievement, adding additional words, and reviewing are the same as those used in the one-minute speed-builder plan.

The chart that follows summarizes the steps in the one-minute speed-forcing plan.

ONE-MINUTE SPEED-FORCING PLAN

Letter material: 270 words
Goal: 80 wam

1st Minute:	Dictate at 70 wam Dictate at 80 wam Dictate at 90 wam Dictate at controlled rate of 80
2d Minute:	Same as first minute
3d Minute:	Same as first 2 minutes
3 Minutes:	Dictate at 80 wam for controlled writing

Many teachers follow the practice of dictating a letter, supposedly using a repetitive one-minute speed-builder plan. When they finish practicing one letter, they go on to the next. If the letters are approximately one minute long, this procedure is satisfactory; however, if the letters are of different lengths, the time base changes according to the length of the letter, and it is impossible for either the teacher or the student to determine the speed-building progress resulting from the repetitive practice. For example, a letter of 60 words dictated at 60 wam would be dictated in one minute; dictated at 80 it would require only 45 seconds, and at 100 only 36 seconds. In this case the dictation declines from one minute to just over a half minute. True, the student's writing rate has increased, but since the length of the dictation period has decreased by nearly half, it cannot be determined whether the student could have maintained the dictation rate of 100 wam for a full minute. Maintaining the one-minute time base not only helps the teacher measure the students' performances, but also motivates the students, since they, too, can better evaluate their speed-building progress.

A SAMPLE ONE-MINUTE SPEED-BUILDER LESSON PLAN
(Gregg Shorthand, Series 90)

Today's Homework:	Lesson 67
Tomorrow's Homework:	Lesson 68

Assignment:	Lesson 67—Read and write paragraphs 597 through 600 twice. Self-dictate and punctuate paragraph 601. Study transcription drill *one of* and vocabulary words *bearable, eventful,* and *milestones.*

Warmup:	From Lesson 66, dictate paragraph 591 (brief-form emphasis) for two minutes at 70 wam. (Used previous day for speed building—entire class should be able to get this dictation easily.)
	(3 min.)

New-Matter Dictation:	Have individual students read paragraphs 604, 605, and 606, Lesson 68, pages 303 and 304. Students read in punctuation and give the reason for the punctuation.

Preview letter 604 on chalkboard or transparency.

Dictate for one minute letter 604 at 60, 70, 80, and 90 wam. Review the preview list between dictations and add other troublesome words.

Preview letter 605 on chalkboard or transparency.

Dictate letter 605 for one minute at 60, 70, 80, and 90 wam. Review the preview list between dictations and add troublesome words.

Preview letter 606 on chalkboard or transparency.

Dictate letter 606 for one minute at 60, 70, 80, and 90 wam. Review the preview list between dictations and add other troublesome words.

Review all preview lists. Combine letters 604, 605, and 606 and dictate at 80 wam for controlled writing.

Instruct students to silently read their notes and insert needed punctuation and coded reasons. Select students to read aloud their shorthand notes, identifying needed punctuation and reasons for choices.

(24 min.)

Transcription Review: Ask students to read and punctuate paragraph 608, page 305, giving applicable punctuation rules.

(3 min.)

USING THE 30-SECOND SPEED-FORCING PLAN. The 30-second speed-forcing plan is similar to the one-minute speed-forcing plan. In this plan, the material used is a series of 30-second takes. Each 30-second take is repeated at successively higher rates in the following manner:

1. Dictate the first 30 seconds at 70 wam.
2. Repeat the first 30 seconds at 80 wam.
3. Repeat the first 30 seconds at 90 wam.
4. Dictate the first 30 seconds at the control rate of 80 wam, or omit this step if desired.

191

5. Dictate the next 30 seconds at 70, 80, and 90 wam.
6. Continue with this procedure until six 30-second takes have been dictated at 70, 80, and 90 wam.
7. Dictate the entire three minutes at 70 wam without pause.

It is, of course, assumed that the teacher will preview and review between dictations and add any needed words.

USING THE SENTENCE SPEED-BUILDING PLAN. As the name implies, this plan uses sentences as the base for speed building. Assuming that the students are now taking dictation at 70 wam, the teacher would follow these procedures:

1. Select three letters of approximately 100 words each.
2. Preview the first letter on the chalkboard.
3. Dictate the first sentence at 120 wam.
4. Dictate the second sentence at 120 wam.
5. Dictate the first two sentences at 120 wam.
6. Dictate the third sentence at 120 wam.
7. Dictate the first three sentences at 120 wam.
8. Continue this procedure until all the sentences in the letter have been dictated at 120 wam.
9. Dictate the entire letter at 100 wam.
10. Follow the same procedure for the next two letters.
11. Dictate the three letters at 90 wam.

A variation of the above plan omits Steps (4) and (6). In this case the procedure is as follows:

1. Dictate the first sentence at 120 wam.
2. Dictate the first and second sentences at 120 wam.
3. Dictate the first, second, and third sentences at 120 wam.
4. Continue this procedure until all sentences in the letter have been dictated.
5. Dictate the entire letter at 100 wam.

This sentence speed-building plan is especially useful during the first semester of shorthand instruction, using a lower dictation rate.

USING THE STAIR-STEP PLAN. Advocated by Robert L. Grubbs, the stair-step plan is excellent for building speed, endurance, and new vocabulary skills.[18] The plan may be used easily in any speed range and with any business letter content. Although the exact number of words in each letter is not important, letters of about 80 to 100 words are recommended at the beginning of the second semester.

The chart on page 183 illustrates the plan graphically and the explanation that follows it will help to administer the plan.

Choose four or five letters averaging 80 to 100 words in length. On the assumption that the class is attempting to pass a new-matter dictation test at 70, 80, and 90 wam, follow these steps:

Step 1. Preview letter 1 at the chalkboard or overhead projector. Dictate the letter at 80 wam. Determine how many students got the take. Place additional outlines on the chalkboard or overhead. If most of the students were able to write letter 1 at 80 wam, move to Step 2. If necessary, repeat the dictation of letter 1 at 80, or at a lower rate if it appears that 80 is too great a challenge.

Step 2. Dictate letter 1 at 90 wam, and without pause between the closing line and the salutation, dictate letter 2 at 80 wam. As letter 2 is being dictated, place any new or unfamiliar outlines in it on the chalkboard or overhead projector. Determine how many of the students got each individual letter. Read aloud and in concert *all* the words on the chalkboard or overhead projector, adding any student-requested outlines to those already there. Repeat Step 2, if necessary, until all or almost all the students get both letters.

Step 3. Dictate letter 1 at 100 wam. Follow immediately with letter 2 at 90 and with letter 3 at 80, placing the unfamiliar outlines in this letter on the chalkboard or overhead projector. Read all the words, adding any that may be requested. Repeat Step 3, if necessary.

Step 4. Dictate letter 1 at 110 wam, letter 2 at 100, letter 3 at 90,

The Stair-Step Plan

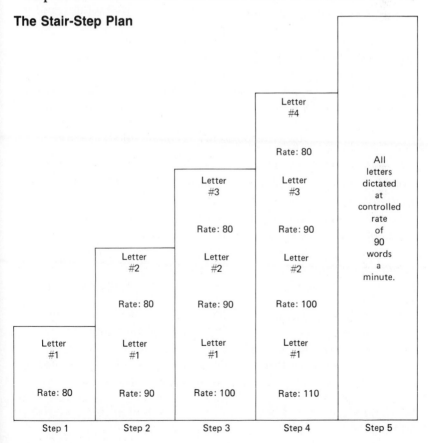

Step 1	Step 2	Step 3	Step 4	Step 5
			Letter #4	
			Rate: 80	
		Letter #3	Letter #3	All letters dictated at controlled rate of 90 words a minute.
		Rate: 80	Rate: 90	
	Letter #2	Letter #2	Letter #2	
	Rate: 80	Rate: 90	Rate: 100	
Letter #1	Letter #1	Letter #1	Letter #1	
Rate: 80	Rate: 90	Rate: 100	Rate: 110	

and letter 4 at 80. Write selected outlines from letter 4 on the chalkboard or overhead projector while dictating it. Have all the preview vocabulary read in concert, and either repeat Step 4 or proceed to Step 5.

Step 5. Dictate letters 1, 2, 3, and 4 without pause at 90 wam. This will be a take of about three minutes' duration. The rate, 90 wam, is enough below the maximum to which students have been pushed, and there have been sufficient repetitions, so that they should be able to write this take with ease and confident control.

Using five letters, without repeating any of the steps, would take about 25 minutes for the complete procedure. The four-letter sequence illustrated would consume about 17 minutes of class time. On days when only three letters are used in the stair-step sequence, consider using the plan twice, using two separate sets of letters for increased vocabulary exposure.

USING THE PYRAMID SPEED-BUILDING PLAN. This speed-building plan developed by Clyde I. Blanchard is designed to increase the students' speed of writing shorthand by 20 wam on a five-minute take.[19] The plan assumes that most students can write for 30 seconds at a speed 50 wam faster than they can write for five minutes, and for one minute at 40 wam faster than they can for five minutes.

To illustrate the plan, assume the students are writing shorthand at a speed of 80 wam on new matter and the goal is to increase their speed to 100 wam on a previewed five-minute take. The strategy is to increase the students' speed to 150 wam for 30 seconds, 140 wam for one minute, 130 wam for two minutes, 120 wam for three minutes, 110 wam for four minutes, and finally reach the goal of 100 wam for five minutes. The following steps are recommended:

Step 1. Preview ten percent of the words contained in a 500-word selection of business letters.

Step 2. Dictate a 240-word segment of the selected take at the students' present shorthand writing speed—80 wam.

Step 3. Preview the first 280-word segment of the take, using the chalkboard or overhead projector screen. Ask students to read the outlines rapidly and then to write them from dictation.

Step 4. Dictate the first four 30-second segments at 150 wam, pausing briefly between dictations. One or two of the segments may be read back.

Step 5. Review and then redictate the four 30-second segments as two one-minute takes at 140 wam. The second one-minute segment of the take should be read back.

Step 6. Repeat the procedure in Steps 4 and 5 for the remainder of the dictation take.

Step 7. Review and then redictate the first 260-word segment as a two-minute take at 130 wam. The final minute of the take should be read back.

CHAPTER 6: DICTATION SPEED BUILDING

Step 8. Review and then redictate the first 360-word segment as a three-minute take at 120 wam. The second minute of the take should be read back.

Step 9. Review and redictate the first 440-word segment as a four-minute take at 110 wam. The second and third minute of the take should be read back.

Step 10. Following a short rest, redictate the entire five-minute take at 100 wam. The second half of the take should be read back.

USING THE INVERTED-PYRAMID SPEED-BUILDING PLAN. Like the stair-step plan, the inverted-pyramid plan is designed to build both speed and sustained writing skill. Although entitled *the inverted-pyramid plan,* it has little resemblance to Blanchard's basic concepts of decreasing speed as the length of dictation increases.

Assuming that a class is able to take dictation at 60 wam and is trying to pass dictation takes at 80, the procedure would be as follows:

1. Preview the letter or letters.
2. Dictate the first minute at 60 wam.
3. Dictate the first minute at 80 wam and the second minute at 60 wam without pausing.
4. Dictate the first minute at 100, the second minute at 80, and the third minute at 60 without pausing.
5. Dictate the first minute at 120 wam, the second at 100, the third at 80, and the last minute at 60 wam.

THE INVERTED-PYRAMID PLAN*

REPETITION	1ST MINUTE	2D MINUTE	3D MINUTE	4TH MINUTE
1	60	—	—	—
2	80	60	—	—
3	100	80	60	—
4	120	100	80	60

*Allien R. Russon, "Methods of Teaching Shorthand Monograph 119," South-Western Publishing Company, Cincinnati, OH, 1968, p. 27.

USING THE 3 × 4 SPEED-BUILDING PLAN. This plan is recommended for second-year shorthand.[20] In the illustration below, it is assumed that the class is working to pass dictation tests at 100 wam.

1. Preview three minutes of a five-minute take.
2. Dictate the first 30 seconds at 140 wam.
3. Dictate the next 30 seconds at 140 wam.
4. Dictate the first two 30 seconds without pausing at 120 wam.
5. Repeat steps 2, 3, and 4 for the third and fourth 30 seconds of dictation.
6. Dictate the entire take at 100 wam for three minutes.

195

THE 3 × 4 PLAN

STEP 1	30 sec. at 140	**STEP 2**	30 sec. at 140
STEP 3		1 min. at 120	
STEP 4	30 sec. at 140	**STEP 5**	30 sec. at 140
STEP 6		1 min. at 120	
STEP 7		3 min. at 100	

USING THE MICROMOLAR SPEED-BUILDING PLAN. The micromolar plan is one of the newer, innovative approaches to speed building. The speed-building dictation is given at the same rate throughout, but copies of the plate material being dictated are gradually withdrawn until the student must finally take the dictation without any reference to the shorthand plates. The plan was originally used in introducing dictation in beginning shorthand and for building speed throughout the shorthand course. A number of modifications of the plan have been developed, but the steps followed are usually those given below:

- Five writing plates are prepared by the teacher for each lesson. The first plate displays the entire passage in shorthand. In the second plate, 20 percent of the shorthand outlines have been omitted. In the third plate, 40 percent of the outlines have been omitted. In the fourth plate, 60 percent of the outlines have been omitted. In the fifth plate, 80 percent of the outlines have been omitted.
- The students write over each plate as the material is dictated, filling in the outlines that are omitted. For instance, during the first dictation they will use the first plate, which contains all the shorthand outlines. On the next dictation they will have to fill in 20 percent of the outlines; on the third dictation, 40 percent, and so on.
- The dictation is given at a constant rate, such as 80 or 100 wam, throughout the course of study.
- Finally, the material is dictated without any of the shorthand outlines visible to the students, again at a constant rate.

The micromolar plan not only gradually withdraws the shorthand plate support from the beginning student but also relies heavily on repetitive dictation, since the material is dictated at least six times, once for each of the five plates and a final time without the assistance of plate material. Developing the five plates needed for each day's lesson is time-consuming, and for that reason the plan is not widely used by classroom teachers.

A number of adaptations of the micromolar speed-building plan have been developed, primarily for research. For instance, a teacher might choose to dictate a ten-word group at 120 wam, followed by a five-second pause until six groups of ten words each had been dictated. The second time, the same material might be dictated in ten-word groups at 120 wam with a four-second pause between groups. During the third dictation, the pause would be decreased to three seconds between groups, and so on, until finally the entire six groups would be dictated without pause at 120 wam in one minute. Regardless of the particular plan followed, the dictation rate remains constant.

USING THE FAST CUE-RESPONSE SPEED-BUILDING PLAN. An adaptation of the micromolar speed-building plan, the fast cue-response plan has been developed primarily for research. Specifically, the plan is executed as follows:

- Select any standard dictation material counted in groups of 20 standard words.
- Divide each 20-word block approximately in half, giving groups of approximately ten standard words.
- 120 wam base speed—each ten-word group should be dictated in five seconds. The length of pauses will depend on the speed of dictation desired.

40 wam =	10-second pause between groups of 10 words of dictation
50 wam =	7-second pause between groups of 10 words of dictation
60 wam =	5-second pause between groups of 10 words of dictation
70 wam =	3½-second pause between groups of 10 words of dictation
80 wam =	2½-second pause between groups of 10 words of dictation
90 wam =	1½-second pause between groups of 10 words of dictation
100 wam =	1-second pause between groups of 10 words of dictation
110 wam =	½-second pause between groups of 10 words of dictation
120 wam =	Continuous dictation at 120 wam

Special-Purpose Speed-Building Drills[21]

Teachers may wish to try a dictation procedure designed to build speed or to develop sustained writing, which would not usually be classified as a speed-building plan. These speed-building techniques can be excellent means of providing variety and interest in the classroom, but it is important to understand exactly what they are designed for and what they can do. They should not be used extensively for speed-building. Some of the procedures which might be so classified are described in the following paragraphs.

PROGRESSIVE WEEKLY PLAN. This plan can be especially effective for a warmup at the beginning of the shorthand period and can build student interest in seeing how much speed can actually be developed on repetitive material in the course of a week. The teacher selects an easy letter, sometimes a phrase or brief-form letter, and challenges the students to try to double their dictation rate on the letter in a week.

- **Day 1:** Dictate the letter at 60 wam, a second time at 70, a third time at 80, and a fourth time at 60.
- **Day 2:** Dictate the letter at 70, 80, 90, and 70.
- **Day 3:** Dictate the letter at 80, 90, 100, and 80.
- **Day 4:** Dictate the letter at 90, 100, 110, and 90.
- **Day 5:** Dictate the letter at 100, 110, 120, and 100.

By the end of the week students should have increased their writing speed on the letter by approximately 40 to 60 wam.

PROGRESSIVE PLAN. This plan is designed for occasional use in second-semester and advanced shorthand. Some teachers use the plan as a warmup before giving dictation takes to be transcribed.

- Preview the entire take.
- Dictate each minute of the take at a faster rate without pausing between takes.
- If most of the class is writing 80 wam, the first minute of the dictation might be at 60; the second, at 80; the third, at 100; and the fourth, at 120.

REVERSE PLAN. This plan is the reverse of the progressive plan.[22] Like the progressive plan, it should be used only occasionally, generally in advanced shorthand.

- Omit the preview if the plan is being used in advanced shorthand.
- Dictate each minute at a lower speed, without pausing between minutes.
- If most of the class is writing at 80 wam, dictate the first minute at 120; the second minute at 100; the third minute at 80; and the fourth minute at 60.
- Place troublesome words on the chalkboard after the dictation is completed.

PROGRESSIVE DICTATION. Progressive dictation may be given as a warmup at the beginning of a dictation period or may be used to stimulate students' interest in increasing their shorthand writing speeds. For this procedure, each line is dictated in six seconds and the dictation rate gradually increases, often finishing as much as 60 wam faster than the first six seconds of dictation. As long as the teacher dictates each line in six seconds, the material will be dictated at the rate indicated at the end of each line. An illustration of material typed for progressive dictation is shown on page 199.[23]

LETTER TYPED FOR PROGRESSIVE DICTATION
(Dictation interval is 6 seconds a line)

	Dictation Rate
Dear Mrs. Johnston: Thank you very much	80 wam
for forwarding to me the interesting din-	80 wam
ner programs for the first annual banquet for	90 wam
the Mary Arden Literature Club. I am always	90 wam
very pleased when our collection will be increased	100 wam
with the mementos and artifacts of our North Texas	100 wam
history, and it was thoughtful of you to think of us as	110 wam
a permanent repository for this club program. Enclosed	110 wam
are three copies of our donor agreement forms. Please sign	120 wam
all three copies and return the carbon copies to us for our	120 wam
permanent records. You may keep the original for yourself. Thank	130 wam
you again, and let me extend to you an invitation to come by the	130 wam
Historical Collection so you can see what we are doing and--further--all	140 wam
we are trying to do. I think you might be much impressed with some of	140 wam
the magnificent items we have recently added to this Historical Collection.	150 wam

To prepare material for progressive dictation, first determine the rates at which each line is to be dictated. More than one line may be dictated at the same rate, but the rate never decreases. Then, using a stroke-count ruler, mark off the number of typing strokes representing the words a minute at which the line is to be dictated. In progressive and spurt dictation by Grubbs, a word is considered to

PROGRESSIVE OR SPURT DICTATION CHART
(Dictation Interval: One-Tenth of a Minute or 6 Seconds a Line)

STROKES	WORDS	DICTATION RATE
25	5	50 wam
30	6	60 wam
35	7	70 wam
40	8	80 wam
45	9	90 wam
50	10	100 wam
55	11	110 wam
60	12	120 wam
65	13	130 wam
70	14	140 wam
75	15	150 wam
80	16	160 wam

be five strokes rather than 1.4 syllables. Thus on the chart on page 199, it can be seen that if a teacher wishes to dictate the first line at 60 wam, 30 strokes, or 6 five-stroke words, would be typed on that line. If the next line is to be dictated at 70 wam, 35 strokes, or 7 words, would be typed on that line, and so on. Six seconds equal one-tenth of a minute; therefore, if 7 words are dictated in 1/10 of a minute, the rate of dictation would be 10 × 7, or 70 wam.

PROGRESSIVE OR SPURT DICTATION CHART
(Dictation Interval: One-Sixth of a Minute or 10 Seconds a Line)

STROKES	WORDS	DICTATION RATE
40	8	48 wam
45	9	54 wam
50	10	60 wam
55	11	66 wam
60	12	72 wam
65	13	78 wam
70	14	84 wam
75	15	90 wam
80	16	96 wam
85	17	102 wam
90	18	108 wam
95	19	114 wam
100	20	120 wam
105	21	126 wam
110	22	132 wam
115	23	138 wam
120	24	144 wam

Because some teachers prefer to dictate in ten-second rather than six-second intervals, the chart shown above indicates the dictation rate when material is marked for ten-second interval dictation.

SPURT DICTATION. Spurt dictation resembles progressive dictation, but the objective is to accustom students to the erratic dictation they will encounter in the office. The material is prepared in exactly the same manner as is material for progressive dictation, but the rates may increase or decrease from line to line as the dictator pauses or dictates in spurts. An illustration of material typed for spurt dictation is given on page 201.

OFFICE-STYLE DICTATION. Office-style dictation[24] simulates conditions under which dictation is taken in the office. Students who can take the smooth, even dictation of the teacher at 100 wam may have difficulty in an office recording irregular dictation that averages only 80 actual wam. The average business dictation may be 80, but students

LETTER TYPED FOR SPURT DICTATION
(Dictation interval is 6 seconds a line)

	Dictation Rate
Dear Mr. Ryan: It is such expertise and	80 wam
professionalism as yours that make us all	80 wam
proud to be in business education today.	80 wam
Your expertise was indeed quite obvious	80 wam
in the comments and responses you gave during	90 wam
the Telelecture sessions with our Issues and	90 wam
Trends class on Monday, January 5, 1980. Enclosed	100 wam
is a copy of the paper presented, which I feel sure	100 wam
could never have been so effectively presented without your	120 wam
own stimulating and enlightening comments and responses.	110 wam
Therefore, Mr. Ryan, I extend to you my sincerest	100 wam
appreciation and heartfelt gratitude for	80 wam
your helpful participation as my Telelecture guest	100 wam
speaker. We plan to publish a monograph in April which will	120 wam
include all of the Telelectures presented by several nationally known	140 wam
business educators to our graduate classes during the past five years.	140 wam
You will, of course, receive a copy of the	80 wam
monograph with my compliments just as soon as	90 wam
it comes off the press. I hope you will find this	100 wam
unusual collection both interesting and valuable.	100 wam

may not be able to cope with the short spurts of 120 to 140 wam of business vocabulary with which they are unfamiliar. Further, the material may be 10 to 20 percent faster than the 80 wam dictation to which they are accustomed because of the syllabic difference in the standard shorthand word and the average word used in business communication. In every comprehensive shorthand program, students should have experience in taking office-style dictation. In a one-year shorthand program, the amount of time devoted to office-style dictation must be limited.

Effective Use of Dictation Speed Building Plans

Various dictation speed-building plans have been discussed in the preceding pages. Teachers will need to determine which are most effective with their students at various times during the shorthand program. Following is a suggested schedule that points out the effective use of three of the plans. The same considerations need to be applied to the other plans that have been discussed.

FIRST HALF OF THE FIRST SEMESTER. The one-minute speed forcing is an effective plan because:

1. The plan is easily adapted to fit the 20-word piece and the 30-second piece in the early stages of dictation speed building.
2. The speeds are at three different rates, thus the speed range is not too great for students to manage.
3. The plan is simple, so students can understand the goals being attempted.
4. The reviews are frequent—at the end of the dictation at each rate.
5. Changing the activity at the end of each dictation from the dictation to a review of words provides built-in rest times.
6. Controlled writing is built into the plan by dropping back to controlled writing at the end of the third repetition of a piece of material.

SECOND HALF OF THE FIRST SEMESTER. The one-minute speed-forcing plan can effectively be continued. The one-minute speed builder can be added to the dictation speed-building program because:

1. Students are now at a stage to manage four different rates of dictation.
2. Students have responded to a great deal of dictation and do not need the frequency of controlled writing at the end of each dictation but can hold on longer to the dictation and work for control at the end of the plan.
3. Greater emphasis is given to sustained dictation during the second half of the semester, and the one-minute speed builder helps to develop sustained writing ability.

Second Semester and the Advanced Course

The one-minute speed-forcing and the one-minute speed-builder are still effective plans to use in the second semester and in the advanced course. However, the stair-step plan is very effective because:

1. Changing the vocabulary of the dictation several times within each step of the dictation motivates the student and helps to develop a wider shorthand vocabulary.
2. Longer pieces of dictation are used with each step, thus strengthening sustained writing ability.
3. The student at the second semester and advanced levels is able to cope with changes in vocabulary without the immediate repetitions provided in the one-minute speed forcing plan and the one-minute speed builder.

4. The five steps and five speeds in the stair-step plan better accommodate the varied speed ranges of these groups of students.

Notes

1. Joe M. Pullis, "Methods of Teaching Shorthand: A Research Analysis," *The Balance Sheet,* September 1970, pp. 16–18, 41.
2. A. E. Klein, "Variations in the Speed of Writing of Symbol Combinations in Gregg Shorthand," doctoral dissertation, New York University, New York, 1961.
3. Mildred C. Hillestad, "Factors That Contribute to the Difficulty of Shorthand Dictation Material," doctoral dissertation, University of Minnesota, Minneapolis, 1960.
4. Elaine Uthe, "An Evaluation of the Difficulty Levels of Shorthand Dictation Materials," doctoral dissertation, University of Minnesota, Minneapolis, 1966.
5. William S. Henrie, "A Comparative Analysis of Difficulty Prediction Formulas for Shorthand Dictation Material," doctoral dissertation, Utah State University, Logan, 1971.
6. Leona May Gallion, "A Comparison of Speed Dictation Development Materials and Methods in Beginning Shorthand," doctoral dissertation, Colorado State College, Greeley, 1968.
7. Delma Jo Prince, "An Experiment Comparing the Achievement in Transcription of Students When the 500 Most-Used Words Were Emphasized With the Achievement of Students When These Words Were Not Emphasized in Beginning Shorthand," master's thesis; University of Maryland, College Park, 1967.
8. Nathan R. Larsen, "The Terminal Effect of Emphasizing the Most Frequently Occurring Words in Intermediate and Advanced Gregg Shorthand," master's thesis, Brigham Young University, Provo, UT, 1970.
9. J. E. Silverthorn, *Word Division Manual for the Basic Vocabulary of Business Writing,* South-Western Publishing Company, Cincinnati, OH, 1968, pp. 85–87.
10. Violet F. Boggess, "Results of Using Dictation Materials of Varying Difficulty for Speed Building Practice in Shorthand Classes," doctoral dissertation, Ohio State University, Columbus, 1970.
11. Margaret A. McKenna, "A Study to Determine the Effect of the Early Introduction of New-Matter Dictation in the Teaching of Beginning Shorthand to College Students," doctoral dissertation, Michigan State University, East Lansing, 1965.
12. Bobbye Sorrels Pershing, "A Classroom Investigation of When to Begin New-Matter Dictation in Gregg Shorthand," doctoral dissertation, University of Oklahoma, Norman, 1966.

13. Devern J. Perry, "Phrasing in Shorthand—Factors Related to Using and Teaching Phrasing," *Balance Sheet,* September 1975, p. 8.

14. Sue Soellers, "The Effect of Previewing Words on Errors in Shorthand Outlines and Transcription in Intermediate Shorthand," doctoral dissertation, University of New Mexico, Albuquerque, 1973.

15. Joe M. Pullis, "Effect of Varying the Duration of Shorthand Dictation," *Delta Pi Epsilon Journal.* February 1970, pp. 17–20.

16. Robert L. Grubbs, "R_x for Effective Shorthand Teaching: How to Build Skill in Second-Semester Shorthand," *Business Education World,* February 1961, pp. 25–28.

17. Catherine M. Pawelski, "An Eperimental Study to Determine the Effectiveness of Fast-to-Slow Dictation in Building Speed in the Second Semester of Gregg Shorthand," master's thesis, The Catholic University of America, Washington, DC, 1966.

18. Grubbs, op. cit.

19. Clyde I. Blanchard, "My Speed-Building Experience," *Business Education World,* December 1940, pp. 345–347.

20. Grubbs, op. cit.

21. Hazel A. Flood, *Brass Tacks of Skill Building,* Prentice-Hall, Inc., Englewood Cliffs, NJ, 1951, pp. 40–41.

22. Allien R. Russon, "Methods of Teaching Shorthand," South-Western Publishing Company, Cincinnati, OH, 1968, p. 28.

23. Grubbs, op. cit.

24. Anthony A. Olinzock, "An Analysis of Business Dictation," doctoral dissertation, University of Pittsburgh, Pittsburgh, PA, 1976.

25. Devern Perry, "An Analytical Comparison of the Relative Word-Combination Frequencies of Business Correspondence with Phrase Frequencies of Selected Shorthand Textbooks," doctoral dissertation, University of North Dakota, Grand Forks, 1968.

Chapter 7

Individualized Instruction in Shorthand

Individualized instruction in any subject area is considered to be a method of instruction that provides for individual differences among students. Such individualization should provide an opportunity for the fast learner to move as quickly as possible through the subject matter, for the average learner to move at a pace consistent with average learning abilities, and for the slow learner to have the repetition and time needed to learn. Individualized instruction should give a student at any learning level an opportunity to spend more time on certain areas of learning when problems occur, and it should provide for a student at any learning level to move more quickly over areas of learning that are easier to master. Teachers should bear in mind that this aspect of individualized instruction is what truly makes for individualization.

Identification of Competencies and Standards

An individualized program of instruction must be complete and contain all the same components as any other instructional strategy. To be certain that this principle is followed, it is important to consider all the competencies or levels of performance that would normally be achieved with in-class instruction. From these competencies or levels of performance, standards would be developed to define the competency levels for various times in the individualized course. Standards that apply to a course taught on an in-class basis should be the same ones that apply to individualized instruction. The difference lies in the amount of time or the number of repetitions it takes for the students to achieve the competency level. On the following pages are some examples of competencies or levels of performance that beginning shorthand students using the *Gregg Shorthand Individual Progress Method* materials would be attempting to attain during the first semester of instruction[1]:

COMPETENCIES AND STANDARDS GUIDELINES FOR
AN INDIVIDUALIZED PROGRAM OF INSTRUCTION

	PHASE I	PERCENT OF GRADE
COMPETENCY 1	The student will read from shorthand plate notes for one minute. The better rate of two readings for each step will be counted.	10

Step 1 (Lessons 1–10)	Step 2 (Lessons 11–20)
70 wam for A	100 wam for A
60 wam for B	90 wam for B
50 wam for C	80 wam for C
	70 wam for D

		PERCENT OF GRADE
COMPETENCY 2	From dictation, the student will write shorthand vocabulary words selected from the lessons for each step, with accurate proportion, line of writing, and theory application.	40

96% accuracy = A
95–88% accuracy = B
87–78% accuracy = C
77–70% accuracy = D

Step 1 (Lessons 1–10)	Step 2 (Lessons 11–20)

		PERCENT OF GRADE
COMPETENCY 3	The student will transcribe homework notes on the typewriter for two minutes, correcting errors as they are made. The two best speeds of four tries will be counted.	20

Step 1 (Lessons 10–15)	Step 2 (Lessons 16–20)
The student will become familiar with the transcription process, performing transcription drills from plate material.	(From homework notes.)
	25 wam = A
	24–20 wam = B
	19–16 wam = C

		PERCENT OF GRADE
COMPETENCY 4	The student will take dictation tests from slightly altered practiced material and transcribe on the typewriter with 95 percent accuracy, attaining a speed twice for a grade.	20

Step 1	Step 2
(Beginning with Lesson 5, the student will practice taking dictation from tapes.)	After finishing Lesson 20 and the accompanying dictation tapes, the student will take dictation tests from Lessons 11–20.

60 wam for 3 minutes = A
60 wam for 2 minutes = B
60 wam for 1 minute = C

	PHASE I	PERCENT OF GRADE
COMPETENCY 5	By using the labs regularly and completing homework practice regularly, the student will earn 10 percent of the grade for Phase I.	10

	PHASE II	PERCENT OF GRADE
COMPETENCY 1	The student will read from homework notes for one minute during two different evaluation periods. The better rate of two readings for each step will be counted.	5

Step 1 (Lessons 21–30)	Step 2 (Lessons 31–40)
120 wam = A	130 wam = A
110 wam = B	120 wam = B
100 wam = C	110 wam = C
90 wam = D	100 wam = D

		PERCENT OF GRADE
COMPETENCY 2	From dictation, the student will write shorthand vocabulary words from the lessons for each step. Grade will be based on accuracy of proportion, line of writing, and theory application.	20

96% accuracy = A
95–88% accuracy = B
87–78% accuracy = C
77–70% accuracy = D

Step 1 (Lessons 21–30)	Step 2 (Lessons 31–40)	Step 3 (Lessons 1–40)
		All brief forms, and all phrases from textbook.

		PERCENT OF GRADE
COMPETENCY 3	The student will take dictation tests from slightly altered practiced material and transcribe on the typewriter with 95 percent accuracy, attaining a speed twice for a grade.	50

Step 1	Step 2
After finishing Lesson 30 in the textbook and the accompanying dictation speed-building tapes, the student will take dictation tests:	After finishing Lesson 40 in the textbook and the accompanying dictation speed-building tapes, the student will take dictation tests:
(Lessons 21–30)	**(Lessons 31–40)**
70 wam for 3 minutes = A	80 wam for 3 minutes = A
70 wam for 2 minutes = B	80 wam for 2 minutes = B
60 wam for 3 minutes = C	70 wam for 3 minutes = C
60 wam for 2 minutes = D	70 wam for 2 minutes = D

	PHASE II	PERCENT OF GRADE

Step 3

After considerable dictation speed-building practice on new material, the student will take dictation on new, unpreviewed material and transcribe on the typewriter with 95 percent accuracy, attaining each speed twice to establish a grade.

80 wam for 3 minutes = A
70 wam for 3 minutes = B
70 wam for 2 minutes = C
60 wam for 3 minutes = D

COMPETENCY 4 The student will transcribe homework notes on the typewriter for 3 minutes, correcting errors as they are made, attaining each speed twice for a grade. The two best speeds of four tries will be counted. 20

Step 1 (Lessons 21–30)	Step 2 (Lessons 31–40)
30+ wam = A	38+ wam = A
25–29 wam = B	37–35 wam = B
20–24 wam = C	34–30 wam = C
	29–25 wam = D

COMPETENCY 5 By using the labs regularly and completing homework practice regularly, the student will earn 5 percent of the grade for Phase II. 5

These competencies may be tested in class or individually. In either case, it is essential that recordkeeping be accurate and test security maintained. In addition, it is important that following the testing and scoring, the teacher or the laboratory assistant review test materials with the student and recommend remedial help as necessary.

In individualized learning, it helps to break the semester or quarter into learning phases or short segments which the learner can see as having beginning and ending times and achievable goals. In the preceding example, the beginning course was divided into two phases with steps identified and competencies defined for each. Seeing the quarter or semester as a whole is perhaps too overwhelming for a learner. In addition, the phase approach encourages more efficient time management as the learner knows when half the course is finished and how much time should be devoted to the second half. Such phase or step development and competency identification can be applied to all levels of shorthand instruction. Total shorthand instruction at the beginning, intermediate, or advanced levels can be individualized.

Methods of Organization

Many different approaches have been attempted to determine the most effective organization and operation of individualized instruction. Some arrangements have used the in-class individualized approach, others the totally individualized approach, and still others a combination approach. Factors such as philosophy of the school or department; availability of space, learning materials, and audio and visual equipment; amount of time allowed for the instruction and laboratory practice; and teacher and laboratory assistant time allocated for laboratory supervision determine the instructional approach to be employed.

In-Class Individualized Approach

The proponents of in-class instruction, with opportunities for individualized instruction within the class, will probably maintain a total-class organization, meeting the class at the scheduled time each day. Students who need extra reading or dictation-recording practice, typewritten transcription drill, shorthand vocabulary development, language arts or English skill development, and/or mailable letter practice would be assigned extra sessions in a laboratory or an educational materials center to work with learning materials designed to help develop deficient areas. Another type of arrangement would be to assign these needed drill and practice activities as part of the daily class work. Such learning activities would then be supervised by the classroom teacher during the class period.

Diagnosing each student's progress at all times throughout the course is the important factor in making this organizational scheme successful. Some teachers applying in-class individualization will prefer, or be required by space or personnel restrictions, to have the additional learning materials in the classroom and check them out to individual students for out-of-class study. Still other teachers may wish to devote part of the in-class time to individualizing instruction and adapting the room space and learning materials to fit the needs of each individual.

Average and above-average students will need careful supervision to see that they are stimulated to use the learning materials necessary to make their progress continuous. The teacher's task for all three student ability levels will be to diagnose and prescribe and to provide a challenging, interesting, and rewarding learning environment.

Totally Individualized Approach

Shorthand instruction at the beginning, intermediate, and advanced levels can be totally individualized. The learning activities that teachers have adapted to, and used in, individualized instruction include development of shorthand reading ability, shorthand vocabulary competency, dictation-recording ability, typewritten transcription ability, transcription-element information, and mailable-letter-production ability. The evaluation of these abilities can also be individualized. The totally individualized approach is more often used in postsecondary or college settings than in the secondary school. The "open laboratory" physical arrangement lends itself well to totally individualized instruction.

An open laboratory organization allows the student to come and to go when the laboratory is open. In addition, the student may choose the learning material to study and the amount of time to spend studying. Some teachers who have used the open laboratory approach have found that not all students are sufficiently self-disciplined to schedule themselves into the open laboratory frequently enough to derive maximum learning. Shorthand, being a skill-development course, needs to be studied regularly. An orientation period at the beginning of the course is recommended to instruct the students on the best procedures for studying to make the maximum progress. In addition, it will be necessary for the laboratory assistants or teacher to keep records of lab attendance and the learning materials used. The teacher and laboratory assistants may need to use conferences, mail, or telephone to reach the student and recommend certain study procedures, laboratory attendance times and frequency, and learning materials.

It is of great importance for the successful operation of an open laboratory to have certified faculty members as laboratory assistants or supervisors. It is essential that students be able to get help with equipment, subject matter, testing, remedial work, and diagnostic and prescriptive counseling when needed. Consideration must also be given to the arrangement of equipment, learning materials, and tests for their maximum security and care.

Combination Approach

Some teachers have developed the combination approach as the most successful solution to individualizing shorthand instruction. One such organizational structure is to have the students meet in class for the first three to four weeks of the semester or quarter. During this time most of the different learning activities will be experienced. In the beginning shorthand class, for example, the student will experience the beginning stages of development of reading ability and the administration of reading rates, practice in writing shorthand, sound/spelling and pronouncing shorthand vocabulary words from a transparency or chalkboard, writing shorthand outlines according to theory principles, dictation speed building, and typewritten transcription. For intermediate or advanced shorthand courses, this orientation period of two, three, or four weeks could be spent (1) reviewing shorthand vocabulary, (2) identifying dictation-recording and type-written transcription goals and practicing procedures for achieving these goals, (3) diagnosing areas of learning that need special attention for various students and helping them understand the program they need to follow to progress toward the end goals, (4) identifying the ways mailable letter production can be improved, and (5) reviewing areas of mailable letter production.

During these orientation weeks of in-class instruction, the teacher would be informing the student about the procedures being used, how these procedures would be completed on an individualized basis, and how testing will be conducted. By the end of the third or fourth week, the student would have made a decision between staying in class or progressing individually.

To help the student make a schedule, it is helpful for the teacher to recommend the amount of time to spend in the laboratory each week for normal progress and also to recommend the most ap-propriate sequencing of the learning materials. For example, a beginning shorthand student would use a presentation tape and/or video tape of the theory presentation first, followed by study of the new lesson. Then the student would return to the laboratory and play a reading tape for the lesson, followed by the dictation speed-building tape and the typewritten-transcription-drill tape for that lesson, and finally the new presentation tape and/or video tape of the next lesson. Such a learning sequence would be similar to the activities in a beginning shorthand class. Similar recommendations for sequenc-ing learning activities would need to be made for the intermediate and advanced students.

Some teachers like to give the students an opportunity to move back and forth from individualized to in-class instruction. Theoreti-cally, there may be value to such a procedure; but practically, frequent changing of personal goals may be too confusing for some students to grow and progress adequately throughout the course.

In this combination approach the teacher would continue to meet in class the students who prefer not to go into a totally individualized learning program.

As part of the combination approach, some teachers have found a partially structured organization to be worthwhile in individualizing instruction. Partially structured may mean that the students are forced into a testing schedule. The students would need to keep up with a study schedule and be ready for testing when in-class students are tested. The individualized group would report to class on test days. Such a structured system keeps the individualized student moving through the materials, and it still allows for a time differential, because the individualized student can spend more time or less time on certain areas of study than the in-class group would spend. What it does not do is (1) allow a student who learns more quickly to finish the course before the in-class group, and (2) allow the student who needs greater repetition and time to continue beyond the end of the semester to complete the competencies designed for the course. To be realistic, most secondary schools and many community colleges and universities must adhere to a quarter or semester calendar and cannot allow incompletes for unfinished work, unless the student has a valid reason such as illness.

To assist in partially structuring individualized instruction, a calendar could be prepared to show both groups of students, the in-class and the individualized, the material to be covered each day in class. The daily class activities and the tests would be indicated on the calendar so the individualized students can see what should be accomplished each day and when it is necessary to report to the classroom for testing. Two weeks of such a calendar for a beginning shorthand class might look like the calendar on page 213.

Similar calendars of daily class activities could be developed for other semesters of shorthand instruction.

Open Entry and Open Exit Procedures

Some schools, especially the community colleges and some universities, have been able to organize their individualized work on an open-entry open-exit basis. Students may enter the program on Monday of any week and exit whenever they have fulfilled the requirements for the course. The recommendations for the totally individualized approach would need to be observed for this arrangement. Counseling, follow-up, identification of goals, and confirmation of testing results would need to be precise and frequent so students do not get lost along the way and merely drop out rather than complete the course.

Shorthand Laboratories

The most common use of shorthand laboratories over the years has been for dictation speed building. In a truly individualized setting, all shorthand learning activities can be performed in the shorthand laboratory. The various types of shorthand laboratories will be discussed in the following paragraphs.

The Classroom Shorthand Laboratory

In secondary schools, the classroom shorthand laboratory is the type found most frequently. It may consist of three, four, or five channels, either wired to a console or wireless. One of the very common uses

Week of:	Monday	Tuesday	Wednesday	Thursday	Friday
	Review L6, 7. Present L8. Read from L7 at A rate. Dictation speed building, L6 and 7.	Review L7, 8. Present L9. Read from L8 at A rate. Dictation speed building, L7, 8.	Review L8, 9. Present L10. Read from L9 at A rate. Dictation speed building, L8, 9.	Review L9, 10. Read from L10 at A rate. Dictation speed building, L9, 10.	Review L8, 9, 10. Read from L10 at A rate. Dictation speed building, L9, 10. Transcription drill, L10.

Week of:	Monday	Tuesday	Wednesday	Thursday	Friday
	Present L11. Dictation speed building, L10. Reading rates,* L1–10 Theory test, L1–10	Review L10, 11. Present L12. Read from L11 at A rate. Transcription drill, L11.	Review L11, 12. Present L13. Read from L12 at A rate. Reading rates, L1–10 Theory test, L1–10	Review L12, 13. Present L14. Read from L13 at A rate. Dictation speed building, L13.	Review L13, 14. Present L15. Transcription drill, L14. Dictation speed building, L14 and/or Related material.

*Underscores indicate group testing

213

of multichannel listening equipment is to help the student develop dictation-recording ability. In such a situation, the teacher will determine which groups of students will listen to the various channels; select the appropriate dictation speed to help the students gain the desired speeds for testing; set goals to be attempted; intervene at appropriate times to keep motivation high; and finally, at the end of the practice, will check achievement and set goals for future practice.

In another form of classroom laboratory, individual playback recorders are used. Several students may be using one recorder, which is playing dictation at speeds most appropriate for their dictation-recording development. Each student would have earphones; and by means of a multiple jack arrangement, students can be seated in clusters around the classroom taking dictation at rates designed for their individual development. Still other classrooms have individual tape recorders for each student, to allow individualized instruction on dictation speed building and other aspects of shorthand instruction. In the classroom shorthand laboratory, some students could be taking dictation from the playback units for dictation speed building or mailable letter transcription; some could be taking brief-form tests while others take shorthand vocabulary tests; others could be listening to directed drills to improve shorthand vocabulary, brief-form and brief-form-derivative usage, phrase usage, or transcription-element usage; and the teacher could be working with another group in a "live" situation. On other days in the same classroom, students could be getting individualized typewritten-transcription-drill practice, or they could be transcribing sets of mailable letters taken from the tapes.

Various laboratory components can be purchased when developing a classroom shorthand laboratory. Some shorthand instructors like to be able to listen to the material the students are hearing. For this purpose, especially designed listening capabilities can be built into the laboratory. Other teachers like to "cut into" the dictation at times, and for this an especially designed intervention system can be provided.

The Open Laboratory

The open laboratory is probably most often found in postsecondary schools or colleges. The dictation speed building equipment for the open laboratory could be similar to that described for the classroom. The operation of the open laboratory would be different, however, from that of the classroom laboratory. If a console arrangement is used, usually a laboratory assistant or supervisor will operate the tape decks. Students might request various rates to be played; or a program for the day, based on expected student needs, might be outlined by the shorthand instructor. The laboratory in which this type of equipment is used is usually a "quiet" laboratory, and the students listen to the tapes with earphones.

Some open laboratories have been planned so that students get their own equipment and materials from open shelves or cabinets and return them when finished.

The Learning Materials Center

In some schools, laboratory assistants or supervisors, open laboratories, and classroom laboratories may not be available, or an extension of these services may be desirable. In such situations, learning materials and equipment can be placed in the library or learning materials center to be used there or checked out to be used elsewhere. Individual study carrels equipped with playback recorders or a quiet area that can be used for listening are usually provided.

Some secondary schools provide a learning center as a part of their business education department area. Teachers are assigned to the center at various times of the day, and students come in for specific learning activities: to use resource materials, to practice keyboarding from both taped and untaped material, to practice typewritten transcription from both taped and untaped material, and the like.

Planning for Laboratory Media and Equipment

The media and materials needed for individualized instruction in shorthand will be as varied as the schools applying the procedures. For the most part, individualized-instruction arrangements at the secondary school level will consist of multichannel listening-station units or individual tape playback units, individual listening areas within an educational materials center, or a practice laboratory area of the business education department.

In considering individualized instructional materials and equipment, attention should be given to the listening types (tapes and records), the listening/viewing types (video tapes, Sound-Page, sound-slide), and the printed-material types (programmed instruction, learning activity packets, job instruction sheets, books, magazines, and the like).

Sound-Page equipment lends itself very well to many elements of learning necessary in shorthand. With this equipment, a short narrative of approximately 3 to 4 minutes is recorded on a disk on the reverse of a sheet of specially treated paper. On the top side of the paper are sentences or exercises for punctuation, number expression, possessives, one-word and two-word combinations, capitalization, hyphenation, and the like. The student listens to material that has been recorded by the instructor on the disk and responds by writing on a separate answer or drill sheet. The same type of learning

215

situation could be set up with short cassette recordings and drill and response sheets.

Many shorthand teachers express concern that some individualized learning materials do not have a video component and students have difficulty learning the direction of writing and the way strokes are joined into words. Such concern would certainly be valid for the shorthand beginner. Video tapes can be easily made of the lesson presentation or of the writing direction, stroke joinings, and sounding of symbols. The "quiet" laboratory would then have video tape playback equipment for viewing and listening.

Sound-slide equipment and overhead projectors would both have a place in such a shorthand classroom or laboratory. Some classrooms and laboratories are equipped with tape-copying equipment, which copies tapes very quickly so that students can take them home for additional study. Tapes purchased from companies may be reproduced only with written permission from the publisher.

In planning shorthand laboratories of any type, special consideration should be given to providing storage for tape and other learning materials; adequate space for good working positions; easy access to the learning materials by the laboratory assistants, instructors, and/or students; and security for equipment and materials.

Media specialists within educational institutions or sales personnel of distributing companies can provide helpful information such as storage units available and desirable storage temperatures and space allotments to prevent tape deterioration.

Appropriate and Effective Uses

Discussion to this point has centered around individualizing instruction in the beginning, intermediate, and advanced shorthand courses. At the secondary school level, individualized instruction is used more frequently in the second semester and advanced courses than in the beginning course. The entire intermediate or advanced course can be taught on an individualized basis similar to that discussed for the beginning course. Often, however, only certain learning activities are supplemented by the use of the shorthand laboratory. Dictation speed building, shorthand vocabulary reviews on tape or video tape, learning activity packets for refinement of transcription skills, typewritten transcription tapes for speed and accuracy development, mailable-letter-production tapes, and various types of testing all lend themselves well to laboratory use for the intermediate and advanced classes.

Even though it is not recommended, some shorthand teachers are faced with the situation of teaching beginning and advanced students in the same classroom during the same period. The preceding suggestions regarding individualizing instruction can help students with varying degrees of individual differences at both levels to realize greater achievement and more successful performance.

216

Since the beginning of the use of multichannel equipment and individualized learning laboratories, frequent cautions have been given that the equipment must not replace the teacher. In totally individualized instruction, the laboratory takes the place of the teacher more than is true for in-class instruction supplemented by the laboratory or multichannel equipment. However, even with individualized instruction, the teacher is a vital part of the learning process to supplement instruction, recommend further action, help give direction to the student, and lend encouragement when needed.

When individualized learning equipment supplements the in-class instruction, most teachers find that students tire of the activity when it is used day after day and when it is used for entire class hours. The optimum length of time for a single individualized learning activity, such as dictation speed building, to be used in the classroom without teacher intervention, would be about 15 to 20 minutes. For some students this may be too long. The teacher will need to be the judge and observe when fatigue, boredom, and lack of motivation set in. A rule of thumb is that the individualized learning activity may be effective for about the same length of time as the teacher would spend "live" on the activity in the classroom.

For in-class dictation speed-building instruction, multichannel equipment can help the teacher better meet individual needs by allowing a variety of dictation speeds. Individualized learning equipment and materials for the in-class situation can be helpful in fitting learning materials to students' individual needs—some may need a learning activity packet or Sound-Page presentation of the use of possessives, others may need a shorthand vocabulary review from the video or audio tape or a transparency, and so on. A valuable aid to making the use of the individualized learning equipment meaningful to the student is for the teacher and the student to set goals for each practice. For example, to test the attainment of a dictation goal, a sample 3-minute dictation-recording test at the goal rate could be given at the end of the practice.

Individualized learning equipment frees the teacher to teach, and more important, it allows the teacher to focus on a group of learners with approximately the same level of ability. If the teacher gives attention to each group at least two or three times during a half-hour session, the probability of violating fundamental learning principles is lessened considerably.

Here is one way in which fundamental skill-building principles can be observed in an in-class shorthand laboratory operated with commercially prepared or teacher-prepared tapes:

1. The teacher should carefully preview the dictation on each tape and determine the most appropriate times for stopping the dictation.

217

2. Learners who are working on the same speed level should be seated together in one section of the shorthand room or the laboratory. It is suggested that the class be broken into no more than four groups.

3. One student in each group should be given a bell or signaling device and instructed to signal the teacher to stop the tape at the time designated by the teacher.

4. When the student bell is rung, the teacher should spend approximately 3 minutes with the group, participating in one or more of the following activities:

   a. Postviewing difficult outlines that have just been dictated.
   b. Previewing difficult outlines that will appear in the next segment of dictation.
   c. Setting reading goals and listening to students read back part of the material that was just dictated at controlled rates.
   d. Checking proportion and fluency of outlines that were written in the controlled dictation.
   e. Listening to students read back and insert the punctuation in the material just dictated at controlled rates.
   f. Setting goals for the next portion of the dictation.
   g. Motivating and encouraging individual students in the group.

The success of the plan depends to a great extent on how the teacher schedules these contacts with student groups. The short 2- or 3-minute sessions must be staggered so that students do not have to stop taking dictation and wait for the teacher to turn attention to their group. Equally important, the teacher must know exactly what the students in each group have recorded in dictation, so immediate focus can be given to their particular problems and needs.

Evaluation of Shorthand Laboratories

New learning materials are constantly being developed for laboratory use and new equipment annually appears on the market. Shorthand teachers will need to keep abreast of the new materials available and include updating as part of the evaluating procedure. Although it will not be necessary to replace equipment often, teachers need to be aware of new developments in the equipment lines and choose wisely that which will do the best job for their students and in their situation.

Consider the following questions when evaluating the shorthand laboratory:

1. Is the laboratory conveniently located near the shorthand classrooms and other business education classrooms?
2. Is the tape storage and learning material storage easily

accessible to the laboratory assistant, or to the students if it is a self-serve system.

3. Is the recordkeeping and checkout system adequate to ensure security of the equipment and learning materials?

4. Is the laboratory open sufficient hours and the best hours for adequate student use?

5. Is the audio equipment flawless in listening quality?

6. Is the video equipment operating with a good quality of picture and sound?

7. Are there adequate copies of learning materials to enable all students wishing to use the laboratory at a particular time to have materials and equipment available?

8. Is the laboratory physically large enough to accommodate the expected number of students?

9. Is the "quiet" laboratory really a quiet area so students can study and work without interruption?

10. Is the multichannel equipment easy to operate and easy to maintain?

11. Is the service policy of the equipment companies reliable so equipment is not in need of repair for long periods?

12. Is there adequate help provided by certified laboratory assistants or teachers?

Other questions pertaining to the equipment and learning materials in particular laboratories could be added to this list. Probably of greatest importance is that a responsible person should be in charge of the laboratory and its use. The shorthand laboratory can be a golden opportunity for meeting individual needs—it should not be abused.

Learning Materials

Many learning materials have been developed for use in individualized instruction. In choosing materials the teacher must evaluate them to see if they will do the job required for individual study. Major components to consider are presentation of the subject matter; clarity of instructions; adherence to known effective psychological principles of skill development and learning; availability of printed, audio, and video materials; and physical ease of using the materials.

Published Materials

Existing combination programs of printed and taped materials are *Gregg Shorthand Individual Progress Method, Programmed Gregg Shorthand,* and *Gregg Shorthand Structured Learning Method* which have been published for use in the first semester; the *Gregg Dictation and Transcription Individual Progress Method* for use in the second semester;

Transcription 36 designed for use the last 36 lessons of the first year, at the beginning of the advanced course, or in a cooperative office-related class; and *Refresher Course in Gregg Shorthand* for use as a review or for brush-up training.[2,3,4,5,6,7] These six published materials provide the textbook, lesson-presentation tapes, and dictation speed-development tapes. *Transcription 36* also provides a series of office-style dictation tapes and transparencies. All six of these materials are designed to be used in individualized, in-class, or combination approaches.

In addition to the published tapes, *Shorthand Speed-Testing Tapes* and *Shorthand Speed Development*, which are correlated with the textbooks, there are workbooks, transparencies, multichannel tapes, records, filmstrips, filmstiks, student transcripts, shorthand dictionaries, and posters available that provide unlimited opportunities for individualizing instruction in the beginning, intermediate, and advanced shorthand classrooms.[8,9]

Teacher-Made Materials

Some teachers prefer to include additional instructional materials in the individualized instruction courses in the form of additional taped material, transparencies, Sound-Page recordings, learning activity packets, and drill sheets. Students respond well to teacher-made tapes because the voice is familiar to them, and teachers can build into the narrative on the tapes motivating comments and cues that they know will appeal to their students.

VIDEO TAPES. Teachers have expressed concern about teaching beginning shorthand on an individualized basis without a visual teaching medium for the student to see the direction, fluency, size of strokes, and the line of writing. To alleviate this concern, some teachers have made video tapes of each lesson. The teacher's voice is on the tape, and the lesson is taught as it would be in class. A similar procedure could be used for reviewing and refining theory for the courses following the beginning course. In another situation of video taping, a teacher has made video tapes that briefly point out the writing principles, the sounds of strokes, and the line of writing, and direct the student through a practice of sample words of the lesson. These tapes have been used in combination with the *Gregg Shorthand Individual Progress Method*. The recommended way to use the tapes is to view the video tape and then listen to the Presentation Tape of the lesson. Each video tape is about 15 to 20 minutes long. These video tapes have been made in the following pattern:

VT 1—Lessons 1 and 2	VT 4—Lessons 7 and 8
VT 2—Lessons 3 and 4	VT 5—Lessons 9 and 10
VT 3—Lessons 5 and 6	VT 6—Lessons 11 and 12

VT 7—Lessons 13 and 14   VT 12—Lessons 24, 25, 26
VT 8—Lessons 15 and 16   VT 13—Lessons 27, 28, 31
VT 9—Lessons 17 and 18   VT 14—Lessons 32, 33, 34
VT 10—Lessons 19 and 20   VT 15—Lessons 35, 36, 37
VT 11—Lessons 22 and 23   VT 16—Lessons 38, 39, 40

The ease of making video tapes is an important consideration. The tapes described above, which provide a brief overview of the writing of the symbols and sample words, were simply made by having an assistant stand behind the instructor with the video tape camera and recorder. The instructor was seated at a desk with a microphone nearby, with notebook and arms in correct writing position. Only the arms, notebook, and desk were shown in the picture. While describing the symbols, strokes, briefly stated rules, line of writing, and proportion of writing, the instructor wrote in the notebook and directed the student to practice writing certain outlines.

READING TAPES.   To help students develop fluent, accurate reading at a rapid rate, some teachers have prepared reading tapes for the first semester. The preparation of such tapes is simple. The teacher reads letters of the homework lesson at a designated rate, perhaps the A rate for this point in the course, and asks the student to drypen and read along. The student drypens the plate in the early stages, but after about six weeks the drypenning is from homework written notes. After reading together at the A rate the first three or four letters of the homework assignment, the teacher could ask the students to place superior figures in the remaining letters of the lesson as their correct location is indicated. As a self-test, the students aim to read the remaining letters at the A rate, and the teacher gives an audible signal, such as tapping a bell, to indicate when the student should be at each superior figure to be reading at the designated rate. The reading tapes should be used after the homework lesson has been studied. The reading tape serves as a guide for the student to determine if study has been adequate and helps develop additional reading skill. These reading tapes are very short—approximately 8 to 10 minutes.

DICTATION SPEED-BUILDING TAPES.   To supplement the dictation tapes published for the first and second semester *Individual Progress Method,* for the *Programmed Instruction,* and for additional taped material for the second, third, and fourth semester, some teachers like to make their own dictation speed-building tapes. Such teacher-made tapes can include directions to the student regarding using the open book during the beginning stages of dictation speed development, looking back and forth from the book to the notebook, the weaning process of looking at the notebook after several repetitions of the dictated piece, and practicing certain outlines between dictations, with motivational comments such as "write a shorthand outline for every word" or "start with the first sounds." In addition, dictation patterns that the teacher prefers and finds helpful to student growth can be used on the tapes; such as using the 20-word piece in the early stages of dictation development (or at any time in any semester to help students break away from plateaus), or using the half-minute piece, the stair-step plan, and spurt and progressive dictation plans, along with directions to the students to use the preview sheet of words and phrases between practices to build a sound shorthand writing vocabulary. The teacher can point out the goals being attempted so the student can understand why practice is at a level from 20 to 30 or 40 wam above that of the dictation test they are trying to pass.

TRANSCRIPTION DRILL TAPES. If a teacher is interested in beginning typewritten transcription early, the drills that would be done in an in-class situation can be taped and the individual student with a typewriter, cassette playback recorder, and cassette tape can perform the drills. Using transcription drill tapes for each lesson and three-minute transcription-rate practice tapes will enable the student to develop fast and accurate typewritten transcription. Teaching cues regarding transcription elements will need to be built into the tape recording in the same way as these transcription elements would be taught in class. Students react well to hearing quiet music on the tape during the actual transcribing.

DICTATION TESTING TAPES. If the student is going to take dictation tests from taped material, the teacher may wish to make the tapes. The dictation test tapes should begin with a 3 to 4 minute warmup at from 20 to 30 wam above the test rate that will follow. After the warmup, the test rate is announced and the test dictated. Following the dictation of the test, the directions for turning in the test tape, transcribing, and turning in the notes and transcript are given. The laboratory assistant or teacher will need to arrange security of test tapes and honesty in taking the test. If the competency states that the dictation test rate must be passed twice in order to fulfill the competency, probably nine or ten test tapes at that particular speed will need to be recorded.

SHORTHAND VOCABULARY TESTING TAPES. Shorthand vocabulary tests on tape are administered similarly to those given in class. At the beginning of the tape the teacher gives directions about numbering, dating, identifying lessons covered, and placement of student's name on the shorthand notebook page. The procedure for administering the test by pronouncing at the rate of 10 wam is announced and then the words are dictated. At the end of the word pronunciation, directions are given regarding looking over the words and rewriting any poorly written outlines. At the end of approximately three to five minutes for a 40- or 50-word test, the teacher says on the tape that the test and the tape should now be given to the laboratory assistant.

If instructional tapes, including video tapes, are to be used in the preceding situations, new formats incorporating teacher directions must be included on the tapes. The content of these tapes will vary with teaching preferences and objectives. However, teachers can be reasonably sure of effective tape formats if the following principles are adhered to:

1. Students should know the exact objectives for which they are striving on a particular tape.
2. Students should know if they meet the specific objectives immediately after completing each tape.
3. Students should develop their skills through short, intensive bursts of effort.
4. Students should participate in a variety of shorthand activities while completing each tape.
5. Students should be more than writing machines. Learning requires the active involvement of the learner. Repetitive dictation over an extended period does not encourage active involvement, motivation, or thinking. On the contrary, it encourages passiveness, even though students are actively involved with the physical activity of writing. Students should be required to think about what they are going to do, how they are going to do it, whether they did it, and how they did it.

PREVIEW SHEETS. In situations where the student is taking dictation from either multichannel equipment or individual playback units, many teachers have found the preview sheet to be a necessary part of the instruction. The preview sheets contain words with which students may need help while listening to the tape or record. It is recommended that the student study the preview sheet and practice writing the words for each segment of the dictation before taking the dictation. Teacher-made tapes can build in directions to the student for appropriate uses of the preview sheets during the practice. A sample preview sheet is illustrated on pages 224 and 225.

In the classroom, students can be assigned to distribute the preview sheets before the practice. In an open laboratory with multichannel equipment, the preview sheets can be placed in folder pockets on a bulletin board with the folder labeled by channel. A program of the various rates can then be posted by channel number so the student can select speed and preview sheet for the desired practice.

Preview sheets such as the one illustrated on pages 224 and 225 can be easily made on master carbons by ruling light pencil lines on the writing side of the carbon before removing the tissue sheet. Proportion and line of writing can then be observed by using the pencil lines as guides. Multiple copies of the preview sheets can then be available for classroom or laboratory use. Some shorthand instructors laminate the preview sheets to preserve them; however, care should be taken that the lamination does not produce a glare or shine that makes looking at the sheet difficult.

<u>PREVIEW</u> <u>SHEET</u>

(SERIES 90)   REEL 81

DIRECTIONS: PLEASE STUDY THESE WORDS BEFORE
             LISTENING TO THE TAPE AND STUDY AGAIN
             AT VARIOUS REST PERIODS.

<u>TRACK 1</u>

1.

2.

3.

4.

5.

<u>KEY</u>:

<u>1st Minute</u>: greater, dependent, correct,
             competition, existed, essential,
             alternative, analysis
<u>2d Minute</u>:   judgments, included, development,
             programs, men and women, number
<u>3d Minute</u>:   simply, confined, genius, commercial,
             recognize, published, countless,
             articles, current, sports
<u>4th Minute</u>: writers, ability, Institute, America,
             assignments, reporters, individual,
             analyze
<u>5th Minute</u>: professional, editors, constant,
             aptitude, observation

DIRECTIONS: PLEASE STUDY THESE WORDS BEFORE
              LISTENING TO THE TAPE AND STUDY AGAIN
              AT VARIOUS REST PERIODS.

TRACK 2

1.
2.
3.
4.
5.

KEY:

1st Minute: judging, of course, pennies, however,
            to make, replacements, dependable,
            American
2d Minute: obtain, advantages, destination,
            transportation, fastest, circumstances,
            discuss, convenience
3d Minute: very much, dangerous, airport,
            increasingly, exposed, control, modern,
            common sense
4th Minute: major, personal, thousands, usual,
            distinction, themselves, essential,
            equipment, found
5th Minute: telephone, supervise, scattered,
            recreation, wholesome, combination,
            practical

225

INCORPORATE STUDENT ACTIVITIES IN TEACHER-MADE MATE-RIALS. The types of student activities are limited only by the ingenuity and objectives of the individual teacher. The following examples show how student involvement can be incorporated into teacher-made tapes:

Description of Tape. Two or three sentences giving a general orientation to the content and organization of each tape will enable learners to develop proper mind sets or to mentally prepare for the tasks ahead. For example, "This 15-minute speed-building tape contains four different letters about the insurance industry. The first three letters, which range in length from 75 to 115 words, will each be dictated twice at speeds ranging from 60 to 90 words a minute. The final letter consisting of 80 words will be dictated once at the rate of 80 words a minute."

Performance Objectives. After the brief introduction, specific performance objectives should be enumerated. The inclusion of such objectives provides specific short-term goals toward which to strive. A performance goal stated in the following manner certainly provides direction: "After completing the practice letters on this 15-minute tape, you should be able to (a) write the final letter in shorthand at a speed of 80 wam for one minute, and (b) read back your shorthand notes accurately within 30 seconds, or at a rate of 160 wam."

Previews. Ideally, previews of difficult outlines should be recorded on student preview sheets as well as on tape. However, if preview sheets are not used, the following method of tape previewing is suggested: *appreciate, a-p-r-e-ish-ea-t, appreciate.* Students should be instructed to listen to the word as it is first pronounced and then spelled. When the word is dictated again, it should be recorded in shorthand.

Dictation. The 1-minute speed builder or 1-minute speed-forcing plans are certainly appropriate for dictation speed building on teacher-made tapes, but research does not reveal that they are superior to other methods. Almost any of the repetitive plans currently in use is satisfactory. However, it would be a serious mistake to develop a tape library that incorporated only one type of dictation speed-forcing plan. All plans that are suitable to the time limitations of a 15- or 30-minute tape should be used.

Some of the speed-building tapes should include nonrepetitive dictation. A series of letters dictated in a nonrepetitive pattern and related to the same general subject will help refine shorthand vocabulary and develop listening skills. Even when repetitive dictation is used, it is suggested that occasional words be changed each time the letter is dictated.

Reading. Tapes should provide for reading back part of the controlled writing from dictation because this allows students to determine whether they have met established goals, and permits short rest periods between intensive writing efforts.

There are several ways to program reading practice on tapes. One effective method includes using soft background music to indicate the timing. For example, "Your goal is to read back the letter at a rate of 150 words a minute. Begin reading when the music starts; if you finish reading the letter before the music stops, you have met your goal."

Paced reading is another way of setting reading goals. After the student has recorded a letter from dictation, the following instructions for paced reading would be given: "Your goal is to read back your shorthand at 150 words a minute. I will pace you by reading the letter very quietly at 150 words a minute. Try to read more rapidly than I, and finish reading your notes before I finish. If you complete your reading before I finish, you have met the goal for this tape. Ready . . ."

Miscellaneous Teacher Comments. It is not inappropriate to include teacher comments on dictation speed-forcing tapes, provided they do not consume excessive valuable time. Such comments can provide valuable transcription training as well as give a brief respite from dictation and writing. The following are samples of comments appropriate to speed building.

- Why is a comma placed after the clause, "If you think you will be able"? (Pause) You are correct if you identified it as an introductory *if* clause.
- Read the first sentence of your notes and insert the proper punctuation. (Pause) You punctuated the sentence correctly if you inserted a comma between the words *manufacturing* and *but*. A comma is usually inserted between two independent clauses that are connected by a conjunction such as *but*.
- Spell the word *Massachusetts* that appeared in the dictation. (Pause) You are correct if you spelled it M-a-s-s-a-c-h-u-s-e-t-t-s.
- Check your first sentence and find the words *debate team*. (Pause) Note that the *d* in debate should be from two to three times as long as the *t* in team.
- Find the number *eighteen* which appears near the middle of your notes. (Pause) Should it be typed as a figure or written out? (Pause) You are correct if you indicated it should be typed as a figure. In ordinary business correspondence, spell out both exact and approximate numbers from 1 through 10; use figures for numbers above 10.
- This letter will be dictated at 120 words a minute. Make a real effort to record something for every word. Do not be overconcerned with proportion or penmanship. Ready . . .
- This letter will be dictated at a controlled rate—only 80 words a

minute. Concentrate on accuracy and proportion of outlines so that you will be able to read it back at 160 words a minute. Ready . . .

Special Purpose Tapes. A series of special teacher-made transcription-development tapes may be particularly valuable for students who lack knowledge relating to spelling, word usage, and punctuation. With comparatively little effort, a teacher can design a series of tapes for remedial practice in these skills.

Punctuation Tapes. A series of sentences requiring punctuation can be enumerated and recorded. The student would be expected to record each dictated sentence in shorthand and very quickly insert the correct punctuation. After the punctuation has been added, the dictator would read the sentence again, inserting the punctuation marks. For example, the following could be recorded: "Sentence 1. I will be pleased to meet you on January 21, but we must schedule the meeting late in the afternoon. (Pause while the student reads the sentence and inserts the comma). A comma should be placed between *21* and *but* because commas separate two independent clauses connected by a conjunction."

Word Usage Tapes. A series of sentences requiring proper word usage could also be enumerated and recorded, and students could follow the same learning procedure as on punctuation tapes. The following is an example of what might be recorded: "Sentence 1. I will be pleased to meet you on January 21, but you must schedule the meeting before 4 p.m. (Pause) Indicate how 4 p.m. should be typed. (Pause) You are correct if 4 is written as a figure and if the letters *p.m.* are written in lower case with a period after *p* and after *m*. There should be no space between the two letters."

Spelling Tapes. A series of remedial spelling tapes can be helpful for students who need special study on the spelling of commonly used business words. There seems to be no one method for effectively teaching spelling to everyone. Therefore, the basic purpose of these tapes should probably be diagnostic so that students can identify the specific words they need to learn.

Spelling tapes might be recorded in the following manner: "This is spelling tape 1 of the most frequently used words in business letters. Fifty words will be dictated in groups of ten. As you hear each word, write it in longhand. After ten words have been dictated, the correct spelling for each word in that group will be given. Check your work and record each incorrectly spelled word in a special notebook. Practice the spelling of these words so that you can spell them correctly for your teacher. Ready . . ."

Shorthand Vocabulary Review Tapes. Research has shown that there is a definite relationship between ability to construct theoretically correct outlines and dictation speed. Although shorthand texts provide a built-in shorthand vocabulary review, individual students may need special remedial drill. The following is a format example which could be used for a series of shorthand vocabulary review tapes. If this format is used, the student should have easy access to a beginning shorthand text and a shorthand dictionary. "Theory Review Tape 20, the *ses* blend. Practice writing the words and dictation emphasizing the *ses* blend. If you need a quick review of the *ses* blend, turn to page 57, paragraph 71 in the beginning shorthand book.

"First write the following words that contain the *ses* blend: Ready ... *analysis, finances, Moses, nurses, basis, losses, prices, services, advances, chances, addresses, promises, causes, places, offices, leases, versus, sister, system, systematic, criticism.*

"Check your shorthand outlines as they are spelled in shorthand. If you are unsure how to write an outline correctly, after listening to the spelling, consult the shorthand dictionary. *Ready* ... a-n-l-ses, f-e-n-a-n-ses, M-o-ses, n-e-r-ses, b-a-ses, l-o-ses, p-r-i-ses, s-e-r-v-e-ses, a-d-v-a-n-ses, chay-a-n-ses, a-d-r-e-ses, p-r-o-m-e-ses, k-o-ses, p-l-a-ses, o-f-e-ses, l-e-ses, v-e-r-ses, ses-t-r, ses-tem, ses-tem-a-t-e-k, k-r-e-t-ses-m.

"If there are outlines that you need to check in the dictionary, turn off your tape player and do it now. (Pause)

"Now, write the same words as many times as possible as they are dictated. Ready ... *analysis, finances, Moses, nurses, basis, losses, prices, services, advances, chances, addresses, promises, causes, places, offices, leases, versus, sister, system, systematic, criticism.*"

A letter emphasizing the use of *ses* such as the one given on page 137 of Chapter 4 would be dictated at 60 wam.

Brief-Form Tapes. Every library should include a series of brief-form tapes. The dictation on these tapes should be progressively faster, and the order of the brief forms should vary from tape to tape. Common brief-form derivatives should also be included in the recordings.

Suggestions for Successful Use of Individualized Instruction and Individualized-Instruction Learning Materials

Care must be taken not to overload the student learner, when learning is completely individualized, with more than can possibly be accomplished. It is very tempting to think of all the remedial instruction that would help the student and forget that there is a logical maximum of time and effort that can be expected from the student. For this reason, it is well for the teacher who has taught in an in-class situation to try to provide for an amount of practice time equivalent to that usually required from students in a class, plus the homework that each group would be expected to do.

Experience has shown that some type of orientation manual is helpful. Such a manual for beginning shorthand instruction could include:

1. A brief statement about the student's responsibility in an individualized learning situation.
2. A laboratory schedule.
3. A calendar recommended for progress and testing.
4. The competencies required for fulfillment of the course.
5. A brief description of the learning materials, identifying their purpose, the best study procedures, the coding for the materials, and the approximate time length of each.
6. A brief explanation of what is meant by dictation speed development when writing for speed and when doing controlled writing.
7. A brief explanation of what is meant by typewritten-transcription development when practicing for transcription speed and when practicing for controlled transcription.
8. A check-off list of the learning materials for the student to keep a record of those used.

Coding the tapes will be necessary for the student to quickly ask for the materials or locate them on an open-shelf arrangement. A suggested coding, followed by the number of the tape, might be: *RT* for *reading tapes, PT* for *presentation tapes, VT* for *video tapes, SBDT* for *speed-building dictation tapes, TDT* for *transcription drill tapes, DTT* for *dictation test tapes,* and *SVT* for *shorthand vocabulary tapes.* In addition, an inventory of the learning materials available and the sources used will need to be maintained. Such an inventory is invaluable to the instructors in making additional tapes and using the test recorded material only for testing.

A major learning principle must be followed by the teacher, laboratory assistant, and learner: There must be adequate practice before testing. For the most part, it is pedagogically unsound to take tests on a trial-and-error basis when sufficient skill has not been developed to probably pass the test.

One can see from this discussion that individualizing instruction is not an easier way to teach. Organization, motivation, follow-up, developing and using appropriate learning materials, and providing a good learning environment are very important and no simple task. Teachers who have worked with individualized instruction usually comment that the work and time are well rewarded by the success the learner experiences.

Notes

1. Louis A. Leslie, Charles E. Zoubek, and Oleen M. Henson, *Gregg Shorthand Individual Progress Method, Diamond Jubilee Series,* McGraw-Hill Book Company, New York, 1972.
2. Ibid.
3. Russell J. Hosler, Arnold Condon, Robert L. Grubbs, and Harry Huffman, *Programmed Gregg Shorthand,* McGraw-Hill Book Company, New York, 1969.
4. Eleanor Skimin and Patsy McMurtrie, *Gregg Shorthand, Structured Learning Method,* McGraw-Hill Book Company, New York, 1972.
5. Louis A. Leslie, Charles E. Zoubek, A. James Lemaster, and Oleen M. Henson, *Gregg Dictation and Transcription, Individual Progress Method, Diamond Jubilee Series,* McGraw-Hill Book Company, New York, 1974.
6. A. Condon, G. Condon, D. H. Crank, and A. C. Lloyd, *Transcription 36,* McGraw-Hill Book Company, New York, 1976.
7. Madeline S. Strony, M. Claudia Garvey, and Howard L. Newhouse, *Refresher Course in Gregg Shorthand, Diamond Jubilee Series,* McGraw-Hill Book Company, New York, 1970.
8. John Peterson and Kay Mendenhall, *Shorthand Speed Testing Tapes,* McGraw-Hill Book Company, New York, 1976.
9. Louis A. Leslie, *Gregg Shorthand Speed Development Tape Library,* McGraw-Hill Book Company, New York.

Chapter 8

Transcription Ability Development Process

The development of transcription ability is a multifaceted process combining several factors into a marketable skill:

1. The ability to read shorthand outlines.
2. The ability to write correctly from dictation.
3. The ability to spell correctly.
4. The ability to recognize possessives and hyphenated-word usages.
5. The ability to correctly punctuate sentences.
6. The ability to make correct choices among similar words.

When use of the typewriter is combined with transcription, the following factors also are added as necessary parts of the whole:

1. The ability to type accurately and speedily.
2. The ability to make correct and rapid decisions about word division.
3. The ability to apply correct number expression and capitalization rules.
4. The ability to make undetectable corrections.

These factors are combined with the ability to transliterate—to see a shorthand outline and transform the shorthand symbol into a typed word in the mind and finally into a correctly typed word on the page. One only needs to look at the elements of this multifaceted process to realize that this is a complex communication skill—one to be taught both thoughtfully and thoroughly.

Too often, transcription is the least-stressed learning component of shorthand instruction, although teachers and learners alike know the end product of all shorthand instruction is the mailable copy of a dictated piece of material.

Historically, when it was thought most students would study shorthand for two years to acquire a marketable skill, authors wrote of the desirability of not emphasizing transcription until the second year of instruction. Now, with a high percentage of high school shorthand students taking only one year of shorthand, it is mandatory that greater emphasis be placed on transcription in the first year. Thus students who take only one year of shorthand will be able to use the skills achieved to work in an entry-level stenographic position. The second year of instruction at the high school level will then further refine transcription skills to the level that high school students can enter true secretarial positions. In addition, early-transcription emphasis may place in proper perspective for the student the real purpose of shorthand instruction; thus encouraging the student inclined to stop after one year of study to visualize realistically the end-product in its refined form and hence pursue a second year.

Discussion in this chapter will address itself to the development of nontyping transcription learning and the development of typewritten-transcription abilities and learning.

Nontyping Transcription Learning Activities

Application of the language arts skills, or English skills, is essential to transcription. Studies such as those by Barras, Vought, and Swanson tell shorthand teachers that spelling, punctuation, typing, capitalization, grammar, and syllabication are essential parts of shorthand learning and must be included in the class activities.[1,2,3] Some teachers prefer to review these skills prior to the use of the typewriter for transcription. Others prefer to review these skills along with the typewritten-transcription work. Textbooks, student transcripts, workbooks, transparencies, special drills, and learning activity packets are some of the sources helpful in reviewing and refining the language arts skills or knowledge of transcription elements.

Diagnostic Testing

During the first few days of the beginning shorthand class, the teacher may wish to give a diagnostic test to determine the prior knowledge and application levels of the class in spelling, punctuation, hyphenation, number expression, use of possessives, word choice, and capitalization. Such a diagnostic test may be a part of a published test or one the teacher has designed. Information derived from diagnostic testing will help the teacher know which students need special drill work and how much information the class already has.

Use of the Textbook

The textbook is a rich source of information for reinforcement and refinement of transcription-element knowledge. The vividly printed marginal reminders emphasize spelling, possessives, transcription typing style, compound adjectives, and so on. Each lesson contains a list of three or four vocabulary words pertinent to the letters being studied, which helps to improve the student's vocabulary. At times, spelling lists and application of spelling rules are part of the lesson. Beginning with Lesson 31 of the first semester, a punctuation review is included in the textbook lessons. The punctuation is included in the plate material, with the coded reason for the punctuation appearing above it. This procedure is continued in all succeeding semester textbooks. In addition, at various places throughout the text, there is narrative related to effective transcription procedures and realistic office situations.

It is important during the preview of each day's lesson to point out to the student how to study these transcription elements. It is also important on the following day to make the student accountable for knowing the application of these transcription elements by reviewing a sampling of the transcription-element information and including some of this material in chapter testing. The textbook is a powerful learning instrument, and both teacher and student will want to make full use of the information in it.

Use of the Student Transcript

The student transcript is a self-study aid containing a written key to the shorthand plate material contained in the text. In the early stages of the first semester, the transcript is essential in helping the student become a fluent reader. The student must be taught to use the two-finger approach (one index finger on the student transcript and the other on the text plate), or the approach of drypenning over each outline in the plate while reading, with the other index finger following at the approximate location in the student transcript. This enables the student to quickly find the word causing the problem, go back to the textbook and spell and say the word, and quickly continue reading.

Students will read the lesson with much greater enthusiasm and more times if the student transcript is available while they are studying. Good reading ability is important to transcription, for a person cannot transcribe accurately and fluently without reading accurately and fluently.

The transcription elements found in the student transcript (spelling, punctuation, number expression, hyphenation, capitalization, possessives, spelling of proper nouns) are all part of homework study. Seeing these items in typescript provides reinforcement for the learner. Therefore, students should be advised to study these transcription elements in the student transcript as part of homework preparation. When computing three-minute transcription rates, the student transcript is a source from which the student can determine the total words transcribed. For these reasons, the student transcript is a recommended student learning aid throughout all semesters of shorthand study.

Use of the Workbook

The workbook is an excellent source for vocabulary development, root-word refinement and derivative formation, punctuation review, transcription-knowledge development, and spelling. Teachers use the workbook in a variety of ways. Some remove certain pages to use for testing, others have the student complete the workbook in class, while still others require homework assignments from the workbook. Like the student transcript and the textbook, it is another source of information for the student to help "fine-tune" transcription knowledge. When the student comes to class after having completed the workbook assignment, a transparency of the completed work can be displayed on the screen for checking and discussion.

Use of Nontyping Drills

Nontyping drills can be in the form of responses to transparency drills; oral or written responses to duplicated review sheets; spell-downs; punctuation and other transcription-element games or relays; proofreading exercises; unison or individual reading of the homework lesson from plate or notes, with insertion of punctuation and reason for it; class discussion of the marginal reminders and vocabulary words in the lesson; and lesson or chapter tests on the vocabulary and transcription knowledge covered. A teacher must not neglect the development of transcription knowledge in deference to developing dictation speed. Time spent in building a foundation of transcription knowledge will be evidenced in transcription of dictation tests and mailable letters.

Early Typewritten Transcription

Many teachers are successfully using typewritten transcription in beginning shorthand classes. The practice of developing typewritten-transcription skills early in the shorthand program appears to have gained approval from a substantial number of teachers. Research evidence is conclusive enough to show the feasibility of this practice.

The reasons some teachers have given for wishing to delay type-written transcription have been that the time spent on it would take away from the time available for reading, shorthand vocabulary development, and dictation development. These teachers think it is psychologically more sound to develop reading, shorthand vocabulary,

235

and dictation skills and then fuse these three abilities into transcription skills.

Studies by Brent, DeYoung, Hampton, Hauppa, and Keller show that the introduction of typewritten-transcription drills and transcription-rate work in the first semester of shorthand instruction do not adversely affect achievement in reading rates, shorthand vocabulary knowledge, dictation speed, and mailable-letter production.[4,5,6,7,8]

The strongest argument in favor of introducing typewritten transcription early in the beginning shorthand course is that many students never take an advanced course. The national ratio of beginning to advanced classes is three to one. The major reason, as reported in a study by Crank and others, seems to be that many students do not start their shorthand study at the secondary level until they are seniors; they do not have the opportunity to take the high school advanced course.[9] This clearly indicates that shorthand teachers must help inform counselors, students, administrators, parents, and other teachers of the advisability of starting shorthand study in the junior year. Students wishing to develop a strong vocational shorthand ability would then be able to improve shorthand vocabulary, dictation, and transcription abilities to a level that would enable them to succeed in secretarial positions at the time of secondary school graduation.

The student who has time for only one year of shorthand study in high school or the student who attends a small high school where only one year is offered can, by the end of one year, if typewritten transcription has been begun early, transcribe at the typewriter with greater confidence and produce mailable letters with a minimum of revision or correction.

Another argument in favor of early typewritten transcription is that the realism of the practice is powerfully motivating. Students enjoy the opportunity to use the typewriter as the output instrument of their shorthand study, because it is the output instrument in the business office.

Suggested Starting Time for Typewritten Transcription

Condon was one of the first advocates of early typewritten transcription.[10] In his teaching and experimentation, Condon began typewritten transcription in the first few days of beginning shorthand classes. The studies conducted by Brent, DeYoung, Hampton, and Hauppa and the teaching at Northern Illinois University have worked with the Condon concept and advocate beginning typewritten transcription about the third week of the first semester of the beginning shorthand course.

Two prerequisites must be fulfilled if typewritten transcription is to begin early, or about the third week of the study of shorthand:

(1) The students should have completed a year of typing before enrolling in beginning shorthand, and (2) beginning shorthand must be taught in a classroom where there is a typewriter available for each student.

Teachers should realize, however, that even when students have not learned typing before beginning shorthand, typewritten transcription can be started about the fifth or sixth week of the first semester of shorthand if the students are currently enrolled in beginning typing. These students would have learned the typewriter keyboard by this time and probably would be stroking, on short timings, at approximately the rate of 20 wam. The transcription drills in the beginning stages will be timed for short periods of 30 seconds and 1 minute; the material will be familiar homework material; transcription elements of spelling, hyphenation, and the like will be heavily previewed; and the drills will be repetitive. The expected rates of transcription in the first semester are low enough that students currently enrolled in beginning typing can attain the prescribed transcription goals.

Teachers with only two or three beginning shorthand students concurrently enrolled in beginning typing and all other students having completed a year of typing, could begin typewritten transcription the tenth or eleventh day as recommended. The two or three beginning typing students can still benefit from the classroom discussion of the transcription elements and can be practicing simple typing drills, developing reading abilities by paired reading, or working with individual audio-listening equipment to develop dictation abilities. Teachers with the majority of beginning shorthand students currently enrolled in beginning typing would be wise to wait until about the fifth or sixth week to begin any typewritten transcription.

Planning Typewritten-Transcription Activities

The greatest benefits are derived from typewritten-transcription practice when a specific schedule is planned and followed. Such a schedule generally contains the following sequence:

1. *Teacher demonstration of correct position, posture, and height of chair and/or typewriter; followed by the student's use of correct position, posture, and height of chair and/or typewriter.* For an electric typewriter, the chair and typewriter should be at a height that fingertips are only slightly above elbow level. This height helps the student avoid the use of the large arm muscle and maintain quiet hand and finger movement. The teacher instructs the student repeatedly that the fingers should "hug the keyboard." For a manual machine, the chair and typewriter should be at

a height that the level of the fingertips is about 6 inches above the elbow level. This height helps the student use the large arm muscle for the staccato, quick, more powerful stroke on the manual typewriter. The student should be a handspan of space from the typewriter, sitting back in the chair, body erect, and leaning forward slightly from the waist. This helps the student develop a relaxed but alert position at the typewriter.

2. *Teacher demonstration and checking of correct stroking techniques.* For the electric machine, the fingers should be curved and the keys struck with a light touch. For the manual machine, the fingers should be extremely curved, and snap or staccato stroking should be emphasized.

3. *Teacher demonstration and practice by the students of the nonkeyboard operations of setting and clearing tab stops; operating tab key or bar; returning carriage or element; quickly and efficiently inserting and removing paper; and setting margins.*

(It is wise to thoroughly review these first three points, because rapid and accurate transcription requires correct typing techniques and motions.)

4. *Teacher demonstration of the correct techniques of transliteration to be applied to typewritten transcription.* The goal is to keep the carriage or element moving continuously and to focus attention on the word being transcribed. Focusing attention on each outline aids in the accuracy of transcription. In addition, to accurately transcribe similar words, such as *their-there, to-too-two, you-your,* it is necessary to read in thought groups.

5. *Performance by teacher and student of guided transcription from shorthand notes written on the chalkboard.* Guided transcription of brief-form sentences shows the student the process of transliteration and smooth, continuous transcription.

6. *Transcription from shorthand plate material for speed or accuracy.*

7. *Goal-setting transcription drills from shorthand plates.*

8. *Goal-setting transcription drills from homework notes.*

9. *One-, two-, and three-minute transcription-rate exercises from homework notes, with students correcting errors.*

A Suggested Weekly Calendar of Typewritten-Transcription Activities for the First Semester of Beginning Shorthand

Transcription drills, like typing drills, should be short and should be continued throughout all semesters of shorthand. As part of the Hampton study, typewritten-transcription patterns and a sequential calendar of activities were developed.[11] Later a printed brochure, "Designs for Teaching Typewritten Transcription in High School and Collegiate Shorthand Classes," was developed and has been used by shorthand teachers throughout the United States.[12] The recommended drills, partial calendars, and descriptions of the drills from the brochure are included here. A specific schedule of transcription drills is essential if all components of shorthand learning are to receive appropriate emphasis. The following weekly calendar of transcription activities is recommended for the first semester of beginning shorthand. The calendar of activities is set up in such a way that three days of a week are used for typewritten transcription, with each day's transcription activities using about 7 to 15 minutes of the class period. Shorthand teachers who use the recommended calendar will need to select the three days of the week that work out best with the other required activities. If shorthand classes meet fewer than five days a week, appropriate adjustments will need to be made in weeks three and four.

WEEKLY CALENDAR OF TRANSCRIPTION ACTIVITIES

Class Week	Class Day	Class Activity
1	—	No typewritten transcription
2	—	No typewritten transcription
3	1 & 2	No typewritten transcription
	3	Review typing techniques
		Guide students in transcribing simple sentences
	4	Review typing techniques
		Guide students in transcribing simple sentences
	5	30-second simple sentence drills from plate notes. One-minute simple sentence drills from plate notes.
4	1 2 3	30-second simple sentence drills from plate notes. One-minute simple sentence drills from plate notes
	4 & 5	No typewritten transcription (From this point on, the typewritten transcription practice may be given during any three days of the week. However, it is advisable to give typewritten transcription practice for three days in succession when possible.
5	1–3	30-second goal-setting drills from plate notes
6	1–3	One-minute goal-setting drills from homework notes
7	1–3	One-minute transcription-rate drills from homework notes
8	1–3	Two-minute transcription-rate drills from homework notes
9	1–3	Two-minute transcription-rate drills from homework notes—erasing and correcting introduced
10	1–3	Three-minute transcription-rate drills from homework notes—corrected transcripts

Class Week	Class Day	Class Activity
11	1–3	One-minute speed-building drills from homework notes (1 day)
		Three-minute transcription-rate drills from homework notes—corrected transcripts (2 days)
12	1–3	One-minute goal-setting drills for speed from homework notes (1 day)
		Three-minute transcription-rate drills from homework notes—corrected transcripts (2 days)
13	1–3	One-minute goal-setting drills for control from homework notes (1 day)
		Three-minute transcription-rate drills from homework notes—corrected transcripts (2 days)
14	1 & 2	One-minute goal-setting drills for speed from homework notes
	3	Three-minute transcription-rate drills from homework notes— corrected transcripts
15	1 & 2	One-minute goal-setting drills for speed from homework notes
	3	Three-minute transcription-rate drills from homework notes—corrected transcripts
16	1 & 2	One-minute goal-setting drills for speed from homework notes
	3	Three-minute transcription-rate drills from homework notes—corrected transcripts
17	1	One-minute goal-setting drills for speed from homework notes
	2	One-minute goal-setting drills for control from homework notes
	3	Three-minute transcription-rate drills from homework notes—corrected transcripts
18	1 & 2	Three-minute transcription-rate drills from homework notes—corrected transcripts

Typewritten-Transcription Drills and Teaching Procedures for the Beginning of Typewritten Transcription

Haney found that students using short transcription drills achieved significantly better results on five-minute transcription tests of pre-viewed material, higher speeds on previewed three-minute dictation tests, and significantly higher speeds on unpreviewed three-minute dictation tests than students not using the drills. The students using the transcription drills also achieved significantly higher and more accurate transcription rates and higher speeds on both previewed and unpreviewed mailable-letter-production tests than students not using these drills.

Typewritten-transcription drills, like all skill and learning development, gradually progress from the very simplest to more complex transcribing procedures. Implementation of correct transcribing techniques, repeated emphasis on correct and well-written shorthand notes, encouragement to learn the transcription elements of the lesson, plus employment of drill procedures laced with "teaching cues" will help the student easily adjust to using the typewriter in the shorthand process. Throughout the drills, the students are instructed to use a five-inch line because five inches is the most-used line length for the average-sized letters transcribed in mailable-production work. The student receives much practice in bell listening, word division, and equalizing side margins while performing short transcription drills and three-minute transcription rates.

The teacher is reminded that the drills being discussed must not take more than 7 to 15 minutes of any class period. They need to be executed quickly to develop good work habits; use class time efficiently; and not neglect the other skill-development areas of reading, shorthand vocabulary, and dictation. Following are descriptions of the drills listed in Weeks 3 through 17 of the first semester in the calendar on pages 239 and 240.

GUIDING STUDENTS IN TRANSCRIBING SIMPLE SENTENCES. About the third day of the third week the students begin transcribing from simple sentences that the teacher has written on the chalkboard or on the overhead transparency. The students read in unison. The teacher then demonstrates at a typewriter the flow of transcribing while reading the sentence aloud. The students then transcribe the sentence as the teacher points to and calls each word in succession. Depending on the amount of time to be used, several sentences could be drilled in this fashion.

THIRTY-SECOND SIMPLE SENTENCE DRILLS FROM PLATE NOTES. About the fifth day of the third week, the teacher selects from the shorthand plate in the textbook (from the previous night's homework assignment) three simple sentences (no internal punctuation) of equal length (10 to 14 words) that occur in succession. The students should have rubber bands around the open parts of the textbook to help keep the book open while transcribing. Copyholders are in position near the typewriter. The procedures recommended are as follows:

1. Review the sentences by reading in unison, students drypenning over the outlines while reading them.
2. Instruct the students to "touch throw" the carriage or the ribbon carrier and transcribe the same sentence again if they

complete the sentence before time is called. Instruct them to double space between each timing. Remind the students that they are not to be concerned about typographical errors.

3. Time the students for 30 seconds on transcribing the first sentence from the plate notes.
4. Repeat the first sentence. Urge the students to strive to transcribe at least one word more on the second timing. Time for 30 seconds.
5. Using the same procedure, give two 30-second timings on the second and third sentences.

ONE-MINUTE SIMPLE-SENTENCE DRILLS FROM PLATE NOTES. As a second part of the preceding drill:

1. Combine all three sentences for one-minute timings. Time for one minute.
2. Urge the students to strive to increase the amount transcribed on a second transcription of the combined sentences. Time for one minute.
3. Urge the students to increase the amount transcribed on the combined sentences. Time for one minute.

THIRTY-SECOND GOAL-SETTING DRILLS FROM PLATE NOTES. Select from the shorthand plate in the textbook (from the previous night's homework assignment) a paragraph containing at least 40 words.

1. Review the paragraph by reading in unison, students drypenning over the outlines while reading them. Have the students insert the superior numbers indicating units of 20 standard words above the proper shorthand outlines in their texts. They may use their transcripts to obtain these numbers, or the locations may be indicated by the instructor during the unison reading so that the class may insert them quickly. Instruct the students to try to reach the first superior number on the first transcription of 30 seconds. Tell them not to be concerned about typographical errors. Time for 30 seconds.
2. Check to see how many reached the goal of 20 words in 30 seconds. Instruct those who did not reach the goal to attempt to reach it on the next timing. Tell those who reached the goal to set a new goal for ten additional words (half way to the next superior number). Time for 30 seconds.
3. Check the achievement of the group. Tell those who reached their goal to set a new goal of ten additional words. Time for 30 seconds.
4. Check achievement and set new goals. Time for 30 seconds.
5. Inform the students that now they should work for control in transcribing by using controlled finger reaches; slowing speed enough to maintain control; and focusing attention on the syllable, letter, or word level. The aim is to transcribe accurately

to the first superior figure (20 words) in 30 seconds. Time for 30 seconds.

6. Students proofread their work and record the number of errors beside the timing. Those who reached the goal of 20 words in 30 seconds with no errors would then attempt to increase their goal by five words. Ask them to place a slash mark in their texts at the point of the new goal. Urge those who did not reach the goal of 20 words in the 30 seconds but had no more than one error to increase stroking rate while still maintaining control. Instruct those who reached their goal but had more than one error to drop back in speed and strive for accurate reading and transcribing of each outline. Time for 30 seconds.

7. Students proofread and respond to questioning regarding achievement.

ONE-MINUTE GOAL-SETTING DRILLS FROM HOMEWORK NOTES. Select from the previous night's homework notes a paragraph containing at least 70 words.

1. Review the paragraph by reading in unison and drypenning. During the unison reading, have the students insert in their homework notes the superior numbers indicating units of 20 standard words. Instruct them to try to reach the second superior number (40 words) on the first timing. Direct the students to ignore paragraphing, space twice at the end of the sentence, and continue typing on the same line. Tell them not to be concerned about typographical errors. Time for one minute.

2. Check achievement. Instruct those who reached the goal of 40 wam to set a new goal for 10 additional words (half way to the next superior number) and encourage the others to reach the 40-word goal on the next timing. Time for one minute.

3. Check achievement. Set goals, with constructive comments for improvement. Time for one minute.

4. Check achievement. Set goals, with constructive comments for improvement. Time for one minute.

5. Check achievement. Make comments for improvement. Time for one minute.

ONE-MINUTE TRANSCRIPTION-RATE DRILLS FROM HOMEWORK NOTES. Select from the shorthand homework notes (from the previous night's homework assignment) a paragraph containing at least 80 words. Use a measurement device such as that described on page 248 to determine three-minute transcription rates.

1. Review the paragraph by reading in unison, discussing and practicing any transcription problems it may contain. Instruct the students to work for speed on the first three timings. The

243

highest of the three will be recorded. Direct the students to ignore paragraphing, to space twice at the end of the sentence, and continue typing on the same line. Time for one minute.

2. Students figure their transcription rates and record beside that timing. Set individual goals for the next timing. Time for one minute.

3. Students figure their transcription rates and record beside that timing. Urge them to strive for at least two more words on the next timing. Time for one minute.

4. Students figure transcription rates, record beside the timing, and circle the highest rate of the three.

5. Instruct the students to adjust their machines for double-spacing and to work for control on the next two timings by dropping back about 5 to 10 wam and concentrating on reading on the syllable, word, or letter level. Time for one minute.

6. Students proofread, figure rate, and record the rate and errors beside the timing. Urge them to strive for a faster transcription rate if accuracy is at the level of two or less errors. If there are more than two errors, ask the students to concentrate on typing technique and focus attention on letter, syllable, and total-word levels of transcribing. Time for one minute.

7. Students proofread, figure transcription rate, record errors and rate beside the timing, and circle the higher rate of the two controlled timings.

This rate work may be the first typewritten-transcription work collected from the student. However, teachers may wish to collect papers before this to evaluate progress.

TWO-MINUTE TRANSCRIPTION-RATE DRILLS FROM HOMEWORK NOTES. From the previous night's homework notes, select material containing at least 140 words.

1. Review the material, discussing any transcription problems. Give particular attention to items introduced in the Punctuation Practice beginning with Lesson 31. For variety, call on one student to read the material to be transcribed, or on several students to read parts of the material. All students are dry-penning during the reading. Instruct the students to transcribe for *control*. Direct them to ignore paragraphing, space twice at the end of the sentence, and continue typing on the same line. Time for two minutes.

2. Students proofread and figure transcription rates (no deduction for errors) and record the wam and number of errors beside the timing. Urge students to try to transcribe five to eight more total words on the next timing, though still maintaining control of no more than three to four errors. Time for two minutes.

3. Students proofread and figure rate the same as above and circle the higher rate of the two timings.

TWO-MINUTE TRANSCRIPTION-RATE DRILLS FROM HOMEWORK NOTES—ERASING AND CORRECTING INTRODUCED. Select from the previous night's homework notes material containing at least 140 words. Erasing and correcting errors (including squeezing and spreading words) should be reviewed the day before this pattern is begun.

1. Review material, discussing any transcription problems. Give special attention to Punctuation Practice illustrations.
2. Instruct the students to work for control, erasing and correcting all errors as soon as they realize they have made them. Inform them that they will have one minute after the timing to further proofread and correct any errors they did not realize they had made. Ignore paragraphing, space twice at the end of the sentence, and continue typing on the same line. Time for two minutes.
3. Allow one minute for proofreading and correcting additional errors. Remove papers from the machine.
4. Instruct students to proofread copy carefully, reading each word and listening as the instructor reads the material, gives the punctuation and reasons, and explains the transcription-element usage. Students figure the transcription rate by deducting from the total words transcribed one word for each transcription error* and ten words for each typing error** not corrected. Divide the remainder by 2 to obtain the wam. Record the rate beside the timing. Urge students to either increase their transcription rates or reduce their errors, whichever is appropriate. Time for two minutes, repeating the same material.
5. Instruct students to proofread and correct additional errors— allow one minute. Remove papers from the typewriter.
6. Students again proofread as teacher reads the material. Students mark -1 or -10 at the point of the error. Students figure rate as indicated in step 4, record it beside the timing,

---

Transcription Error—an error that cannot be classified as a typing error. Transcription errors include incorrectly transcribed outlines, incorrectly spelled words, omitted words, added words, transposed words, punctuation errors, hyphenation errors, possession errors, capitalization errors, errors in correct application of number expression, and so on.

**Typing Error*—an incorrectly typed letter, symbol, figure; poor correction; spacing error; or any error that results from incorrect operation of the typewriter.

and place the better rate at the top of the paper under name and date.

THREE-MINUTE TRANSCRIPTION RATES FROM HOMEWORK NOTES— CORRECTING TRANSCRIPTS. (The recommended measurement device used throughout the remainder of the first semester and throughout second, third, and fourth semesters, or all semesters and quarters of shorthand instruction.) From the previous night's homework notes, select material containing at least 160 words. (The number of words needed will increase as the students' abilities increase. The selected material will always need to consist of more words than the fastest transcriber can transcribe.) Students should correct errors as they realize they are made.

1. Review the material, discussing transcription problems with special emphasis on new punctuation introduced in the lesson. Use some variety in the method of review—unison, one person, several persons. Ignore paragraphing, space twice at the end of sentences, continue transcribing on the same line. Time for three minutes.
2. Allow students one minute to proofread and correct any errors they did not realize they made while transcribing.
3. Draw a straight line at the right edge of the paper, at 80 on the elite machine and at 67 on the pica.
4. Remove papers from the machines. Instruct students to proofread copy as the instructor reads the material, reads in punctuation and reason for the punctuation, and explains the transcription-element usage. Students figure transcription rate by deducting from the total words transcribed one word for each transcription error and ten words for each typing error not corrected. Divide the remainder by three minutes to obtain the wam. Record the rate at the right of the timing. Urge students to either increase their transcription rate or reduce their errors, whichever is appropriate. Insert another sheet of paper (ask that students use clean paper rather than the back of a previous timing, because corrections are difficult to make well when typing on the back of previously used paper). Time for three minutes, repeating the same material.
5. Students proofread and correct errors for one minute.
6. Students draw a straight line at the right edge of the paper at 80 elite, 67 pica; remove papers from the typewriter.
7. Instructor reads material as students proofread their papers, figure rate, record beside the timing, and circle the better of the two attempts. To help students develop an attitude of accuracy in transcription, three-minute transcription-rate work with more than five errors should not be considered acceptable.

To help students learn to listen for the typewriter bell and make quick decisions about correct word division, attention must be given to listening for the bell in drill work and in three-minute transcription-rate work. First, the students must know, for their own particular machine, where the bell rings before the desired end of the line. If the desired end of the line is 80 elite and 67 pica, as it would be for the five-inch line, they must know if the bell is ringing four, five, six or more or fewer spaces before the 80 or 67 and learn to recognize the stopping point for the line. The transfer of this practice and learning is valuable for mailable-letter work. Students practice responding to the bell, word division, an equalizing left and right margins numerous times before the mailable-letter work begins.

To check performance on this task, students will align the plastic card-holder arrow with 80 on the elite and 67 on the pica, roll the paper back up to the first line of the typed transcript, place a pen or pencil in the arrow, hold the pen or pencil firmly, and turn the cylinder to get a vertical straight line down the paper. Decisions then must be made as to whether the typed lines are too long or too short. In the beginning stages the teacher may wish to only write a comment on the students' papers regarding the length of lines. After they have practiced for a time, the teacher may wish to count too-long lines or too-short lines as typing errors which would be a -10 deduction on the three-minute transcription-rate work.

Variations of the one-minute drills can be completed to develop transcription speed and accuracy. Goals will need to be identified and recommendations made for improvement and growth.

The drills that have been discussed can be used during the first semester of the beginning shorthand course if the prerequisites of previous typing instruction and typewriters in the shorthand class-room have been met. If teachers do not wish to spend three days a week in typewritten transcription, two days instruction would be helpful to the students. Whatever alterations are made to the proposed calendar, it is important to move from the simple to the more complex. It is also important to help the students as much as necessary for learning to take place and to withdraw previewing and confirmation as soon as possible in order to help the student gain independence.

Evaluation Procedures

All short drills are designed for drill only; no grade should be assigned to them. A grade can be assigned to the three-minute transcription rate to evaluate growth resulting from the drills. The following grading scale might be applied to the three-minute transcription rates in the first semester of beginning shorthand:

SECOND 6 WEEKS		THIRD 6 WEEKS	
25+ wam	= A	28+ wam	= A
21–24 wam	= B	24–27 wam	= B
16–20 wam	= C	19–23 wam	= C
11–15 wam	= D	14–18 wam	= D

With approximately 7 to 15 minutes a day for three days a week devoted to typewritten transcription, most teachers will want to allocate 10 to 20 percent of the total shorthand grade to the typewritten transcription component. The recommended standards for all four semesters are included in Chapter 10.

Source of Material Used for Transcription Drills and Three-Minute Transcription Rate

For the first three weeks of typewritten transcription, homework plate notes are the source. These notes are correctly written, well-proportioned outlines, so the student will not have a problem trying to read poorly or incorrectly written outlines. By the fourth week of transcription practice the student should be using homework notes as the source. The use of homework notes is recommended for the remainder of the first semester and throughout the second, third, and fourth semesters. The major reasons for this extensive use of homework notes is to encourage students to write the homework; to write homework practice notes accurately and with good proportion; and to know the information required for homework, such as hyphenated words, possessives, capitalization, spelling, number expression, and all other transcription-element information.

Reinforcement and Refinement of Transcription Skills and Knowledge

The shorthand teacher must use every opportunity to teach, refine, and reinforce the components of transcription. In the very beginning of the use of typewritten transcription drills, the transcription elements (spelling, number expression, capitalization, hyphenated words, compound words, and so on) are previewed heavily by the teacher before the students practice the drill. Various previewing techniques can be used, such as chalkboard discussion followed by students practicing typing the word or words; transparency drills; and student response to teacher questioning about the transcription elements, with reinforcement on the chalkboard or overhead.

About the seventh week of the typewritten transcription drill work, there is a gradual decrease in the amount of previewing, and only the items with which students could be expected to have difficulty will need special review or preview.

With Lesson 31 of the first semester textbook, a punctuation review is begun. The students are asked to place the punctuation in the homework notes, circle it, and write in abbreviated longhand the reason (coded reason) for it above the punctuation. Again, the previewing, explanation, and discussion of the punctuation review is heavy in the beginning stages and gradually becomes less with emphasis later only on the more difficult punctuation.

When three-minute transcription rates are administered, the teacher will want to read back the material as the students proofread and score their copy. During this reading, the teacher is again pointing out the reasons for transcription elements, emphasizing various ones, and spelling words.

Special duplicated drill sheets, workbook exercises, learning activity packets, and transparencies are helpful for teaching transcription elements diagnosed as presenting special problems for the class or for individual students. Discussions and practice of transcription elements before drill practice, their implementation during drill practice, and finally a review of the transcription elements at the completion of the practice will provide learning and refinement of transcription-element usage.

Use the Student Transcript to Learn, Refine, and Reinforce Transcription Elements

The student transcript should be a part of each student's study materials during each semester of shorthand study. In addition to helping with reading development, the transcript provides a source for outside-of-class dictation, and for writing homework notes. Most importantly, the student transcript serves as a reference manual for all transcription elements. The student should be made to feel responsible for knowing the transcription elements in each letter. To study a lesson without learning this information gives practice in writing shorthand but not complete development of the cognitive aspect of learning it.

Mailable-Letter Work Continues the Refinement and Reinforcement of Transcription Elements

In the first stage of the mailable-letter procedure, the teacher will discuss with the students the transcription-element usage before their transcription of the letters. This previewing will gradually be reduced and will be supplanted by postviewing the transcription-element usage after the letters have been transcribed. Further treatment of mailable-letter teaching and production appears in Chapter 9.

Development of Typewritten Transcription Speed

Typewritten transcription speed is developed in the same way as speed typing. First, the student must be able to read the material to be transcribed. During the first few weeks the transcription is from homework plate material. The student has drypenned and read repeatedly with the aid of the student transcript; then has self-dictated and written in the notebook as part of the homework preparation. The student has been urged to learn all the transcription elements from the textbook and student transcript of the material during homework.

The plate material to be transcribed is drypenned and read through in unison or by an individual. All transcription elements are discussed from the chalkboard or transparency. At times the student practices typing them. The student is in correct position—height, distance, fingers—and finally a speed goal is set. A speed goal 10 wam above the A rate for the three-minute transcription rate work for that point in the semester is realistic. The students are urged to transcribe rapidly, using correct stroking technique, motions, and posture. Because the material is homework, and all problem areas have been eliminated with the previews, and the drills are short—30 seconds or one minute—the students can successfully reach the speed goal. As each person reaches the goals identified, increased rates of transcription are attempted.

Drills recommended for speed development are the goal-setting, bell-ringing or calling-the-throw, and scribble-transcription drills. Checking on the progress of the class after each attempt and helping each individual set goals will help motivate each student toward increased transcription speed. After the first three weeks of the transcription-drill work, the source of the material is homework notes. At this time, it is necessary for the students to write the notes correctly and with good proportion. In addition, the student must know all transcription-element information (correct number expression, capitalization, hyphenated words, one- or two-word usages, spelling, punctuation) found in the homework material.

When working to develop transcription speed, it is important for the teacher to give cues and recommendations for increasing the speed, which are more helpful than "type faster." Some recommendations that can be made are:

1. Notes must be well written with correct outlines and accurate proportion.
2. Students must know the application of the transcription elements so quick, correct decisions can be made.
3. Position at the typewriter must be correct—head erect and facing the copy, which should be at the right of the machine and tilted to reduce shine; body erect and leaning forward

slightly; shoulders level; body a handspan from the machine, centered opposite the J key; feet apart, firmly braced on the floor, one foot ahead of the other; fingers curved under so that only the tips touch the keys for staccato stroking on the manual machine and quick, light stroking on the electric machine.

Within a drill period, after three or four or five attempts to reach the speed goals, the teacher may wish to give timings to attain accuracy of transcription.

Development of Accuracy in Transcription

The development of transcription accuracy carries many of the same components as the development of transcription speed. It is important that the student be able to read quickly and accurately the plate material assigned for homework and know the transcription-element information. When the source of transcription is homework notes, it is important that they be correctly written with accurate proportion. The transcription-element material must have been studied as a part of the homework preparation.

Transcription accuracy may be the goal for the entire drill, or accuracy drills may be given after three, four, or five speed-goal attempts. The accuracy goals should be about 5 wam above the A level for the three-minute transcription rate for each grading period. Students will need to be taught how to transcribe accurately. First, if the material is homework that has been studied sufficiently for the notes to be read fluently, if the notes are well written, and if the transcription elements have been learned, then the students will need to concentrate on correct typing techniques and the level of reading for accuracy. The position at the machine will need to be correct, as indicated under the development of speed.

Finally, the level of reading is important when attempting to transcribe accurately. The students should be taught how to read words at the letter, syllable, or total-word level. Reading level is individual; probably no two people will read words at the same level. Short, common words such as *to, the, as* will probably be read on the total-word level. A word such as *combination* will probably be read on the syllable and letter level, *com-bin-a-tion,* while a word such as *statistics* will probably be read on the individual letter level, *s-t-a-t-i-s-t-i-c-s.* Students will need to specifically practice transcribing to implement reading levels. After considerable practice, the reading level for accuracy will be a natural way of reading from shorthand notes. As in speed development, it is important to give positive cues to the student. It is not just a matter of slowing down to attain accuracy. Some helpful recommendations follow:

1. Notes must be well written with correct outlines and accurate proportion.
2. Students must know the application of the transcription elements so quick, correct decisions can be made.
3. Position at the typewriter must be correct, with specifics pointed out as needed. Fingers must hug the keyboard, and all non-keyboard reaches must be made by touch, with remaining fingers on the home-row keys.
4. Stroking must be controlled, with each finger directed to the correct key.
5. Reading must be according to the word, syllable, letter, or combination approach, with the mind focusing on the word being transcribed.

Typewritten-Transcription Drills for Second, Third, and Fourth Semesters of Shorthand

During the second, third, and fourth semesters, typewritten-transcription drills may be given on any three days of the week. However, it is advisable to give typewritten transcription drills for three days in succession when possible. The time spent during each class period should range from 6 minutes to about 13 minutes, with 10 minutes being about average. Teachers must continuously make sure that dictation speed building and shorthand-vocabulary refinement are the major skill development and learning components of the second semester and that typewritten-transcription drill takes a minor role.

A suggested partial second-semester calendar follows:

CLASS WEEK	CLASS DAY	CLASS ACTIVITY
1	1	Review typing techniques One-minute goal-setting drills from homework notes
	2	Review correcting techniques One-minute goal-setting drills from homework notes
	3	Three-minute transcription-rate drills from homework notes—corrected transcripts
2	1 & 2	One-minute scribble-transcription drills from homework notes
	3	Three-minute transcription-rate drills from homework notes—corrected transcripts

The remaining weeks of the second-semester calendar include two days of drills chosen from the following possible drills: one-minute goal-setting drills, one-minute scribble-transcription drills, one-minute call-the-return drills, one-minute guided goal-setting drills. The third day of the week is spent doing three-minute transcription rates from homework notes—corrected transcripts.

The one-minute goal-setting drills and three-minute transcription-rate drills were discussed in the first-semester drill descriptions. Goals are higher for the second semester, and transcription-element usage of punctuation, hyphenation, possessives, number expression, capitalization, and the like are more difficult. If two three-minute transcription rates are given in the same class period, each timing should be on different material to give a wider coverage of vocabulary and transcription-element usage. The drills that are new to the second-semester work are described as follows:

ONE-MINUTE SCRIBBLE-TRANSCRIPTION DRILLS FROM HOMEWORK NOTES. Select from the previous night's homework notes, material containing at least 90 words. Instruct students to adjust machines for the five-inch line, to single-space, and to ignore paragraphing.

1. Review the material to be transcribed, discussing transcription problems.
2. Direct students to transcribe as rapidly as possible on the first timing. Time for one minute, calling "return" at the end of the minute.
3. Instruct students to draw a vertical line (with pen or pencil) on paper in machine at the end of the last word transcribed. Tell them to roll back the paper so that it is positioned for retyping the same material on top of the transcription just completed.
4. Urge students to attempt to increase their transcription rates by three to five words beyond the previous transcription. Time for one minute.
5. Check achievement. Instruct students to place a vertical line at the end of this second transcription and to roll back the paper so that it is positioned for retyping directly over the previous two transcriptions.
6. Urge students to increase their transcription rates by three to five words beyond the second vertical line. Time for one minute.
7. Check achievement.
8. Direct students to space down to a clean section of the paper and to set the machine for double spacing. On this transcription, they are to attempt to transcribe the same number of words as in the first transcription (indicated by the first vertical line), *but* with no more than one error. Time for one minute.
9. Have students proofread. Check achievement by having students raise their hands if they transcribed with no errors; with one error.

10. Direct students to space down to a clean section of the paper. Those who achieved the goal equivalent to the first vertical line, with only one error or no errors, should now increase their transcription rates and attempt to transcribe as far as the second vertical line, still maintaining control. Time for one minute.

11. Check achievement with no errors and then with one error.

ONE-MINUTE CALL-THE-RETURN DRILLS FROM HOMEWORK NOTES. From the previous night's homework notes, select material containing at least 180 words (several letters in succession may be used). Instruct students to move the *paper guide* slightly to the left of zero, set the *left margin stop* at zero, and move the *right margin stop* to the end of the scale on the right. Adjust machines for *single spacing*. Ignore paragraphing. The goal is transcription speed.

1. Inform students that on these drills the number (on the horizontal-spacing scale) achieved on the timing indicates the transcription rate for that line. (Example: If the student transcribes to 45 on the horizontal-spacing scale, the transcription rate for that line is equivalent to one-fifth of 45, or 9 words for the 12 seconds. Since 45 strokes equals 9 words and "return" will be called each 12 seconds, or five times in one minute, the rate of 45 wam would be the goal for the one-minute drill.) Help the students locate the horizontal-spacing scale (on the paper bail on most manual machines, on the front of the machine just above the keys on electric machines).

2. Review the material to be transcribed, discussing transcription problems. Use some variety in the method of review—unison, one person, several persons, practicing items written on the chalkboard or an overhead transparency. Direct students to work for speed (ignoring errors) on the first three timings. Instruct students to start the timing from the "45" location on the line scale so the first portion requires a return the same as will all following portions.

3. Tell the students that you will call "return" at the beginning of the timing and at the end of each 12 seconds and that they are to "touch" return the carriage or ribbon carrier immediately, even though they may be in mid-word. They are to continue on the next line of typing, beginning the line with the next word in the shorthand notes. On the first timing, urge the students to strive to transcribe to 45 or beyond on the horizontal-spacing scale each time before the "return" call. Repeat the 12-second timings for one minute (five times), calling "return" at the end of each of the first four 12-second

intervals and calling "return and stop" at the end of the fifth 12-second interval (the minute).

4. Instruct students to quickly check to see how many lines they transcribed to 45 or more on the horizontal-spacing scale, by scanning up or down the page (depending on the location of the horizontal-spacing scale on the typewriter) in line with the 45. Check achievement to see how many transcribed beyond 45 on all five lines; on four lines.

5. Explain to the students that on each timing they are to begin where they left off on the previous transcription. Urge them to transcribe to 50 or beyond on each line on the next timing. Time for one minute, calling "return" at 12-second intervals and "return and stop" at the end of the minute.

6. Instruct students to quickly check how many lines they transcribed to 50 or more on the horizontal-spacing scale by scanning up or down the page (depending on the location of the horizontal-spacing scale on the typewriter) in line with the 50. Check achievement to see how many transcribed beyond 50 on all five lines; on four lines.

7. Urge students to transcribe to 55 or beyond on the next timing. Students are to begin where they left off on the previous timing. Time for one minute, calling "return" at 12-second intervals.

8. Instruct students to quickly check to see how many lines they transcribed beyond 55 on the scale. Check achievement to see how many transcribed beyond 55 on all five lines; on four lines.

9. Direct students to adjust machines for double spacing. Instruct them to transcribe from the beginning of the material and to work for *control* on the next two timings. Urge them to aim to transcribe to 50 or more on the scale, with perfect copy on each line. Remind students that if they are beyond 50 when "return" is called but are making errors, it would be better to reduce their speed slightly or read more carefully and maintain 50 with perfect copy. Time for one minute, calling "return" at 12-second intervals.

10. Have students proofread. Check achievement to determine those who transcribed to 50 or more on each line with no errors for the minute; with one error.

11. Direct students to begin where they left off on the previous timing and to try again for perfect copy while transcribing to 50 on the scale. Time for one minute, calling "return" at 12-second intervals.

12. Have students proofread. Check achievement to determine those who transcribed to 50 on each line with perfect copy for the minute; with one error.

255

A variation of this drill would be to decrease or increase the number of seconds for the "return" call, thus increasing and decreasing the number of lines in the timing. For example, if the 20-second return were used, the student would be transcribing three lines in a minute. If the student reached 45 (9 words × 3 = 27), the rate of 27 wam would have been achieved.

GUIDED GOAL-SETTING DRILLS FROM HOMEWORK NOTES. Select from the previous night's homework notes, material containing at least 100 words. Use the five-inch line and single spacing. Ignore paragraphing. The goal is transcription speed.

1. Review the material to be transcribed, discussing transcription elements. Have the students insert in their homework notes the superior figures indicating units of 20 standard words as the teacher indicates these locations.
2. Explain to the students that they will be guided in their transcription by hearing the superior figures at the proper intervals for the rate of 40 wam. Time for one minute, calling "1" at 30 seconds and calling "2 and stop" at the end of the minute.
3. Check achievement to determine those who reached or surpassed the goal of 40 wam. Direct those who did not reach the superior figures when called to speed up so they will reach the figures on the next timing. Time for one minute on the first two superior figures (40 words).
4. Check achievement to determine those who reached or surpassed the goal of 40 wam.
5. Direct the students to begin at superior figure 2 on the next timing and to strive to reach superior figure 3 at the end of 30 seconds and "4 and stop" at the end of the minute.
6. Check achievement to determine those who reached or surpassed the goal of 40 wam. Direct those who did not reach the superior figures when called to stroke rapidly to reach them on the next timing. Time for one minute beginning at superior figure 2.
7. Check achievement to determine those who reached or surpassed the goal.
8. Direct students to adjust machines for double spacing. Ask students to try for completely accurate transcription at the rate of 40 wam for two minutes as the superior figures are called to guide their transcription. They are to transcribe from the beginning of the material. Time for two minutes, calling the superior figures 1 through 4 at 30-second intervals.
9. Have students proofread material. Check achievement to determine those who reached the goal with perfect copy; with only one error.

Other Appropriate Drills

Variations of the previously described drills can provide similar opportunities for speed and accuracy development on typewritten transcription. Some teachers use a variable-line drill, which is similar to the one-minute call-the-return drill. Basically it is done in the following manner:

1. The student sets a line length of five inches (50 pica, 10 five-stroke words; 60 elite, 12 five-stroke words).
2. "Return" is called each 12 seconds or five times during the minute.
3. The student works toward a goal of 5 × 10 = 50 wam or 5 × 12 = 60 wam.

The goals can be set to provide for individual differences by having students lengthen the line to six inches after reaching the preceding goal. The six-inch line (60 pica, 12 five-stroke words; 70 elite, 14 five-stroke words) would provide for goals of 60 wam pica and 70 wam elite, if the 12-second goal is maintained. With this procedure, individual goals can be set for varying abilities within the class.

In addition to varying the length of lines for this drill, the number of seconds used for the "return calls" can be changed to fit appropriate class goals. For example, calling the "return" each 20 seconds and using the 50-space pica line would mean 10 words × 3, or 30 wam. Likewise, calling the "return" each ten seconds and using the 50-space pica line would mean 10 words × 6, or 60 wam. In summary, the variable-line drill provides for expansion or reduction of goals by varying the length of the line being used and/or by increasing or decreasing the number of seconds between "return" calls.

Many of the short drills used in typing class to develop speed and accuracy can be applied to developing speed and accuracy of type-written transcription. The creativity of shorthand teachers can provide motivating and satisfying experiences for students in this typewritten-transcription learning process.

ADJUST GOALS TO MATCH PROGRESS. When two-thirds or more of the class achieve the goals set for the various drills, the goals can be raised 5 wam. When the superior figures are called in the guided goal-setting drill, the interval chart for dictation of 20 standard-word material can be used. For example, if the goal to be achieved is 50 wam, the superior figures would be called every 24 seconds; for the 60-wam goal, the superior figures would be called every 20 seconds; for the 70-wam goal, the superior figures would be called every 17 seconds. For the 5-wam gains, the following formula could be used to determine the seconds for each superior figure:

$$\frac{\text{Standard Word Count}}{\text{Desired Rate}} \times 60 \text{ seconds} = \text{seconds per superior figure}$$

To determine the seconds per superior figure if calling the 55-wam goal, the following computation would be made: (20 is the standard word count for superior-figure-marked material)

$$\frac{20}{55} \times 60 = 22 \text{ seconds per superior figure}$$

The matching of goals to progress will need to be continued throughout the use of all drills. In all drill work it will be necessary to set the goals in relation to the standards being attempted for a particular grading period of the first, second, third, and fourth semesters.

A THIRD AND FOURTH SEMESTER CONTINUING PROCESS. The drills that have been described are recommended for use in the third and fourth semesters as well as the first and second semesters. The three-minute transcription-rate procedure is recommended for use throughout the four semesters. The standards indicated in Chapter 10, pages 344–355 will provide the basis not only for assigning grades but also for goal setting for the various drills. The amount of time devoted to transcription will depend on the emphases for the semesters as indicated in the standard percentages in Chapter 10, pages 343 and 350 and in the competency emphases outlined in Chapter 2, pages 52–57.

The Jester study points out strongly the need for additional typewritten-transcription instruction.[14] In this study, 62 percent of the time was devoted to nontyping activities involving correcting errors, deciphering shorthand notes, and spelling and punctuation problems. Shorthand problems causing pauses in the transcription process were inability to read shorthand notes, deciphering incorrect shorthand outlines, and reading shorthand for context and meaning.

Transcribers who wrote accurate shorthand outlines were more efficient and faster than those who lost time deciphering incorrectly written outlines. This study further emphasizes the need to write notes correctly as the source for transcription. Teachers can help develop this ability and the attitude of correctly writing notes by repeatedly using homework notes as the source of typewritten transcription and constantly emphasizing that homework notes must be written with correct proportion and outline. When typewritten-transcription drills and three-minute transcription rates are given frequently, each using well-written homework notes as the source, students develop the ability and attitude for writing notes correctly and in good proportion. This skill is then carried over into mailable-letter-production work, because the emphasis when taking dictation is not so much on writing rapidly as on writing correctly and with accurate proportion.

Another aspect of the Jester study that can be applied directly to typewritten-transcription drills and three-minute transcription-rate work is the need to develop more accurate and rapid typing and the ability to make quick decisions about spelling; punctuation; and application of transcription elements of capitalization, number expression, hyphenation, word division, and so on. Using typewritten-transcription drills will give a great deal of practice in all these, and the three-minute transcription rate will help the students see their achievement.

In all typewritten-transcription-drill work and three-minute transcription-rate work, it is essential that the student use transcription elements correctly and apply correct typing techniques. Further, it is necessary that both student and teacher set goals and make genuine efforts to achieve them. The teacher will need to diagnose problems and recommend remedial procedures for continued learning and growth in performance to take place.

Relationship to Mailable-Letter Production

If the students have been doing transcription drills and three-minute transcription rates since the third week of the first semester, or at least during the first semester, they will feel comfortable with transcription when they are ready to move into mailable letters. They have developed a relatively high degree of speed and accuracy of typewritten transcription; learned the importance of correctly written and accurately proportioned notes; and learned how to transcribe, making correct and quick decisions in applying transcription elements. In addition, with the use of the five-inch line for drills and the three-minute transcription rate, the student has developed a sense of bell listening and has had much experience in deciding about word division and completion of lines. The five-inch line is commonly used for the average-length letter, and since most business letters are average length, the carryover from the drills and three-minute transcription rate work should be helpful in mailable-letter production.

Drills and three-minute rate work are continued as part of the transcription emphasis throughout all semesters of shorthand. It is through drills that transcription speed and accuracy are improved. By continuing to use the three-minute transcription rate, an evaluation of progress in transcription speed and accuracy can be made.

Chapter 9 deals with developing the ability to produce mailable letters by introducing the process and detailing a plan for movement from the simple to the more complex tasks involved.

Notes

1. Sister Mary Joanna Barras, "Transcription Achievement of Fourth-Semester Shorthand Students in Selected Catholic

High Schools in the Midwest," master's thesis, University of Wisconsin, Madison, 1961.

2. Barbara Jeanne Vought, "A Study of Transcription Errors Made on Different Transcription Activities by Shorthand I and II Students of Peotone High School," master's thesis, Northern Illinois University, DeKalb, 1968.

3. Dorothy Swanson, "A Study of Nonshorthand Transcription Errors Made on Letters Transcribed by a Shorthand II Class at Moline Senior High School," master's thesis, Northern Illinois University, DeKalb, 1970.

4. Linda C. Brent, "A Study to Determine the Effect of Early Introduction of Typewritten Transcription on Achievement in Beginning Shorthand," master's thesis, Northern Illinois University, DeKalb, 1970.

5. Ron C. DeYoung, "The Effect of Early Typewritten Transcription Practice on Achievement in Shorthand Classes," independent research, Northern Illinois University, DeKalb, 1968.

6. Donald F. Hampton, "The Effect on Achievement in First-Year Shorthand of Introducing Typewritten Transcription Practice at Various Times During the Year," doctoral dissertation, Northern Illinois University, DeKalb, 1971.

7. Dorothy Hauppa, "An Experimental Study to Determine Effect on Achievement When Introducing Typewritten Transcription in First-Year Pitman Shorthand," master's thesis, Northern Illinois University, DeKalb, 1971.

8. John Frederick Keller, "Immediate Introduction to Typewritten Transcription Versus Deferred Introduction to Typewritten Transcription in First-Year Shorthand Classes," doctoral dissertation, University of North Dakota, Grand Forks, 1973.

9. Floyd L. Crank, Doris H. Crank, and Mary Frances Hanrahan, "Why Don't Beginning Shorthand Students Go On?" *Balance Sheet*, December 1971, January 1972, pp. 153–156.

10. Arnold Condon, "A Comparative Study of the Transcription and the Functional Methods of Teaching Elementary Shorthand," doctoral dissertation, New York University, New York, 1946.

11. Hampton, op. cit.

12. Doris H. Crank, Floyd L. Crank, and Donald F. Hampton, "Designs for Teaching Typewritten Transcription in High School and Collegiate Shorthand Classes," independent research, Northern Illinois University, DeKalb, 1973.

13. Annice Mauldin Haney, "The Effect of Selected Shorthand Transcription Drills on Transcription Skill Development,"

doctoral dissertation, North Texas State University, Denton, 1976.

14. Donald D. Jester, "A Time Study of the Shorthand Transcription Process," doctoral dissertation, Northwestern University, Evanston, Illinois, 1959.

Chapter 9

Developing Mailable-Letter Production Ability

The production of mailable letters is the accountability factor in the teaching of shorthand. Shorthand-related components of mailable-letter production are:

1. Reading self-written notes rapidly and accurately.
2. Taking dictation and writing with controlled, correctly written outlines.
3. Making efficient and correct decisions in applying transcription rules of number expression, hyphenation, possessives, spelling, punctuation, capitalization, and sentence structure.

Correct and efficient application of these shorthand-related components must be combined with the typing components of the mailable letter.

The fact that a rather large proportion of students takes beginning shorthand in the senior year and are not in the secondary school for an advanced course vividly tells shorthand teachers that developing a marketable mailable-letter-production ability is an essential emphasis for the first year of shorthand.

Introduction to Mailable-Letter Production

The time to introduce mailable letters in the shorthand program will depend on many factors:

1. The number of semesters or quarters in the total shorthand program.
2. The ability of the students.
3. The availability of typewriters during the first semester of instruction.
4. The amount of time devoted to typewritten transcription in the first semester of instruction.
5. The goals to be accomplished by the end of the first year of high school instruction or two semesters or three quarters of postsecondary instruction.

Each shorthand instructor will need to evaluate these factors in setting emphases for the second and succeeding semesters and quarters of instruction.

Some teachers will recommend introducing mailable-letter production at the beginning of the second semester of the high school beginning shorthand course. If this is done, no doubt less time will be spent on dictation speed building. Learning activities such as continued shorthand vocabulary refinement, continued development of typewritten-transcription speed and accuracy, and further refinement of transcription-element execution would be emphasized. Proponents of this thinking state that it is important to use mailable-letter production as one of the major emphases during the second semester of the beginning course. With this degree of mailable-letter emphasis and less time spent on dictation speed building, the three-minute dictation test on new material could be replaced with production of mailable letters, dictated at the rates of 60 or 70 wam. Toward the end of the second semester, dictation speeds for the mailable letters could be increased to 80 wam whenever possible, and simple office-style dictation could be used.

More teachers probably prefer to spend considerable time developing dictation-recording ability in the second semester of the beginning high school shorthand course and to begin mailable letter production about the midpoint or the seventh or eighth week of this semester. Beginning mailable-letter production at the halfway point of the second semester allows time during the first half of the semester for continued theory refinement, dictation speed building, continued development of typewritten-transcription speed and accuracy, and further refinement of transcription-element execution. If mailable-letter production is started about the seventh or eighth week of the second semester, the students will still have approximately eight or nine weeks of skill development in mailable-letter production.

Three-Day Orientation

Whatever the preference of the shorthand teacher about when to begin mailable-letter work, it is essential that the orientation to mailable letters be a specific teaching procedure with reviews and refinements of the elements involved in their production. The amount of review and the amount of time to be spent on orientation will depend on factors indicated at the beginning of the chapter—length of class period, students' typing experience, and necessary repetitions to develop student understanding. Some teachers may wish to consider the following three-day orientation more of a three-stage orientation, spending more time and giving more drill for each step than the plan indicates. A recommended three-day or three-stage orientation period, consuming about 20 minutes per class hour can be effectively carried out as follows:

FIRST DAY—STEP 1. Distribute to the students a duplicated sample letter style. At the top left corner of the page provide this information as an example: full blocked style, mixed punctuation, average-size letter. Discuss this letter style with the students, having them label the sample letter as the teacher illustrates on the chalkboard or transparency the names of the parts of the business letter and the spacing between them.

FIRST DAY—STEP 2. Have the students insert clean typing paper; set the machine for a five-inch line (appropriate for the average-size letter), single spacing; and practice typing the parts of the letter by executing a series of one-minute timings from the date through the salutation and then several timings from the last line of the body through the enclosure notation. The purposes of practicing these beginning and ending parts of the letter are: (1) to develop a "touch-return" technique on the return key or the correct return of the carriage on a carriage machine, (2) to learn the correct spacing and rapid execution of the spacing between parts of the letter, and (3) to learn the placement of the parts of the letter. If a letter style using indentions is the sample, the teacher will need to emphasize "touch tabbing" with other fingers remaining on the home keys. In the final stage of this Step 2, have the students insert another clean sheet of paper; come down 15 spaces to the date line; and type the entire sample letter with correct technique and motions, spacing, and placement of parts, giving them about six minutes to do this. A direction can be given that if the letter is completed before time is called, turn the paper over and start typing it again.

FIRST DAY—STEP 3. Teach how to estimate the length of a letter from the shorthand notes. Using their shorthand homework notes for the day, select one of the letters, and follow these steps:

1. Count the number of words in the first five lines. Each word in a phrase would count as an individual word.
2. Divide by five to obtain average words per line.
3. Count number of lines of notes in the letter.
4. Multiply average words in a line times the number of lines in the letter to estimate the number of words in the letter.

Feedback and recommendations for more accurate estimating will enable the students to become quite accurate. If they estimate the length of letters for approximately two to three weeks, they will then be able to look at their notes and judge the length of letters. The ultimate goal is for students to be able to look at their notes and see that a certain amount of their writing represents a short letter, a medium-length letter, or a long letter. It is difficult for students to start out at this stage of estimation; therefore, some rather specific method of figuring the length of letters should be used at first so they can develop a base for estimating letter length.

FIRST DAY—STEP 4. Discuss a letter-placement scale from either a reference manual or a duplicated sheet given to each student. Many teachers like to use the same letter placement scale procedures used in the typing classes in their school. One such scale might be:

SIZE OF LETTER		LENGTH OF LINE (Pica-Elite)	MARGINS (Pica-Elite)	SPACES BETWEEN THE DATE AND INSIDE ADDRESS
Short:	0–100 words	4-inch P40 E50	P22–67 E25–80	8
Medium:	101–200 words	5-inch P50 E60	P17–72 E20–85	6
Long:	201–300 words	6-inch P60 E70	P12–77 E15–90	4
Two-page:	over 300 words	6-inch P60 E70	P12–77 E15–90	4

The date begins on Line 15 for all letter lengths. Apply the letter lengths determined in Step 3 to the scale to understand the use of the scale.

SECOND DAY. The preceding activities would take about 20 minutes of the first day. On the second day, quickly review Steps 1 through 4 of the first day. Use the homework notes as a source of letters for length estimation. Provide an inside address and a dictator's name and title on the chalkboard and have the students set up a letter from their homework notes, using the letter style and type of punctuation practiced on the first day. Instruct the students to turn the paper over and start again on the back with the same letter or a different letter if they finish before the eight to ten minutes provided for the transcription.

THIRD DAY. Again review items from the previous two days and then dictate two short letters (up to 100 words) by following this procedure:

1. Heavily preview problem shorthand outlines in the letters by writing them on the chalkboard or a transparency and having students practice writing the words several times.
2. Dictate the two letters at 60 wam. The dictation rate can be at 60 wam because problem words have been heavily previewed, the letters are short, and there is a pause between the two letters. Students should be given individual help during the transcription if there is a problem in reading the notes.
3. After the dictation, allow about four to five minutes for the students to read through their notes individually, to write in the necessary punctuation with coded reason above, and to refine outlines by writing correct outlines above the poorly written ones. Then have the class read through in unison, drypenning as they read and reading in punctuation and reason for it.

265

4. Discuss and place on the chalkboard or transparency the transcription elements, such as correct transcribing of dates, numbers, spelling of unusual words, possessives, hyphens, and so on.
5. Allow about 10 to 12 minutes to transcribe. The amount of time for transcription is based on a 15- to 20-wam production rate and can be figured in the following manner:

Letter 1   75 words in the body of the letter
Letter 2   70 words in the body of the letter
       145 words
  + 38 words added for dates, inside addresses, complimentary closings, name of dictator, title of dictator, reference initials
    183 total words divided by 20 wam production rate = 9+ minutes for the production time,
or   183 ÷ 15 wam production rate = 12+ minutes for production time.

When carbons and envelopes are added, the number of words on the envelope and approximately 15 words for each carbon should be added to the total words before dividing by the 15- to 20-wam production rate.

6. During the first few days, have the students hold up their finished letters so all can see the format; then the teacher will read the letter and comment on the spacing, style, and punctuation. Students will then determine the mailability of their own letters.

From this day on, the mailable-letter production should be done in about the same way, with the following modifications in procedure:

1. After a few days, do not read through the letters in unison before transcription. Read aloud, but individually, for a few more days after unison reading stops.
2. Preview fewer problem shorthand words as time goes on.
3. Do less previewing of transcription elements until only quite difficult items are previewed.

Type of Material and Reinforcement Procedures

In the beginning stage of mailable-letter work, the subject matter of the letters should be relatively easy. The shorthand outlines that could cause writing problems should be previewed from the chalkboard or a transparency. Following the dictation of the letters, the students should have an opportunity to read through their notes, to refine shorthand outlines, to write in punctuation and reasons, and to consult reference sources for information. The necessary transcription information should be discussed and highlighted on the board or a transparency for visual reinforcement. A recommended source for the letters to be dictated is the Instructor's Handbook for the second semester course—not only will these letters consist of relatively easy vocabulary, but their subject matter can be the same as that of the homework studied for the day or for the past few days.

The use of a reference manual is essential during mailable-letter production. Preferably, students should have their own reference manuals, which would always be easily accessible and would become part of their personal libraries when they obtain their first jobs. If it is impossible to require each student to own a reference manual, several copies must be available for ready reference during transcription. Teacher and students must assume responsibility for knowing the topics covered in the reference manual and must know much of the information without needing to refer to the manual. Some reference manual material is not used frequently enough to require memorization, so the student will need to know how to use the reference manual index quickly. Short oral or written drills for locating reference manual information are valuable.

RELATED SUBJECT MATTER. In business offices the secretary will be taking dictation on similar subject matter day after day. For example, in the insurance industry the correspondence dictated will consist, for the most part, of insurance terminology—and the same for other types of industries. Teachers have not always followed this procedure and thus have made the classroom situation more difficult than the real-work situation. Many excellent sources are published in which the dictation materials for mailable letters are categorized by subject areas. While the student is studying public utilities for the homework assignment, letters using the terminology of public utilities can be found in supplementary sources—and the same for most of the subject areas studied in the textbook. By relating the subject matter of mailable-letter dictation to the homework subject matter, the student is experiencing a more realistic business situation; the probability of successful transcription of mailable letters is higher; and shorthand vocabulary, spelling, and word usage will be improved.

Even when the subject matter of the letters in the supplementary sources is not identified, some teachers have found it worthwhile to categorize these letters by subject matter and place them in a subject-labeled notebook for use in mailable-letter dictation, or they have prepared an index of sources of material related to textbook subject areas. Mailable-letter dictation material can be related to the homework lesson throughout semesters 2, 3, and 4. During the semester in which the high school teacher is using *Gregg Transcription*, the supplementary book, *Dictation for Transcription*, is an excellent source for mailable-letter material, because each chapter has a group of related letters or direct answers to the textbook letters. Similarly, in college shorthand classes when the text, *Gregg Shorthand Transcription for Colleges* is being used, the supplementary book, *College Dictation for Transcription* is an excellent source, because the letters are directly related and are oftentimes answers to the letters in the textbook studied for homework.

REINFORCEMENT PROCEDURES CHANGE. In the early stages of mailable-letter work, the problem shorthand outlines are previewed before giving the dictation, and the transcription elements are discussed before the letters are transcribed. As the second semester of work on mailable letters progresses, the teacher will probably wish to reduce the amount of previewing of problem shorthand words and transcription elements. Before the end of the second semester, the student must become as independent as possible. Because of the number of students who may not be going on to a third or fourth semester of shorthand study, the student who completes the second semester must be able to produce mailable letters without teacher assistance on shorthand outlines, transcription elements, letter forms, and punctuation; and must correctly proofread with all errors corrected—the letters must be mailable by any employer's standards. To do less than this by the end of the second semester fails an accountability standard of having attained a marketable skill. Students who have not achieved this level should not be turned out into the labor market but must continue further shorthand instruction.

Transcription-Element Confirmation and a Transcription-Element Teaching Technique

As pointed out in the preceding chapter, the Jester study emphasized the need to develop the ability to make quick, accurate decisions about spelling; punctuation; and the application of transcription elements of capitalization, number expression, hyphenation, word division, and so on.[1]

The following phase approach is designed to help the student learn the correct application of transcription elements and develop the ability to make quick, accurate decisions during mailable-letter production.

Phase One—The First Three to Four Weeks of the Introduction of Mailable Letters

After the dictation of the mailable-letter set, the students read through their shorthand notes to refine outlines and to insert punctuation and coded reasons. They also determine length of letters, look up materials in the reference manuals, and note the number and content of the paragraphs. Following this activity, teacher and students discuss the transcription elements with chalkboard or transparency illustrations of the correct transcription element usage.

Phase Two—The Next Three to Four Weeks of the Second Semester

As the students read through shorthand notes, refining outlines, inserting punctuation and coded reasons, determining length of letters, and noting paragraphing, the teacher can be placing the grid in the figure shown below on the chalkboard or on a transparency as an example:

LETTER	LENGTH OF LETTER	LINE LENGTH	NO. OF PARA- GRAPHS	REQUIRED PUNCTUATION	OTHER TRANSCRIPTION ELEMENTS TO OBSERVE
1			3	ap ⊙ ser ⊙ par ⊙ nc ⊙	2 singular possessives
2			4	par ⊙ intro ⊙	2 compound adjectives before nouns
3			3	ap ⊙ par ⊙ emphasis ⊖ nonr ⊙	1 singular possessive

While the students read through notes and make transcription-element decisions, they check the material on the board to see if they agree with the items and if they can locate all the items listed. Approximately two minutes per letter is given for the reading through and decision-making process. At the end of approximately six minutes for a three-letter set, the teacher discusses the items in the three letters by asking individual students:

1. To give the word or words preceding the punctuation and the punctuation and reason as indicated on the grid on the board. The teacher further explains the punctuation, such as "nc— compound sentence with *no conjunction* between the independent clauses."
2. To indicate the other transcription elements and how they would be transcribed.

Chalkboard confirmation displaying the correct typing of the transcription elements is given by the teacher. Since the paragraphs had been indicated in dictation, only the reasons for the recommended paragraphing are discussed. Finally, the students are asked individually to give the length of the letter in terms of short, medium, or long and the line length to be used. At the end of the discussion, the grid on the board (illustrated on page 269), would be completed as follows, if the letter-placement-scale technique of using margins is used:

LETTER	LENGTH OF LETTER	LINE LENGTH
1	Medium	5-inch
2	Short	4-inch
3	Medium	5-inch

Phase Three—The Remainder of the Second Semester

In the final stages of the second semester, when the goal is to make the student more independent, the teacher may wish to place the required punctuation, other transcription elements to observe, and number of paragraphs in a grid on the chalkboard as shown in the figure below. The information is given under the column headings, but the teacher does not discuss the items with the students. If particular students have difficulty locating information in their notes, they should feel free to consult the teacher for help.

During the final two or three weeks of the semester, nothing is placed on the board except the very unusual, in an attempt to help

LETTER	REQUIRED PUNCTUATION	OTHER TRANSCRIPTION ELEMENTS TO OBSERVE	NUMBER OF PARA-GRAPHS
1	intro ⊙ nc ⊙ nonr ⊙	2 hyphenated compound adjectives	4
2	as ⊙ emphasis ⊖ ser ⊙	1 plural possessive 1 amount of money	3
3	if ⊙ nc ⊙ and omitted ⊙ courteous request ⊙	2 hyphenated compound adjectives 1 plural possessive 1 time expression	4

the student become quite independent of teacher help. The door should still be left open, however, for the student who cannot make the correct decisions and feels the need for help from the teacher.

Third and Fourth Semesters

Such a grid procedure may be helpful during the beginning of the third semester, when students are coming back after a break from shorthand instruction. Such a procedure strongly reinforces the importance of careful decision-making and accurate application of transcription elements.

Some teachers tenaciously insist that students read through their notes and make decisions about punctuation and other transcription elements before transcription throughout the four semesters of shorthand instruction. They think the time spent on such decision making is well spent and will result in a higher level of production and fewer false starts while transcribing. As the students progress through the four semesters, the time spent in such decision-making becomes less and less. These teachers no doubt advise their students to do the same thing on the job to increase their productivity.

Weekly Plans for the Second, Third, and Fourth Semesters (Based on a 50-minute Class Hour)

To give adequate time to the major learning emphases for each semester and to the minor learning that must be covered, the following weekly plans are recommended:

Second Semester

FIRST WEEK OF MAILABLE-LETTER WORK
Days 1, 2, and 3—Introduction to Mailable Letters (20 minutes a day—as explained on pages 263–266)—theory review of old lesson and theory preview of new lesson, dictation speed building.

Days 4 and 5—Production of two or three letters each day—theory review of old lesson and theory preview of new lesson

REMAINING WEEKS OF SECOND SEMESTER
Monday: Theory review of old lesson and theory preview of new lesson, mailable-letter production—three letters, about 75 to 125 words each, production rate = 15–20 wam.
Tuesday: Same as Monday.
Wednesday: Transcription drills and/or three-minute transcription rates from homework notes—15 minutes.

Theory review of old lesson and theory preview of new lesson—10 minutes.
Dictation speed building—25 minutes.

Thursday: Same as Wednesday.

Friday: Dictation testing (if mailable-letter introduction has been delayed to midpoint of second semester; if mailable-letter introduction was at the beginning of second semester, there may be no three-minute dictation testing).

THE LAST TWO OR THREE WEEKS SOME CARBON WORK AND ENVELOPE WORK SHOULD BE DONE.

Third Semester—Speedbuilding Emphasis Semester*

FIRST 9 WEEKS (Grubbs' Chart Plan may be used for this part of the semester—see page 288)

Monday: Transcription drills and/or three-minute transcription rates, theory review of old lesson and preview of new lesson, dictation speed building.

Tuesday: Theory review of old lesson and theory preview of new lesson, mailable-letter production (heavily preview problem words and check on transcription elements before transcribing) three letters (about 150 words each); transcription time based on 18–20 wam.

Wednesday: Transcription drills and/or three-minute transcription rates, theory review of old lesson and theory preview of new lesson, dictation speed building.

Thursday: Transcription drills and/or three-minute transcription rates, theory review of old lesson and preview of new lesson, dictation speed building.

Friday: Theory review of old lesson, theory preview of new lesson, and dictation testing (every week or alternate weeks).

SECOND 9 WEEKS (Mailable Grading Standard may be used—see page 285)

Monday: Theory review of old lesson and preview of new lesson, mailable-letter production with carbons and envelopes (limited previewing and confirming transcription elements—only the very unusual). Use dif-

*Some teachers prefer to emphasize dictation speed building the third semester, and others prefer to emphasize transcription; therefore, the emphasis for the third and fourth semesters are interchangeable.

	ferent types of correspondence, and correspondence and envelopes with special lines.
Tuesday:	Same as Monday.
Wednesday:	Transcription drills and/or three-minute transcription rates, theory review of old lesson and theory preview of new lesson, dictation speed building.
Thursday:	Same as Wednesday.
Friday:	Theory review of old lesson and theory preview of new lesson and dictation testing (every week or alternate weeks).

Fourth Semester: Transcription Emphasis Semester (Mailable Grading Standard Used)

FIRST 9 WEEKS

Monday: Tuesday: Wednesday:	Theory review of old lesson and theory preview of new lesson. Mailable-letter production.
Thursday: and Friday:	Transcription drills and/or three-minute transcription rate Theory review of old lesson and theory preview of new lesson Dictation speed building with dictation testing alternate weeks

or

*Monday:	Transcription drills and/or three-minute transcription rate, theory work, and dictation speed building
Tuesday: Wednesday: Thursday:	Theory review of old lesson and theory preview of new lesson and mailable-letter production
Friday:	Dictation testing alternate weeks

For mailable-letter production—preview only the very unusual problem words in the mailable letters before dictation,

and postview only the very unusual transcription elements before students transcribe the letters.

*If dictation labs are required during the week, dictation speed-building practice on Monday can serve as a goal-setting technique for the week.

SECOND 9 WEEKS

Weekly plans similar to those indicated in the first nine weeks of the fourth semester.

No previewing or postviewing unless material is very technical or unusual.

Mailable-letter production should include much office-style dictation, manuscripts, minutes of meetings, interoffice correspondence, and so on.

Other activities should include in-basket exercises, minisimulations, major office simulations, and the like.

Stages of Difficulty in the Development of Mailable-Letter Production

The development of mailable-letter production should progress from the simple to the complex. Increases in difficulty will include:

1. The difficulty of the subject matter.
2. Faster dictation.
3. Adding office-style and alertness dictation.
4. Performing additional tasks, including typing multiple carbons and extra envelopes.
5. Using a standard letter line (e.g., the six-inch line) for all correspondence, and adjusting spacing between parts for attractive arrangement on the page.
6. Transcribing various forms of material, such as interoffice memos, reports, minutes of conferences or meetings, two-page letters, letters with tables, telephone conversations.
7. Adding special lines on letters and envelopes.
8. Using various sizes of stationery and envelopes.
9. Applying the judgment method of placement on the page using two-inch margins for short letters; one-and-one-half-inch for medium-size letters; and one-inch for long letters.

The study by Olinzock gives helpful information to shorthand teachers considering simulating business dictation for mailable-letter production practice in the classroom.[2] Regarding rates of business dictation, the length of a typical piece of dictation, the syllabic intensity of the material, and a rate pattern of dictators, Olinzock reported:

1. The median overall gross speed of dictation was 63 wam.
2. The highest gross dictation speed for a quarter minute was 216 wam, with a median of 116 wam.
3. The typical piece of dictation contained 157 gross words with a syllabic intensity of 1.65.
4. Speeds of dictation were higher at the beginning and end of each piece of correspondence.

During the third and fourth semesters, it is essential that the student experience as many situations similar to the real world as possible. At this time, the teacher who has had recent office experience can creatively make the advanced shorthand classroom an office-like setting filled with real-work experiences. Minisimulations of one or two days and longer simulations of a week or two should be employed in the advanced course. Opportunities for the student to work or observe as "secretary for a day" in local offices will help bring realism to the advanced instruction.

Length and Type of Letters

Usually in the beginning stages of introduction to mailable letters the letters will be short, averaging from 75 to 100 words. As the second semester progresses, letters of 125 to 150 words should be dictated. During the third and fourth semesters the letters should become somewhat longer, ranging from 150 to 250 words. The teacher should keep in mind that the average business letter is between 125 and 175 words; therefore, most of the letters dictated for classroom production should be within that range. However, the student needs to experience estimating the lengths of letters of varying sizes, using the four-, five-, or six-inch line, using a standard-length line for all sizes of letters, and transcribing the two-page letter, as part of the third and fourth semesters of instruction. Shorthand teachers will need to keep in mind the vast quantity of business correspondence which is interoffice and give adequate practice in using interoffice forms and taking dictation and transcribing interoffice material.

Amount and Types of Material Dictated

After the three-day or three-stage procedure of the introduction to mailable letters, using a set of letters for mailable-letter production more nearly simulates an office situation. The number of letters in the set will depend on the length of the class period. In schools with periods of 40 to 50 minutes, probably the three-letter set will be most practical. If the classs period is 55 to 60 minutes or longer, the four-letter set can be used. In schools with two- or three-hour block programs, mailable-letter production can more nearly simulate an office situation by using seven-, eight-, nine-, or ten-letter sets. However, teachers in the block programs may wish to consider dictating two separate sets of three to five letters and giving a grade for each set. This procedure is an advantage to the student in the earlier stages of the semester, because the timing periods are shorter, and students can often perform better in a shorter period than in an extended period, thus achieving better grades. Before the end of the third or fourth semester, however, students should experience taking dictation and transcribing the longer sets of seven to ten letters.

COLD NOTES. Before the end of the third or fourth semester, students should have an opportunity to transcribe from cold notes, simulating the end of an office day and the resumption of the transcription on the following day or after the weekend. To achieve such a simulation, more letters than can be transcribed in one class period are dictated. The students transcribe during that period, hand in notes and completed letters and envelopes, and resume transcribing the letters during the next class session. Teaching the students to read through all letters, refine outlines, and insert punctuation and coded reason before beginning transcription will help them realize the importance of this procedure in a job situation. Reorienting oneself by reading through the remaining letters before continuing transcription on the succeeding day or days is a helpful habit to develop.

VARIETY OF MATERIAL. Varying the number of copies to be made; dictating some interoffice memos and some external letters; and dictating very short, average, and long letters within the same set will enable the student to make decisions required in an office.

At all stages of the mailable-letter-production work, it is necessary that the teacher review all material that the students have not recently practiced, before they start production work based on this material. For example, when interoffice memos are begun, the teacher will need to use the chalkboard, transparency, bulletin board, or handout sheet to review margins, internal spacing, printed headings and alignment with printed words, and ending lines of the interoffice memo. One cannot assume that information acquired in a typing class will be efficiently and correctly applied in transcribing mailable letters. Other areas that will need review and practice before production are tables within letters, reports, special lines of letters and envelopes, variations in margins for nonstandard-sized stationery, and any types of arrangements that have not been reviewed in the shorthand class and which are part of the transcription of mailable letters.

To produce the best learning and production, the teacher will need to recognize when previewing and reinforcement are necessary and when the student can be expected to perform independently with efficiency and correctness.

Application of Transcription Elements

Heavy previewing of transcription elements is recommended in the early part of mailable-letter production. As the teacher sees that the students are able to handle the transcription element decisions independently, they should be allowed and required to do so. However, even in the third and fourth semester, as transcription elements arise that the students cannot be expected to know because of the specialized nature or unexpected arrangement of the material, the information should be discussed and understood before transcription. Only in the final stages of instruction, when the teacher is trying to help the student understand the necessity for completely independent thinking and decision making, would the totally unexpected be unpreviewed. The emphasis then is on helping the student understand when it is necessary to seek help and where information can be found.

In the beginning stages of mailable-letter work, students should have the opportunity to ask questions individually during the transcription of mailable letters. Mailable-letter production should be treated as a learning rather than a testing experience by both the teacher and the students. Help that is needed should be given. If this is done from the beginning, the teacher will find that the process of helping and of making the students independent thinkers, will be a gradual weaning and the students will, in the final stages of mailable-letter production, be able to produce letters efficiently, quickly, and with a high degree of mailability.

Rates of Dictation

A principle important to consider in the early stages of mailable-letter work and for a major part of the third and fourth semesters is: *The dictation for mailable-letter production should be about 10 wam below the lowest speed dictation test rate of the class.* For example, if the lowest speed dictation-test rate of the class, in the second semester when mailable-letter work is introduced, is 70 wam, then the dictation for mailable-letter work would be 60 wam. Even at this time, if some students are still trying to pass 60-wam on new-material three-minute dictation tests, the mailable-letter dictation can be at 60 wam because: (1) the teacher is heavily previewing shorthand words that could cause writing problems, (2) the letters are read through in unison or individually before transcribing, (3) the transcription elements are previewed heavily, and (4) the letters are short with pauses between each of the three letters in the set. Such a situation is quite different from an unpreviewed three-minute dictation test on new material at 60 wam. In addition, the student who has difficulty reading notes taken for mailable-letter transcription should, in the very early stages, have an opportunity to ask the teacher for help. Soon this need for help will be eliminated.

The students will have much dictation speed-building practice and much 3-minute dictation testing. The teacher must keep in mind and help the student to understand that the purpose of dictation for mailable-letter transcription is not to test dictation rates but to encourage the writing of correct, well-proportioned notes. At times the teacher may wish to dictate a set of letters at varying rates, such as letter 1 at 60, letter 2 at 70, and letter 3 at 80, to help the students learn to adjust writing to different dictation rates, writing at the same speed as the dictation and concentrating on excellent notes.

Dictating mailable letters at 10 wam below the lowest dictation test rate of the class is recommended into the third and fourth semesters. If the teacher follows this procedure, it is essential to keep the rates within the ability range of the entire class so each person can write with controlled notes. Most of the time, the letters should be dictated at one speed, and as the dictation abilities of the class increase the dictation speed for mailable letters can increase, still dictating 10 wam below the lowest dictation test rate of the class.

If a teacher has a class with a wide span of speed dictation test rates such as 70 to 110, it would be helpful to make two tapes of the mailable-letter dictation and dictate one tape at 80 wam for the students who are at the 90, 100, and 110 levels of speed dictation testing and the other tape at 60 wam for the students at the 70- and 80-wam speed dictation levels.

At other times, the teacher will wish to spurt for a few seconds at top speed ranges for the class. Students sometimes ask, "Why do we work to attain speed-dictation-test levels of 110 or 120 or 140 words a minute, when letters in business are dictated at 80 or less words a minute?" One answer to this question can be found in the results of an investigation by H. H. Green on the speed of office-style dictation.[3] Upon analyzing the speed patterns of 72 dictators in business, he concluded that shorthand writers taking dictation at 80 wam for three minutes could take 48 percent of all material dictated and those taking dictation at 100 wam for three minutes could take 75 percent of all material dictated.

Green also determined that during 60 percent of the dictation time the dictator was either groping or thoughtful and the other 40 percent, confident or sprinting. With this explanation, students can better understand the necessity of having 110- to 140-wam dictation abilities to take care of the sprinting and confident phases of the dictation patterns in offices.

COACH FOR WELL-WRITTEN NOTES IN MAILABLE-LETTER DICTATION. Shorthand students are very accustomed to, and heavily drilled on, writing rapidly during the dictation speed-building practice and during three-minute dictation testing. Unless they are coached to do otherwise, they will tend to take mailable-letter dictation in the same manner. For this reason, it is necessary for the teacher to say during mailable-letter-production dictation that the dictation will be at a rate about 10 wam below the lowest dictation test rate of the class and to specify the rate to be used. The teacher should also ask the students to write only as fast as they must to keep up with the dictator and to concentrate on writing accurate, well-proportioned outlines.

For example, the teacher must direct students not to write at 110 to 120 wam rates when the material is being dictated at 60 wam. The writer must learn to adjust to the rates of the dictator and the changes in pace of dictation, still striving for accurately written outlines.

Therefore, the emphasis on knowledge and refinement of theory, correctness of proportion, and writing with control during all semesters of shorthand will help students to respect these elements when taking dictation for mailable-letter production in the classroom and ultimately on the job.

CREATE APPRECIATION FOR CORRECT POSITION AND CORRECT NOTEBOOK HANDLING WHILE TAKING MAILABLE-LETTER DICTATION. From the beginning of dictation speed development and throughout the four semesters, students will need to be reminded of the following points regarding position and notebook handling:

1. The notebook should be flat on the desk, open so both front and back are on the desk, because this enables the student to hold down the notebook with the nonwriting hand, and the edge at the bottom of the notebook becomes less and less of an obstacle for the hand to move over as the student progresses through the notebook.
2. Both arms should be supported on the desk.
3. The notebook or page should be moved up gradually as the writer progresses down the column so that the writing arm is always supported on the desk.
4. The pages are turned quickly and efficiently so there is no loss of time.
5. Dictation is taken by writing through the notebook in one direction and then turning the book around to write through the book using the backs of the pages.

As mailable-letter dictation begins, the student should also:

1. Date the notebook on the outside cover for the period of time it is used.
2. Date the beginning of the day's dictation at the bottom of the first page of notes.
3. Number the letters.
4. Leave three or four lines between letters for added instructions given by the dictator or for notes written by the student.
5. Print words or names that are spelled by the dictator, because these are usually words that could present spelling problems.
6. Underscore words to be all in capitals.
7. Leave the second column free for notations and changes in dictation if the dictator frequently makes corrections or changes.
8. Incorporate other notebook techniques that the teacher has developed from personal work experience.

Appreciation of the correct position for taking dictation and insistence that it be used will take kind, persistent effort by the teacher. The expected carryover is that when the students become employees they will help their employers understand the necessity for enough writing space so the notebook can be flat and the arms supported on the desk. The students must realize that this is their career. Work conditions that can help them to produce better are in their interest. Employers cannot be expected to know the necessary conditions without the help of the employee. The movie and television image of the secretary taking dictation on the knee is not the day-by-day position necessary for the high-level production expected of professional secretaries.

DICTATION OF PARAGRAPHS.   In the beginning stages of mailable-letter production, the paragraphs should be dictated. Some time before the completion of the final shorthand course work, the elements of paragraphing should be reviewed; practice in determining paragraphs should be given on successive days; and finally the letters should be dictated without paragraphs indicated and the student should independently determine the paragraphing. On the days that determining paragraphs is being practiced, the teacher may wish to use the board diagram idea to help the student select the paragraphs.

	Recommended Paragraphs
Letter 1	3
Letter 2	4
Letter 3	3

While the student is reading through, refining notes, inserting punctuation, and looking up reference information, decisions are made about paragraphing by consulting the board diagram to see the number recommended. During the discussion that follows, reasons for the paragraphing are discussed.

Office-Style Dictation and Transcription

During the latter half of the third semester (especially if it is the final semester of instruction), and again during fourth semester, instruction must be provided on office-style dictation and its transcription. In a one-year shorthand program, teachers may wish to include parts of this information and give some experience in applying office-style dictation procedures.

Office-style dictation in the shorthand classroom is meant to simulate as nearly as possible dictation given on the job. The Olinzock and

Green studies both show that the rates of office dictation are not constant, that the dictation is spasmodic, halting, rapid, slow, and at times nonexistent. Published tapes are available that will give office-style dictation experience to students. Published books have material designed to be dictated office-style. Teachers can become quite expert at office-style dictation by applying their own work experience.

Both teacher and student need to be conscious of special practices to bridge the gap between constant-speed dictation and realistic office-style dictation. Following are some procedures that teachers can use to help students develop the ability to take office-style dictation:

1. Coach students to write only as fast as is necessary to keep up with the dictator and to concentrate on writing accurate, well-proportioned outlines.
2. Start with simple office-style dictation procedures and work into the more complex; for example:
   a. Start with uneven dictation. Dictate some parts of sentences more rapidly than other parts. Dictate the beginning and ending of the letter faster than the middle.
   b. Include one- or two-word insertions and deletions.
   c. Include longer additions and deletions.
   d. Add and delete paragraphs.
   e. Stop dictation to simulate answering a telephone or talking to someone who has entered the office. Resume the dictation by asking a student to read back the last paragraph, last sentence, or entire letter to that point.
   f. Move around during the dictation so the voice is not always equally loud and clear, but is always loud enough to be understood.
   g. Include directions during the dictation such as how the letter should be mailed, sending an extra copy to another person, looking up information needed for the correspondence, special directions about spelling proper names, special directions about underscoring and capitalizing, and the like.
   h. Include intentional errors so that the student will need to be alert to such errors and make corrections in the material.
3. Teach students how to deal with office-style instructions in their shorthand notebooks. The following revision marks should be introduced:
   a. Use a caret (∧) to include single-word insertions.

    b. Use a slash (/) or (\) to cancel out single-word deletions.

    c. Use a wavy line through words to cancel them.

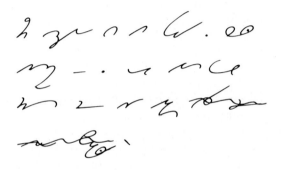

    d. Use circled capital letters to show insertion of a larger piece of material, and write the words to be inserted in a second column or in another location on the page.

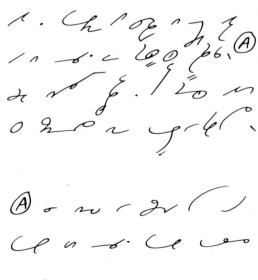

e. Use the turn-around mark (∽) to show transpositions of words.

f. Use one wavy line under material to be typed in all capital letters.

g. Use only the left-hand column in the notebook if the dictator makes frequent substantial changes or indicates directions during the dictation.

h. Leave three to four lines between letters for special instructions that may be given during dictation.

4. Teach students to read through and refine outlines while waiting for the dictator to resume dictation. They should be ready to read the last paragraph, entire letter, or last few sentences of the material when the dictator is ready to continue.

These are only suggestions, and many other techniques and procedures can be added to help students bridge the gap between evenly timed classroom dictation and office-style dictation. The teacher should also coach and insist that during the reading-through process after the office-style dictation of a set of mailable letters the student:

1. Write in better shorthand forms, any above previously written outline that might cause a reading problem while transcribing.
2. Insert punctuation and a coded reason above it.
3. Look up spelling words in a reference book and write them in longhand above the shorthand outlines.
4. Insert paragraphs if they were not dictated.
5. Make notes of any questions that should be asked before beginning transcription.
6. Look up transcription elements in a reference manual and write the correct transcription form in longhand in the notes.
7. Determine the lengths of the letters.
8. Make decisions about special directions given.

Before transcribing, the student is coached to have all reference materials, stationery, carbons, envelopes, and correction materials, conveniently and efficiently located at the work area; to think carefully before beginning transcription; and to aim to work without having to start letters over because of errors. On completion of a letter (or part of a letter, if it is necessary to stop within a letter) the notes should be cancelled out with a diagonal line and dated.

If correct position has been stressed and demanded during transcription drill, three-minute transcription-rate work, and transcription of three-minute dictation tests, the student is accustomed to correct position during typewritten transcription. See the typing position recommendations discussed on pages 237 and 238.

In drills, the student has been expected to transcribe from the notebook on a copyholder and to keep the eyes on the notebook during transcription. This technique is still observed during the transcription of mailable letters.

Judging the Placement of Letters and Other Dictated Materials

In the beginning stages of mailable-letter production, some teachers instruct students to determine the length of letters by the procedures discussed on page 264. After several days of determining the length of letters in this manner, the students will be able to estimate by looking at the notes whether the letter would be short, average, long, or two-page and would be able to apply the correct line length from a letter-placement scale similar to the one on page 265.

As part of the advanced course, teachers may wish to have the students practice setting up letters using a standard line for all letter lengths. Information should then be provided regarding varying the space between the date and inside address and between the complimentary closing and dictator's name and title to allow for varying lengths of letters.

Because not all material in a business office will be in standard letter form, it will be necessary to review with the student the styles and margins as they first produce interoffice memos, reports, minutes, and various other dictated materials.

Evaluation of Mailable-Letter Production

Mailable-letter production should be a learning experience and not always considered a testing situation. For this reason, the teacher may wish to use some of the following procedures to evaluate student work:

Teaching and Practicing With No Grading During the First Four Weeks of the Mailable-Letter Work in the Second Semester.

During these four weeks there would be as much previewing, helping, reviewing, discussing, and practicing as necessary for the student to learn how to produce mailable letters. Starting about the fifth week of this unit of instruction, the three-letter set of mailable letters would be graded:

3 letters mailable   = A
2 letters mailable   = B
1 letter mailable   = C
1 letter correctable = D

Correctable can mean various things. It can mean that there is one error in the letter that can be corrected to make the letter mailable, and the student must find this error and correct it at the beginning of the next class meeting when the letters are returned to the students. If the letter is made mailable, the grade on the set could be changed to reflect its mailability. Teachers may not wish to continue the correctable aspect of evaluation for the entire second semester or at all in the third or fourth semesters.

A three-letter-set grading plan used by a high school teacher in Illinois and applying the correctability concept follows:[4]

3 mailable	A
2 mailable, 1 correctable	A − or B +
2 mailable	B
1 mailable, 2 correctable	B −
1 mailable, 1 correctable	C +
1 mailable	C
3 correctable	D +
2 correctable	D
1 correctable	D −

For information regarding other grading scales for mailable-letter production, including allowance for letters of varying lengths, see Chapter 10, pages 346–356.

Retranscriptions of Mailable-Letter Attempts

During the first part of the mailable-letter work in the second semester and perhaps the first half of the third semester, allowing the students to retranscribe any unmailable letters of the set for an improved grade is one way to help them learn, and experience success on, certain items not known on the first attempt. Such retranscriptions can be done either in or outside of class. The retranscription procedure may be used as follows: The set of mailable letters are transcribed in class and the notes are stapled underneath the set of mailable letters, carbons, and envelopes. When the set is handed back the next day, it has been graded, for a four-letter set:

4 letters mailable = A
3 letters mailable = B
2 letters mailable = C
1 letter mailable = D

or for a three-letter set:

3 letters mailable = A
2 letters mailable = B
1 letter mailable = C

For the retranscription, emphasis would be on using the notes and not the typed letter. If necessary, notes could be removed from the set, and the graded letters returned to the teacher after the student has had an opportunity to understand the mistakes. A student direction sheet and possible grading scale for such retranscription work follows:

Retranscriptions of Mailable Letters

Four-Letter Set: If you transcribed all four letters and:
None was mailable and you retranscribe all four into *mailable* form, grades will be assigned as follows:

1st retranscribed and mailable = D−
2d retranscribed and mailable = D
3d retranscribed and mailable = D+
4th retranscribed and mailable = C−

One was mailable and you retranscribe the remaining three into *mailable* form, grades will be assigned as follows:

1 mailable   = D
2d retranscribed and mailable = D+
3d retranscribed and mailable = C−
4th retranscribed and mailable = C

Two were *mailable,* grades will be assigned as follows:

2 mailable   = C
3d retranscribed and mailable = C+
4th retranscribed and mailable = B−

Three were *mailable,* grades will be assigned as follows:

3 mailable   = B
4th retranscribed and mailable = B+

Three-Letter Set: If you transcribed all three letters and:

None was mailable and you retranscribe all three letters into *mailable* form, grades will be assigned as follows:

1st retranscribed and mailable = C −
2d retranscribed and mailable = C
3d retranscribed and mailable = C +

One was *mailable*, grades will be assigned as follows:

1 mailable   = C
2d retranscribed and mailable = C +
3d retranscribed and mailable = B −

Two were *mailable*, grades will be assigned as follows:

2 mailable   = B
3d retranscribed and mailable = B +

The student retranscribes the letters, either in class or outside class, staples the new set on top of the previously transcribed letters (or just the notes if the letters had been removed), and hands in the material to be reevaluated. Grades are then adjusted according to the preceding scale. In using this procedure one might wish to build in a rule that only those letters transcribed in the original production of the set could be retranscribed. If this is not done, students may spend too much time transcribing one or two letters of a set during the original transcription, with the idea that the remaining ones could be transcribed during retranscription. Such a practice would defeat the purpose of the activity.

It has been found that in using this procedure the students really learn the items missed on the first transcription, they feel a sense of accomplishment in transcribing the letters correctly, and their attitude toward the mailable-letter work is positive and success-oriented. The grade improvement is very slight, but it does allow for a better grade average. The entire value seems to be in the learning experienced and the positive attitude acquired. One must remember that this procedure is not continued throughout a semester. It is not a realistic evaluation of mailable production, and the student must come to realize that mailability means mailable on the first attempt.

Choosing a Sampling of the Mailable-Letter Sets for Grade Application

If mailable-letter production is to be a learning experience and not only a testing situation, the teacher may choose only a sampling of the mailable-letter opportunities for grading. For example during a grading period, the teacher may have nine mailable-letter-set grades recorded. Perhaps choosing the best four or five of these nine will provide the information needed for grading. Cancelling out the poorest will help the teacher and student to keep in perspective the true meaning of practicing and learning and not to be overwhelmed with the idea of mailable-letter-production days being testing days. To be successful one must experience success, and to be successful one must maintain a positive attitude. Selecting the best attempts helps maintain this positive attitude.

Grubbs' Chart of Transcription Laboratories

Again, during the first half of the third semester, using the Grubbs' charts can be a positive help to student learning without grading too rigidly by *mailable* versus *unmailable* standards. The emphasis that the students most need should be the major emphasis for the point system. The chart can be placed on the bulletin board and the goals for transcription of the mailable-letter set for a particular day explained to the students—and/or the chart can be duplicated and become the cover page for the set of mailable letters that will be completed and submitted by the student. The chart shown here is an example of the Grubbs' plan when the major emphasis is *Transcription Rate (Transcribed Words a Minute—Twam):*

TRANSCRIPTION SELF-APPRAISAL CHART 1[5]

Emphasis: Transcription rate (Twam)		90–100 = A
Lab Time: 30 minutes (minimum rate, 20 twam)		80–89 = B
		70–79 = C
		60–69 = D

The Job	Points per letter	Total
4 letters (600 words) completed	15	60
Bonus Points		
A. 30 or more twam (20 minutes or less)	4	(16)
25 to 29 twam (24 minutes or less)	3	(12)
B. English applications 100% accurate	2	8
C. Message 100% accurate, verbatim	2	8
D. Transcript appearance: clean, balanced, etc.	2	8
Total possible points:		100

Other charts could be used when the major emphases are transcript accuracy, English application, or transcript appearance. It is recommended that a particular chart be used for two or three or more mailable-letter sets so the student can keep the major emphasis in focus and make sincere attempts to improve. Another use of the charts would be to help individualize mailable-letter production. Certain students may need one emphasis while others may need another. With duplicated sheets indicating the chart to be followed, individuals can concentrate on the emphasis most needed for their individual growth.

In using the charts, four letters comprise a set, and each letter completed is awarded 15 points, giving a base of 60 points for the four letters. If class time does not permit the dictation and transcription of four letters, three letters could be used and each completed letter awarded 20 points, still giving a 60-point base. This plan can also be changed by lengthening the letters to increase the difficulty of the task. The *Job* in the chart is based on letters of approximately 150 words.

Teachers must keep in mind that the use of the Grubbs' charts is a learning and teaching procedure. Students could receive passing scores without having mailable letters; therefore, these charts probably should not be used throughout the entire third semester. Sometime before the end of the third semester the students should be required to produce mailable copy, and the grading standard should be based entirely on high standards of mailability.

The Mailable Letter Is a "Million-Dollar" Skill

To produce mailable letters consistently time after time is a "million-dollar" skill. Not only must the shorthand notes be written in correct and well-proportioned form, but the transcriber must be able to quickly and correctly read the notes, apply information about transcription elements and the style of the letter and its parts, apply information from reference manuals regarding special instructions, transcribe, and make corrections that will not show. With the cost of letter production constantly rising, it is necessary for this part of shorthand introduction to be taught step-by-step so the student learns thoroughly, is able to perform consistently, and has an attitude of respect for the job being completed.

Iannizzi reported that advanced shorthand students had a higher number of transcription errors from correct outlines than beginning students.[6] She suggested that this is probably because the "advanced student attempts to increase quantity at the expense of quality." Shorthand teachers will need to help advanced students keep in "proper perspective" the necessity for accuracy and quality of production first, with quantity of production as a secondary consideration.

To help develop this appreciation for the job and move the students from one level of this task to another, it is important to keep them motivated and confident. To do this will take much encouragement from the teacher and methods of teaching and evaluation that will not threaten the students but will enable them to grow gradually in mailable-letter-production.

A Suggested Daily Plan for Mailable-Letter Production

Approximately the 13th week of
Intermediate Shorthand (college class)

or

Second semester (high school class)
55-minute class hour—1:00–1:55

Today's Lesson: 41
Tomorrow's Lesson: 42

Performance Objectives

The students will:

1. Write correctly the brief forms and derivatives of Lesson 41.
2. Demonstrate knowledge of vocabulary words of Lesson 41 by writing the shorthand and giving definitions orally.
3. Understand the phrases of the new Lesson 42 and respond by saying and writing sample words.
4. Take dictation of new material for mailable-letter production at 70 wam.
5. Transcribe into mailable form the set of letters dictated, performing at a 15 to 20 wam production-rate level.

Teaching Materials:

1. *Gregg Shorthand for Colleges,* 2d Ed., Vol. 2, and Student Transcript (or high school second-semester textbook and Student Transcript)
2. Stopwatch and interval chart.
3. Sabin, *The Gregg Reference Manual,* 5th Ed.
4. Instructor's Handbook for *Gregg Shorthand for Colleges,* Vol. 2 (or high school second-semester instructor's handbook).

Learning Activities:

1. Review of Lesson 41. Pronounce the following words and ask students to write each once:

Place shorthand outlines on the chalkboard for students to check accuracy of writing.
Ask students to write the shorthand for selected vocabulary words: *striving* and *Common Market.* Discuss definitions.
2. Preview of Lesson 42. Explain omission of minor words in phrases and penmanship points to observe as phrases are placed on the board:

Students say words rapidly and then write each phrase several times.

3. Homework procedures: (Teacher would determine which items need careful explanation.)

a. Take a self-test on the phrases on page 234. Check accuracy and practice words incorrectly written until they are known. Practice in groups of three words, three times; example:

b. Write in groups of three (each group three times) the geographical expressions. Learn the spelling of each geographical location.

c. Learn the uses of *past* and *passed* and develop a business sentence for each of these two words.

d. Learn the business vocabulary words:

Know the spelling, the shorthand outline, the definition, and the correct use of the word in business sentences.

e. Drypen and read quickly each of the letters 352–357. Quickly spell any word that causes problems in reading. Use the student transcript as needed to read quickly.

f. Self-dictate letters 352–357 as rapidly as you can speak. Write only in the first column of your notebook; reserve the second column for practice on individual problem words. If you come to a word that you think could cause problems on a theory test or in taking dictation, practice it repeatedly in the second column, spelling the shorthand sounds of the word as it is written.

g. Self-dictate letters 352, 354, and 356 (or all letters 352–357) at a controlled writing rate. Emphasis is on excellent notes. Insert the punctuation, encircle it, and write the reason for it above. Write in both columns of the notebook on this writing. These are the notes that will be used for typewritten transcription drills and/or three-minute transcription rate tomorrow in class.

291

       h. Study the marginal reminders to be sure all spelling and transcription elements are learned from the lesson. As a final review, read through the letters from the Student Transcript, observing and understanding the transcription elements.

4. Dictation of mailable letters (start by 1:10)*

       a. Warmup dictation on one letter at the rate of 90 wam—letter 38 of instructor's handbook). Postview phrases and dictate again at 100 wam.

       b. Dictate the mailable-letter set following these steps:

Directions to the student: (Students use shorthand to take directions)

1) Today's letters are related to Lessons 39, 40, and 41—you may use your student transcript and the Sabin manual as reference sources.

2) The addresses are 39, 40, and 41 in the back of your textbook, and your dictator is number 42. The dictator's title is Assistant Manager.

3) Use the blocked style on page 26 of your textbook. Use the style shown on page 26 for reference initials. Use *Enclosure* as your style for the enclosure notation.

4) Use open punctuation; make one carbon copy for the file, with all corrections made so they do not show.

Dictate the following letters (from instructor's handbook) at 70 wam:

Letter 39 102 words
Letter 40 115
Letter 41 113

    330 words ÷ 70 wam = 5 min. of dictation
    135 words   inside addresses, dates, endings
     45 words   allowed for carbons
    510 words ÷ 20 twam = 26—transcription time allowance

*In planning for mailable-letter-production days, it is necessary to plan the amount of time needed for the entire mailable-letter work: dictation, reading through, discussion, and transcription. The teacher would then determine the time in the class hour that the mailable-letter work must begin in order to give students enough time to complete the set as planned. For example, the total time needed might be 45 minutes, and dictation would have to begin at 1:10. The remainder of the class hour would be spent on Learning Activities 1, 2, and 3.

c. Timing of Step 4:

Warmup dictation	3 minutes
Dictation of mailable-letter set	5 minutes
Time to read through notes, refine outlines, insert punctuation, determine length of letters	6 minutes
Discussion of necessary transcription information	4 minutes
Time to transcribe	<u>26</u> minutes
	44 minutes

d. While students are reading through the letters, place the grid below on the board:

LETTER	LENGTH OF LETTER	LINE LENGTH	SPACES BETWEEN THE DATE AND INSIDE ADDRESS	REQUIRED PUNCTUATION	OTHER TRANSCRIPTION ELEMENTS TO OBSERVE
1	Medium	5-inch	6	intro ⊙ courteous request ⊙	Transcription of "$\mathscr{C}\ 20\ \mathscr{a}$"
2	Medium	5-inch	6	conj ⊙ as ⊙ nc ⊙ if ⊙	1 singular possessive Transcription of amount of money Transcription of a date
3	Medium	5-inch	6	ap ⊙	1 plural possessive Transcription of an amount of money, a date, and a time of day

e. During the discussion following the reading-through process, the information regarding length of letter, line length, and spaces between date and inside address (in parentheses above) is inserted in the grid. The degree of discussion of "required punctuation" and "other transcription elements to observe" would depend on the time in the semester and the students' abilities.

The preceding is only a sample plan to indicate the necessary considerations on a mailable-letter-production day. The plan would vary depending on the time in the semester and the semester itself:

- Problem shorthand words might be previewed before dictation of a mailable-letter set.
- Four or more letters might be dictated as a set, or two letters might comprise a set.
- When additional tasks are added, such as typing envelopes and extra carbons to be mailed (which will also require extra envelopes), additional words need to be added to obtain total words.
- When extra carbons are made, students will need to have information regarding style for carbon copy notations and envelope addresses for extra copies.
- Extent of discussion of transcription information will vary depending on time in the course and in the program.
- Completeness of directions will vary depending on time in the course and in the program.

A major requirement in lesson planning for mailable-letter production is to "teach and help" when this guidance is needed but to work toward a time in the semester and the program when the student will be able to perform independently.

Minisimulations and Decision-Making Activities

During the third semester if only three semesters are offered, or during the fourth semester in schools offering four semesters of shorthand instruction, experiences with minisimulations and decision-making activities should be provided. Such minisimulations usually will be developed by the teacher. The teacher could visit businesses in the employment community to observe secretaries at work and organize a two-, three-, or four-day minisimulation based on the observations. Or several secretaries might be asked to complete task-analysis forms, on which a two-, three-, or four-day minisimulation could be based.

An in-basket exercise similar to the one completed in the Certified Professional Secretary examination is a culminating experience for advanced shorthand students. Such an in-basket exercise could be a two- or three-day in-class activity in which on the first day the students individually make decisions about the priority ranking of the seven or eight items in the in-basket packet. Following the individual decision making, the class as a whole could discuss their reasons for the priority rankings. As a final activity, certain in-basket items could be selected, and the students would specify the action to be taken and then complete the work on these items. Tape-recorded letters could be used for the dictation aspect of this in-basket, or the directions only could be dictated as is sometimes done on the CPS examination.

Considerations for Community College, Four-Year College, and High School Shorthand Teachers

The basic procedures discussed in Chapters 8 and 9 would not differ for high school, community college, or four-year college students. Teachers will need to analyze the goals, abilities, maturity levels, and past experiences of their students and adjust the degrees of repetition, reinforcement, and pacing to ensure optimum learning. Fortunately, publishers of shorthand textbooks and supplementary materials have adjusted the levels of the materials to the learning levels of these three groups of students. Wisely using well-chosen teaching techniques, strategies, and methodologies can be an exciting task for the teacher.

In Summary

Correct methodology, prudent use of materials, and positive reinforcement and confirmation from the teacher will help students become productive transcribers.

If typewritten transcription is begun in the early stages of the first semester, the students experience many opportunities to read and transcribe from well-written shorthand notes, develop quick and accurate decision making, use transcription elements correctly, develop accurate and rapid transcription, and practice directing their abilities and knowledge toward the proper goal of all shorthand instruction—*THE MAILABLE PRODUCT.*

Notes

1. Donald D. Jester, "A Time Study of the Shorthand Transcription Process," doctoral dissertation, Northwestern University, Evanston, Illinois, 1959.
2. Anthony A. Olinzock, "An Analysis of Business Dictation," doctoral dissertation, University of Pittsburgh, Pittsburgh, PA, 1976.
3. Harold H. Green, "The Nature of Business Dictation," doctoral dissertation, University of Pittsburgh, Pittsburgh, PA, 1951.
4. Diane S. Cavosie, "A Grading Plan for Mailable Letters," *The Balance Sheet,* September 1973, pp. 20, 30.
5. Robert L. Grubbs, "Rx for Effective Shorthand Teaching: Student Self-appraisal in Transcription," *Business Education World* June 1961, pp. 23–28.
6. Elizabeth Iannizzi, "Transcription and Shorthand Errors Among Elementary and Advanced High School Writers of Simplified and Diamond Jubilee Gregg Shorthand," doctoral dissertation, New York University, New York, 1967

Chapter 10

Shorthand Grading and Standards

Shorthand skills, because of their objectiveness, are relatively easy to measure. However, shorthand teachers are still faced with many of the problems associated with converting a series of skills and complex knowledge into a composite letter grade.

The failure of the business community to communicate its specific needs and standards contributes to the confusion surrounding the evaluation of shorthand performance. Additionally, the uniqueness of school systems promotes a multiplicity of evaluation procedures, with differences determined by attitudes toward grading, differing objectives and emphases in shorthand classes, differing expectations and philosophies of shorthand teachers, differences in the abilities and aptitudes of shorthand students, varying lengths of time available for shorthand instruction, and lack of uniformity in instructional equipment and teaching aids.

Accordingly, grades generally provide a rough estimate of a student's ability and potential within a given classroom; but they are almost meaningless to anyone but shorthand students and their teachers. For example, an A does not necessarily mean superior achievement when it is compared with superior achievement in another school, nor does a C indicate average ability in all schools.

The implications of the inconsistencies in shorthand evaluation are obvious. Shorthand teachers must develop grading plans appropriate to the uniqueness of their schools and students, but based on commonly accepted procedures and standards.

This chapter should assist shorthand teachers in developing, or adapting existing, grading plans. A discussion of characteristics associated with effective grading plans and standards and commonly used evaluation procedures follows.

Characteristics of Effective Shorthand Testing Programs

Leslie, while recognizing that there are pertinent minor factors, lists four major characteristics of shorthand testing:[1]

1. It emphasizes desirable objectives for the subject matter being tested.
2. It requires the use of good teaching and learning procedures for success in the test.
3. It provides a substantially just and accurate rating of the learners tested, without requiring an unreasonable amount of time for administration and correction.
4. It verifies and improves the teacher's knowledge of the state of learning of the students.

Harms and Stehr indicate that evaluation techniques should follow a consistent pattern, should be accepted by students, and should stress those factors that form the foundation of the course.[2]

According to Pullis, the effectiveness of an evaluation procedure should be measured not only in terms of its validity, reliability, and objectivity; but also with respect to the degree to which it promotes and encourages the type of study that contributes to shorthand proficiency.[3]

Russon states that because shorthand is a perceptual and motor skill and the emphasis is on *doing*, performance tests are most important.[4] She believes that performance tests should correlate with the stated objectives of each unit of instruction, and she identifies other characteristics of effective testing, including setting higher and higher goals and helping students become aware of their individual goals.

Other writers who attempt to describe positive characteristics of effective testing and grading programs are in general agreement with the authors mentioned, although additional characteristics are often listed. There seems to be general, although not unanimous, agreement that the following principles or guidelines should be considered when developing a shorthand evaluation program:

The Shorthand Testing Program Should Incorporate Both Internal and External Grading Methods

External standards are defined as standards set by the teacher based on knowledge of, and experience with, business standards. Internal standards are based on relative class standing. By using both types of standards, the teacher can balance general class abilities with business standards.

The Major Portion of the Final Grade Should Be Based on Achievement of External Standards

The final goal of shorthand instruction is to record dictation at a speed acceptable for employment and to transcribe the dictation into mailable copy. If external standards are used for evaluation, the grade is more likely to reflect actual business requirements.

External Standards Should Approximate Vocational Standards

Dictation rates and transcription performance must be geared to the expectations of business, or there is little justification for formal evaluation in shorthand. For example, A, B, or C grades should indicate the ability to use shorthand in business.

All Elements of the Total Shorthand Skill Should Be Evaluated, but With Differing Emphases

Shorthand involves a series of complex skills, all of which are important to achieving final objectives. Consequently, emphasis must be given to any skill bearing on the ultimate objective.

Shorthand Grades Should Reflect the Major Objectives of the Grading Period

As discussed in Chapter 2, learning activities receive varying degrees of emphasis during each quarter/semester. The percentage of the grade for each learning activity should correspond to the time allotted to it during the grading period. The ability to read shorthand is probably the most important objective of the first grading period, whereas ability to record dictation would be one of the major objectives of later grading periods.

The Emphasis on a Particular Element of Shorthand Skill Development Should Change as the Course Progresses

Objectives change as shorthand skill develops. Therefore, the evaluation emphases should also change.

Final Grades for a Course Should Reflect the Most Important Objectives of the Course

The relative importance of objectives changes as a student moves from one level of shorthand instruction to the next. Although other elements of shorthand skill development cannot be ignored, a grading plan should be weighted so that the most important objectives are most strongly reflected in the final evaluation.

Testing Should Comprise a Comparatively Small Proportion of Total Classroom Activity

The time spent in measuring achievement could often be spent more profitably in other learning activities. If substantial portions of class time are used for evaluation, less time is available for more meaningful activities. Leslie writes: "Almost everything that happens in the properly conducted shorthand classroom is, in a sense, a test of the skill the learner has acquired. No school subject has less real need of formal testing than shorthand; probably no school subject has leaned more heavily on testing in the past than shorthand."[5]

Testing Programs Should be Easy for the Students to Understand and for the Teacher to Administer

Testing in shorthand classes should be similar to the day-to-day learning activities. Students need to be told before a test how it will be administered and specifically what it will cover.

Students Should Be Aware of the Standards and Objectives for Particular Grading Periods

The knowledge of goals and standards is a powerful motivator. Although it is important to have a knowledge of end-of-year-objectives, it is even more crucial for students to be aware of specific intermediate goals and standards. The ability to set goals, attain those goals, and set new ones is a key to successful learning.

Positive Approaches Should Be Used when Evaluating Progress Toward External Standards

Achievement of a particular speed on a dictation test is to be rewarded, but failure to achieve such a speed should not be punished. When students take a dictation-recording test, they should consider the test as merely another opportunity to reach an established goal. Russon states: "If the testing program is to motivate the student, test scores should be expressed positively whenever possible. Two psychological principles operate here: (1) nothing succeeds like success and (2) nothing fails like failure."[6]

Most Shorthand Tests Should Contain an Element of Speed and Should Be Timed

Speed is largely a habit and the testing program should help develop the habit. In most shorthand testing, students should be attempting to work within time constraints.

Directions for All Shorthand Tests Should Be Thoroughly Understood Before Tests are Administered

Students will normally perform better if they know what is expected of them. For example, they should know the time limitations on timed tests, the criterion of evaluation, and the directions to be followed during the administration of the test.

Testing Procedures Should Conform to Established Norms

To attempt to maintain consistency of standards, achievement, and test administration, testing and evaluation should be conducted similarly from one school to the next. A recommended source for administering and scoring various types of tests is the booklet published for the Gregg Awards program.

Test Results Should Be Made Available to the Student as Soon as Possible

If possible, test results should be received while the details of the test are still fresh in the students' minds. If this is done, they are more apt to look at the details of the test from a remedial viewpoint rather than just from the point of a grade.

The End Result of All Testing in Shorthand Is the Development of the Ability to Produce Mailable Transcripts

Throughout all semesters of shorthand instruction, teachers and students alike must keep in focus that all reading, dictating, recording, and transcribing activities are directed toward the major objective of a correct transcript.

The Major Purpose of All Testing Is to Promote Learning

Testing should have a function broader than evaluation. For the student, it should be a basis for motivation, remedial study, and future objectives. For the teacher, testing should help identify the remedial work, the drill procedures necessary, and the immediate goals to be attempted.

Shorthand Testing Programs Must Accurately Assess Student Performance

The testing program should accurately assess student growth from one testing time to the next and the ability of the student to perform the day-to-day learning activities.

Shorthand Skills Are Most Accurately Assessed by Measuring Performance

Direct measures of what students can do are more effective than indirect measures. Tests that require students to read, write, or transcribe shorthand are more meaningful measures of performance than tests that evaluate knowledge of rules or require answering questions.

Part of the Evaluation of Shorthand Learning Should Be Informal

Shorthand teachers should continually make mental estimates of the day-to-day performances of individual students and of the entire class. Informal assessment, while not used for grading, allows the teacher to determine progress toward objectives, to determine proper remedial measures, and to communicate with and motivate students.

Commonly Used Shorthand Tests

This section describes tests commonly used in shorthand evaluation programs at both the high school and collegiate levels. Procedures for administration and standards for these tests are discussed. However, recommended standards should be interpreted as guidelines, and teachers may need to adjust standards according to the conditions under which they teach.

Longhand Transcription from Shorthand Plates

Testing student ability to transcribe in longhand from shorthand plates is done during the introductory phases of shorthand skill development. Usually, transcription is from the plate material of the current homework lesson.

Although used by some teachers, the practice of transcribing in longhand is questioned because the rate of longhand writing influences the rate of transcription. Most teachers today agree that reading shorthand plates aloud provides a more accurate assessment of reading ability. In many schools, longhand transcription from plate material has been replaced by typewritten transcription of the homework lesson. In situations where typewriters are not available, some teachers use longhand transcription to check the degree of preparation, spelling ability, and recognition of outlines. It is not recommended that longhand transcription take the place of oral-reading-rate evaluation.

Reading Skill Evaluation

Research indicates a positive relationship between reading ability and dictation-recording ability. Accordingly, shorthand teachers should stress heavily the development of reading skills in the first half of the first semester.

The methods recommended for developing reading ability are detailed in Chapter 5. Many teachers start the reading evaluation by using homework plate material and then move to the use of homework notes as the reading source. They need not feel that they are neglecting reading if the evaluation is done primarily in the first half of the first semester, because the following shorthand activities are still strongly based on reading ability: typewritten-transcription drills and three-minute transcription rates, reading from notes taken for dictation testing, reading from self-written notes taken for mailable-letter transcription, reading from shorthand outlines in the work-books, reading from self-written notes taken for class lectures in other subjects, reading from self-written notes taken for personal use. In addition, reading skill is employed every time a student sound/spells and pronounces words from the chalkboard or responds to previews, reviews, and postviews during dictation speed building. Finally a student cannot respond to dictation material without mentally reflecting on the word, which is somewhat like a reading process. Therefore, reading takes place throughout shorthand learning, but evaluation procedures must focus on the activities most relevant at a particular time in a course.

During the last few years, an increasing number of shorthand teachers have developed specific reading goals that students are expected to attain during a grading period.

Setting specific reading goals and determining whether students meet standards is valuable because of the objectivity given to evaluation and because learners have specific objectives to strive for. A description of administering one-minute and 30-second reading rates is given in Chapter 5, pages 148–149.

The following recommendations will help the student and teacher set and obtain reading-rate goals:

1. Assign specific words-a-minute reading goals for use in preparing homework lessons. If students are given a reading-goal speed chart, they can reread each homework letter until speed goals have been met. The reading-goal speed chart provided here gives learners a simple way to check whether goals have been achieved. To use this chart, the length of the homework letter must be determined. Locate the corresponding letter length in the left column of the chart. Reading goals are printed across the top of the chart. The number where the appropriate reading-speed goal and the appropriate letter

length intersect represents minutes and/or seconds allowed to meet the speed goal.

2. Select, or ask for volunteers of, five or six students daily during the first semester to read for one minute or 30 seconds from the homework lesson to determine reading rates.

3. Make reading tapes as recommended in Chapter 7 for the students to use at the beginning of the class hour while the teacher is busy with taking roll and other administrative duties, to take home for homework study, or to use in the library or learning center; and for class use for students who need special reading help.

The following recommendations from writers and researchers may help teachers who wish to establish specific words-a-minute reading standards:

- The authors of Pennsylvania Bulletin 277 state that the evaluation of oral reading of homework notes should be based on an average of several 30- or 60-second timings.[7] They suggest these standards:

A	180 wam
B	160 wam
C	140 wam
D	120 wam

   They recommend that the same grading scale be used for beginning and advanced shorthand because the shorthand material in textbooks becomes increasingly difficult.

- Pullis writes that during the fourth week of instruction students should be expected to read at a minimum of 40 wam, with an increase of 20 words for each successive grade.[8] He believes that the minimum rate should be increased by 10 words every two weeks until a base minimum rate of 160 words is reached sometime during the second semester.

- Dick found that less than one-third of the Wisconsin teachers in her sample graded on reading skill at the end of the second semester.[9] For those teachers who evaluated reading skills, the standards reported varied widely. However, there was a clustering around 200 wam for A grades, 120 to 140 wam for B, 100 wam for the C level, and 80 wam for D.

- Seals found that only 10 of the 50 Utah teachers in her sample indicated reading rates were associated with grades.[10] Eight of the ten indicated that students had to read contextual material within the 180- to 200-wam range for A's. Most of them stipulated a range of 150 to 170 wam for B's, and 100 to 140 wam for C's.

Although there seems to be no ready answer regarding the most appropriate words-a-minute standards to apply for oral reading from the homework lesson, the standards given in pages 343, 344, 346,

READING GOAL SPEED CHART

(WORDS A MINUTE)

WORDS IN LETTER	70	80	90	100	110	120	130	140	150	160	170	180	190	200	210	220	230	240
50	43	38	34	30	27	25	23	22	20	19	17	17	16	15	14	14	13	13
52	44	39	35	31	28	26	24	22	21	20	19	17	17	16	15	14	14	13
54	46	41	36	32	29	27	25	23	22	20	19	18	17	16	16	15	14	14
56	48	42	37	34	31	28	26	24	22	21	20	19	17	17	16	15	14	14
58	50	44	38	35	32	29	27	25	23	22	20	19	18	17	17	16	15	14
60	52	45	40	36	33	30	28	26	24	23	21	20	19	18	17	16	16	15
62	53	47	41	37	34	31	29	26	25	23	22	20	19	19	18	17	16	16
64	55	48	43	38	35	32	29	28	26	24	23	22	20	19	18	17	17	16
66	57	49	44	40	36	33	30	28	26	25	23	22	21	20	19	18	17	17
68	58	51	45	41	37	34	31	29	27	25	24	23	22	20	19	19	18	17
70	1:00	53	47	42	38	35	32	30	28	26	25	23	22	21	20	19	18	18
72	1:02	54	48	43	39	36	33	31	29	27	25	24	23	22	21	20	19	18
74	1:03	55	49	44	40	37	34	32	30	28	26	25	23	22	21	20	19	19
76	1:05	57	51	46	41	38	35	33	30	28	27	25	24	23	22	21	20	19
78	1:07	58	52	47	43	39	36	33	31	29	28	26	25	23	22	21	20	20
80	1:09	1:00	53	48	44	40	37	34	32	30	28	26	25	24	23	22	21	20
82	1:10	1:01	55	49	45	41	38	35	33	31	29	28	26	25	23	22	21	20
84	1:12	1:03	56	50	46	42	39	36	34	32	29	28	26	25	24	23	22	21
86	1:14	1:04	57	52	47	43	40	37	34	32	31	29	27	26	25	23	22	22
88	1:15	1:06	59	53	48	44	41	38	35	33	31	29	28	26	25	24	23	22
90	1:17	1:08	1:00	54	49	45	42	39	36	34	32	30	28	27	26	25	23	23
92	1:19	1:09	1:01	55	50	46	42	39	37	34	32	31	29	28	26	25	24	23

WORDS IN LETTER																	
94	23	25	26	27	28	29	31	33	35	38	40	43	47	51	56	1:03	1:10	1:21
96	24	25	26	28	29	31	32	34	36	38	41	44	48	52	58	1:04	1:12	1:22
98	25	26	27	28	29	31	32	35	37	39	42	45	49	53	59	1:05	1:13	1:24
100	25	26	27	29	30	32	34	35	38	40	43	46	50	55	1:00	1:07	1:15	1:26
102	26	27	28	29	30	32	34	36	38	41	43	47	50	56	1:01	1:08	1:16	1:27
104	26	28	28	30	31	33	35	37	39	42	44	48	52	57	1:02	1:09	1:18	1:29
106	26	28	29	30	31	34	35	37	40	42	45	49	53	58	1:04	1:11	1:19	1:31
108	27	29	29	31	32	34	36	38	40	43	45	49	54	59	1:05	1:12	1:21	1:33
110	27	29	30	31	32	35	36	39	41	44	46	50	54	1:00	1:06	1:13	1:23	1:34
112	28	30	31	32	33	35	37	40	42	45	47	51	55	1:01	1:07	1:15	1:24	1:36
114	28	30	31	32	34	36	37	40	43	46	48	52	56	1:02	1:08	1:16	1:25	1:38
116	29	31	32	33	34	36	38	41	43	46	49	53	57	1:03	1:10	1:17	1:27	1:39
118	29	31	32	34	35	37	38	41	44	47	49	54	58	1:04	1:11	1:19	1:28	1:41
120	30	32	33	34	35	38	40	43	45	48	50	54	58	1:05	1:12	1:20	1:30	1:43
122	30	32	33	35	35	38	40	43	46	49	51	55	59	1:07	1:13	1:21	1:31	1:45
124	31	33	34	35	36	38	41	44	46	49	51	56	1:00	1:08	1:14	1:23	1:33	1:46
126	32	34	34	36	37	39	42	44	47	50	52	57	1:01	1:09	1:16	1:24	1:34	1:48
128	32	34	35	37	37	40	43	45	48	50	53	57	1:02	1:10	1:17	1:25	1:36	1:50
130	32	34	35	37	38	40	43	46	49	51	54	58	1:03	1:11	1:18	1:27	1:38	1:51
132	34	35	36	38	38	41	43	47	49	52	55	59	1:04	1:12	1:19	1:28	1:39	1:53
134	34	35	37	38	39	41	44	47	50	53	56	1:00	1:05	1:13	1:20	1:29	1:40	1:55
136	34	35	37	38	40	43	44	48	51	54	57	1:01	1:06	1:14	1:22	1:31	1:42	1:57
138	35	37	38	39	41	43	46	49	52	54	57	1:02	1:07	1:15	1:23	1:32	1:43	1:58
140	35	37	38	40	42	44	46	49	53	55	58	1:03	1:08	1:16	1:24	1:33	1:45	2:00
142	35	38	39	40	43	44	47	50	53	56	59	1:04	1:09	1:17	1:25	1:35	1:46	2:02
144	36	38	39	41	43	45	47	51	54	57	1:00	1:05	1:10	1:19	1:26	1:36	1:48	2:03
146	37	38	40	42	44	46	48	52	55	58	1:01	1:06	1:11	1:20	1:28	1:37	1:49	2:05

Courtesy William Perry, Collier County Vocational-Technical Center, Naples, Florida

347, and 360 of this chapter provide further information on rates to be expected and weighting of reading in comparison with all other shorthand learning activities during a grading period. The reading-rate standard will be somewhat lower if the students are expected to drypen while reading.

Shorthand Vocabulary Testing

The research of Pullis, Goetz, Karaim, and others indicates that the more accurately students write shorthand outlines, the faster they write from dictation.[11,12,13,14] In addition, research such as that of Fermenich, Dortch, Cook, Haggeblade, Klaseus, and others has also found a significantly positive correlation between accuracy of shorthand outlines and accuracy of transcription.[15,16,17,18,19] From these studies and from experience in working with students, many teachers today believe that testing the students' ability to write theoretically correct outlines is an important part of learning and evaluation.

Three types of shorthand vocabulary tests are commonly used. They include (1) brief, unannounced shorthand vocabulary tests including words from homework lessons, (2) chapter shorthand vocabulary tests covering five or six lessons from the textbook, and (3) complete theory.

BRIEF, UNANNOUNCED SHORTHAND VOCABULARY TESTS. These tests focus student attention on the importance of writing correct shorthand outlines. Their objective is to promote learning through more thorough homework preparation. When such tests are used, the teacher selects 10 to 25 words from the current homework lesson and administers the tests from one to three times a week. Several types of shorthand vocabulary tests can be used, depending on the stage of learning.

The first type is recommended during the first few days of learning, before students have done very much shorthand writing. The teacher writes 10 to 25 isolated shorthand outlines from the word lists of the homework lesson on the chalkboard. Students are expected to transcribe the outlines in longhand within a prescribed time limit.

Another type that can be used the first few days is to write words on the chalkboard or on a master carbon in shorthand and ask students to write the shorthand sounds and then the transcribed word.

Example:

student response: s-t-r-a-n-j—strange

The third type of shorthand vocabulary test is probably the most used and is recommended after students have attained a degree of writing facility, usually after about three to five weeks of instruction. The teacher selects 10 to 25 isolated shorthand outlines from the word lists of the homework lesson and dictates at the rate of one word every six seconds. Students are evaluated on the number of theoretically correct outlines they are able to write. In the early stages, incorrect or poor penmanship, proportion, and position on the writing line are not counted as errors. The teacher will help the students understand the importance of these elements by writing the word correctly on the quiz paper. Building remedial work into the next class drill will help improve penmanship, proportion, correct symbol usage and joinings, and position on line of writing. In the early stages, to help the students attain higher grades on such tests, they may be asked to transcribe the shorthand outline into a longhand word; thus on a 20-word test, the grade would be based on 40 items— 20 outlines and 20 transcribed words. After sufficient time has been given to practice correctness of line of writing and proportion (about seven to eight weeks of the first semester), penalties should be made for irregularities.

Some teachers like to use short, unannounced shorthand vocabulary tests throughout the entire two years of shorthand instruction. When this practice is followed, the dictation rate is increased to one word each five seconds or less. Brief shorthand vocabulary tests in the second, third, and fourth semesters give the student more immediate feedback on knowledge of writing words correctly than do one-chapter or two-chapter tests. Short, unannounced shorthand vocabulary tests also give the student a basis for studying for the chapter or two-chapter test. In the second, third, and fourth semesters, some teachers choose shorthand vocabulary words from within the paragraph material as well as from the word lists. This procedure helps emphasize knowing the correct writing of words within the paragraph material as well as those in the word lists.

CHAPTER TESTS. Such tests are given at six-lesson intervals in the first semester and at five-lesson intervals in the remaining semesters. During the first semester, the tests include words illustrating theory principles presented in the word lists in the preceding five lessons and review Lesson 6. In other semesters, the test items will be chosen from the word lists and the paragraphs of the lessons within the chapter.

Usually 25 to 50 words are selected from the five to six lessons previously studied. These words are dictated at the rate of an outline every six seconds. After all outlines have been dictated, the students are given a couple of minutes to look them over and to cancel out and rewrite outlines. The tests are scored in the same way described for brief, unannounced shorthand vocabulary tests.

In administering the shorthand vocabulary part of chapter tests and short unannounced shorthand vocabulary tests, as in all testing, **307** the teacher should lessen test anxiety as much as possible. Following are suggestions to alleviate test anxiety in shorthand vocabulary testing and to help the students perform successfully:

1. Give the same directions for preparing student notebook paper for each test. Example:
   a. "Number in the first column from 1 to 20; in the second column, from 21 to 40.
   b. Write your name on the lower left line, date on the lower right line, and the lesson number or chapter in the center."
2. Say the number of each item, and pronounce each word twice so no one will have difficulty hearing it.
3. Use past tense and plurals, or any other word that may be difficult to distinguish because of sound, in sentences.
4. Do not go back and repeat words once the next word has been pronounced. Hearing words other than the one on which the student is concentrating, causes confusion.
5. Ask the students to write fluently and quickly, writing only shorthand as they hear the words pronounced.

The shorthand vocabulary section of the chapter test is often only one of several sections. Many teachers also include spelling, business vocabulary, and punctuation tests. Samples of items to test spelling, business vocabulary, and punctuation, are given on pages 326–330 of this chapter.

Chapter tests should be used primarily for student and teacher information. On the basis of test results, teachers can determine the amount of reteaching and review necessary for individual students or the entire class. However, assigning and recording grades for these tests should encourage better homework preparation and more active involvement in classroom learning activities. Suggested standards and weightings for the chapter tests are shown on pages 343 through 356 of this chapter. Many teachers like to record shorthand vocabulary, spelling, business vocabulary, and punctuation grades separately in order to be able to see at a glance how well a student is doing in each area. This procedure also helps the student to see areas that need more study and areas where they are successful.

COMPLETE THEORY TESTS. These tests usually include 100 words designed to assess mastery of brief forms and phrases and the ability to write theoretically correct high-frequency vocabulary.

Teachers who use these tests find the annual *Gregg Tests and Awards Booklet* a valuable source for testing. Five complete tests are published every year in these booklets.

Directions for administration of these tests are as follows:

1. Instruct students to number from 1 to 100 in their shorthand notebooks, or distribute duplicated forms numbered from 1 to 100.

2. Dictate the words at the rate of about one every six seconds.
3. When all words are dictated, instruct students to transcribe all the shorthand outlines in longhand, in the order dictated.
4. Allow approximately 20 minutes for longhand transcription of the 100 words.
5. Deduct half a point for each shorthand outline incorrectly written, and another half point for each incorrect longhand transcription.

Teachers who often use complete theory tests, for giving awards to students who perform well, need to contemplate the following disadvantages to complete theory tests:

1. Much valuable class time is consumed in administering a 100-word test according to directions given above (10 minutes to administer; 20 minutes to transcribe).
2. Results are often discouraging to the student and to the teacher because review for such a test cannot be focused on any one segment of the book or theory learning.
3. With the wide range of possible shorthand vocabulary words that could be covered in a complete theory test, it is difficult for the student to meaningfully review for such testing.

Many teachers find from experience that students can more easily learn theory application when it is concentrated on a portion of the material studied—such as a chapter or two chapters. By studying designated lessons, the student is refining theory knowledge and ability to write correctly.

Practiced-Matter Dictation

Most practiced- or familiar-matter dictation during the first semester is selected from homework lessons. The ability to record previously practiced dictation is an important step toward learning to record new-matter dictation. Therefore, administering dictation-recording tests on slightly rearranged practiced homework material is common during the first two-thirds of the first semester of instruction.

The authors of the *Instructor's Handbook for Gregg Shorthand* suggest that such tests be about three minutes in length.[20] The students transcribe the test on the typewriter if they have begun typewritten transcription or in longhand if typewritten transcription has not begun. The Gregg authors recommend a three-step approach to the dictation testing of homework material.

The first step in using homework lesson material for dictation-recording testing is to inform the students exactly what material will be dictated, and give them a few days to practice. As skill develops, the second step is used; students are told that the test material will be selected from a range of specified letters. For example, two letters could be selected for dictation from ten that have previously been identified by the teacher. Of course, students are encouraged to practice all ten letters in order to ensure passing the test. In the third stage, the test material would be taken from any previous homework lesson without preparatory notice.

Quite a number of teachers today are delaying practiced-dictation testing until about the seventh or eighth week of the first semester. This means that from the first day of dictation practice up to the seventh or eighth week, all dictation practice is for speed building. The methodology explained in dictation speed building, Chapter 6, of starting with small pieces, using an open book, and so on, is all part of this dictation procedure. For the first dictation-recording test at the seventh or eighth week, students are told the letters that will be used for the dictation test material. This material would be taken from the letters used in class during the week for dictation speed-building practice. For example: Monday—letters practiced in class were 288, 290, 291; Tuesday—letters 298 and 300; Wednesday—letters 309, 313, 314; Thursday—letters 321, 324, 325. The students' homework for Friday would be to practice drypenning and reading, writing selected sentences or parts of the letters, and writing selected words in these letters that seem to be troublesome. The most important direction regarding homework is that they not attempt to memorize the letters, because the wording will be changed slightly and it will only confuse them if they try to memorize rather than studying as recommended. Before class the next day, the teacher selects the material to be dictated for the test. If the test is to be a three-minute, 60-wam test, 180 words will need to be selected. Letters can be shortened and dictated in succession without breaks to get the 180 words. With a pencil and the student transcript, the material is changed slightly by rearranging words; shortening sentences or paragraphs; and changing names, dates, series; and so on. No new words are used, only words that have been studied in the paragraphs.

On Friday in class, after theory preview of the new lesson is completed, three to five minutes of warmup would be given at 70 or 80 wam, about 10 to 20 words above the dictation-test rate of 60 wam. After the test is dictated, the students would transcribe it on the typewriter using a six-inch line, double spacing, and five-space paragraph indention. At completion, the notes would be stapled under the test and handed to the teacher.

Weekly dictation tests similar to this would be given throughout the completion of theory presentation, Lesson 48. After Lesson 48, new material should be the source of dictation speed-building drill and of dictation testing.

Another way to test familiar-material dictation-recording ability is suggested for consideration. During the last grading period of the first semester, or when the theory introduction is completed with Lesson 48, apply the following standards for familiar-material dictation-recording testing.

GRADE	RATE	LENGTH	ACCURACY
A	80	3 min.	95%
B	70	3 min.	95%
C	60	3 min.	95%

In preparation for testing, peruse the previously covered textbook lessons looking for combinations of letters which when combined would equal about three minutes of dictation at speeds of 80, 70, and 60 wam. Record on tape the equivalent of five, three-minute takes at 80 wam. On another tape, record the equivalent of five, three-minute tests at 70 wam, and on a third tape record five tests at 60 wam. The 80-wam tape is labeled as the A tape; the 70-wam tape as the B tape, and the 60-wam tape as the C tape. There will be 15 minutes of dictation on each tape, or a total of 45 minutes.

Instruct students that the dictation-recording tests will be administered directly from the tapes, but tell them that they can use the tapes for out-of-class practice before the test days. When testing, randomly select a dictation take from each of the tapes. Tell students that they will have several opportunities to pass tests with 95 percent accuracy and that they will receive credit for the highest speed passed.

Preparation of these testing tapes consumes valuable teacher time, but students are encouraged to practice for the tests. They know the exact nature of the tests and recognize that they have a chance to perform well if they spend enough time practicing the 45 minutes of dictation.

In the first semester, a 95 percent accuracy standard is usually used to determine whether students have passed dictation-recording tests.

The following are recommended first-semester dictation-test standards used by teachers in selected areas of the country for familiar-material dictation:

- Pullis outlines conditions for practiced-dictation-recording testing— unpreviewed, not practiced in class, previously written for homework and within a five-lesson range—and states that students should be capable of the following minimum rates with 95 percent accuracy:

  Week 12—50 wam
  Week 15—60 wam
  Week 18—70 wam

  He writes that the above standards are for C grades and recommends raising the rate 10 wam for B and 20 wam for A.[21]
- Crank outlines the following grading scale for dictation-recording

testing of familiar material during weeks 8 to 12 of the first semester (each rate must be passed twice to establish the grade):[22]

GRADE	RATE	LENGTH	ACCURACY
A	70	3 min.	95%
B	70	2 min.	95%
C	60	3 min.	95%
D	60	2 min.	95%

In grading a dictation-recording test to determine if the student has passed two minutes of it, the three-minute test is used and the one-minute intervals marked off on the student's paper. The number of errors for each of the minutes is recorded to the right on the student's transcribed copy. If the student has not passed the three-minute test within the 5 percent error allowance, the teacher checks to see if the first two minutes or the last two minutes were passed within the 5 percent error allowance. If the same material is used to check passing either two minutes or three minutes, extra dictation tests do not need to be given for two minutes.

- Dick concluded that the first-semester standards used by Wisconsin shorthand teachers varied considerably for practiced-matter dictation.[23] However, there was clustering around 80 wam for A grades; 60 wam for B or C; and 50 wam for D. The majority of teachers who used practiced-matter dictation tests required students to pass two, three-minute tests with 95 percent accuracy.

New-Matter Dictation-Recording Tests

Evaluating the ability to record and transcribe new-matter dictation is common after the presentation of shorthand theory and introduction of new-matter dictation. Such tests essentially assess the ability to record sustained, new-matter dictation at specified speeds for three or five minutes. Many teachers move completely into this new-matter dictation-recording testing at the completion of theory in the first semester, which might be about the twelfth week. Teachers differ on whether longhand or typewritten transcription errors are considered dictation-recording-test errors. In the beginning stages, the teacher may wish to note the correct punctuation and reason and the correct transcription-element usage for the student to observe. Within a few weeks, the student should be held accountable for correctness of these aspects of transcription. New-matter dictation-recording tests and mailable-letter tests are major vehicles for determining progress toward terminal course objectives, and they are an integral part of every shorthand program. Despite their frequent use, there is lack of conformity in *how* they are used. An examination of shorthand teacher practices reveals differences in test lengths, speed standards, error allowances, and test administration. Because there is no uniformity from school to school, it is difficult to compare results without analyzing the conditions under which the tests are given.

A discussion of the factors associated with dictation tests follows:

LENGTH OF TESTS. Research completed by Pullis (Chapter 6, page 180) shows that the median average difference between three-minute and five-minute tests is 20 wam.[24] Although five-minute dictation tests were once the most prevalent standard for measuring speed of new-matter dictation recording, today most authors recommend three-minute tests. The rationale for decreasing test length relates to economizing on class time, providing for more dictation test opportunities during a class hour, and more closely simulating the length of continuous business dictation.

Surveys of teacher practices reveal that three-minute tests are most commonly used, but that some teachers use a variety of other lengths. Wedell found that almost 60 percent of the teachers in his sample used three-minute tests.[25] However, another 25 percent of the respondents used either one- or two-minute progress tests, and approximately 11 percent used tests that were longer than three minutes. Dick, who surveyed Wisconsin shorthand teachers, concluded that the majority of the respondents dictated for at least three minutes, and Seals found that three-minute tests were used by approximately 80 percent of the teachers in Utah high schools.[26,27]

Teachers should strongly consider using three-minute dictation tests. Although other lengths are defensible, the adoption of a three-minute test could be the first step toward a uniform expression of achievement and standards.

ACCURACY REQUIREMENTS. There is almost unanimous agreement among teachers that a liberal error allowance should be given in determining whether students have passed dictation-recording tests. Since the goal of dictation-recording testing is to encourage maximum speed development, an ample error allowance should allow students to move toward higher speed goals more quickly and with less frustration. Leslie states that the only value of a shorthand speed test is to indicate when the learner is ready to advance to a new speed level.[28]

Accordingly, students who exceed error limits should be told that they will not be penalized for not meeting the standard and that there will be other opportunities to pass tests at the speed level they failed to achieve.

Leslie cautions about using rigid accuracy requirements by stating: "There can be no quarreling with almost any reasonable accuracy requirement for a terminal speed test. But for shorthand speed tests given as progress tests, too high an accuracy requirement serves only to hamper the learner's progress."[29]

Russon writes: "Dictation speed tests are scored on the basis of 95

313

percent accuracy as passing. Students are encouraged to move forward as rapidly as they can."[30]

Like Russon, most writers recommend a 5 percent error allowance, and surveys reveal a 95 percent accuracy standard is used in most classrooms throughout the country. Surveys by Dick and Wedell indicate that the 95 percent recommendations are being followed by most teachers.[31,32] However, there are still teachers using standards ranging from 90 to 94 percent, and some instructors are using standards of from 96 to 100 percent. Some teachers prefer to use the 95 percent accuracy standard for the first three semesters and a 97 percent accuracy standard for the final semester, believing that the final semester should aim for refinement and greater control of writing, without necessarily building higher dictation speeds. Post-secondary and college shorthand teachers often will use the 95 percent standard for the first semester and the 97 percent standard for the succeeding semesters.

Some teachers will use a 97 percent accuracy requirement on three-minute dictation tests and a 95 percent accuracy requirement on five-minute dictation tests in order to try to balance out the differences in achievement when using the two different lengths of tests, or to better equate the three-minute test with the five-minute test.

FREQUENCY OF DICTATION-RECORDING TESTS. Administering dictation-recording tests consumes valuable class time that could be devoted to dictation speed building and other learning activities. When students transcribe dictation tests in longhand or at the typewriter, they are proving their ability to record dictation at specific speed levels, but they are not improving shorthand skills. Thus, the overuse of dictation-recording testing may hinder speed development. Ideally, individual students should take dictation tests only when they can potentially pass them, but most teachers work with groups of students. As a result, dictation-recording tests are scheduled according to group rather than individual needs. Although there are no ready answers regarding the optimum frequency of dictation testing, teachers should not administer dictation-recording tests more than once a week. In fact there may be occasions, particularly early in the second semester or during the initial stages of the second year, when two-week intervals between dictation tests would be advantageous. Basically, dictation-writing skill should be developed before dictation testing is done. Dictation speed building should be a major part of the class activity three days of the week to help the student build dictation skill for successful achievement on dictation-recording testing. When schools, especially postsecondary schools, have laboratory situations, out-of-class time can be spent on dictation speed development thus allowing in-class time to be spent on other learning activities.

Closely associated with the frequency of dictation-recording testing is the question of how many times students must pass dictation tests before credit is given for attaining a speed. Teacher practice reveals no strong consensus. Shorthand teachers require from one to three dictation-recording tests with a minimum of 95 percent accuracy for proof of satisfactory performance. Requiring three satisfactory performances at a given speed level may force teachers to administer an excessive number of speed tests, and valuable class time is stolen from other learning activities. Students should be spending their class and practice time in moving to new, challenging speed goals rather than in continuing to prove they can record dictation at a particular speed level.

Many teachers today agree that passing a particular dictation speed twice in relatively close succession is assurance that the student is capable of writing dictation at that speed—the student then progresses to the next rate. Other teachers allow students to move on to new speeds without having passed two tests at a particular rate, even though the standard for the course may require two to be passed at a particular rate for a grade. Having an opportunity to bypass a second test motivates students, because they try diligently to keep moving ahead. However, there is another point to be considered. Since dictation material varies greatly in difficulty, sometimes students may pass their first test of a rate on an "easy" test and move on to the next highest speed. They may then become very discouraged when the next rate seems impossible to attain. For this reason, some teachers require that two tests be passed before moving to the next highest rate.

ADMINISTRATION OF DICTATION-RECORDING TESTS. Because of individual differences, teachers usually dictate several dictation-recording tests, covering a range of speeds, on days when such tests are scheduled. Therefore, the following procedures are recommended:

- Provide three to five minutes of warmup dictation at rates that are 10 to 20 wam above the fastest dictation test to be given. For example, if the fastest rate to be given is 120 wam, the warmup dictation should be at 130 and 140 wam.
- Dictating the tests in descending order (for example, 120, 110, 100, and 90 wam), gives students trying to pass tests at lower speeds additional warmup opportunities by taking at least part of each of the faster rates. Also students trying for 100, for example, may be able to write the 110 and transcribe it rather than the 100. Students taking the higher rates can be reading through notes, refining outlines by canceling out and writing better outlines above the poorly written ones, looking up materials in reference manuals, and so on, while the teacher is dictating the slower rates.

Recommendations for lending uniformity to dictation-testing procedures include the following:

- After theory introduction is completed, with Lesson 48 in the first semester, dictation testing for the remainder of the first semester and throughout the second, third, and fourth semesters should be new material. Students should not have practiced or heard it previously.
- Words should not be previewed.
- Dictation should be given once and within the time prescribed.
- Punctuation marks should not be dictated.
- Paragraphs are dictated.
- Students should transcribe at the typewriter. If the early typewritten transcription drills have been used as described in Chapter 8, the students will be ready to use the typewriter for transcribing by the time dictation testing is begun at the seventh or eighth week of the first semester. If typewriters are not available, the transcription must be done in longhand.
- When the typewriter is used for transcribing dictation tests, the material should be set up with a six-inch line, double spacing, and a five-space paragraph indention. If the material is set up in letter style, the students tend to confuse the goals of mailable-letter production with those of verbatim dictation recording. Teachers must try to keep the goals separate in the minds of the students. Advantages to setting the dictation-recording test up in double-spaced form allows the student to proofread and correct errors more easily. It also allows space for the teacher to write in the shorthand outline of words missed, the punctuation and reason for punctuation, and other notes when correcting the transcript.
- Students should be encouraged to consult dictionaries and reference manuals when transcribing.
- Some teachers have found that it is wise to require students to transcribe a dictation test at the test rate they are attempting to achieve, or one higher, each time that dictation tests are given, even if they think they cannot pass the test within the 5 percent error allowance. Much can be learned from transcribing—correct spelling; correct transcription usage; and if the typewriter is used, correct typing style. Students will need encouragement to always transcribe their dictation-recording test. The first test at a new dictation speed is sometimes difficult, but transcribing from notes written at that particular speed will help the student do a better job the second and succeeding times that this rate is taken. Another element enters into this situation—if students know that the test must be transcribed, usually they try harder to get the dictation.

An exception to this requirement might be if the class dictation testing is from 120 down to 80. For example, students at the 120, 110, 100, and 90 test rates could take the 80 wam test material for mailable-letter production if they were not successful at getting their own particular dictation-recording test speed. Such a practice would work any time after mailable-letter work has been started. This procedure makes the day's effort worthwhile and gives another opportunity for a mailable-letter grade. Other teachers like to have the students use multichannel equipment, records, or individual tape recorders for extra practice if they are unable to record the dictation test at the assigned test rate.

- Students should be given ample time to transcribe the dictation. Most teachers agree that the transcription rate, whether in longhand or on the typewriter, should be at least between 15 and 20 wam. If a teacher takes the number of words to be transcribed at the highest speed for the day and divides by 15, the number of minutes to be allowed for transcription can be determined. Example: 120 wam $\times$ 3 minutes $= \dfrac{360 \text{ words}}{15 \text{ twam}} = 24$ minutes for transcription. Therefore, if the class period is 50 minutes, and the rates to be dictated are 120, 110, 100, 90, and 80, the timing allowances for the class might be as follows:

Preview of new lesson:	5 minutes
Dictation warmup:	3 minutes
Dictation of tests:	5 × 3 = 15 minutes + pauses between dictation = 17 minutes
Transcription time:	25 minutes

- Have the students staple shorthand notes under the transcript before submitting it. When the paper is handed back, the notes are there for the students to compare teacher notations on the corrected transcript with the notes taken during dictation.

CORRECTING DICTATION-RECORDING TESTS. Teachers, rather than students, should correct dictation-recording tests to ensure fairness and consistency, as students have differing levels of proof-reading ability.

The following scoring rules should be followed to determine whether students have passed the test within the accuracy standards used on dictation tests.

- Check only the handwritten or typewritten transcript. Ignore errors in the shorthand notes. However, a quick, informal evaluation of shorthand notes may be helpful in diagnosing individual or group learning deficiencies. Scanning the notes can reveal fluency of writing; wasting space at the beginning or end of lines, which causes loss of time in moving the hand down the page and from page to page; inclusion of longhand writing, and the like.
- Deduct one word for each of the following: incorrectly transcribed words, omitted words, added words, transposed words, and other deviations in the copy.
- Deduct 1 for punctuation errors that change the context of the

material. In the early stages teachers will be more liberal in error deduction for punctuation and deduct for punctuation only as it is reviewed in the textbook.

- Deduct 1 for each misspelling. If the same word is misspelled more than once, make only one deduction.
- Deduct 1 for each uncorrected typographical error if the transcript is typed.
- Do not deduct for irregularities in paragraphing, capitalization, and arrangement. If paragraphs are dictated, the teacher may deduct for incorrect paragraphing. In the second and succeeding semesters, as capitalization is reviewed, deductions may be made for incorrect capitalization.

Once the transcript has been checked, errors should be totaled and the percentage of accuracy determined. Percentage of accuracy can be computed by dividing the total of correctly transcribed words by total words in the dictation material. For example, a three-minute take dictated at 60 wam contains the equivalent of 180 words. If a transcript contains six errors, 174 words are divided by 180 words, or 96.6 percent.

The chart on page 319 can be used for making quick calculations of percentage of accuracy.

Some teachers use a method of determining the maximum number of errors for the test to be passed within the error allowance and count the dictation test either "passed" or "not passed" based on the number of errors allowed. Following are examples of the number of errors allowed at various rates on three-minute tests, if the standard for passing is 95 percent accuracy:

120 wam, 18 errors
110 wam, 17 errors
100 wam, 15 errors
90 wam, 14 errors
80 wam, 12 errors

When the paper is scored, the number of errors can be recorded at the top of the paper with a notation; for example, for a 110 wam test:

$$\frac{15 \text{ errors OK}}{\text{passed}} \quad \text{or} \quad \frac{19 \text{ errors NO}}{17 \text{ allowed}}$$

SPEED STANDARDS FOR DICTATION-RECORDING TESTS. Setting speed standards for dictation-recording tests requires balancing business expectations and needs with typical attainment by shorthand students after one and two years of study. If both factors are not considered, speed standards may be unattainable by students or standards may be too low to meet their vocational needs.

ERROR ALLOWANCE AND PERCENT OF ACCURACY

ERRORS	60 wam		70 wam		80 wam		90 wam		100 wam		110 wam		120 wam	
	3 min.	5 min.	3 min.	5 min.	3 min.	5 min.	3 min.	5 min.	3 min.	5 min.	3 min.	5 min.	3 min.	5 min.
1	99.4	99.7	99.5	99.7	99.6	99.8	99.6	99.8	99.7	99.8	99.7	99.8	99.7	99.8
2	98.9	99.4	99.1	99.4	99.2	99.5	99.3	99.6	99.3	99.6	99.4	99.6	99.4	99.7
3	98.4	99.0	98.6	99.2	98.8	99.2	98.9	99.3	99.0	99.4	99.1	99.5	99.2	99.5
4	97.8	98.7	98.1	98.9	98.4	99.0	98.5	99.1	98.7	99.2	98.8	99.3	98.9	99.3
5	97.3	98.4	97.6	98.6	98.0	98.8	98.1	98.9	98.3	99.0	98.5	99.1	98.6	99.2
6	96.7	98.0	97.1	98.3	97.5	98.5	97.8	98.7	98.0	98.8	98.2	98.9	98.3	99.0
7	96.1	97.7	96.7	98.0	97.1	98.2	97.4	98.4	97.7	98.6	97.9	98.7	98.1	98.8
8	95.6	97.4	96.2	97.8	96.7	98.0	97.1	98.2	97.3	98.4	97.6	98.5	97.8	98.7
9	95.0	97.0	95.7	97.5	96.3	97.8	96.7	98.0	97.0	98.2	97.3	98.4	97.5	98.5
10		96.7	95.2	97.2	95.9	97.5	96.3	97.8	96.7	98.0	97.0	98.2	97.2	98.3
11		96.4	94.8	96.9	95.4	97.2	96.0	97.5	96.3	97.8	96.7	98.0	96.9	98.2
12		96.0		96.6	95.0	97.0	95.6	97.3	96.0	97.6	96.4	97.8	96.7	98.0
13		95.7		96.3		96.8	95.2	97.1	95.7	97.4	96.1	97.6	96.4	97.8
14		95.4		96.0		96.5	94.8	96.8	95.3	97.2	95.8	97.5	96.1	97.7
15		95.0		95.8		96.2		96.6	95.0	97.0	95.5	97.3	95.8	97.5
16				95.4		96.0		96.4		96.8	95.2	97.1	95.6	97.3
17				95.1		95.8		96.2		96.6	94.9	97.0	95.3	97.2
18				94.9		95.5		96.0		96.4		96.7	95.0	97.0
19						95.2		95.7		96.2		96.5		96.8
20						95.0		95.5		96.0		96.4		96.7
21								95.3		95.8		96.2		96.5
22								95.1		95.6		96.0		96.3
23								94.9		95.4		95.8		96.2
24										95.2		95.6		96.0
25										95.0		95.5		95.8
26												95.3		95.7
27												95.1		95.5
28												94.9		95.3
29														95.2
30														95.0

Courtesy Donald Beringson, Oregon State University, Corvallis, Oregon

Relatively little is known about business standards, although 80 wam is commonly mentioned as a marketable rate. There is some research to substantiate the 80-wam theory. For example, the secretaries in Scammon's sample who used shorthand estimated that shorthand speeds of 80 to 100 wam were equal to the dictation they encountered, and 60 percent of the personnel managers in the same study specified a necessary speed range of 80 to 100 wam.[33]

Green analyzed the dictation habits of 72 dictators in 1951.[34] Although his data is limited by sample size and is not recent, the research provides an in-depth look at the actual dictation process. His analysis reveals that a range of dictation-recording speeds is required to meet business needs and implies that there is no universal minimum-speed standard.

The following table illustrates the range of speeds required to meet the needs of the individual dictators:

ANALYSIS OF BUSINESS DICTATION SPEEDS AND ABILITY TO RECORD DICTATION

WRITING SPEED FOR 3 MIN.	% OF DICTATORS FROM WHOM ALL DICTATION WOULD BE RECORDED	% OF DICTATORS FROM WHOM ALL DICTATION WOULD NOT BE RECORDED
70 words a minute	20	80
80 words a minute	40	60
90 words a minute	60	40
100 words a minute	75	25
110 words a minute	85	15
120 words a minute	95	5
130 words a minute	98	2
140 words a minute	100	0

Courtesy Harold Green, "The Nature of Business Dictation," doctoral dissertation, University of Pittsburgh, Pittsburgh, 1951.

Green's research also reveals dictation patterns, and this reinforces the argument that absolute speed standards are lacking.

Olinzock's study was similar to Green's earlier research.[35] He found that the overall gross dictation speed of dictators was 63 wam. However, the quarter minute gross speed of dictators reached a maximum of 216 wam, and the median maximum speed was 116 wam.

The research available seems to indicate that there are no absolute dictation-recording speed standards, but that 80 wam is minimal for employment. However, an 80-wam attainment on a dictation-recording test with a 5 percent error allowance will probably not meet vocational expectations. Dictators are apt to adjust dictation rates to meet the skill levels of secretaries, but they are not so prone to vary their transcription standards. Ability to prepare a usable transcript containing no major errors within an acceptable time is the major criterion for shorthand job success. Thus, attainment of 80 wam with 95 percent accuracy on a three-minute dictation-recording test will probably not meet minimum job requirements.

A review of the literature reveals little consistency in dictation-recording test speed standards. The diversity of teacher practices associated with test length, accuracy requirements, and methods of administration have heightened the confusion surrounding speed requirements after one and two years of instruction. The following are examples of speed achievement or recommended standards after one year of high school instruction.

- Wedell asked shorthand teachers to estimate the single highest achievement for each of their students on unpreviewed, new-matter dictation, at the end of one year of instruction, assuming three-minute tests and a 95 percent accuracy standard.[36] The teachers reported that 157 students, or 3.9 percent, could not pass a dictation test of at least 40 wam. Estimated mean speed achievement for the 3,842 students who passed at least one speed test at 40 wam or higher was 71.69 wam. The performance of the majority of students, 2,445 or 61.1 percent, was estimated at 60 to 80 wam. The median speed achievement was estimated at 65.5 wam, and the mode estimated achievement was 60 wam.
- Haueisen surveyed teachers in Central Ohio to determine grading standards being used.[37] The median new-matter dictation-recording requirements and grades after one year of instruction were:

80 wam	A
70 wam	B
60 wam	C
50 wam	D

PATTERN OF DICTATION OF SELECTED DICTATORS

PHASE OF DICTATION	SLOW DICTATORS	AVERAGE DICTATORS	RAPID DICTATORS	VERY FAST DICTATORS
Groping (15% of time)	0–30 wam	0–40 wam	0–40 wam	0–50 wam
Thoughtful (45% of time)	40–60 wam	50–80 wam	50–90 wam	60–100 wam
Confident (30% of time)	75–90 wam	85–105 wam	100–130 wam	110–140 wam
Sprinting (10% of time)	100 wam up	120 wam up	140 wam up	150 wam up

Courtesy Harold Green, "The Nature of Business Dictation" doctoral dissertation, University of Pittsburgh, Pittsburgh, 1951.

- Seals surveyed Utah high school teachers to determine the speed standards being used at the end of a year of instruction.[38] She stated that, in general, the speed and accuracy requirements for new-material, three-minute dictation tests for each grade were:

  A   Must have passed three 80- to 100-wam dictation takes with a maximum of 18 errors

  B   Must have passed three 60- to 90-wam dictation takes with a maximum of 14 errors

  C   Must have passed three 50- to 80-wam dictation takes with a maximum of 14 errors

  D   Must have passed three 50- to 60-wam dictation takes with a maximum of 10 errors

- Coburn, in studying the criteria used to evaluate high school shorthand students in Southwestern Missouri, (new-material, three-minute dictation tests) concluded that the dictation standards used most frequently during the second semester were: 100 wam for an A, 80 wam for a B, 60 wam for a C, and 50 wam for a D.[39]

- Dick, in surveying the grading practices of Wisconsin shorthand teachers, found a wide variety of speed standards being used for new-material, three-minute dictation tests during the first year of instruction.[40] However, she found that about two-fifths used 80 wam for A grades and 70 wam for B. She also found that more than half the teachers expected a 60-wam performance for a C, and about 44 percent of her sample expected students to write at 50 wam for a D.

- Leslie writes that after 150 to 200 class periods of instruction, the majority of students will be ready to pass an 80 wam five-minute test within the 5 percent error limit.[41] He adds that the few at the bottom of the group will succeed in passing a test at 60 wam and the few in the top group will be passing tests at 100 wam or better.

- Pullis states, "On unpreviewed, new-matter, three-minute tests requiring 95 percent accuracy, the high school student should be expected to attain the following minimum standards: week 24, 50 wam; week 30, 60 wam; and week 36, 70 wam."[42]

- The authors of *Pennsylvania Bulletin 277* recommend the following standards for new-material, three-minute speed tests with a 5 percent error allowance at the end of the second semester: A, 80 wam; B, 70 wam; C, 60 wam; D, 60 wam.[43] They differentiate between C and D grades by suggesting that a 98 percent accuracy standard be used for C.

There are no ready answers to establishing speed standards for dictation tests. Teachers must make a thoughtful assessment of all the factors associated with shorthand performance before arriving at specific speed standards for dictation tests. Subject to wide variations, the following might be considered as standards (on new-material, unpreviewed, three-minute dictation tests, at a standard of 95 percent accuracy) that balance typical high school student performance after one year of instruction with industry expectations:

A   80–100 wam
B   70–90 wam
C   60–80 wam
D   60   wam for two minutes to 70 for three minutes

Information on speed standards for second-year high school shorthand is scant. Although recommended standards can be found in the literature, little research has been conducted to determine the standards actually applied in shorthand classrooms. Depending on the transcription emphasis during the second year, speed standards on three-minute, unpreviewed, new-material dictation tests with a standard of 97 percent accuracy should probably be increased from 20 to 40 wam on dictation tests from the first to the second year. If such an increase were used, the following grades and standards would be applied:

A   100–120 wam
B   90–110 wam
C   80–100 wam
D   70–90 wam

A Plea for the Future With Respect to Dictation Practice, Testing, and Standards

Would teachers be willing to abandon all use of the 50-wam dictation practice or testing? How about a 60-wam dictation test as the minimum rate ever used, and giving credit for passing 60 wam for three, two, or one minute.

Almost anyone can write dictation in longhand at 50 wam. Do shorthand teachers wish to continue a practice that allows shorthand to be written at the same speed as longhand? Why then study shorthand? Some teachers never dictate below 60 wam for practice or for testing. In that case the dictation procedures outlined in Chapter 6 will need to be followed and credit given to a student for passing 60 wam for one minute and two minutes. It does work and students like it!

Brief-Form Tests

Mastery of the 115 brief forms representing 132 words in the Series 90 Gregg system is important to maximum dictation-recording speed development. Consequently, shorthand teachers usually provide intensive brief-form drill and review, until students can write and transcribe brief forms with almost automatic facility.

When brief forms are being presented and learned during the theory-learning stage, mastery can be encouraged by administering brief, unannounced shorthand vocabulary tests and chapter shorthand vocabulary tests in which brief forms have been included. A common practice is to evaluate competency by administering complete brief-form tests after all brief forms have been presented. Absolute brief-form standards are not available, and there is little consensus on the most appropriate grading criteria.

The following are examples of teacher practice in selected areas of the country, which may help in developing brief-form test standards:

- Dick found that the majority of Wisconsin teachers considered brief-form tests in determining grades at the end of the first semester of shorthand.[44] The majority of the respondents used a maximum error allowance of 0 through 5 percent for A grades, 1 through 10 percent for B, 2 through 20 percent for C, and 2.9 through 25 percent for D. Standards for the second semester of shorthand ranged from 0 to 2 percent for A, 0.5 through 6 percent for B, and 1 to 10 percent for C. Half the respondents allowed a maximum error allowance of 2 through 12 percent for D.

- Seals found that Utah teachers tended to use the following standards for brief forms during the last grading period of the school year: A, 90 to 100 percent; B, 80 to 97 percent; C, 70 to 94 percent; and D, 60 to 94 percent.[45]

Although teachers should set their own standards, the following plan and standards are suggested for evaluating brief-form mastery:

Prepare brief-form testing sheets, numbered from 1 to 115 in columns. Vertical space should be allowed between numbers to simulate the spacing of the shorthand notebook line so that proportion of writing can conform to notebook size.

Record three brief-form tapes. Identify the first as the beginning brief-form testing tape; the second could be labeled as the intermediate brief-form testing tape; and the final tape could be designated as the advanced brief-form testing tape.

The beginning tape is designed for use during the first semester after all brief forms have been presented. All brief forms on the beginning tape are recorded in their exact order of presentation, at the rate of one brief form about every six seconds. Students are informed that the testing tape is available for out-of-class practice before the administration of the test. The test is administered directly from the tape, and students are told to transcribe all brief forms after all outlines have been written. Deduct half a point for each incorrectly written brief form and another half a point for each error in transcription. Use the following scale in assigning grades:

A   96 percent or higher
B   91–95 percent
C   86–90 percent
D   80–85 percent

Tell students who are not satisfied with their performances that they may retake the examination outside of class and their highest grade will be recorded and used in computing the grade.

The intermediate testing tape is designed for use during the first 12 weeks of the second semester. Brief forms are dictated in random order at the rate of one approximately every four seconds, and students are encouraged to use the tapes for out-of-class practice. The test is administered directly from the tape, and students are asked to record and transcribe each brief form. Half a point is deducted for each incorrectly written or mistranscribed brief form. The accuracy standard is increased to the following:

A   98 percent or higher
B   95–97 percent
C   91–94 percent
D   88–90 percent

Students who want to improve their brief-form grades are allowed to retake the examination during a free period or after school, and the highest grade achieved is used as a part of the grade for that marking period.

The advanced-level testing tape would be used near the end of the school year to assess the degree of brief-form mastery. The tape contains brief forms as well as selected derivatives dictated in random order at the rate of one every three seconds. As with the previous tapes, students are encouraged to use the tape for out-of-class practice, and the test is administered directly from the tape. A half-point penalty is used for incorrectly written outlines or incorrectly transcribed brief forms. The recommended accuracy scale is even more rigid than the previous brief-form tests:

A   100 percent
B   98–99 percent
C   95–97 percent
D   92–94 percent

As with previous tests, students are allowed to retake the advanced brief-form test if they believe they can improve performance.

The results of brief-form tests should constitute a greater portion of the grade during the first semester because considerable time is spent trying to automatize the brief forms. There will be declining emphasis on brief-form tests during the remaining semesters.

In order to conserve time, some teachers have students transcribe only the brief forms that stand for more than one word; example:

⌣   *hour, are, our*

Homework Evaluation

Teachers assume that completion of daily reading and writing assignments has a direct relationship to shorthand success. To encourage completion of daily assignments, written homework notes are collected and a tabulation of completed assignments made. The number of written assignments completed determines part of the grade at the end of the marking period.

Unfortunately, this evaluation assesses quantity but not quality of homework. Students should be preparing their written homework assignments from self-dictation for optimum learning efficiency. Without self-dictation, there is little association between what students see and what they write, and the result may be the preparation of fluent-looking pictures. Various homework procedures are discussed in Chapter 5.

Because it is difficult to assess the quality of homework preparation, comparatively little grading emphasis should be given to the number of assignments completed. Glancing at homework notes occasionally, recording reading rates from shorthand plates or homework notes, using the homework notes for typewritten transcription drill and rates, and administering brief, daily shorthand vocabulary tests should encourage more purposeful homework preparation than does merely checking and recording whether assignments have been completed.

Keeping a log containing the number of assignments completed is certainly justifiable if teachers believe that it will encourage students to complete daily work. However, valuable teacher time can be used in record-keeping that has little relationship to teaching or learning. Certainly, placing much grading emphasis on homework quantity is unsatisfactory, because the mindless copying of shorthand plates to meet a requirement has little bearing on shorthand learning.

Language Arts Tests

Language arts fundamentals—spelling; punctuation; vocabulary; and the transcription elements including hyphenated words, possessives, number expression, and capitalization—are taught throughout the four semesters of the shorthand program. Short paper-and-pencil tests are commonly administered to encourage students to study and master these basics. The chapter or two-chapter test used in all four semesters is an excellent vehicle for pulling together the information studied about spelling, vocabulary, and punctuation. Samples of these parts of chapter tests are given in the illustrations that follow:

Samples of Parts of Chapter Tests or Special Tests

Sample 1:
Directions: Read each sentence quickly. Punctuate, circle the punctuation, and give the reason for punctuation at the right.

1.

1. _____

2.

2. _____

(There might be eight to ten such sentences to a test, taken from the textbook lessons assigned as review for the test.)

Sample 2:
Directions: Read each sentence and determine if an apostrophe is needed. Rewrite the word or words in longhand on the blank at the right and show the correct use of the possessive. Write only the word or words that contain the apostrophe.

1.

1. _____

(There might be four or five such sentences to a test, taken from the textbook lessons assigned as review for the test.)

Sample 3:
Directions: Punctuate the following sentences and write in longhand the spelling words indicated by number in the space provided at the bottom of the sheet. Write the reason for punctuation on the blank to the right.

1.

1. _____

2.

2. _____

Spelling words

1. _____
2. _____

(There might be eight to ten such sentences chosen from the textbook lessons assigned as review for the test.)

Sample 4:
Directions: Determine if the sentence is correct or incorrect as it is printed. Mark C or I. If the sentence is incorrect, rewrite it in longhand.

_____ 1. I attended the conference this year, but I shall not attend next year.
_____ 2. The letters in the tray, and those in these folders are all to be filed.

(There might be 10 to 20 such sentences taken from textbook lessons assigned as review for the test or from reference manual reviews.)

Sample 5:
Directions: Write the following sentences from dictation. The sentences will be dictated at a rate at which you can write legible and accurate notes. Each sentence will be repeated a second time, during which you should check the accuracy of your notes.
(The teacher dictates eight to ten sentences selected from the textbook lessons assigned as a review for the test. Each sentence is dictated twice.)

Directions (Continued): Read through your notes of the sentences, inserting the correct punctuation and making necessary decisions about all transcription elements. Then transcribe the sentences on the typewriter, using a six-inch line, double spacing. Your aim is to have each sentence completed in mailable form—all corrections made so they are not detectable. When you have finished proofreading the transcribed copy, remove it from the typewriter, and write in longhand above each mark of punctuation the reason for the punctuation in abbreviated longhand form:
Example: *ap* for apposition, *nc* for no conjunction, and so on.

Sample 6: Spelling
Directions: Insert this sheet into your typewriter, align with the shorthand outline, and spell correctly the outline shown.

328

1.

2.

3.

(There might be eight to ten such words selected from the lessons reviewed.)

Sample 7: Vocabulary

Directions: Insert this sheet into your typewriter, align with the shorthand outline, spell the shorthand outline correctly, and type a brief definition of the word.

1.

2.

3.

(There might be eight to ten such words selected from the lessons reviewed.)

Sample 8: Spelling

Directions: Insert a sheet of paper into the typewriter, and set your left margin at 15 and tabs at 50 and 75. Type in the number 1 at the left margin and wait. Set the typewriter on double spacing. Now listen twice for the pronunciation of the spelling word before you begin to type. Do not begin typing until you have heard the word pronounced twice. Visualize the word in your mind in its typed form, type the word correctly, return your carriage or carrier, type in the next number at the left margin, and wait to hear the next word. If you should make an error on the first typing of the word, tab to 50 and retype the word a second time. If you still have a mistake, tab to 75 and type the word a third time. Full credit is received for typing the word correctly in the first column, half credit for typing it correctly in the second column, and one-third credit for typing it correctly in the third column.

(The teacher has chosen 10 to 20 words from the homework lessons reviewed for the test, pronounces each word twice, waits until the last student has typed in the next number, and pronounces the next word twice, and so on. The procedure takes a little disciplining in the early stages to get students to wait until they have heard the word twice before they type. Emphasis is on visualizing the word in its correct form before typing and on typing it correctly the first time. Students do not erase in this procedure; they tab to 50 or to 75 to retype, if they know the word is incorrect. After all words are pronounced, they have an opportunity to look through the list and tab to the 50 or 75 location to retype words they recognize are incorrect.)

Sample 9

Sample 5 describes sentences being dictated and then transcribed. A dictation procedure can be used for vocabulary words and spelling words also. The teacher would pronounce 10 to 20 spelling words, and the students would write the words in longhand. At the end of the test, they could be asked to write the correct shorthand outline beside the spelling word. For the vocabulary section of the test, five to ten words could be pronounced and the students would write the vocabulary word in longhand. After the pronunciation, they would go back and write the vocabulary word in shorthand and give a brief definition.

These are only suggestions of ways in which testing can be done on the spelling, vocabulary, and transcription-element-application parts of a chapter. Many other types of tests can provide effective evaluation.

Administering and Scoring the Chapter Test

The chapter or two-chapter test described on pages 327–330 might include the following parts and number of items:

Part I	Shorthand Vocabulary Words	20–40 items—chosen from the word lists and/or the letters within the lessons
Part II	Spelling	10–20 items—chosen from the marginal reminders and/or spelling lists within the lessons
Part III	Vocabulary	5–10 items—chosen from the Business Vocabulary Builders within the lessons
Part IV	Sentences	8–10 sentences—chosen from the letters within the lesson

Because of the need to use time wisely, the chapter or two-chapter test should not take more than 25 to 30 minutes to administer and for the student to complete. During this same class period, the remaining time could be spent previewing the new lesson and drilling on transcription-element usage, vocabulary usage, shorthand vocabulary development from a particular letter, brief-form drills, or any other short drills that might take 20 to 25 minutes. Many teachers like to keep the scores of the four parts separate rather than combining them into one grade. This helps the student to understand which areas of work are being done very well and which need more attention during homework preparation. As the teacher peruses the student's record in a counseling session with student or parent, specific areas of strengths and weaknesses can be seen at a glance. The results of the individual parts are not hidden in one grade.

Transcription Evaluation

The ultimate objective of all shorthand instruction is to develop the ability to produce mailable letters from shorthand notes written under pressure of dictation. If students are unable to produce mailable letters, there can be little justification for offering shorthand as a vocational subject. Although some teachers begin typewritten transcription in the first semester, the major emphasis on typewritten transcription occurs during the later stages of instruction. The degree of emphasis varies, depending on whether shorthand is offered as a one- or two-year program. If two years are offered, the major transcription emphasis is reserved for the second year, but basic typewritten-transcription skills and transcription-element usage are usually developed during the first year. If only one year of shorthand is offered, the teacher is faced with an awesome responsibility. Dictation-recording skills must be achieved, but typewritten-transcription skills must be developed and polished to vocational proficiency.

Chapters 8 and 9 of this material give a detailed suggested procedure for developing typewritten-transcription and mailable-letter-transcription abilities. Incorporating these procedures into the one-year or the two-year course can help students reach vocational proficiency.

Mailability Standards

Most shorthand teachers use a "mailability" standard when evaluating mailable letters. Determining whether transcripts are mailable or unmailable is an attempt to lend realism to the transcription process by simulating the standards for business usability. Correspondence containing one or more of the following errors is judged and marked not mailable:

1. Misspelled words or names
2. Material added, omitted, or substituted that changes meanings

3. Typewriter strikeovers
4. Omission of letter parts
5. Transposed words
6. Errors in figures
7. Raised capital letters
8. Serious errors in punctuation or capitalization
9. Serious errors in word division
10. Serious irregularities in format
11. Untidy corrections

Although not all teachers use these criteria, their application should ensure a high standard for transcription accuracy.

The ways of expressing mailability are varied. Some teachers use "mailable plus" (M+) for a perfect letter, "mailable" (M) for an acceptable one, "mailable minus" (M−) for a letter that would be mailed with reluctance under certain conditions, and "not mailable" (NM) for a letter containing one or more errors in the preceding list. Other teachers use only "mailable" or "nonmailable," in evaluating performance. They believe that correspondence is either usable or unusable and that degrees of mailability are unrealistic. Teachers using this method usually prefer to record a three- or four-letter set by showing the evaluation for each letter rather than one grade for the total set. They can then look at mailability notations to see at a glance how often mailability is being achieved by a student. The mailability factor is not hidden in a score.

Teachers who evaluate mailable-letter production by mailability standards sometimes convert expressions of mailability to points for grade-book recording. Common practices include:

4 points for a perfect (M+) letter
3 points for a mailable (M) letter
2 points for a mailable with reservation (M−) letter
0 points for a nonmailable (NM) letter

1 point for a mailable letter
0 points for a nonmailable letter

3 points for a mailable letter
2 points for a correctable letter
0 points for a nonmailable letter

3 points for a perfect or M+ letter
2 points for a mailable letter
1 point for a mailable with reservation letter
0 points for a nonmailable letter

Ways of expressing mailability and their accompanying point values are relatively unimportant compared to other aspects of transcription training, and teachers should make their own determination based on personal preferences.

Weighting Point Values by Letter Length

Weighting point values according to letter length is an important consideration. Teachers often compensate for length by assigning more point values to longer letters.

Leslie and Zoubek suggest the following scale for assigning point values by letter length:[46]

Number of Words in Letter	POINTS		
	Perfect	Mailable	Unmailable or Correctable
Up to 125	2	1	0
126–250	4	2	0
251–375	6	3	0
376–500	8	4	0

Courtesy Leslie and Zoubek, *Instructor's Handbook for Gregg Transcription, Diamond Jubilee Series*, Gregg Division, McGraw-Hill Book Company, New York, 1972.

They also advocate adding 15 words to the copy length to compensate for letter parts that must be typed but are not normally dictated, adding another 20 words if carbon copies are required, and 10 extra words if preparation of an envelope is required.

Teachers who do not weight the point values of letters by length usually limit the length of letters that are dictated and transcribed to material of 75 to 175 words. They cite three advantages to not weighting point values: Evaluation is simplified, short and medium length letters are far more frequent in business, and evaluation validity is decreased if long letters are evaluated by mailability concepts.

There are no ready answers to the question of weighting point values by letter length, although there is certainly justification for limiting length to between 75 and 175 words in first-year transcription. The time available for developing transcription skills is limited, and teachers can provide only the basics of transcription during the first year. During the second year, when more time is available, students should be transcribing letters of various lengths, manuscripts, memorandums, and so on; and there is greater justification for adding point values to longer transcripts.

Converting Point Values to Grades

Mailable-letter-production point values accumulated at the end of the grading period are converted to grades in a variety of ways. Some teachers specify that students must acquire a definite number of points during a grading period to achieve specific grades. For example, if 40 letters are dictated during the marking period, given points on a mailable (1 point) and unmailable (0 points) basis only, the following table illustrates how a grade could be derived:

A	35–40 points
B	30–34 points
C	20–29 points
D	15–19 points

An obvious disadvantage to this plan is that students who are unavoidably absent are penalized, or the teacher must help them make up the mailable-letter production.

Other teachers use a *percentage-of-mailability* standard. The number of letters dictated is divided into the number of mailable letters produced during a marking period to arrive at a mailable-letter-production grade. For example, if 40 letters were dictated to a student who transcribed 30 mailable copies, the percentage-of-mailability score would be 75 percent. The percentage score would then be applied to a standards table similar to the following:

A	88–100%
B	75–87 %
C	50–74 %
D	38–49 %

Another method of converting point values to grades is to divide the total letters dictated to a student into the total points accumulated to arrive at an average point value per letter. For example, if a grading system of four points for M+ letters, 3 points for M letters, 2 points for M− letters, and 0 points for nonmailable letters were used, and 40 letters were dictated during the marking period, the following might be used as a grading scale:

A	3.0–4.0
B	2.0–2.99
C	1.0–1.99
D	.5– .99

Other teachers do not set specific standards for grading mailable-letter performance but base their evaluations on overall class ability. Point values are accumulated by one of the methods previously discussed, and scores are arrayed from high to low. Usually a subjective analysis, based on class ability and other factors, is used to determine mailable-letter-performance grades.

Although accumulation of point values is common, there are

teachers who convert mailable-letter performance to grades at the time of production and accumulate grades during the marking period. The teacher often dictates three or four short to medium-length letters to be transcribed during a 30-minute period (or a period of time based on a 15–20 wam transcription rate) and evaluates according to a predetermined four-letter standard such as the following:

A	four letters mailable		A	three letters mailable
B	three letters mailable		B	two letters mailable
C	two letters mailable		C	one letter mailable
D	one letter mailable			

Further discussion of mailable-letter evaluation appears in Chapter 9, pages 284–289.

Measuring Transcription Rates

Teachers realize that secretarial performance is evaluated by both speed and accuracy of transcription. Accordingly, some teachers measure and evaluate transcription words-a-minute performance when students produce mailable letters. Such a practice has several advantages, including encouraging better work organization, motivating students to constantly improve their transcription rates, and basing grading practices on business evaluation standards. Information on specific words-a-minute standards is limited, and little is known about the conditions under which the standards are maintained.

The typewritten transcription drills and three-minute transcription rates detailed in Chapter 8 have been developed and used to help students become accurate and rapid transcribers of mailable letters. Through the drills, which are given to develop speed and accuracy of transcription as well as decision-making abilities regarding application of transcription elements, the production of mailable letters should be improved.

In addition, through extensive use of typewritten-transcription drills and three-minute transcription-rate work, a respect for knowledge of transcription elements within the lesson and for the benefits derived from accurately written shorthand outlines can be developed. These drilled and learned procedures are combined in the production of mailable letters. As a result of timing and drilling on typewritten transcription (accuracy and speed of transcription and decision-making regarding transcription-element usage) teachers have found they can apply a transcription-rate standard to mailable-letter production. Nationally the transcription-rate standard that appears to be applied is 20 twam. A more detailed description of the timing of mailable-letter work is given in Chapter 9, page 266.

335

Description of a Comprehensive Mailable-Letter Grading Plan

A mailable-letter grading plan that includes the measurement of three variables—letter length, transcription accuracy, and transcription speed—appears in the *Instructor's Handbook for Gregg Transcription*.[47] The plan is recommended for second-year shorthand, when typewritten transcription is the primary objective.

A weekly mailable-letter transcription report similar to the form appearing on page 337 is duplicated for each student. After the daily dictation and transcription activities have been completed, letters are read by the teacher and corrected by students in class. The daily results are recorded by students on their report forms. At the end of each week, the completed report forms as well as all mailable letters are submitted to the teacher for evaluation.

The large number 27 in the upper left-hand corner of the report form (A) is merely a helpful device for handling the record. After the students' names have been alphabetized, assign a number to each student in the roll book and instruct the students to place that number on all papers turned in to you. The papers submitted may be arranged much more readily in numerical order than in alphabetical order.

When the letters are read back in class, the teacher provides identification numbers of the letters and the total number of words in each letter, and students record that information in columns 1 and 2. Students make an assessment of letter quality and indicate corresponding point values for perfect letters in column 3 and for mailable letters in column 4. Double credit is given for perfect letters, single credit for mailable letters, and no credit is provided for unmailable letters. Point compensation for various letter lengths is provided by using Leslie's chart on page 333.

The students add the number of words in the letters listed in column 2, putting the total number of words for each day in column 5. The note at the foot of the Weekly Transcription Report gives the students directions for recording incomplete letters. Students also add points accumulated in columns 3 and 4, and record the total in column 6, Day's Total Points. The day's transcription speed is computed by dividing total words transcribed by the minutes allowed for transcription. Average transcription speed is recorded in column 7. After entries have been made in columns 1 through 7, students are instructed to draw a horizontal line under the day's mailable-letter performance.

Each day's mailable letter performance is recorded in the same manner. The letter B on the form indicates that mailable-letter performance was not evaluated on the third day. The student completed two dictation-recording tests, one at 120 wam with 38 errors and one at 100 wam with nine errors. These scores are for information and are not used to determine the weekly transcription score.

Weekly Transcription Report

(A)→

| 27 Number | Name Rader, Charles | Week Ending Nov. 12 | Score 96 |

WEEKLY TRANSCRIPTION REPORT--BLANKTOWN SCHOOL

1	2	3	4	5	6	7	8	9	10	11
Letter Number	Number of Words	Points		Day's Total Words	Day's Total Points	Day's Trans. Speed	Week's Total Words	Week's Total Points	Week's Average Speed	Score for the Week
		P.	M.							
230	72		0				3,811	48	24	96
231	107	2								
232	127		1							
233	147		2							
234	145	4								
235	176	4								
236	185		0	959	13	24				
237	129	2								
238	105		0							
239	150		2							
240	151	4								
241	136	4								
242	168		2							
243	158		0	997	14	25				

(B)→ { 120-38
100-9

SCORE is obtained by adding *twice* the week's average speed to the week's total points.

1	2	3	4	5	6	7
244	67	2				
245	97	2				
246	118		1			
247	150	4				
248	155		2			
249	354		–	941	11	23
250	78		0			
251	35		–			
252	149	4				
253	187		2			
254	465		4	914	10	23

Note: If a letter is completed but unmailable, place a zero in Column 4. If the letter was not started, place a dash in Column 2 and a dash in Column 4; if not completed, a dash in Column 4 and the number of words completed in Column 2.

Courtesy Louis A. Leslie, Charles A. Zoubek, A. James Lemaster, and John C. Peterson, *Instructor's Handbook for Gregg Transcription, Series 90*, Gregg Division, McGraw-Hill Book Company, New York, 1979, pp. 19–23.

At the end of the week, students summarize weekly mailable-letter performance by completing columns 8 through 11. Column 8, Week's Total Words, is computed by adding entries in column 5. Column 9, Week's Total Points, is determined by adding scores appearing in column 6; and column 10, Week's Average Speed, is computed by finding the average of the scores in column 7. As a final step, students determine a weekly transcription score by doubling the week's average speed in column 10 and adding that figure to the week's total points. With the week's scores arranged in order, it is a simple matter to distribute the class grades.

The plan appeals to teachers for the following reasons:

1. Learners initially correct their own transcripts and learn to judge standards of mailability.
2. Learners have a great deal of information on which to analyze their performances and strive for improvement.
3. Teachers have a wealth of information from which to judge mailable-letter performance.
4. All variables associated with mailable-letter performance, except rate of dictation, are measured and used for evaluation.

Teachers who choose not to use the plan would probably cite the following disadvantages or limitations:

1. The plan cannot be used effectively in schools where a single period is available for shorthand instruction. (Although it is possible to use it by reducing the number and lengths of the letters.) Because the plan consumes a great deal of class time, it could most feasibly be used in schools that offer double periods for shorthand and transcription.
2. The plan is too complicated. Not all the information provided is necessary or desirable.
3. The plan provides limited opportunity for teaching and for basic mailable-letter skill development. Students are constantly tested on ability to produce mailable copy and on transcription speed.
4. The plan requires too much record keeping and paper checking for students and teachers.
5. The composite weekly score includes too much emphasis on speed and not enough on accuracy.
6. The application of the mailability standard is not as strong in this plan as in some other grading plans.

For variety in the advanced class or for a mailable-letter-production block in an office procedures class, limited use might be made of this plan.

Production Tests

Such tests are commonly introduced during the latter stages of the first year and administered during the third and fourth semesters. Russon states that production tests are the most reliable and valid tests for measuring competency in shorthand and transcription and that these tests should be weighted more than any other shorthand-transcription activity during the second year of instruction.[48]

Teachers who use these tests commonly dictate from four to six letters at moderate speed, and students are timed for at least 30 minutes to determine production efficiency. Letters are evaluated according to a mailability standard, and points are accumulated or averaged by one of the methods described earlier in the chapter.

Since the primary purpose of production tests is to determine the number of mailable letters that can be produced within a specified time, the variable, dictation speed, should not be considered. For example, teacher dictation beyond the normal writing rates of individual students may yield test results that are not indicative of transcription proficiency. Consequently, a moderate dictation rate, approximating class recording speeds, is suggested. Some teachers dictate at a rate 10 wam below the lowest dictation test rate of the class.

If the rate-of-dictation variable is considered important, teachers may wish to occasionally administer a modified production test. The letters are dictated at varying speeds; for example, 100, 90, 80, 70, and 60 wam. Students transcribe as many letters as possible within a 30-minute period, and grades are based on the number of mailable letters produced.

However, accuracy of transcription is more important than speed of dictation, and the two types of production tests should be weighted accordingly.

The production test referred to here is similar to the three- and four-letter set referred to and described in Chapter 9.

Three-Minute Transcription Rate

The three-minute transcription rate is a measurement that can be used in all four semesters of shorthand instruction. As described in Chapter 8, if typewritten transcription is started early in the first semester, three-minute transcription rates can be part of the evaluation process during the first semester. The procedure would then be continued into the remaining semesters. The details of the execution of the transcription rate and the standards are explained in Chapter 8, pages 246 to 248. Further information about standards for the three-minute transcription rate is given on pages 344 to 356 of this chapter.

The advantages of using the three-minute transcription rate are many: (1) The student must have prepared the homework in order to participate, (2) homework notes must be accurately written, (3) knowledge of transcription-element usage is applied frequently, (4) decision-making skills are sharpened, because constantly decisions must be made under the pressure of time, and (5) emphasis on speed and accuracy of transcription becomes natural and expected.

Evaluation and Its Relationship to Objectives

Types of evaluations used and their contribution to final grades are determined by major semester objectives. Although some differences exist in the semester goals sought by shorthand teachers, the following are common major objectives for each semester of high school instruction.

First Semester

- To develop a knowledge of shorthand vocabulary
- To develop shorthand reading skills
- To develop dictation-recording skills on practiced and new material
- To develop brief-form reading and writing facility
- To develop initial typewritten transcription ability
- To provide transcription readiness by developing vocabulary skills and transcription-element application

Second Semester

- To review and refine shorthand vocabulary and brief-form knowledge
- To refine and maintain shorthand reading skills
- To develop dictation-recording skills on new material
- To improve typewritten transcription skills and transcription-element application
- To develop mailable-letter-production ability

Third Semester

- To refine and extend shorthand vocabulary and brief-form knowledge
- To increase dictation-recording skills on new material
- To improve and refine typewritten transcription skills and transcription-element application
- To improve mailable-letter-production ability and extend its application to varied types of office correspondence

Fourth Semester

- To extend shorthand vocabulary and brief-form-derivative knowledge into new vocabularies
- To increase dictation-recording skills on new material
- To refine typewritten transcription skills and transcription-element application
- To refine mailable-letter-production ability and extend its application to simulated office situations

A more detailed statement of competencies and emphases is located in Chapter 2.

Test Emphasis

Testing and evaluation programs should promote and measure progress toward major objectives during each grading period. The table that follows provides general guidelines for test emphasis during each semester of high school shorthand instruction. Major consid-

RECOMMENDED GUIDELINES FOR EVALUATION EMPHASES

TYPE OF EVALUATION	DEGREE OF EMPHASIS			
	Semester 1	Semester 2	Semester 3*	Semester 4*
Longhand transcription of short-hand plates	minor or no	no	no	no
Oral reading rates of shorthand plates	major	minor or no	no	no
Oral reading rates of shorthand homework notes	moderate	minor or no	no	no
Brief, unannounced shorthand vocabulary tests	major or moderate	minor	minor	minor
Chapter or two-chapter tests	moderate	moderate	moderate	moderate
Complete brief-form tests	major	moderate	minor	minor
Practiced-matter dictation-recording tests	moderate	no	no	no
New-matter dictation-recording tests	moderate	major	major	minor
Homework evaluation	minor	minor	minor	minor
Typewritten-transcription rates	minor	moderate	moderate	moderate
Mailable-letter production	no	moderate	moderate	major

*Evaluation emphases may be reversed, according to teacher philosophy and preferences. In 3-semester programs, the fourth semester shown may become the third semester emphases.

eration should be given to the following when interpreting and using the table:

1. The table does not necessarily imply the extent of contribution to grades.
2. The table is based on common practices and does not account for differences in teaching methodology and objectives.
3. The table lists most of the frequently used shorthand tests. Teachers will probably not use all the tests in their evaluation programs, and individual teachers may supplement their testing programs with other evaluation procedures not described in this chapter.

Test Frequency

Testing should consume relatively little class time. The suggested frequencies in the following table are maximums, and accurate performance assessments can often be made with less frequent testing.

SUGGESTED FREQUENCY FOR ADMINISTRATION OF COMMONLY USED SHORTHAND TESTS

TYPE OF TESTS	SUGGESTED FREQUENCY
Longhand transcription of shorthand plates	Used sparingly in the first weeks of first semester instruction
Oral reading rates of short-hand plates	8 to 10 minutes a day, 3 or 4 days a week during first 6 weeks of first semester
Oral reading rates of short-hand homework notes	8 to 10 minutes a day, 2 or 3 days a week during last 12 weeks of the first semester
Brief, unannounced short-hand vocabulary tests	Three times weekly during first semester; twice weekly during remaining semesters
Chapter or two-chapter tests	At the end of each chapter in the first semester; at the end of each chapter or two chapters in the remaining semesters
Complete theory tests	Once or twice a semester, if used
Practiced-matter dictation-recording tests	Weekly from about week 7 to completion of theory introduction in the first semester
New-matter dictation-recording tests	Weekly after completion of theory introduction in the first semester and throughout remaining semesters
Complete brief-form tests	Two or three times a semester in first year
Homework evaluation	Informal daily evaluation through all semesters
Three-minute typewritten-transcription rates	Two to three times weekly during each semester
Mailable-letter production	Once a week in the second semester, once or twice a week in third semester, three times a week in fourth semester

Grading Plan Examples

Pages 343 through 356 contain grading plans developed by Crank.[49] These plans are suggested in the Illinois Curriculum Guide, *Business Education in the 70's,* for use by high school teachers. The new Illinois Curriculum Guide, *Business Education into the 80's,* recommends almost identical standards. The recommended weighting for various components of shorthand skill that are evaluated each nine weeks is shown below. Suggested tests and standards recommended for each of the grading periods are given on the following pages.

RECOMMENDED EMPHASIS FOR FIRST-YEAR HIGH SCHOOL SHORTHAND

SEMESTER 1

First 9 Weeks (Weeks 1–9)		Second 9 Weeks (Weeks 10–18)	
Reading rates	20%	Reading rates	10%
Chapter tests and quizzes	25%	Transcription rates	20%
Transcription rates	20%	Dictation-recording speed	30%
Dictation-recording speed	20%	Chapter tests and quizzes	30%
Homework and/or lab	15%	Homework and/or lab	10%
	100%		100%

SEMESTER 2

Third 9 Weeks (Weeks 19–27)		Fourth 9 Weeks (Weeks 28–36)	
Dictation-recording speed	50%	Dictation-recording speed	50%
Transcription rates	20%	Transcription rates	20%
Chapter tests and quizzes	20%	Mailable letters	10%
Homework and/or lab	10%	Chapter tests and quizzes	10%
	100%	Homework and/or lab	10%
			100%

RECOMMENDED GRADING PLAN FIRST-YEAR HIGH SCHOOL SHORTHAND

(9-Week Quarter System)

	PERCENT OF GRADE
FIRST 9 WEEKS (Weeks 1–9)	
READING: First 6 weeks students read a short selection from *shorthand plate* material and next 3 weeks from *homework notes.*	20

100 wam	A
80 wam	B
60 wam	C
40 wam	D

CHAPTER TESTS AND QUIZZES: As soon as writing begins, short quizzes of about ten words each may be given. Students write outlines from dictation. | 25

FIRST 9 WEEKS (Weeks 1–9)

Chapter tests include sampling of shorthand vocabulary words, spelling and business vocabulary words, sentences containing transcription-element usage.

95%	A
88%–94%	B
77%–87%	C
70%–76%	D

TRANSCRIPTION RATE: Transcribe on the typewriter from shorthand home-work notes. Transcribe for 3 minutes. Penalize one word for each transcription error and ten words for each uncorrected typing error. Papers containing more than five errors, after correction, are not acceptable.   20

24 wam	A
20–23 wam	B
15–19 wam	C
10–14 wam	D

DICTATION-RECORDING SPEED: *Practiced* material, dictated for 3 minutes, to be transcribed on the typewriter, if possible, with a minium of 95% accuracy. Each speed must be passed at least twice to establish a grade.   20

Rate	Grade
70 for 3 minutes	A
70 for 2 minutes	B
60 for 3 minutes	C
60 for 2 minutes	D

HOMEWORK AND/OR LAB PRACTICE: 15

SECOND 9 WEEKS (Weeks 10–18)

READING: Students read a short selection from *homework notes*.   10

120 wam	A
100 wam	B
80 wam	C
60 wam	D

TRANSCRIPTION RATE: Transcription on the typewriter from homework notes. Timing and scoring same as first grading period.   20

28 wam	A
24–27 wam	B
19–23 wam	C
14–18 wam	D

DICTATION-RECORDING SPEED: *New Material,* dictated for 3 minutes, to be transcribed on the typewriter with a minimum of 95% accuracy. Each speed must be passed a minimum of two times in close succession to establish a grade.   30

		PERCENT OF GRADE

SECOND 9 WEEKS (Weeks 10–18)

Rate	Grade
70 for 3 minutes	A
70 for 2 minutes	B
60 for 3 minutes	C
60 for 2 minutes	D

CHAPTER TESTS AND QUIZZES: Chapter tests include sample of shorthand vocabulary words, spelling and business vocabulary words, sentences containing transcription-element usage.   30

95%	A
88%–94%	B
77%–87%	C
70%–76%	D

HOMEWORK AND/OR LAB PRACTICE: 10

THIRD 9 WEEKS (Weeks 19–27)

TRANSCRIPTION RATE: Transcription on the typewriter from homework notes.   20
Timing and scoring same as first grading period.

32 wam	A
28–31 wam	B
23–27 wam	C
18–22 wam	D

DICTATION-RECORDING SPEED: New material, dictated for 3 minutes, to be   50
transcribed on the typewriter with a minimum of 95% accuracy. Each speed must be passed a minimum of two times in close succession to establish a grade.

Rate	Grade
90	A
80	B
70	C
60	D

CHAPTER QUIZZES AND TESTS: Chapter tests include sample of shorthand   20
vocabulary words, spelling and business vocabulary words, sentences containing transcription-element usage. Grade on same scale as Second 9 Weeks.

HOMEWORK AND/OR LAB PRACTICE: 10

FOURTH 9 WEEKS (Weeks 28–36)

TRANSCRIPTION RATE: Transcription on the typewriter from homework notes.   20
Timing and scoring same as first grading period.

35 wam	A
31–34 wam	B
26–30 wam	C
21–25 wam	D

FOURTH 9 WEEKS (Weeks 28–36)

**PERCENT
OF GRADE**

DICTATION-RECORDING SPEED: New material, dictated for 3 minutes, to be transcribed on the typewriter with a minimum of 95% accuracy. Each speed must be passed a minimum of two times in close succession to establish a grade.   50

Rate	Grade
100	A
90	B
80	C
60	D

MAILABLE LETTERS: Three letters, dictated at 60 wam, each letter containing 75–125 words, to be transcribed with complete mailability at a minimum transcription rate of 20 wam.   10

3 letters mailable	A
2 letters mailable	B
1 letter mailable	C
1 letter correctable	D

CHAPTER TESTS AND QUIZZES: Chapter tests include sample of shorthand vocabulary words, spelling and business vocabulary words, sentences containing transcription-element usage. Graded on same scale as second 9 weeks.   10

HOMEWORK AND/OR LAB PRACTICE: 10

RECOMMENDED GRADING PLAN FOR
FIRST-YEAR HIGH SCHOOL SHORTHAND

(12-Week Quarter System)*
(Weeks 1–12)

FIRST QUARTER—FIRST 6 WEEKS (Weeks 1–6)

READING: Students read a short selection from *shorthand plate* material.   40

100 wam	A
80 wam	B
60 wam	C
40 wam	D

CHAPTER TESTS AND QUIZZES: As soon as writing begins, short quizzes of about ten words each may be given. Students write outlines from dictation. Chapter tests include sampling of shorthand vocabulary words, spelling and business vocabulary words, and sentences containing transcription-element usage.   40

95%	A
88%–94%	B
77%–87%	C
70%–76%	D

HOMEWORK AND/OR LAB PRACTICE: 20

*This plan is broken into two 6-week terms to give shorter term goals for the quarter system and to provide a 6-week grading plan for teachers who assign grades each 6 weeks.

FIRST QUARTER—SECOND 6 WEEKS (Weeks 7–12)

PERCENT OF GRADE

READING: Students read a short selection from *homework notes*.   10

100 wam	A
80 wam	B
60 wam	C
40 wam	D

DICTATION-RECORDING SPEED: Practiced material, dictated for 3 minutes, to be transcribed on the typewriter if possible. Must be transcribed with a minimum of 95% accuracy. Each speed passed a minimum of two times to establish a grade.   30

Rate	Grade
70 for 3 minutes	A
70 for 2 minutes	B
60 for 3 minutes	C
60 for 2 minutes	D

TRANSCRIPTION RATE: Transcription on the typewriter from *homework notes*. Transcribe for 3 minutes. Penalize one word for each transcription error and ten words for each uncorrected typing error. Papers containing more than five errors, after correction, are not acceptable.   20

25 wam	A
21–24 wam	B
16–20 wam	C
11–15 wam	D

CHAPTER TESTS AND QUIZZES: Chapter tests include sampling of shorthand vocabulary, spelling, business vocabulary, and sentences applying the transcription-element usage.   30

95%	A
88%–94%	B
77%–87%	C
70%–76%	D

HOMEWORK AND/OR LAB PRACTICE: 10

SECOND QUARTER—FIRST 6 WEEKS (Weeks 13–18)

READING: Students read a short selection from *homework notes*.   10

120 wam	A
100 wam	B
80 wam	C
60 wam	D

DICTATION-RECORDING SPEED: New material, dictated for 3 minutes, to be transcribed on the typewriter with a minimum of 95% accuracy. Each speed must be passed a minimum of two times in close succession to establish a grade.   30

347

		PERCENT OF GRADE

SECOND QUARTER—FIRST 6 WEEKS (Weeks 13–18)

Rate	Grade
70 for 3 minutes	A
70 for 2 minutes	B
60 for 3 minutes	C
60 for 2 minutes	D

TRANSCRIPTION RATE: Transcription on the typewriter from homework notes. Timing and scoring same as Second 6 Weeks—First Quarter.   20

28 wam	A
24–27 wam	B
19–23 wam	C
14–18 wam	D

CHAPTER TESTS AND QUIZZES: Chapter tests include shorthand vocabulary, spelling, business vocabulary, and sentences applying the transcription-element usage.   30

95%	A
88%–94%	B
77%–87%	C
70%–76%	D

HOMEWORK AND/OR LAB PRACTICE: 10

SECOND QUARTER—SECOND 6 WEEKS (Weeks 19–24)

DICTATION-RECORDING SPEED: New material, dictated for 3 minutes, to be transcribed on the typewriter with a minimum of 95% accuracy. Each speed must be passed a minimum of two times in close succession to establish a grade.   50

Rate	Grade
80 wam	A
70 wam	B
60 wam	C
60 for 2 minutes	D

TRANSCRIPTION RATE: Transcription on the typewriter from homework notes. Timing and scoring same as Second 6 Weeks—First Quarter.   20

30 wam	A
26–29 wam	B
21–25 wam	C
16–20 wam	D

CHAPTER TESTS AND QUIZZES: Chapter tests include sampling of shorthand vocabulary, spelling, business vocabulary, and sentences applying transcription-element usage.   20

95%	A
88%–94%	B

	PERCENT OF GRADE
SECOND QUARTER—SECOND 6 WEEKS (Weeks 19–24)	

77%–87%　C
70%–76%　D

HOMEWORK AND/OR LAB PRACTICE:　　　　　　　　　　　　10

THIRD QUARTER—FIRST 6 WEEKS (Weeks 25–30)
DICTATION-RECORDING SPEED: New material, dictated for 3 minutes, to be　　50
transcribed on the typewriter with a minimum of 95% accuracy. Each speed
must be passed a minimum of two times in close succession to establish a
grade.

Rate	Grade
90	A
80	B
70	C
60	D

TRANSCRIPTION RATE: Transcription on the typewriter from homework notes.　　20
Timing and scoring same as Second 6 Weeks—First Quarter.

32 wam	A
28–31 wam	B
23–27 wam	C
18–22 wam	D

CHAPTER TESTS AND QUIZZES: Chapter tests include sampling of shorthand　　20
vocabulary, spelling, business vocabulary, and sentences applying transcription-element usage.

95%	A
88%–94%	B
77%–87%	C
70%–76%	D

HOMEWORK AND/OR LAB PRACTICE:　　　　　　　　　　　　10

THIRD QUARTER—SECOND 6 WEEKS (Weeks 31–36)
DICTATION-RECORDING SPEED: New material, dictated for 3 minutes, to be　　50
transcribed on the typewriter with a minimum of 95% accuracy. Each speed
must be passed a minimum of two times in close succession to establish a
grade.

Rate	Grade
100	A
90	B
80	C
70	D

TRANSCRIPTION RATE: Transcription on the typewriter from homework notes.　　20
Timing and scoring same as Second 6 Weeks—First Quarter.

	PERCENT OF GRADE

THIRD QUARTER—SECOND 6 WEEKS (Weeks 31–36)

35 wam	A
31–34 wam	B
26–30 wam	C
21–25 wam	D

MAILABLE LETTERS: Three letters, dictated at 60 wam, each letter containing 75–125 words, to be transcribed with complete mailability at a minimum transcription rate of 20 wam.   **10**

3 letters mailable	A
2 letters mailable	B
1 letter mailable	C
1 letter correctable	D

CHAPTER TESTS AND QUIZZES: Chapter tests include sampling of shorthand vocabulary words, spelling, business vocabulary, and sentences applying transcription-element usage.   **10**

95%	A
88%–94%	B
77%–87%	C
70%–76%	D

HOMEWORK AND/OR LAB PRACTICE: **10**

RECOMMENDED EMPHASIS FOR SECOND-YEAR HIGH SCHOOL

SEMESTER 1—SPEED BUILDING EMPHASIS

First 9 Weeks (Weeks 1–9)		Second 9 Weeks (Weeks 10–18)	
Dictation-recording speed	30%	Dictation-recording speed	40%
Transcription rate	20%	Transcription rate	10%
Mailable-letter production	20%	Mailable letters	20%
Chapter tests and quizzes	20%	Chapter tests and quizzes	20%
Homework and/or lab work	10%	Homework and/or lab work	10%
	100%		100%

SEMESTER 2—TRANSCRIPTION EMPHASIS

First 9 Weeks (Weeks 19–27)		Second 9 Weeks (Weeks 28–36)	
Transcription rate	30%	Transcription rate	20%
Mailable letters	30%	Mailable letters	50%
Chapter test and quizzes	20%	Chapter tests and quizzes	10%
Dictation-recording speed	20%	Dictation-recording speed	20%
	100%		100%

RECOMMENDED GRADING PLAN FOR
SECOND-YEAR HIGH SCHOOL SHORTHAND

(9-Week Quarter System)

	PERCENT OF GRADE

THIRD SEMESTER—DICTATION SPEED-BUILDING EMPHASIS*
First 9 Weeks (Weeks 1–9)

DICTATION-RECORDING SPEED: New material, dictated for 3 minutes, to be transcribed on the typewriter with a minimum of 95% accuracy. Each speed must be passed a minimum of two times in close succession to establish a grade.   **30**

Rate	Grade
110	A
100	B
90	C
80	D

TRANSCRIPTION RATE: Transcription on the typewriter from homework notes. Timing and scoring the same as first 9-week quarter—first year.   **20**

37 wam	A
33–36 wam	B
27–32 wam	C
22–26 wam	D

MAILABLE LETTERS: Dictated at 70 wam, each letter containing 100–150 words; address envelopes; use carbons—length of production time based on 20 wam.   **20**

3 letters mailable	A
2 letters mailable	B
1 letter mailable	C
1 letter correctable	D

CHAPTER TESTS AND QUIZZES: Chapter tests include sampling of shorthand vocabulary words, spelling, business vocabulary, and sentences applying transcription-element usage.   **20**

95%	A
88%–94%	B
77%–87%	C
70%–76%	D

HOMEWORK AND/OR LAB PRACTICE: **10**

THIRD SEMESTER
Second 9 Weeks (Weeks 10–18)

DICTATION-RECORDING SPEED: New material, dictated for 3 minutes, to be transcribed on the typewriter with a minimum of 95% accuracy. Each speed must be passed a minimum of two times in close succession to establish a grade.   **40**

*Third and fourth semesters may be reversed if a teacher prefers to allocate transcription emphasis to the third semester and speed-building emphasis to the fourth semester.

		PERCENT OF GRADE

THIRD SEMESTER
Second 9 Weeks (Weeks 10–18)

Rate	Grade
120	A
110	B
100	C
90	D

TRANSCRIPTION RATE: Transcription on the typewriter from homework notes. Timing and scoring same as first grading period.   10

40 wam	A
36–39 wam	B
30–35 wam	C
25–29 wam	D

MAILABLE LETTERS: Three letters, dictated at 80 wam, each letter containing approximately 125–150 words; address envelopes; use carbons—length of production time based on 20 wam.   20

3 letters mailable	A
2 letters mailable	B
1 letter mailable	C
1 letter correctable	D

CHAPTER TESTS AND QUIZZES: Chapter tests include sampling of shorthand vocabulary words, spelling, business vocabulary, and sentences applying transcription-element usage.   20

95%	A
88%–94%	B
77%–87%	C
70%–76%	D

HOMEWORK AND/OR LAB PRACTICE: 10

FOURTH SEMESTER—TRANSCRIPTION EMPHASIS*
First 9 Weeks (Weeks 19–27)

TRANSCRIPTION RATE: Transcription on the typewriter from homework notes. Timing and scoring the same as first grading period.   30

46 wam	A
42–45 wam	B
36–41 wam	C
31–35 wam	D

MAILABLE LETTERS: Four dictated at 90 wam, each letter containing approximately 125–175 words; address envelopes; use carbons—length of production time based on 20 wam.   30

*Third and fourth semesters may be reversed if a teacher prefers to allocate transcription emphasis to the third semester and speed-building emphasis to the fourth semester.

	PERCENT OF GRADE

FOURTH SEMESTER—TRANSCRIPTION EMPHASIS
First 9 Weeks (Weeks 19–27)

4 letters mailable	A
3 letters mailable	B
2 letters mailable	C
1 letter mailable	D

CHAPTER TESTS AND QUIZZES: Chapter tests include sampling of shorthand   20
vocabulary words, spelling, business vocabulary, and sentences applying
transcription-element usage.

95%	A
88%–94%	B
77%–87%	C
70%–76%	D

DICTATION-RECORDING SPEED: New material, dictated for 3 minutes, to be   20
transcribed on typewriter with a minimum of 97% accuracy. Each speed must
be passed a minimum of two times in close succession to establish a grade.

Rate	Grade
120	A
110	B
100	C
90	D

FOURTH SEMESTER—TRANSCRIPTION EMPHASIS
Second 9 Weeks (Weeks 28–36)

TRANSCRIPTION RATE: Transcription on the typewriter from homework notes.   20
Timing and scoring the same as first grading period.

55 wam	A
50 wam	B
45 wam	C
40 wam	D

MAILABLE LETTERS: Dictated at 90 wam and office-style dictation, varying   50
lengths of letters, interoffice memos, minutes, reports, etc.; production time
based on minimum of 20 wam.

4 letters mailable	A
3 letters mailable	B
2 letters mailable	C
1 letter mailable	D

CHAPTER TESTS AND QUIZZES: Chapter tests include sampling of shorthand   10
vocabulary words, spelling, business vocabulary, and sentences applying
transcription-element usage.

95%	A
88%–94%	B
77%–87%	C
70%–76%	D

	PERCENT OF GRADE

FOURTH SEMESTER—TRANSCRIPTION EMPHASIS
Second 9 Weeks (Weeks 28–36)

DICTATION-RECORDING SPEED: New material, dictated for 3 minutes, to be transcribed on the typewriter with a minimum of 97% accuracy. Each speed must be passed a minimum of two times in close succession to establish a grade. **20**

Rate	Grade
130	A
120	B
100	C
90	D

RECOMMENDED GRADING PLAN FOR SECOND-YEAR HIGH SCHOOL SHORTHAND

(12-Week Quarter System)

FIRST QUARTER—DICTATION SPEED-BUILDING EMPHASIS (Weeks 1–12)
DICTATION-RECORDING SPEED: New material, dictated for 3 minutes, to be transcribed on the typewriter with a minimum of 95% accuracy. Each speed must be passed a minimum of two times in close succession to establish a grade. **40**

Rate	Grade
110	A
100	B
90	C
80	D

TRANSCRIPTION RATE: Transcription on the typewriter from homework notes. Timing and scoring the same as in the First Year—First Quarter. **20**

38 wam	A
34–37 wam	B
28–33 wam	C
23–27 wam	D

MAILABLE LETTERS: Dictated at 70 wam, 125–150 word letters; address envelopes; use carbons—to be transcribed with complete mailability at a minimum transcription rate of 20 wam. **20**

3 letters mailable	A
2 letters mailable	B
1 letter mailable	C
1 letter correctable	D

CHAPTER TESTS AND QUIZZES: Chapter tests include sampling of shorthand vocabulary words, spelling, business vocabulary, and sentences applying transcription-element usage. **10**

95%	A
88%–94%	B

		PERCENT OF GRADE
FIRST QUARTER—DICTATION SPEED-BUILDING EMPHASIS (Weeks 1–12)		

77%–87%	C
70%–76%	D

HOMEWORK AND/OR LAB PRACTICE: 10

SECOND QUARTER—TRANSCRIPTION EMPHASIS (Weeks 13–24)

TRANSCRIPTION RATE: Transcription on the typewriter from homework notes. Timing and scoring the same as in the First Year—First Quarter. 30

48 wam	A
44–47 wam	B
38–43 wam	C
33–37 wam	D

MAILABLE LETTERS: Dictated at 80 wam, 150–175-word letters; address envelopes; use carbons—to be transcribed with complete mailability at a minimum transcription rate of 20 wam. 30

4 letters mailable	A
3 letters mailable	B
2 letters mailable	C
1 letter mailable	D

CHAPTER TESTS AND QUIZZES: Chapter tests include sampling of shorthand vocabulary words, spelling, business vocabulary, and sentences applying transcription-element usage. 20

95%	A
88%–94%	B
77%–87%	C
70%–76%	D

DICTATION-RECORDING SPEED: New material, dictated for 3 minutes, to be transcribed on the typewriter with a minimum of 97% accuracy. Each speed must be passed a minimum of two times in close succession to establish a grade. 20

Rate	Grade
120	A
110	B
100	C
90	D

THIRD QUARTER—TRANSCRIPTION EMPHASIS (Weeks 25–36)

TRANSCRIPTION RATE: Transcription on the typewriter from homework notes. Timing and scoring the same as in the First Year—First Quarter. 20

55 wam	A
51–54 wam	B
45–50 wam	C
40–44 wam	D

	PERCENT OF GRADE

THIRD QUARTER—TRANSCRIPTION EMPHASIS (Weeks 25–36)

MAILABLE LETTERS: Dictated at 90 wam and office-style dictation, varying lengths of letters, interoffice memos, minutes, reports, etc.; production time based on minimum of 20 wam. — 50

4 letters mailable	A
3 letters mailable	B
2 letters mailable	C
1 letter mailable	D

CHAPTER TESTS AND QUIZZES: Chapter tests include sampling of shorthand vocabulary words, spelling, business vocabulary, and sentences applying transcription-element usage. — 10

95%	A
88%–94%	B
77%–87%	C
70%–76%	D

DICTATION-RECORDING SPEED: New material, dictated for 3 minutes, to be transcribed on the typewriter with a minimum of 97% accuracy. Each speed must be passed a minimum of two times in close succession to establish a grade. — 20

Rate	Grade
130	A
120	B
110	C
90	D

A Plan for a One-Year High School Shorthand Program

As was pointed out in Chapter 2, some high schools in the United States offer only one year of shorthand. From earlier discussions it is obvious that a three- or four-semester program can help provide more thorough learning and the development of skills necessary on the job. However, since teachers are faced with the situation of only one year of shorthand, the following plan attempts to answer that problem.

The plan described on the following pages illustrates how time constraints must influence methodology, objectives, and evaluation. It is presented to emphasize the importance of developing or modifying existing grading plans to meet the unique characteristics of individual classes or schools. There is no one grading plan that can be universally adopted to meet the needs of all shorthand teachers.

This plan is developed for a one-year high school shorthand program in a school with six-week grading periods. Because instruction is limited to one year, the plan includes tests and procedures that consume a minimum of class time.

The following describe the rationale for tests used in the plan:

LONGHAND OR TYPEWRITTEN TRANSCRIPTION FROM HOMEWORK SHORTHAND PLATES AND NOTES. Longhand or typewritten transcription rates from shorthand plates and homework notes are used only during the first four grading periods. During the first grading period, the contribution to the final grade is 25 percent, and the emphasis is reduced to 10 percent during the second and third periods of the first semester. The typewritten-transcription-rate work is 20 percent during the fourth marking period because of the emphasis given to transcription speed and accuracy development and transcription-element usage prior to mailable-letter work in the fifth and sixth grading periods. Rates are administered and evaluated according to the procedures and standards outlined earlier in this chapter.

READING RATES FROM HOMEWORK PLATE OR HOMEWORK NOTES. Reading rates of the homework material are taken throughout the first semester. Contribution toward final grades decreases from 30 percent during the first grading period to only 15 percent during the last grading period of the first semester.

Almost every teacher calls on students to read the homework lesson as part of the daily routine. Usually, they are called on randomly to read for half a minute or one minute. This assessment allows teachers to record reading rates for six to eight students daily. Little class time is consumed in testing reading, and good homework study habits are promoted through the use of this reading-evaluation procedure.

CHAPTER AND SHORTHAND VOCABULARY TESTS. Short, unannounced shorthand vocabulary tests are administered two or three times a week throughout the year to encourage thorough homework preparation and shorthand vocabulary mastery. Chapter tests covering a sampling of shorthand vocabulary, spelling, business vocabulary, and sentences applying transcription-element usage are given at the end of each chapter in the first semester and at the end of each two chapters in the second semester. Grading emphasis given to these tests ranges from a high of 30 percent during the first two grading periods to 10 percent during the sixth grading period.

BRIEF-FORM TESTS. Formal testing of all brief forms is initiated during the third grading period after the last brief forms have been presented in Lesson 31. Fifteen percent of the third period's grade is associated with brief-form mastery. After this time, brief-form testing is included in the grades for chapter and shorthand vocabulary tests during the fifth and sixth grading periods. The brief-form tests are administered and scored according to the procedures and standards outlined earlier in this chapter.

DICTATION-RECORDING TESTS. Dictation is introduced during the first week of the first semester, and dictation tests are administered during all grading periods. Contribution of dictation-recording ability

357

to final grades varies from a low of 10 percent in the first grading period to a high of 50 percent during the fourth and fifth periods.

Primary testing emphasis during the first two grading periods is on recording dictation tests on practiced-matter dictation and passing the test with at least 95 percent accuracy. A series of three tapes consisting of previously practiced material are recorded at three different speeds to evaluate A, B, and C performance during the first 12 weeks when familiar material is the source for dictation speed building. For example, five one-minute takes at 60 wam are used as a C tape, five one-minute takes at 70 wam as the B tape, and five one-minute takes at 80 wam as the A tape during the first six weeks. Students are given an opportunity to use the tapes for practice, and the one-minute letters used for testing are randomly selected and administered directly from the tapes. Two or three opportunities are provided for testing, and students are given credit for the highest speed they are able to record with 95 percent accuracy.

The same procedures and rates are used for the second period, although the length of dictation is increased to two minutes. In the third period the length of dictation is still two minutes, but the material is "easy" new-material dictation. During the fourth six weeks, the length of dictation is three minutes, the material is easy new material, but the speed standards remain the same.

Graded new-matter dictation is introduced in Lesson 36 of the first semester using Lessons 49 through 55 of *Gregg Shorthand, Series 90* as the source. These lessons review the theory presented in each chapter, so dictation contains only theory principles that have been presented and learned by students when the following schedule is used:

HOMEWORK LESSON	LESSON SOURCE FOR NEW DICTATION
36	49
37	49
38	50
39	50
40	51
41	51
42	52
43	52
44	53
45	53
46	54
47	54
48	55

After completion of the introduction of theory in Lesson 47 and new-matter dictation practice from the theory review lessons, students should be ready to meet the two-minute standards outlined for the third grading period. During the fourth grading period, the length of dictation is increased to three minutes, and the standard length through the fifth and sixth grading periods is three minutes of new-matter dictation.

DICTATION STANDARDS

GRADING PERIOD	LENGTH	TYPE	SPEED	GRADE
1	1 min.	Familiar material	60	C
	1 min.	Familiar material	70	B
	1 min.	Familiar material	80	A
2	2 min.	Familiar material	60	C
	2 min.	Familiar material	70	B
	2 min.	Familiar material	80	A
3	2 min.	Easy new material	60	C
	2 min.	Easy new material	70	B
	2 min.	Easy new material	80	A
4	3 min.	Easy new material	60	C
	3 min.	Easy new material	70	B
	3 min.	Easy new material	80	A
5	3 min.	New material	60	C
	3 min.	New material	70	B
	3 min.	New material	80	A
6	3 min.	New material	70	C
	3 min.	New Material	80	B
	3 min.	New material	90	A

All tests are graded on a 95 percent accuracy standard using evaluation criteria previously described.

TYPEWRITTEN-TRANSCRIPTION EVALUATION. Typewritten-transcription is introduced early in the first semester. Typewritten-transcription performance is 25 percent of the grade in the first grading period and 10 percent during the second and third grading periods of the first semester. Approximately 30 minutes a week are reserved for transcription activities during the first three grading periods. The transcription drills and rates explained in Chapter 8 and the evaluation of transcription rates explained earlier in this chapter are used as the methodology and evaluation for the typewritten transcription.

During the fourth grading period, 20 percent of the grade is reserved for three-minute typewritten-transcription rates from homework notes and for evaluating ability to produce mailable letters. One or two short letters are dictated once or twice a week, and students strive for mailability. Evaluation is based on the number of letters produced during the grading period.

Dictation of sets of letters for mailable letter production is begun in the fifth grading period, and 25 percent of the grading emphasis is based on mailable letters produced in 30-minute periods, or at a production rate of 15 to 20 twam. At the end of the fifth and sixth grading periods, students are evaluated on the average point values attained per letter dictated or on a mailable-letter standard, with the poorest grades being dropped in the averaging. The major parts of two class periods a week are devoted to typewritten-transcription activities during the final six weeks, and grading emphasis on mailable-letter production and three-minute transcription-rate work are combined and increased to 45 percent of the final grade. Part of one class hour is used for typewritten-transcription rates, typewritten-transcription drills, and transcription-element teaching. The major part of a second class hour is devoted to mailable-letter-production work. Grades are computed as described in the preceding paragraphs.

SUMMARY OF EMPHASES FOR A ONE-YEAR SHORTHAND PROGRAM. This plan is presented to illustrate how a grading plan reflecting the time constraints of a one-year shorthand program can be developed. The following Table summarizes the learning activities and the weightings for each activity.

GRADING PERIOD	SKILL	PERCENT
1	Reading rates from homework plate or homework notes	30
	Longhand or typewritten transcription from homework shorthand plates and homework notes	25
	Chapter and shorthand vocabulary tests	30
	Dictation-recording tests on familiar material	10
	Homework assignments completed	5
2	Reading rates from homework notes	25
	Longhand or typewritten transcription from homework notes	10
	Chapter and shorthand vocabulary tests	30
	Dictation-recording tests on familiar material	30
	Homework assignments completed	5
3	Reading rates from homework notes	15
	Typewritten transcription from homework notes	10
	Chapter and shorthand vocabulary tests	25
	Complete brief-form tests	15
	Dictation-recording tests on new material	30
	Homework assignments completed	5
4	Chapter and shorthand vocabulary tests	20
	Complete brief-form tests	5

GRADING PERIOD	SKILL	PERCENT
	Dictation-recording tests on new material	50
	Typewritten transcription from homework notes and introduction to mailable-letter production	20
	Homework assignments completed	5
5	Chapter and shorthand vocabulary tests	20
	Dictation-recording tests on new material	50
	Mailable-letter production and three-minute typewritten-transcription rates	25
	Homework assignments completed	5
6	Chapter and shorthand vocabulary tests	10
	Dictation-recording tests on new material	40
	Mailable-letter production and three-minute typewritten-transcription rates	45
	Homework assignments completed	5

Computing Grades

A perusal of the following illustration reveals that two methods, averaging or best performance(s), are used to assess components of shorthand and transcription skill development when determining grades.

SUGGESTED METHODS FOR CALCULATING MARKING PERIOD GRADES FROM EVALUATIONS

TYPE OF EVALUATION	SUGGESTED CALCULATION METHOD
Longhand transcription of shorthand plates	better half of the rates
Oral reading rates of shorthand plates	better half of the rates
Oral reading rates of shorthand homework notes	better half of the rates
Brief, unannounced shorthand vocabulary tests	average accumulated grades or points
Chapter tests	average accumulated grades or points
Complete theory tests	best performance(s)
Familiar-matter dictation-recording tests	best performance(s)
Complete brief-form tests	best performance(s)
New-matter dictation-recording tests	best performance(s)
Homework evaluation	total assignments
Three-minute transcription rates	better half of the rates
Mailable letters	better half of the sets dictated or average of accumulated points

Averaging Grades

Averaging grades usually involves converting grades to point values. Commonly used conversion scales are:

GRADE	POINTS	GRADE	POINTS
A	4	A+	12
B	3	A	11
C	2	A−	10
D	1	B+	9
F	0	B	8
		B−	7
		C+	6
		C	5
		C−	4
		D+	3
		D	2
		D−	1
		F	0

After grades have been converted to point values, total points are divided by number of grades to arrive at an average point value. Average point values are converted to grades using the scale from which the point values have been derived. For example, C+, D+, A−, and C are converted to 6, 3, 10, and 5. The total 24 is divided by number of grades 4. The result 6 is reconverted to a C+ average grade.

Best Performance Grades

Best performance is usually applied to a specific standard that students are expected to meet. For example, students are usually expected to meet specific standards for new-matter dictation to attain an A, B, or C grade. Comparing standards with best performance(s) allows an easy translation from performance to grade.

Weighting Grades

After grades have been derived for all components of shorthand skill that are being evaluated, they are weighted according to emphasis suggested in the grading plan. The following might be the weights assigned for the first nine weeks of the first year.

Reading homework assignments from plate material and homework notes	20%
Transcription rate from homework notes	20%
Chaper tests and quizzes	25%
Dictation-recording speed tests	20%
Homework and/or lab work	15%

Suppose a student had an A average in reading, a B average in transcription rate from homework notes, a C average in chapter tests and quizzes, and a D in dictation testing. The percentages used in weighting are converted to decimals; for example, 25 percent is .25 and 15 percent is .15. These decimals are multiplied by the point values achieved and totaled to arrive at a marking period grade. For example, the A in reading is converted to 4 and multipled by .20, resulting in .80. Accordingly, the above student's grade for the grading period would be calculated:

Reading homework assignments from plate material and homework notes, A average	$4 \times .20 = .80$
Transcription rate from homework notes, B average	$3 \times .20 = .60$
Chapter tests and quizzes, C average	$2 \times .25 = .50$
Dictation-recording testing, D standard	$1 \times .20 = .20$
Homework and/or lab work, A average	$4 \times .15 = .60$
TOTAL	2.70

The student's grade of 2.70 on a four-point scale is converted to a B− grade for the grading period.

Collegiate Standards

Community college and four-year college and university teachers use methods of testing and evaluation similar to those described earlier in this chapter. However, achievement expectations are greater and performance standards are generally higher than those used in high schools. Because postsecondary students are expected to have a higher degree of maturity and motivation and represent a more homogeneous population, collegiate teachers can expect and obtain better results than most high school shorthand teachers.

Grever's study provides comprehensive and authoritative data on shorthand programs in public community colleges and four-year colleges and universities.[50] A total of 400 schools participated in the study, and data pertaining to grading and standards provided by 129 community colleges and 107 colleges and universities operating on semester plans is reported in this section. Because of space limitations, only basic data is reported. More detailed information may be obtained by consulting Grever's dissertation.

Collegiate Grading Plan Components

An analysis of the data appearing in the tables on pages 365 and 366 reveals more similarities than differences between community colleges on one hand and colleges and universities on the other in grading-plan components and their influence on shorthand grades.

GRADING PLAN COMPONENTS IN FIRST SEMESTER. The data in the table on page 365 reveals that, at the community college level, the skill components having the greatest influence on semester grades are dictation-recording speed, shorthand vocabulary, production of mailable letters, typewritten-transcription rates, and brief-form knowledge. The data reveals that teachers who introduce and teach typewritten transcription during the first semester consider these skills important in determining grades.

Teachers in colleges and universities are most apt to place greatest emphasis in their grading plans for the first semester on: dictation-recording speed, shorthand vocabulary tests, mailable-letter production, typewritten-transcription rates, reading rates, and brief-form mastery.

GRADING PLAN COMPONENTS IN SECOND SEMESTER. For the final grades in the second semester of instruction, community college teachers place greatest emphasis on dictation-recording-speed tests, mailable-letter production, typewritten-transcription rates, tests on transcription elements, and shorthand vocabulary tests.

College and university teachers give greatest grading emphasis to dictation-recording speed, mailable-letter production, typewritten-transcription rates, shorthand vocabulary tests, and tests on transcription elements.

A review of the table on page 365 indicates that postsecondary teachers rely heavily on results from dictation-recording-speed tests and that aspects of typewritten transcription are common to most grading plans during the second semester.

GRADING PLAN COMPONENTS IN THIRD SEMESTER. The table on page 366 reveals commonly used components of third-semester community college grading plans. Major grading emphasis is apt to be on dictation-recording speed, mailable-letter production, typewritten-transcription rates, tests on transcription elements, and shorthand vocabulary tests.

A similar pattern is evident for college and university grading plans. Greatest grading emphasis is on dictation-recording speed, mailable-letter production, typewritten-transcription rates, and tests on transcription elements.

The grading plan components and emphases given to them reveal that the development of dictation-recording speeds and increasing typewritten-transcription efficiency are common major objectives of most programs.

GRADING PLAN COMPONENTS IN FOURTH SEMESTER. Dictation-recording speeds, mailable-letter production, typewritten-transcription rates, and tests on transcription elements make the greatest contribution to final fourth-semester grades in community colleges.

Those components most emphasized in determining grades in fourth-semester college and university grading plans are dictation-

MEAN PERCENTAGE OF TOTAL GRADE GIVEN EACH COMPONENT OF FINAL GRADE FOR SEMESTERS I AND II IN COMMUNITY COLLEGES AND FOUR-YEAR COLLEGES AND UNIVERSITIES

	Community Colleges		Colleges/Universities	
SEMESTER I COMPONENTS	Freq[1]	Mean %	Freq	Mean %
Brief-form tests	87	16.6	73	15.7
Class attendance	24	10.0	21	7.5
Dictation speed rates	98	40.8	78	43.2
Homework	77	10.5	37	8.8
Lab attendance	19	8.3	12	6.4
Mailable letters	16	21.9	13	20.3
Reading rates	62	14.9	49	16.3
Theory tests	93	24.2	79	24.0
Transcription elements	40	13.8	30	12.6
Typewritten-transcription rates	26	21.7	28	17.3
SEMESTER II COMPONENTS				
Brief-form tests	49	10.9	46	9.6
Class attendance	23	5.6	14	10.3
Dictation speed rates	104	42.7	83	46.0
Homework	49	8.7	25	8.8
Lab attendance	22	6.6	11	6.8
Mailable letters	65	24.0	62	25.2
Reading rates	32	9.3	26	11.2
Theory tests	60	16.0	62	14.7
Transcription elements	60	16.1	43	12.8
Typewritten-transcription rates	50	18.1	41	14.8

[1]Data based on 114 community colleges and 93 four-year colleges and universities for semester I, and 113 community colleges and 95 four-year colleges and universities for semester II. Caution should be used in interpreting this table and all succeeding tables in this chapter. The means appearing in the tables represent a composite averaging of responses from community colleges and four-year colleges and universities.

recording-speed tests, mailable-letter-production tests, typewritten transcription-rates, tests on transcription elements, and brief-form tests.

Collegiate Reading Standards

The table data on page 367 reveals that collegiate teachers often use specific reading goal standards for each semester of instruction. The standards for A, B, and C grades are listed for both the first and second semesters. Although differences exist between community colleges and four-year collegiate institutions, there is a pattern of agreement for reading rate standards. Teachers from both types of institutions expect reading rates on plate materials after a year of

MEAN PERCENTAGE OF TOTAL GRADE GIVEN EACH COMPONENT OF FINAL GRADE FOR SEMESTERS III AND IV IN COMMUNITY COLLEGES AND FOUR-YEAR COLLEGES AND UNIVERSITIES

SEMESTER III COMPONENTS	Community Colleges		Colleges/Universities	
	Freq[1]	Mean %	Freq	Mean %
Brief-form tests	26	7.2	23	9.5
Class attendance	18	4.2	8	10.8
Dictation speed rates	104	37.6	77	38.2
Homework	48	7.9	20	9.2
Lab attendance	19	6.3	12	8.7
Mailable letters	81	33.5	70	35.8
Reading rates	14	8.9	12	8.1
Theory tests	32	11.3	31	10.0
Transcription elements	57	16.9	39	14.2
Typewritten-transcription rates	58	20.6	48	18.3
SEMESTER IV COMPONENTS				
Brief-form tests	11	8.2	4	12.2
Class attendance	12	7.4	3	6.0
Dictation speed tests	62	32.3	36	31.7
Homework	24	7.9	9	10.4
Lab attendance	12	7.4	7	7.1
Mailable letters	60	41.9	35	43.7
Reading rates	6	8.3	4	6.7
Theory tests	13	10.8	8	7.6
Transcription elements	41	17.0	15	16.1
Typewritten-transcription rates	41	19.4	20	20.6

[1]Data based on 111 community colleges and 86 four-year colleges and universities for semester III, and 73 community colleges and 43 four-year colleges and universities for semester IV.

instruction to be around 200 wam for A grades, 170 to 180 wam for B, and 140 to 160 wam for C.

Collegiate Shorthand Vocabulary Testing Standards

Shorthand teachers in collegiate institutions were asked to state the percentage of accuracy required on shorthand vocabulary tests for A, B, and C grades. Their mean responses appear in the table on page 367. A 90 percent or higher accuracy performance is commonly required for A grades throughout all four semesters of instruction. In both types of institutions, B performance is generally in the high 80 percent range and C performance is generally in the low 80 percent accuracy range.

Dictation-Recording Standards

Three-minute dictation recording tests are most frequently used throughout the four semesters of college shorthand, but five-minute standards are still frequently applied, particularly during the second, third, and fourth semesters. A 95 percent accuracy criterion is commonly used to determine satisfactory performance on dictation-recording tests, although a substantial number of college teachers use 97 or 98 percent accuracy standards. Usually students are required to pass two or three dictation-recording tests to receive credit for writing at a particular speed level.

FIRST-SEMESTER DICTATION-RECORDING-SPEED STANDARDS. The speed most frequently cited for an A in community colleges is 80 wam, with 60 and 70 wam also commonly associated with A performance during the first semester.

College and university A standards are similar to community college requirements. Approximately 65 percent of the respondents specify 80 wam as A performance, but 60 to 70 wam are frequently mentioned.

MEAN WORD-A-MINUTE READING STANDARDS USED IN COMMUNITY COLLEGES AND FOUR-YEAR COLLEGES AND UNIVERSITIES

	Community Colleges			Colleges/Universities		
SEMESTER 1	**A**	**B**	**C**	**A**	**B**	**C**
Number of words read per minute from homework notes	127.3	110.5	95.5	135.3	118.1	99.2
Number of words read per minute from plates	139.3	121.2	103.7	148.9	128.6	105.6
SEMESTER 2						
Number of words read per minute from homework notes	171.7	153.6	134.6	203.0	180.5	159.5
Number of words read per minute from plates	206.0	181.0	157.0	198.0	171.5	143.5

MEAN PERCENTAGE OF ACCURACY REQUIRED FOR THEORY TESTS IN COMMUNITY COLLEGES AND FOUR-YEAR COLLEGES AND UNIVERSITIES

	Community Colleges			Colleges/Universities		
SEMESTER	**A**	**B**	**C**	**A**	**B**	**C**
Semester 1	92.9	86.1	78.9	94.3	89.1	82.8
Semester 2	94.4	88.4	81.5	95.2	90.0	84.1
Semester 3	94.0	88.2	81.5	95.8	91.1	85.7
Semester 4	92.9	88.7	81.9	95.3	89.9	83.9

SECOND-SEMESTER DICTATION-RECORDING-SPEED STANDARDS. About half of the community college teachers indicate that 100 wam is the A standard for the second semester. Approximately one-third of the instructors designate either 80 or 90 wam for A.

Dictation-recording-speed standards in colleges and universities cluster around 100 wam for A performance. Other A standards commonly cited are, in order of frequency, 110 wam, 80 wam, and 90 wam.

THIRD-SEMESTER DICTATION-RECORDING-SPEED STANDARDS. Almost half of the community college teachers specify 120 wam for A. Another 25 percent use 100 wam, and 110-wam achievement is designated as A performance in 13 percent of the community colleges.

Colleges and universities are most apt to apply a 120-wam standard for A. However, about 36 percent require either 100 or 110 wam for an A grade.

FOURTH-SEMESTER DICTATION-RECORDING-SPEED STANDARDS. Speeds from 120 to 140 wam are most frequently cited as A performance in community colleges, with 120 wam required in about 56 percent of the institutions.

An almost identical pattern of standards is used in colleges and universities. Ninety percent equate A achievement with writing speeds between 120 and 140 wam.

Collegiate Typewritten-Transcription-Rate Standards

Shorthand teachers in collegiate institutions were asked to specify standards for typewritten-transcription rates. The table shown below indicates the mean responses for four semesters of instruction. The responses indicate general agreement on typewritten-transcription-rate standards between teachers in the two types of institutions. During the first semester, speeds of approximately 26 wam are

MEAN RATE OF TYPEWRITTEN TRANSCRIPTION REQUIRED IN COMMUNITY COLLEGES AND FOUR-YEAR COLLEGES AND UNIVERSITIES

| | Mean Transcription Rate Standards | | | | | |
| | Community Colleges | | | Colleges/Universities | | |
SEMESTER	A	B	C	A	B	C
Semester 1	25.5	21.3	17.1	26.7	22.8	18.6
Semester 2	31.9	28.6	23.6	31.7	27.3	22.5
Semester 3	38.5	34.1	29.3	39.0	34.1	28.3
Semester 4*	36.1	33.2	29.6	34.6	29.6	23.2

*The lower speed standards for semester 4 are probably attributable to reporting mean scores. Evidently, many teachers who specified the highest rates reported standards for the third semester, but did not respond for the fourth semester.

required for A performance; during the second semester, speeds of approximately 31 wam are associated with A; and during the third semester, speeds around 38 wam are evaluated as A performance.

Notes

1. Louis Leslie, *Methods of Teaching Gregg Shorthand,* Gregg Division, McGraw-Hill Book Company, New York, NY, 1953, p. 197.
2. Harm Harms and B. W. Stehr, *Methods of Vocational Education,* 2d ed., South-Western Publishing Co., Cincinnati, OH, 1963, p. 167.
3. Joe M. Pullis, "Shorthand and Transcription Evaluation Procedures," *The Journal of Business Education,* Vol. XLVII, No. 1, p. 23, October 1971.
4. Allien Russon, *Methods of Teaching Shorthand,* Monograph 119, South-Western Publishing Co., Cincinnati, OH, April 1963, p. 46.
5. Leslie, op. cit., p. 196.
6. Russon, op. cit., p. 45.
7. Department of Public Instruction, *Shorthand for Business Education Departments in Pennsylvania's Public Schools,* Bulletin 277, Commonwealth of Pennsylvania, 1968, p. 74.
8. Joe M. Pullis, *Methods of Shorthand Instruction, A Research Analysis,* South-Western Publishing Co., Cincinnati, OH, November 1973, p. 50.
9. Judith Dick, "An Analysis of the Standards Used in Determining Grades in First-Year Shorthand in Selected Secondary Schools in the State of Wisconsin," master's thesis, University of Wisconsin, Whitewater, 1972.
10. Carolyn Seals, "Grading Criteria Used to Evaluate Beginning Shorthand Students in Utah High Schools—A Study of Similarities and Differences," master's thesis, Brigham Young University, Provo, UT, 1972.
11. Joe M. Pullis, "The Relationship Between Shorthand Vocabulary Outline Errors and Dictation/Recording Transcription Errors With the Effects of IQ Partialed Out," independent study, Louisiana Tech University, Ruston, 1979.
12. Joe M. Pullis, "The Relationship Between Competency in Shorthand Accuracy and Achievements in Shorthand Dictation," doctoral dissertation, North Texas State University, Denton, 1966.
13. Leo G. Goetz, "The Relationship Between Symbol Mastery and Selected Dictation Speeds in Gregg Shorthand," doctoral dissertation, University of North Dakota, Grand Forks, 1966.
14. William J. Karaim, "A Comparison of the Writing Practices of Two Diverse Achievement Groups of Shorthand Students

When Writing From Dictation," doctoral dissertation, University of North Dakota, Grand Forks, 1968.

15. William F. Fermenick, "An Analysis of the Relationship Between Applications of Some Principles of Gregg Shorthand Simplified and Errors in Transcription," master's thesis, Mankato State College, Mankato, MN, 1959.
16. Neil R. Dortch, "A Study to Determine the Relationship Between Shorthand Outlines Constructed According to Theory and the Accuracy of the Transcript," doctoral dissertation, University of Wisconsin, Madison, 1976.
17. Romayne Reed Cook, "Transcription Achievement of Eight Shorthand Classes in Milwaukee, Wisconsin," master's thesis, University of Wisconsin, Madison, 1966.
18. Berle Haggeblade, "Factors Affecting Achievement in Shorthand," doctoral dissertation, University of California, Los Angeles, 1965.
19. Richard C. Klaseus, "An Analysis of Some of the Factors That Contribute to the Difficulty of Transcription Materials in Gregg Shorthand—Diamond Jubilee Series," master's thesis, Mankato State College, Mankato, MN, 1964.
20. John Robert Gregg, Louis Leslie, and Charles Zoubek, *Instructor's Handbook for Gregg Shorthand, Series 90,* Gregg Division, McGraw-Hill Book Company, New York, 1978, p. 41.
21. Joe M. Pullis, *Methods of Shorthand Instruction,* p. 51.
22. Doris Crank, "Standards, Grading, and Testing for First-Year Shorthand," *Secretarial Education with a Future,* American Business Education Yearbook, 1962, pp. 164–183. (Standards later modified by Crank.)
23. Dick, op. cit.
24. Joe M. Pullis, "Effect of Varying the Duration of Shorthand Dictation," *Delta Pi Epsilon Journal,* February 1970, pp. 17–20.
25. Richard L. Wedell, "An Analysis of Selected Practices in Teaching First-Year Gregg Shorthand in United States High Schools," doctoral dissertation, University of North Dakota, Grand Forks, 1978, pp. 102–103.
26. Dick, op. cit.
27. Seals, op. cit.
28. Leslie, op. cit., p. 203.
29. Leslie, op. cit., p. 202.
30. Russon, op. cit., p. 47.
31. Dick, op. cit.
32. Wedell, op. cit.
33. Samuel M. Scammon, "An Analysis of the Need for and Use of Shorthand by Secretaries in Large Businesses as Indicated by Secretaries, Managers, and Personnel Directors," doctoral dissertation, Michigan State University, East Lansing, 1974.

34. Harold Green, "The Nature of Business Dictation," doctoral dissertation, University of Pittsburgh, Pittsburgh, PA, 1951.
35. Anthony A. Olinzock, "An Analysis of Business Dictation," doctoral dissertation, University of Pittsburgh, Pittsburgh, PA, 1976.
36. Wedell, op. cit.
37. Mariwyn Haueisen, "Grading Standards in Office Machines, Shorthand, and Typewriting in the Public Secondary Schools of Central Ohio," master's thesis, Ohio State University, Columbus, 1964.
38. Seals, op. cit.
39. Evelyn Coburn, "An Analysis of Criteria Used to Evaluate First-Year Shorthand Students in Public High Schools in Southwest Missouri," master's thesis, Kansas State College of Pittsburg, May 1974.
40. Dick, op. cit.
41. Leslie, op. cit., pp. 211–212.
42. Joe M. Pullis, *Methods of Shorthand Instruction*, p. 52.
43. Commonwealth of Pennsylvania, Bulletin 277, p. 76.
44. Dick, op. cit.
45. Seals, op. cit.
46. Louis Leslie and Charles Zoubek, *Instructor's Handbook for Gregg Transcription, Diamond Jubilee Series*, Gregg Division, McGraw-Hill Book Company, New York, 1972, p. 21.
47. Louis A. Leslie, Charles A. Zoubek, A. James Lemaster, and John C. Peterson, *Instructor's Handbook for Gregg Transcription, Series 90*, Gregg Division, McGraw-Hill Book Company, New York, 1979, pp. 19–23.
48. Russon, op. cit., p. 47.
49. Doris Crank, "Business Education for the Seventies," Office of the Superintendent of Public Instruction, Springfield, Illinois, 1972, pp. 127–138.
50. Jean Grever, "A Survey and Comparative Analysis of Shorthand Courses and Course Offerings in Public Community Colleges and Four-Year Colleges and Universities in the United States," doctoral dissertation, Northern Illinois University, DeKalb, 1975.

Chapter 11

Research in Shorthand and Transcription

Throughout each chapter in this text, the methods of teaching shorthand presented and discussed have been based on the findings of research in the field whenever such findings were available. In the past 15 to 20 years there has been a renewed interest in attempting to determine whether the shorthand teaching methods recommended for many years were in fact the best procedures to follow. Likewise, researchers have attacked many other problems of current interest, the findings about which can be helpful to every classroom teacher. However, unless the classroom teacher is aware of such research, that teacher is unable to use those findings in a meaningful way in teaching shorthand.

In this chapter some of the findings of these research studies will be summarized, together with their implications for the classroom teacher. No attempt has been made to include all research in shorthand and transcription that has been completed in the last 20 years, but rather to summarize for the reader areas of agreement and disagreement upon which the conclusions given at the end of this chapter are based.

Shorthand Accuracy

Effect of Shorthand Accuracy on Shorthand Achievement

In the past it has often been stated that the accuracy of the students' shorthand outlines is unimportant—that as long as they can decipher their outlines, the way the outlines are written makes little difference. However, research findings of the past 20 years refute these claims.

Pullis studied the relationships between students' ability to write theoretically correct shorthand outlines and achievement in shorthand dictation. He checked the accuracy of the shorthand outlines written from the dictated vocabulary tests as well as the transcripts of those outlines. Dictation-recording competency was measured by three-minute dictation-recording tests. He found a significant positive relationship between the students' ability to write accurate shorthand outlines and achievement in shorthand dictation. A significant positive relationship also existed between the ability of students to write accurate shorthand outlines and their ability to transcribe those outlines. The students' competency in transcription increased with competency in shorthand accuracy.[1] Pullis concluded that the degree of mastery of shorthand vocabulary that students possessed by the end of the course established limits on achievement in future shorthand courses.[2] The extent to which students increase their dictation rates may depend on the accuracy of their outlines as does the ability to transcribe shorthand outlines. Goetz and Karaim also found that students with the highest dictation-recording speed attained the highest degree of symbol mastery.[3,4] Pullis further found that the ability to write accurate outlines was established by the first six months of shorthand instruction; appreciable increases did not occur later. Goetz concurred with these findings and concluded that the major part of the students' symbol mastery was attained during the first semester.

Patrick, in his analysis of selected brief forms and principles in shorthand notes of beginning Gregg shorthand students, reported that 96 percent of the students' ability to transcribe brief forms correctly and approximately 90 percent of their ability to transcribe correctly written outlines were directly associated with the theoretical accuracy of the shorthand outlines written from dictation.[5]

In an evaluation of systematic repetition of brief forms through specially constructed dictation materials, Minnick found that the use of materials designed to provide systematic recurrence of brief forms and their derivatives enabled students to write and transcribe brief forms more accurately than did students not using those materials.[6]

Hallman compared classes using material providing a systematic review of shorthand principles and found a significant difference in accuracy of writing outlines in favor of the group using these materials. However, there was no difference between the groups in writing brief forms, transcribing brief forms, knowledge of principles, and speed achievement approximately six weeks after the completion of the special dictation materials.[7]

Effect of Shorthand Accuracy on Transcription

In 1959 in a study of the relationship between application of some principles of Gregg Shorthand Simplified and errors in transcription, Fermenick found that high-frequency words presented less difficulty in both shorthand outlines and transcription than words of lower frequency.[8] He also reported that one type of shorthand rule seemed to cause no more difficulty than another. Cook found that errors in outlines were the greatest contributing factor to inaccurate transcription.[9]

Haggeblade examined 11 selected factors in the achievement of fourth-semester shorthand students and found a significantly high correlation between the ability of students to write theoretically correct outlines and their achievement in transcription. He recommended that teachers stress the value of writing theoretically correct shorthand outlines for the majority of words found in business dictation. Haggeblade pointed out that complete mastery of brief forms was necessary, but teachers should realize that mastering the brief forms alone was not sufficient for satisfactory achievement in shorthand.[10]

In analyzing some of the factors contributing to the difficulty of transcription materials in *Gregg Shorthand Diamond Jubilee Series*, Klaseus found that correctly written outlines were transcribed correctly 96 percent of the time but incorrect outlines were transcribed correctly less than 59 percent of the time.[11] His findings are supported by those of Dortch, who reported a statistically significant correlation at the .01 level of confidence between the accuracy of shorthand outlines and the accuracy of transcription.[12] Dortch also reported that the sense of a sentence often made it possible for a student to transcribe it correctly even though some shorthand outlines were omitted. Further, he concluded that students were apparently poor listeners, or were indifferent to accuracy, or were so conditioned to writing something down that they wrote any character they knew.

Ellingson, in an analysis to determine the critical nature of errors students make in shorthand outlines and in transcripts, reported nearly 58 percent of all words correctly transcribed fell at a low-frequency range even though only 10 percent of the dictation was in this range. She reported a significant relationship between uncommon shorthand outlines and inaccuracy and difficulty of transcription; correct shorthand outlines tended to be transcribed correctly.[13]

In studying the relationship between knowledge of shorthand principles and transcription errors, Howard reported that a significant number of students did not know the basic shorthand alphabet and were therefore unable to apply the principles effectively in taking dictation.[14]

In addition to studying the effect of accuracy of shorthand outlines on transcription, Crewdson also studied the factor of context in transcription. She reported she could find no conclusive evidence that context alone was the major factor in transcription. However correctly written outlines were as important as context in arriving at a mailable transcript. She concluded that students should be encouraged to write correct outlines and recommended more emphasis on shorthand vocabulary tests, especially early in the students' training.[15]

Gallenberg studied the relationship of theoretically correct shorthand outlines to accuracy of transcription of those outlines. The shorthand outlines with few or no errors were transcribed with the highest percentage of accuracy. However, some incorrectly written outlines were transcribed with a high degree of accuracy. Poor proportion caused transcription errors as did some phrases students did not recognize as phrases when transcribing. Gallenberg concluded that a correct shorthand outline does not ensure accuracy of transcription. Sentence structure and word usage were also contributing factors.[16]

Pullis, in a study of the relationship between accuracy of shorthand notes and correctness of transcription, found that of the total transcription errors, 32 percent were from correctly written outlines and 68 percent were from incorrectly written outlines. Based upon a chi-square analysis, he concluded that an incorrectly written outline was appreciably more likely to be incorrectly transcribed than was a correctly written outline. When the transcription of dictated material was deferred for one week, a correctly written shorthand outline was more than 60 times as likely to be correctly transcribed than was an incorrectly written outline.[17]

Peters studied the types of errors found in shorthand outlines and reported that unrecognizable outlines were the type of error that appeared to affect the transcript most frequently on all material dictated. Omission of strokes more often resulted in transcription errors than did addition of unnecessary strokes. Incorrect proportion was a frequent error causing transcription difficulties. The errors increasing most with increases of speed were proportion errors.[18]

Hooven investigated the effect of intensive practice of shorthand outlines for 500 high-frequency words on achievement in first-year shorthand at the high school level. A total of 97 control and 99 experimental students participated in the study. The first word-list test was administered upon completion of the Gregg theory. For the next 25 periods the experimental classes intensively practiced the 500 target words in 18-minute treatment sessions. Otherwise, the control and experimental classes were taught in the same manner. A posttest was given at the conclusion of the study.

Hooven reported that the experimental group had significantly higher achievement than the control group in the following areas: recording outlines for vocabulary in both word list form and contextual form; constructing outlines for unfamiliar words in word list form; and transcribing contextual material. Students in both the higher and lower GPA levels in the experimental classes had significantly higher mean achievements than corresponding control students in recording target words and in transcribing. Further, students who entered the second semester with lower levels of shorthand performance tended to benefit most from intensive practice on the 500 high-frequency words.[19]

Student Errors in Theory Application

In recent years few researchers have analyzed students' shorthand errors, since such studies had frequently been made in the past. As in earlier studies, Klaseus reported that the most frequent error in substitution was the *o* and *oo* hook.[20] Crewdson also found that words using the *o* and *oo* hook gave students the most difficulty in transcription.[21] Klaseus found the substitution of *i* and *e* caused errors and attributed the problem to students' writing according to spelling rather than sound. He attributed many of the omissions in the students' transcripts to totally illegible outlines.

Gaffga found that shorthand writers wrote essentially plate shorthand during employment, although certain key elements in Gregg shorthand were not followed accurately. The most common errors were in past tense, confusion of *o* and *oo*, using the left *s* for the right *s* and vice versa.[22]

Doerr analyzed the difficulties 100 beginning shorthand students had in learning selected principles of the Gregg shorthand system (*s, th, nt-nd, mt-md, den-ten, dem-tem, men-mem, rd-ld, rt-lt*). He selected for analysis and evaluation the principles other investigators had reported as most difficult for students to learn. Doerr found in all the exercises in the study, the percentage of shorthand outlines for familiar words using the selected principles ranged from 5.3 to 93.4 percent. The percentage of shorthand outlines for familiar words written exactly according to the Gregg shorthand dictionary ranged from 0.0 to 81.3 percent. The percentage of shorthand outlines for new words using the selected principles ranged from 5.3 percent to 73.6 percent. The percentage for words written exactly according to the Gregg shorthand dictionary ranged from 0.0 to 93.4 percent. Doerr concluded that even though students might apply the selected principles when writing familiar words, fewer students could be expected to apply these same principles when writing shorthand outlines for new words.[23]

Methods of Teaching Theory

In 1965 Schloemer compared the achievement attained through two methods of teaching shorthand—a theory approach versus a nontheory approach. Grading in the nontheory class was based on students' transcripts; while in the theory class, grading was based half on word list tests and half on student transcripts. The students were compared on practiced material at the end of the first semester, on three minutes of new-matter dictation at the end of the second semester, and on results of a 100-word shorthand vocabulary test each semester. At the end of the first semester the two groups were able to take practiced dictation at almost identical speeds of 60 wam or more. Students in the theory class were able to write more accurate outlines on the 100-word shorthand vocabulary tests given at the end of the first and second semesters than were the students in the nontheory group. Schloemer concluded that the study showed that when two classes were taught by the same teacher, neither approach to teaching beginning shorthand was superior to the other.[24]

In 1969 Pullis compared two methods of teaching shorthand. The control group was taught according to the methods recommended by the authors of Gregg shorthand (functional method). In the experimental group, the procedures emphasized (a) accuracy of outline construction; (b) weekly shorthand vocabulary tests; (c) early introduction of writing (Lesson 6); (d) textbooks closed during dictation of familiar material; (e) early introduction of new-matter dictation (week 6); (f) observation of students' writing habits by the teacher; (g) intensive as well as extensive homework practice; (h) timing of reading rates; and (i) reading of cold notes. Pullis found a significant difference in favor of the experimental group in rate of dictation speed, shorthand accuracy, and shorthand transcription ability.[25]

Clippinger analyzed two methods of shorthand theory presentation. The control method consisted of presenting shorthand theory according to the instructions in the *Instructor's Handbook for Gregg Shorthand* while the experimental method involved analyzing reading, recycling the textbook material, and tracing some textbook-connected matter (13 lessons). Subjects were 190 first-year shorthand high school students. Comparisons were made of three aspects of shorthand achievement: theory mastery, recording speed, and transcription accuracy. Clippinger reported that both teaching methods had an equal effect on shorthand theory mastery. However, the experimental method was superior in promoting shorthand recording speed in the upper ability level (IQ of 110 and above). Students in the upper ability level were superior to those in the lower ability level (IQ of 109 and below) in each aspect of shorthand recording achievement.[26]

Lipova conducted an experiment to determine the value of stressing thought units during the first semester of shorthand. She found that marking the shorthand copy into thought units increased shorthand reading speed from the textbook. Emphasis on reading shorthand in thought units had a slightly positive effect on accuracy of writing isolated vocabulary words in shorthand and produced more accurate transcripts when students transcribed from their own notes. However, emphasis on thought units had little effect on the speed of dictation transcribed and adversely affected transcription from plates in the textbook. Lipova further concluded that emphasis on thought units was more beneficial to students of high ability than to those of low ability.[27]

Barber, in an experimental study in teaching using the tachistoscope, found that the tachistoscope was not effective in increasing accuracy of writing or accuracy of transcribing shorthand outlines. It appeared to be best utilized to increase reading speed, to automatize the learning of brief forms and phrases, and as a motivational device. Barber concluded that the tachistoscope should be used as a supplement to regular teaching procedures rather than as a complete year-long program.[28]

In 1969 Githens compared shorthand achievement of students using the student transcript with those not using the transcript and found that the use of the transcript did not make a significant difference in achievement of students in beginning Gregg shorthand.[29] Another study in 1964 by Young compared the effect of choice-making (choosing between left and right *s* and over and under *ith*, and so on) on the speed of writing symbol combinations in Gregg and Pitman shorthand. In this case it was determined that choice-making of shorthand outlines actually had an adverse effect on shorthand dictation-recording speed.[30]

Manwaring found that, in most schools, doubling the time spent presenting each lesson of Gregg shorthand theory resulted in no significant differences in ability of the experimental and control groups to record dictation at 70 wam for three minutes at the end of one year. Further, the procedure of doubling the amount of time spent teaching shorthand theory did not affect the end-of-year accomplishment of students of average or lower general scholastic ability.[31]

Shorthand Reading

Is there a relationship between shorthand reading ability and shorthand achievement?

In 1972 Pullis conducted a study to determine whether a significant relationship existed between the ability of shorthand students to read connected plate material from their text and their achievement in recording dictation. The coefficient of correlation between fluency of reading and achievement in dictation was .72. In the first semester of shorthand, significant differences in reading rate existed between the dictation rate levels of 50 and 70; 50 and 80; and 60 and 80. The second-semester coefficient of correlation between fluency of reading and achievement in dictation was .61. Significant differences in reading rates existed between dictation-rate levels of 80 and 100 and 80 and 110. Fluency in writing shorthand appeared to be related to and fostered by fluency in reading shorthand in both semesters.[32]

A study by Beringson also indicated a significant relationship between the ability to read shorthand and to take shorthand dictation. He also found that reading from a shorthand plate of a particular difficulty level was not any more closely associated to writing ability than reading from a plate of another level of difficulty.[33]

Osborne also reported a statistically significant relationship between the ability to read shorthand symbols in context with the ability to transcribe shorthand notes taken from dictation.[34]

Jensen compared the terminal achievement of students in beginning shorthand who were not assigned letter grades for their oral reading ability with students who were assigned letter grades. No significant difference existed in achievement tests at the end of the semester.[35] Prueher, in studying the effect of setting daily reading goals on success in first-semester shorthand, reported that shorthand grades did not differ between classes emphasizing reading goals and those not having reading goals.[36]

Homework

What is the most effective type of homework assignment in shorthand? Is extensive or intensive homework practice preferable?

In trying to determine whether the reading approach or the writing approach was superior in shorthand homework, Toulouse found that students who used the extensive reading approach in their homework practice attained approximately the same level of competency as did students using the intensive writing approach in all aspects of shorthand—brief-form accuracy, vocabulary, shorthand accuracy, and transcription accuracy.[37]

A number of researchers have been interested in determining the effect of practicing a part of the homework from print. Arnold attempted to determine whether copying shorthand plates *and* writing shorthand from printed materials for homework would produce effects different from those produced by *only* copying shorthand when students using each procedure spent the same amount of time on homework. Arnold found that copying only shorthand plates for homework produced higher textbook reading rates, while the combination of plates and printed material produced higher reading rates from shorthand homework—but differences were insignificant in most cases. Students copying only shorthand plates made more errors on word-list tests, but no significant differences were found between the two groups in writing unfamiliar material or in reading brief forms. Neither copying shorthand plates nor combination homework practice produced significantly different rates of incorrect transcription of correctly written familiar-word outlines, correct transcription of incorrectly written outlines, or incorrect transcription of incorrectly written outlines. No difference was found between the two groups on rate of transcription.[38]

Hayes added to her analysis of print versus shorthand plates for homework the factor of vocabulary expansion. She reported that the procedure of writing some homework from print was as good as copying shorthand plates. The practice on printed materials, which

379

included more infrequently used words than occurred in the textbook, did improve shorthand dictation and transcription skills more than copying textbook material. She concluded that "practice on material which provides an exposure to a significantly greater number of less frequently used words does improve ability to take and transcribe unfamiliar dictation."[39]

In his comparative study of two methods of writing shorthand homework, Gregory had one group copy the shorthand plate from the text while the other group transcribed on the typewriter the plates in the text and then wrote shorthand outlines for the printed lines of typewriting. No significant difference was found in memorizing brief forms or in ability to construct outlines for difficult words from dictation; but students doing homework by the typescript method recorded letter dictation at a progressive rate significantly better, as measured by the ability to transcribe their own notes on the typewriter, than did shorthand students copying the plates from homework.[40]

Hanson sought to determine whether there were significant differences in performance between first-semester college Gregg shorthand classes doing homework by self-dictation from textbooks (visual stimuli) and classes doing homework from textbook and tape-recorded dictation of the text plate material (combined audiovisual stimuli). The control students practiced from the text while the experimental students practiced from tapes with their text open for reference. After the first 36 lessons, new-matter dictation with preview sheets was used in the experimental class. Hanson found beginning students who wrote homework by self-dictation from the textbook achieved a knowledge of shorthand superior to those who wrote homework from recorded dictation with the textbook open for reference. Neither homework method proved superior for developing skill in reading plate material, in writing from practiced-matter dictation, or in writing from new-matter dictation.[41]

Perry measured the effect of selected homework procedure on the shorthand performance of second-semester first-year high school students. The experimental group read the homework only and was given individual reading rate goals for each semester. The control group followed the same procedure but was instructed to write isolated outlines they considered unfamiliar or difficult. Perry reported that (1) the use of reading goals to encourage accurate high-speed reading during the second semester of the high school shorthand program served as a legitimate substitute for the traditional reading or writing the homework assignment once; (2) second-semester students who were expected to meet specific reading-rate goals *and* who practiced unfamiliar shorthand outlines attained significantly higher dictation-recording speeds than students who only met reading goals or who read or wrote the lesson only once; (3) the type of homework assignment would probably have little effect on the dictation-recording ability at the beginning of the second semester; and (4) ability of students to write theoretically correct outlines was not affected significantly by the nature of the homework assignment.[42]

Both Stutte and Waters studied the effectiveness of programmed homework materials when in-class instruction was the same for students using these materials and those completing the traditional homework assignment from the text. Stutte's experiment was conducted in a beginning course and Waters' on the intermediate level. Both studies reported a significant difference in students' achievement with the difference favoring the programmed approach.[43,44]

Pankhurst studied the relationship between shorthand achievement and two plans of homework in beginning and intermediate shorthand. Similar class procedures were used with the experimental and control groups. The control class completed homework in the traditional manner, while the experimental classes practiced each step of the homework learning activity in a manner as near the expert level of performance as possible. One part of the plan required the use of dictation tapes. Dictated word-list tests and dictation tests given at the end of the semester indicated the achievement of the intermediate experimental group was significantly better at the .05 level than that of the intermediate control group on the 80-wam dictation test. A significant positive relationship at better than the .05 level was also found between the mean word-list test scores and the mean dictation test scores. Pankhurst concluded that the use of the controlled plan of homework, requiring students to practice each step of the shorthand learning activities more nearly as performed by the experts, was likely to produce better results on word-list tests and dictation tests than traditional homework procedures, and that achievement in dictation transcription was significantly related to the students' ability to construct accurate shorthand outlines.[45]

In his study of two homework methods, Jensen compared the dictation achievement and shorthand vocabulary achievement of one group of college students in beginning shorthand who practiced homework from shorthand tapes accompanying each lesson with another group who practiced homework following the traditional read-and-copy approach. Both groups received identical classroom instruction and both devoted the same amount of time to homework.

At the end of two semesters seven achievement tests were administered to the two groups: four three-minute constant-level dictation tests at 50, 60, 70, and 80 wam; one three-minute dictation test at speeds ranging from 50 to 80; a 100-item Speedform test; and a 100-item vocabulary test based on the 2,500 words most used in business. No significant differences were found between the experimental and the control groups on constant-level dictation at 50, 60, and 70 wam; progressive dictation at the same speed levels; Speedforms; and shorthand vocabulary. Significant differences were found on the dictation test and the progressive dictation test at 80-wam, which appeared to indicate that, as the dictation speed progressed upward, students practicing homework from tapes might have an advantage over those practicing shorthand by the read-and-copy approach.[46]

Shorthand Dictation Materials

Predicting the Difficulty Level

Hillestad and Uthe were among the first to give serious consideration to a study of those factors which might be used to predict more accurately the difficulty of shorthand dictation material. Hillestad's study conducted in 1960 was designed to estimate the efficiency of several factors in predicting the number of shorthand outline errors made in Gregg shorthand notes written from dictation and to analyze the number and kinds of outline errors found in the shorthand notes. She found that the difficulty of dictation material with respect to shorthand outline errors could be predicted by the number of syllables in the dictated material and the number of words not included among the 1,500 words most frequently used in business communications according to Silverthorn's list. The vocabulary level, as measured by the frequency of use of the words, was found to be the most important determiner of difficulty of text material. Brief forms were the easiest words for students to write, while brief-form derivatives were the most difficult. Students' shorthand outline errors tended to include vowels that, according to theory, should be omitted. Hillestad concluded that students needed a broader vocabulary coverage with more practice on the less frequently used words in order to be able to write accurate shorthand notes containing these words.[47]

In 1966 Uthe used the Hillestad dictation tests, and procedures comparable to those of Hillestad, to develop a multiple regression equation that would predict the number of outline errors students would be likely to make in their shorthand notes when recording a dictation test. One hundred letters of 160 actual words were dictated to 25 groups of fourth-semester high school students. Uthe reported that syllabic intensity had a simple linear r value of $-.13$ with the number of shorthand outline errors made by students, and that the multiple regression equation that was best and most practical for predicting the number of outline errors made on the 100 letters written from dictation included the number of brief forms in the letters, the number of words beyond the 1,500 most frequently used, and word endings. According to Uthe, the regression equation for predicting shorthand outline errors was valid for use in classifying the dictation letters as "easy," "average," and "difficult" with respect to predicting the number of shorthand outline errors that would be committed.[48]

Henrie compared four difficulty prediction formulas and concluded that only Hillestad's formula was reasonably reliable for predicting transcription errors, while the least reliable method was simply using syllabic intensity. Syllabic intensity and the Mellinger prediction formula were considered the easiest formulas to calculate. The two most reliable prediction formulas contained more than one variable and both included the number of words beyond the first 1,500 most frequently used words in the Silverthorn list.[49]

Mickelson studied the relationship between word frequency and the difficulty of shorthand dictation materials. Three three-minute dictation tests with extremely varying high-frequency indexes were constructed, all having a syllabic intensity of 1.43. The tests were dictated at 80 wam to 117 high school fourth-semester shorthand students to determine whether a statistically significant difference existed among the mean raw scores on the three tests when the measure was based on the completed shorthand transcript. Since significant differences were found to exist among the means and between every possible pair of means, it was concluded that the three indexes of high-frequency words used in the study were successful in determining three distinct dictation levels. Familiarity of vocabulary appeared to be a highly significant factor in determining the difficulty of stenographic dictation materials.[50]

Wedell, in his study of the relationship of syllabic intensity, word frequency, and shorthand stroke intensity to the difficulty of shorthand dictation materials, reported that the number of errors increased as the number of syllables per word increased; that the errors increased as the use of the word decreased; and that errors increased as the number of shorthand strokes per word increased. He concluded that word frequency should not be used as a single measure in determining difficulty of shorthand dictation material. He also concluded that computation of dictation-material difficulty should be made within each minute of dictation to ensure uniformity throughout dictation materials.[51]

Pullis has conducted a number of studies of factors affecting the difficulty of shorthand materials. In one study he analyzed whether high-frequency words, average word length, and syllabic intensity within published dictation texts could be used as an accurate measure of shorthand dictation-take difficulty when shorthand transcription errors were used as the criterion. Pullis concluded that the combination of these three variables did not appear to reflect accurately the real difficulty of published shorthand dictation materials and that these published dictation takes varied extremely in difficulty.[52]

In a second study Pullis tested the validity of using syllabic intensity and percent of high-frequency words as a measure of difficulty of published shorthand dictation materials. He determined that published dictation takes controlled on the basis of syllabic intensity and percent of high-frequency words were not necessarily of comparable difficulty. In other words, students might perform satisfactorily on a published dictation test at a given rate, yet on another published dictation take with the same syllabic intensity and percentage of high-frequency words and dictated at the same rate, they might make a significantly larger number of transcription errors. The difference in student performance on dictation takes might well be due to the differences in difficulty of the published dictation material and not to a difference in the students' ability to record and transcribe their notes.[53]

In a later study of the relationship between syllabic intensity and percentage of high-frequency words within published shorthand dictation texts, Pullis found that of sixty 100-wam takes analyzed, the syllabic intensity ranged from 1.31 to 1.55. The number of actual words per take ranged from 452 to 536, and the number of brief forms per take ranged from 167 to 288 (38 percent to 57 percent). The percentage of words per take falling within the first 100 words of highest frequency ranged from 45 to 63 percent; in the first 500, from 65 to 83 percent; and in the first 1,500, from 80 to 94 percent. The percentage of words per take falling beyond the 1,500 most frequently used words ranged from 6 to 20 percent. Since variability in syllabic intensity reflected only approximately 10 percent of the variability in the percentage of high-frequency words within the published dictation takes, Pullis concluded that syllabic intensity was not a sensitive index of the percentage of high-frequency words within the material. He further concluded that if difficulty of dictation material is significantly related to the percentage and number of high-frequency words contained within the dictation material, then appreciable differences exist within published shorthand dictation takes that are not reflected by the syllabic intensity of the material.[54]

In determining whether a relationship existed between frequency of occurrence of words, as measured by a business vocabulary index, and difficulty of published shorthand dictation materials, Nickerson established that the vocabulary index as measured by Perry's list of 5,000 frequently used words was 183.37. This difficulty index did not identify the three difficulty levels of "hard," "average," and "easy" in published dictation materials. However, the hypothesized "hard" level did differ significantly from both the "average" and "easy" levels. In relating transcription errors to dictation-material difficulty, Nickerson reported that transcription errors were a function of the interaction between relative shorthand skill proficiency and relative difficulty of dictation material. The absolute number of transcription errors alone could not be considered an indicator of the difficulty of the shorthand dictation takes for all students of varying proficiency levels. Nickerson concluded that published shorthand dictation materials were not of similar difficulty. Also, while the majority of the 60 dictation takes analyzed evidenced vocabulary distributions not statistically different from the vocabulary distributions of business communication, about one-third of the 60 takes did contain vocabulary distributions that varied significantly from the distribution of words common to business correspondence.[55]

In 1977 Condon conducted a study to determine (a) the extent to which Gregg shorthand principles occur in 500-word segments of a composite word-frequency list of the 5,000 most-used words and (b) the number of word characteristics, such as syllables for each word, of the 500-word segments of the 5,000 most-used words.

Condon reported that the Gregg shorthand theory principles consisting of alphabet characters, abbreviating principles, and joining principles found in the 500, 1,000, 1,500, and 2,000 most-used words were not the same as those found in the list of 5,000 most-used words. Neither were the brief forms, word beginnings, word endings, abbreviated words, disjoined words, and hyphenated words found in these 500-word segments the same as those in the 5,000 most-used word list. However, the word characteristics classified as typing stroke intensity, shorthand stroke intensity, and syllabic intensity found in the 500, 1,000, 1,500, and 2,000 most-used words were not significantly different from those word characteristics found in the total list of 5,000 most-used words.

Condon concluded that shorthand practice material restricted to the 500, 1,000, 1,500, or 2,000 most-used words would not provide the student with practice in writing the theory principles and word types found in the 5,000 most-used words.[56]

Controlled Versus Uncontrolled Materials

Prince reported that students who used dictation materials for transcription that emphasized the 500 most frequently used words in Silverthorn's *Most Used Words* attained higher transcription achievement, on both material emphasizing these words and material not emphasizing these words, than did students who used other types of copy. However, the emphasis on these high-frequency words in the experimental class was limited to the second six weeks of the second semester, when ten minutes a day for four days a week was spent drilling on this vocabulary, and to the following six weeks' period, when five minutes once a week was devoted to drill on these words.[57]

Rice compared shorthand dictation and accuracy of students who learned shorthand theory using programmed vocabulary materials based on the 2,500 most commonly used words in business letters with the achievement of students using text materials. She found differences in dictation speed in favor of students using the controlled vocabulary materials, with some of these differences being statistically significant. However, Rice did not indicate whether these differences were due to the controlled vocabulary or to the design of the programmed materials. Also the small size of the sample limits its validity.[58]

Larsen reported that intermediate and advanced shorthand students, when given dictation composed of the 2,800 most frequently occurring words in business correspondence, attained approximately the same terminal achievement as those students who were exposed to a larger uncontrolled vocabulary.[59]

In a study using vocabulary-controlled materials in beginning shorthand, Gallion found students receiving vocabulary-controlled dictation material achieved slightly higher means than students receiving dictation from textbook materials. However, no overall statistically significant differences in achievement were found between students practicing vocabulary-controlled material based on the 1,500 most frequently used words and those practicing from the textbook.[60]

The real issue in whether to use controlled or uncontrolled materials is, of course, the effect on the student's skill development. Perhaps researchers need to give some consideration to the use of both controlled and uncontrolled materials. For example, controlled vocabulary for theory presentations and shorthand vocabulary lists might prove to be highly beneficial to first-semester students, yet their reading practice might be limited only to the extent necessary to prevent the inclusion of principles not yet presented. Such material is likely to sound less contrived and at the same time introduce students to a wider range of vocabulary than is otherwise possible. However, whether such a mix would be beneficial to student achievement is yet to be determined.

Syllabic Intensity

Is a syllabic intensity of 1.4 no longer a valid estimate of the syllabic intensity of contemporary business communications?

In 1965 Mellinger pointed out that the average syllabic intensity of all 200,000 words in Silverthorn's *Word Division Manual* was 1.56.[61] In 1968 Perry noted that the average syllabic intensity of words appearing in business letters had increased to 1.63.[62] Thus a person writing shorthand at 100 wam using 1.4 as a standard word would in effect be writing only 85.89 wam on the basis of actual business correspondence. While no one questions the accuracy of the foregoing studies, the task of re-counting all the current shorthand materials on the basis of 1.6 syllables per standard shorthand word would be a formidable one that neither scholars nor publishers have undertaken. The most important implication of the preceding research, however, is that regardless of the use of 1.4 syllables as the standard word, dictation material purported to be reflective of contemporary business communications should have an actual syllabic intensity of approximately 1.6.

In 1976 Olinzock studied three aspects of shorthand dictation: dictation speed, dictation methods and procedures, and materials used. He reported that not only did dictation rates vary greatly from dictator to dictator but from one piece of dictation to another by the same dictator. These variations were attributed to differences in ability of the dictators and the type and difficulty of the dictation. The highest gross dictation speed for a quarter minute was 216 wam, with the median being 116 wam. Dictation speed tended to be faster at the beginning and end of each piece of dictation. Olinzock also reported that a typical piece of dictation of the median level of difficulty of the materials analyzed would contain 157 gross words, with 68 percent being common words, 35 percent brief forms, and 31 percent speed forms. The syllabic intensity of the correspondence would be 1.65, the median overall gross dictation speed would be 63 wam, and the median gross rate of dictation would be 58 wam. He concluded that current instructional materials overrate students' dictation speed by 18 percent.[63]

Building Shorthand Dictation-Recording Skills

What procedures are most effective in building shorthand dictation-recording skills?

In 1967 Sloan and Boss both conducted investigations of the micromolar behavior theory as it related to dictation skills in beginning shorthand. The beginning students in the experimental classes were given dictation practice at a constant rate of 100 wam. In the control classes, dictation was given by a modified pyramid approach. Both Sloan and Boss reported no statistically significant differences in the achievement of the students taught by the micromolar behavioristic approach and those taught by the traditional method of dictation skill building. Both reported that the rapid dictation used for short periods in beginning classes was feasible, though Boss indicated that the students in both groups seemed to generalize best to a speed of 90 wam.[64,65]

Anderson, in her investigation of the micromolar approach in 1969, gave all dictation at 90 wam. In this study one group of students referred to previewed word lists while taking dictation, and the other group traced the shorthand outlines using textbook material. Anderson found no significant differences in achievement of students using a micromolar speed-building plan in which one group used a word preview technique and the other, a tracing method. Further, the mean achievement scores of students receiving dictation from textbook material were not different from those of students receiving controlled material.[66]

Langemo also found that beginning secondary school shorthand students using the fast cue-response method of taking dictation progressed as quickly and attained the same speed rate as students taught by traditional speed-building plans.[67]

According to Pawelski, there was no evidence that either the fast-to-slow or the slow-to-fast dictation procedure was better for developing dictation speed. Further, the speed-building method had no effect on the mastery of theory.[68]

Dye compared various practice patterns used to develop skill in writing shorthand dictation and concluded that the writing pattern at which practice dictation is given in shorthand classes does not affect the level of achievement when writing shorthand from dictation on speed takes.[69]

In the experimental study by Stocker of the use of the DictaTutor as a teaching aid in beginning shorthand, the control group copied shorthand from plates in the text while the experimental group wrote shorthand by self-dictation from the DictaTutor. Stocker reported that students using the DictaTutor recorded a letter dictated at progressive rates of speed significantly better at the .05 level of significance, as measured by ability to transcribe accurately their own notes, than did the students in the control group. The DictaTutor students constructed 100 dictated shorthand outlines significantly better at the 95 percent level of confidence and also transcribed significantly better, as measured by the ability to transcribe their own notes accurately, than did students in the control group. There was no significant difference between the two groups in memorizing brief forms, as measured by their ability to write 100 dictated brief forms, or in their transcription speed, as measured by their ability to transcribe their own notes on the typewriter.[70]

Boggess conducted a study to determine the results of using easy, average, or difficult dictation material for speed practice during the last 12 weeks of first-year shorthand. She concluded that, given the level of difficulty of material used in this study, it made no difference which level of difficulty was used to develop the ability to take and transcribe dictation.[71]

McIntosh studied the effects of repetitive versus nonrepetitive dictation in shorthand speed development on the high school level. The study was conducted for 60 class periods, with 130 students receiving repetitive dictation and 105, nonrepetitive dictation. No statistically significant differences were found in the mean achievement test scores.[72]

Soellers tested the effect of previewed words on errors in shorthand outlines and reported that students who had practiced 10 percent of the words as previews made significantly fewer errors than students who had not previewed the words. Students taking dictation at 60 wam benefited more from the previews than students taking dictation at 80 wam.[73]

McKenna, Pershing, Baird, and Ward conducted experiments to determine the effect of early introduction of new-matter dictation in the teaching of beginning shorthand. McKenna introduced new-matter dictation in the first group after two weeks of instruction. In the other group new matter was deferred until all shorthand theory had been introduced. There was no statistically significant difference between the two groups on dictation tests or on the two shorthand vocabulary tests. Transcription achievement, as measured by the dictation tests, correlated with shorthand vocabulary competency, as measured by shorthand vocabulary tests, in each section and in the two sections combined.[74,75,76,77]

Pershing, in a study to determine when to introduce new-matter dictation in Gregg shorthand, found no significant difference in achievement in theory, familiar-matter dictation, and new-matter dictation in classes in which new-matter dictation was introduced at the beginning of the shorthand course and used continuously there-after and in classes in which new-matter dictation was delayed.[78]

In a study at the high school level, Baird introduced new-matter dictation in Lesson 25 in the experimental class and postponed new-matter dictation in the control class until Lesson 54. He concluded that the early introduction of new-matter dictation in beginning shorthand classes did not reduce the time required to transcribe unpracticed material dictated at 60 wam for three minutes. Further-more, the early introduction of new material had no discernible effect on student achievement.[79]

On the other hand, Ward in his study of the effect of early introduction of new-matter dictation on the achievement of first-year shorthand students, found a significant positive difference in the achievement of students taught with the early new-matter ap-proach.[80]

In comparing differences in writing performance of first-year students writing at 80 wam and second-year students writing at 120 wam, Palmer reported that students writing at 120 wam showed significant improvement in writing unfamiliar words. However, error percentages for shorthand and transcription were high for both groups. Difficult words not only caused hesitations and increased writing time, but also affected the writing of the word that followed.[81]

In 1970 Pullis analyzed the effect of the duration of shorthand dictation and found that the mean average difference between three-minute and five-minute dictation tests was 16 wam. The median average difference between three-minute and five-minute dictation tests was 20 wam. On the five-minute tests not passed, there was a high concentration of errors during the last two minutes.[82]

Individualized Instruction

In 1972 Shank studied the use of autoinstructional materials for learning Gregg shorthand. No significant difference was found when comparing the means of the autoinstructional treatment (individual instruction) group and the means of the traditional treatment group on the mastery of Gregg theory, level of reading and writing skills, and instructional time needed to attain proficiency in transcribing.[83]

In 1975 Simcoe investigated the effectiveness of the Gregg Shorthand Individual Progress Method and reported that students using the Individual Progress Method could achieve as much or in some instances more than students taught by the traditional method.[84] Gilmore found that at the end of two semesters of shorthand, inner-city students made fewer errors in writing shorthand theory when using IPM materials and concluded the method was more effective than conventional methods for teaching shorthand principles to such students. These students also made fewer errors and took less time when transcribing dictation than students taught by the traditional approach. She concluded that students in the lower socioeconomic group appeared to benefit most from the IPM materials.[85]

Hardy compared the relative effectiveness of three instructional methods (individualized, teacher-taught, and taped instruction for group study) on student achievement in intermediate and advanced collegiate shorthand. Students in the individualized group checked out cassettes, working at their own rates. Students using taped-instruction-for-group-study attended class four times a week and were assigned to a class according to their initial shorthand speed, advancing to the next speed level as they met the dictation speed requirements. The teacher-taught classes also met four days a week. The 161 students were administered pretests that included a 130-word brief-form test, a 150-word shorthand vocabulary test, and a progressive dictation test. Three comparable posttests were administered at the end of the semester.

The pretest and posttest scores were subjected to analysis of covariance to determine if significant differences in achievement existed. A statistically significant difference existed in favor of the teacher-taught group over the individualized group in ability to transcribe brief forms, write shorthand outlines using selected theory principles and transcribe these outlines, and to write and transcribe progressive dictation at speeds ranging from 80 to 140 wam.

The teacher-taught group improved significantly more than the taped-instruction-for-group-study students in ability to write short-hand outlines using selected principles, to write brief-form outlines, and to write and transcribe progressive dictation. Students in the individualized group improved more than students in the taped-instruction group in ability to transcribe shorthand outlines using selected shorthand principles.[86]

In Sigler's study, a videotaped individualized-instruction approach was used to teach beginning shorthand to 127 students while 91 were taught by the traditional method. Students using the videotaped instructional materials passed the same number of tests at 50, 60, and 70 wam as students using the traditional approach. Students using the videotaped materials achieved a level of skill significantly higher, as measured by number of takes passed at 70 wam with a higher percentage of accuracy, than did students using the traditional approach.[87]

In 1963, Taylor developed some programmed materials that were used for the presentation of theory in beginning shorthand classes. She found no significant differences on vocabulary or dictation achievement measures between students taught with the programmed materials and those taught with the shorthand text. Also there were no significant differences between the time required for completing the programmed lesson and achievement measures at the close of the study.[88] These findings are similar to those of Henson and DeYoung, who reported that no significant differences were found to exist in student achievement on theory quizzes, transcription rates, and vocabulary tests between students using programmed instructional materials and those using traditional materials.[89,90]

Henson prepared programmed materials for the first five chapters of the beginning high school shorthand text and evaluated the effectiveness of these materials during the first nine weeks of instruction. The experimental group used the programmed materials both during the class and for homework, receiving no group instruction or chalkboard drill. The control group was taught by conventional methods. Henson reported the experimental group completed the theory lessons a week ahead of the control group and the mean vocabulary scores of this group were significantly higher than those of the control group on three of the five end-of-chapter tests. It should be noted that although students were equated on a number of factors, only 16 students in each group participated in the study.

Both O'Connell and Henson conducted studies to determine whether significant differences in student achievement would exist between students using programmed materials and those using traditional materials. After nine weeks of instruction, Henson reported the programmed group made significant gains on transcription skills. However, O'Connell found no significant differences existed between student achievement on theory tests, transcription rates, dictation rates, and vocabulary tests at the end of first-semester shorthand on the high school level.[91,92]

Waters conducted an experimental study of programmed shorthand homework in 1964. In-class instruction was the same for both control and experimental groups. The control classes followed traditional homework procedures, including the introduction of new shorthand outlines before the end of each class period, followed by an assignment of reading and writing practice. Students in the experimental classes were given instruction for preparing their homework on programmed materials. Waters reported a significant difference in shorthand achievement at the intermediate collegiate shorthand level when programmed homework materials were used in place of traditional homework procedures.[93]

In another study on the college level, Clark reported students learned shorthand theory through the use of programmed homework and were able to take shorthand significantly faster than students not using these materials. However, the effectiveness of the programmed materials could not be adequately determined, since the experimental class received more dictation during class than did the control group.[94]

Moyer and Perkins developed programmed materials to review punctuation and transcription. Moyer reported that students using the programmed materials punctuated printed materials in transcripts as well as students who were exposed to conventional methods of review in advanced classes.[95] Perkins developed a self-instructional package combining the basic punctuation rules of business correspondence. A total of 389 high school students participated in the study. The experimental group devoted 10 to 15 minutes daily studying these materials, while students in the control group were given traditional instruction on these rules by the teacher. Perkins reported that the gain score analysis showed the programmed materials were significantly and appreciably more effective than the conventional methods in producing instructional behavioral changes. The mean gain for the experimental group was 43.7 percent; for the control group, 19.75 percent.[96]

Taped Instruction

Coleman sought to determine whether there would be any significant difference in terminal achievement of two equated groups of beginning shorthand students, one group being taught in a multichannel tape laboratory and the other in a traditional manner. She reported that the group taught in the traditional manner performed significantly better than did the group taught with the multichannel tape system.[97] In another study of the effectiveness of taped versus teacher dictation, Palmer reported that the terminal-achievement results indicated no significant difference at the .05 level of confidence between classes using teacher dictation and those using taped dictation.[98] In a study completed in 1971, Laird reported finding no significant difference between college shorthand classes using teacher dictation and classes using taped dictation.[99]

Lensing, in a study of terminal achievement in second-semester shorthand classes taking dictation from the teacher and classes taking dictation from a range of tape-recorded materials, also reported that there were no significant differences between the classes in terminal speed in writing shorthand.[100]

Hess studied the effects of a varied shorthand laboratory schedule on students' achievement. In one method the shorthand laboratory was used only during the regular class period. In the second method the shorthand laboratory was used during the regular class period and for homework assignments. The results obtained with these two methods were compared with those obtained with traditional teaching methods in which a shorthand laboratory was not used. Hess reported that on both posttests dictated at 80 and at 100 wam, the differences in terminal performance of the three groups in intermediate shorthand were not statistically significant. Hess concluded that the use of a shorthand laboratory showed no significant influence on the terminal achievement of students in intermediate collegiate shorthand.[101]

A study by Tingey sought to determine student acceptance of taped instruction as a method of teaching intermediate shorthand and to compare student achievement in intermediate shorthand at Brigham Young University for three fall semesters. The first fall the classes were taught by the traditional method with Dictaprint (self-dictating and writing shorthand from print) used for homework. The next fall 30 minutes of each class period was used for taped instruction, and the third fall, Dictaprint was used and all class instruction was tape recorded. There was no significant difference between any two of the three years for speed or transcription-error frequency. While students seemed to have a favorable opinion of taped instruction, most felt a combination of taped instruction and teacher instruction would improve the course.[102]

In a study to determine the effectiveness of taped instruction in shorthand, Stoddard had two groups that received "live" dictation and a third, multichannel tape dictation. One of the first two groups transcribed in longhand while the other group transcribed on typewriters. The group receiving taped dictation practice also transcribed on typewriters. Stoddard concluded that there was no significant difference in student achievement among the three groups.[103]

Transcription

Introduction of Typewritten Transcription

In a study of the effect of early introduction of typewritten transcription on achievement in beginning shorthand, Brent reported that no significant differences existed in reading rates, dictation speed, mailable letter averages, or transcription rates between groups with and without early introduction of typewritten transcription. A significant difference did exist on the theory test scores in favor of the group in which typewritten transcription was introduced later, near the end of the first year.[104]

Hampton also studied the effect on achievement in first-year shorthand of introducing typewritten-transcription practice at various times during the year. He found that the time at which typewritten-transcription practice was introduced had no effect on shorthand theory knowledge, three-minute transcription rates, and three-minute dictation speeds attained by the students in the classes.[105] Keller also determined that immediate introduction and delayed introduction to formal typewritten transcription produced comparable results in dictation writing and in typewritten-transcription speed.[106]

Shorthand Transcription Achievement

In a study by Barras to determine transcription achievement of fourth-semester shorthand students in selected Catholic high schools in the Midwest, three business letters were dictated at 80 wam, with 30 minutes allowed for transcription of the 400 standard words in the letters. Barras found the average transcription rate was 14.3 wam, with a range from 6.6 to 27.8 wam. Only 4 percent of the students attained a rate of 20 wam or higher. English errors accounted for 17 percent of all errors. Errors included typographical, poor erasures, spelling, punctuation, English usage, letter mechanics, and syllabi-cation.[107]

In a study of shorthand and transcription errors among elementary and advanced high school shorthand writers, Iannizzi found that 45 to 50 percent of all transcription errors were related to shorthand outline errors. Of the transcription errors, 50 to 55 percent were from shorthand outlines that had been correctly written according to the shorthand dictionary. Chi-square tests of independence, however, indicated that accuracy of transcript was highly related to accuracy of outline construction.[108]

Talbot reported that only 0.4 percent of the first-year shorthand students and 15.7 percent of second-year shorthand students for a total of 99 (4.31 percent) of the test population of 2,297 students tested in his study could transcribe the test material dictated at 80 wam with 95 percent accuracy. First-year students using typewriters did significantly better than those who did not use typewriters. Test scores of urban and rural students in first-year shorthand showed no significant difference, but in second-year shorthand, rural students did significantly better. First-year shorthand students did significantly better in class sizes with 21 to 25, 31 to 35, and 40 or more students. Second-year students did significantly better in classes with at least 16 but no more than 30 students.[109]

In 1961 Frink reported that although teachers stated that they required 100 wam at the end of two years of shorthand and 60 wam at the end of one year, in general, stenographic students were not capable of producing either mailable letters or verbatim transcripts of material of 1.4 syllabic intensity dictated at rates not over 80 wam.[110]

Rate and Duration of Dictation—Effect on Transcription

Kimbrel studied the equivalencies of shorthand dictation at differing speeds, duration, and transcription levels. She found that the higher the dictation speed, the more rapidly transcription accuracy decreased as duration of dictation increased. Likewise, at any given duration of dictation, transcription accuracy decreased as dictation speed increased.[111]

Transcription Procedures

Bose prepared special materials for her experimental study designed to determine the effect of immediate versus delayed knowledge of results on initial learning and retention of selected related learnings in transcription classes. Immediate knowledge of correct response had no significant effect on initial learning in beginning transcription but significantly facilitated learning in advanced transcription. Immediate knowledge of correct response appeared to have no significant effect on retention in either beginning or advanced shorthand transcription. Bose concluded that there was no particular need to design teaching aids and materials to give immediate knowledge of correct response in transcription classes, since such materials had no significant effect on initial learning and retention of selected related learnings in transcription.[112]

McGuire used shorthand slides for pacing transcription. She found that their use appeared to have no greater and no less effect on transcription speed development than did the use of transcription timed from plate material.[113]

In 1976 Haney studied the effect of the use of selected transcription drills in beginning shorthand on the ability of students to produce both typed copy and mailable letters from shorthand notes. She found that students using transcription drills achieved higher percentages of all speed scores on three-minute dictation tests except at 40 wam than did students not using drills. Students in the experimental group passed 61.82 percent of all three-minute dictation tests, while students in the control group passed 38.18 percent. Students using transcription drills achieved significantly higher and more accurate transcription rates and higher speeds on both previewed and unpreviewed mailable-letter-production tests than students not using these drills, with the results being statistically significant at the .01 level.[114]

The Transcription Process

One of the best-known studies in the area of transcription is a time study of shorthand transcription completed by Jester in 1959. Jester found that only 38 percent of the overall transcription time was devoted to typing activities; 62 percent was devoted to nontyping activities such as erasing and correcting errors, deciphering shorthand notes, and dealing with spelling and punctuation problems. Since the duration of typing activity was less than 30 seconds for 93 percent of the intervals, Jester concluded that typing drills used to build transcription skill should be short. Transcribers typed at approximately half their straight-copy speed during the time they were actually striking the keys. A significant correlation did exist, however, between the typing speed while transcribing and the straight copy rate of the transcribers. The overall production rate of transcribers was between 14 and 36 percent of the straight-copy typing rate, generally centering around 20 percent of their straight-copy speed. One-fourth of the transcribers' time was spent erasing and correcting and proofreading and correcting. Shorthand problems causing pauses in transcription were inability to read shorthand notes, deciphering incorrectly written outlines, and reading shorthand for context and meaning. Although incorrectly written shorthand outlines were often correctly transcribed, time was lost attempting to decipher them; and a significant linear correlation of positive .79 was found to exist between the number of theory errors on a shorthand test and the number of problems occurring during transcription because of incorrectly written outlines. Transcribers who wrote accurate shorthand outlines were more efficient and faster transcribers than those who lost time deciphering incorrectly written outlines.[115]

Shorthand and Language Arts

Language Arts Skills of Shorthand Students

In 1975 Johnson conducted a study to determine whether beginning shorthand could be identified as a course that could be taken for the development and improvement of language arts skills. He found that shorthand students performed significantly better than nonshorthand students in the language arts skills of punctuation, spelling, and vocabulary, with the highest degree of significance between the groups being in spelling. Shorthand students did not perform specifically better in the language arts skills of capitalization and word usage or in the area of reading comprehension.[116]

Bolan reported a significant relationship between knowledge of spelling, punctuation, capitalization, and grammatical usage, and the application of that knowledge in transcription from shorthand dictation. There was a significant relationship between knowledge of syllabication, writing numerals, and sentence structure and paragraphing, and the application of that knowledge in transcription from shorthand dictation. Bolan concluded, however, that it could not be assumed students would automatically apply the knowledge they acquired in English classes to transcribing from shorthand dictation.[117]

In an analysis of spelling errors in transcription in advanced shorthand classes, Anderson found that over half the spelling errors were made on words from the 1,500 most frequently used words in the Silverthorn list. Errors also occurred in homonyms, silent letters, failure to double letters, and unnecessary doubling of letters.[118]

Student Errors in Transcription

Vought found the most frequently occurring types of errors in transcription in both beginning and advanced shorthand were related to language skills and typing rather than shorthand transcription errors. Types of errors occurring most frequently were errors in punctuation, typing, spelling, capitalization, grammar, and format placement.[119]

Swanson determined that sound errors were the greatest cause of misspelled words resulting mainly from mispronunciation or substitution. Rule errors caused the second highest percentage of spelling errors, with formation of the possessives accounting for over half of such errors. Confusion of homonyms ranked high. Comma errors caused the greatest percentage of punctuation errors, with 64 percent being commas omitted and 21 percent, commas incorrectly inserted. The comma-conjunction rule was most often violated, followed by the omission of the comma after an introductory clause.[120]

Dupree attempted to determine whether a relationship existed between the number of punctuation decisions required of shorthand students and the transcription time and accuracy in punctuation. A test consisting of five-minute letters was dictated at 80 wam to 449 second-year shorthand students in 24 high schools. Dupree found that the transcription time and number of punctuation errors increased significantly with an increase in the number of punctuation decisions required. The error occurring most frequently was failure to use a comma to separate two independent clauses joined by a conjunction. The least common error was in the use of the possessive pronoun.[121]

Prognosis

A number of researchers, including Spann, Varah, Durso, Byers, and Utley, have reported that factors such as phonetic understandings, spelling, grade point average, English grades, symbol retention, and

397

auditory and visual stimuli can be used to some extent to predict success in first-year shorthand.[122,123,124,125,126]

Moskovis found that personality traits and attitudes were significantly related to success in first-semester shorthand but that they were not reliable in predicting transcription achievement.[127]

In an analysis of the subtests of the Turse Shorthand Aptitude Test, Pauk found that the four verbal subtests combined predicted shorthand success better than the combined three mechanics-of-shorthand subtests (.66 vs .34); that the verbal subtests individually and in combination predicted shorthand success with the same magnitude (.56 to .66) as the total Turse test (.63); and that the general score of the ACE predicted shorthand success as well as the total Turse test (.63 vs .63).[128]

In 1967 O'Connell conducted a study to determine the relationship between scores on the Turse test and the GPA to achievement in shorthand. She reported that it could be predicted with a high degree of accuracy that students with GPAs of less than C who also ranked in the lower quartile on the Turse test would not attain minimum achievement in shorthand. Based on the two factors of GPA and aptitude test scores separately, success or failure could not be predicted with the same degree of accuracy. The correlation coefficient between shorthand grades and GPA was .68 compared to .54 as the correlation between shorthand grades and the Turse test, indicating that neither criterion should be used separately in predicting shorthand success. O'Connell concluded that in counseling students about their chances of success in shorthand, one should use as many factors as possible in making recommendations.[129]

Rittenhouse, in a study of certain factors influencing success in the learning and achievement of shorthand, concluded that personality factors within the teacher might be related to the students' success with different methods of shorthand teaching. The psychological tests used in the study—School and College Ability Tests (Verbal), the Rokeach Dogmatism Scale, the Test of Critical Thinking and selected subtests (Order, Change, Consistency) of the Edward's Personal Preference Schedule were of no significant value in determining which students would learn shorthand efficiently, when students used the workbook for supplementary homework or used only conventional homework practice.[130]

Lambrecht reported that the use of all six shorthand aptitude subtests of the revised edition of the Byers' *First Year Shorthand Aptitude Tests* to predict shorthand achievement was no more effective for prediction than a selected battery of fewer aptitude subtests. The validity of the shortened battery version was no different from that of the complete aptitude battery in the cross-validation sample.[131]

Handorf and Holderness attempted to develop a formula for predicting success in first- and second-year shorthand. The criterion variables for first-year shorthand were a theory test, a transcription test, students' ability to transcribe their own notes at the end of the first semester, and a three-minute take dictated at 80 wam at the end of two semesters. The correlations between the shorthand criterion variables for first-year shorthand were .93 for the theory tests; .77 for the transcription test; and .68 for the dictation test. The predictor variables for beginning shorthand were Part 3, Phonetic Spelling of ERC Stenographic Aptitude Test, Paired Associates Section of the Modern Language Aptitude Test, and overall grade-point average. The second-year shorthand criterion variables were a 100-wam dictation test, mailable-letter test dictated at 80 wam, and a mailable transcription rate. Correlations with predictors were .65 for the dictation test and .60 for mailable transcription rate. The predictors for second-year shorthand were Part 1, Speed of Writing of the ERC Stenographic Aptitude Test, Part 3, Phonetic Spelling of the ERC Stenographic Aptitude Test, Symbol Writing, and overall grade point average for previous shorthand achievement.[132]

Skaff attempted to develop and evaluate a prognostic test for first-semester shorthand. The predictive test had five parts: phonetic understanding and spelling, symbol retention, manual dexterity, proofreading and punctuation, and sentence retention and writing speed. Phonetic understanding, proofreading, and punctuation scores on the aptitude test showed a close relationship to first-semester shorthand grades. Students with vocational interests in shorthand achieved higher grades than students who were enrolled in the course for other reasons.[133]

Shane compared personal background factors and/or characteristics of successful and unsuccessful students in beginning shorthand to determine the relationship of these personal background factors and/or characteristics to achievement in beginning shorthand. A total of 148 students in beginning shorthand were analyzed in terms of personality, major area of study, type of courses pursued, parental occupation, advisement preference, social relationships, motor skill development, study habits and attitudes, foreign language grades, English grades in the ninth and tenth grades, and final grade in beginning shorthand. The factors found to be significant at the .001 level in predicting achievement in beginning shorthand were education acceptance, English grades in the ninth and tenth grades, motivation, social relationships, motor skill development, teacher approval, family income range, work methods, and delay avoidance.

Shane concluded that there is a significant relationship between certain personal background factors and/or characteristics and achievement in beginning shorthand, that students who scored high on the social relationships, motor skill development, and study habits and attitudes tend to perform satisfactorily in beginning shorthand, and that students who achieve successful English grades in the ninth and tenth grades tend to achieve successful grades in beginning shorthand.[134]

Nennick, in attempting to find a predictor index for use in elementary shorthand, measured the extent to which Form A of the Nelson-Denny Reading Test, a cloze test, and a spelling-dictation test would successfully identify higher risk students. She found that the cloze test was a short, useful technique for identifying high-risk and low-risk students in elementary shorthand classes at two-year colleges.[135]

Hammers, in attempting to predict the success of students in individualized and traditional beginning shorthand courses, administered five instruments to 51 beginning shorthand students—Phonetic Spelling (subtest of the Stenographic Aptitude Test), Symbol Writing and Transcription of the Bennett Aptitude Test, Myers Briggs Type Indicator, Rotter Internal and External Control Scale, and a student information form. Hammers found a significant relationship between the Stenographic Aptitude Test (Phonetic Ability) scores and end-of-semester achievement in the traditional beginning shorthand course. A similar relationship was found to exist between this test and the end-of-semester achievement for students in the individualized shorthand course. Extroverts were found to be more successful in the traditional shorthand course while introverts were more successful in the individualized course.[136]

Ellington found that variables including the MLAT scores, grade point average, language achievement, the cloze procedure, and modern language aptitude test scores failed to yield a correlation sufficiently high with the shorthand criterion (three-minute dictation tests) to justify use of the battery as a predictor.[137]

Foster, in a study of the factors for predicting success in beginning Gregg shorthand, found that achievement in beginning Gregg shorthand appeared to result from emphasis on a combination of factors during all development stages. Achievement in reading appeared to be a function of achievement in theory and reading; achievement in three-minute typewritten-transcription rates was largely dependent on achievement in theory, reading, and one-minute transcription rates; and achievement in three-minute dictation speeds appeared to be a function of achievement in one-minute dictation speeds and theory. Foster concluded that the combination of one-minute dictation speeds and theory scores at the end of the first semester could be used as a predictor of performance on three-minute dictation speeds at the end of the first year of instruction.[138]

Teachers sometimes feel their students have difficulty learning shorthand because they have no understanding of phonetics. In a study by Bell, formal phonics instruction was given to four groups of beginning shorthand students during regular classes. It was found that such training did little to increase knowledge of phonics, as measured by the California Phonics Survey, and that there was little relationship between phonics knowledge and shorthand achievement, as measured by the number of correct handwritten words a minute transcribed from shorthand plates.[139]

Miscellaneous

Skabo conducted a study of the relationship between the time used for selected class activities and achievement in shorthand theory. The four most common class activities were reading connected matter from text, 14.86 percent; independent study, 12.99 percent; writing familiar dictation, 11.86 percent; and miscellaneous teacher activities, 9.88 percent.

In first-semester shorthand 35 percent of the time was spent in reading and 25 percent in writing. In the construction of theoretically correct shorthand outlines and transcription of students' disconnected shorthand outlines, achievement was higher for classes using more time for reading and writing activities. Achievement was also higher on these two measures for classes using more time for reading and writing chalkboard outlines. Achievement was higher for construction of correct shorthand outlines, transcribing disconnected shorthand outlines, and reading and writing familiar dictation when less time was used for independent study (homework). Achievement was higher in constructing connected outlines for classes using more time for chalkboard demonstrations by the teacher. Classes spending more time on writing activities had higher achievement on transcription of students' disconnected shorthand outlines.[140]

Rees reported that intermediate and advanced shorthand students who attended class four consecutive days a week or who attended class three days a week on a Monday-Wednesday-Friday schedule developed approximately the same degree of competency as students attending class five days a week.[141]

Hanrahan's findings supported those of Rees. She found that students did not differ in shorthand vocabulary knowledge, reading rates, dictation speed, and typewritten transcription at the end of the beginning college course whether they attended class four or three days a week. However, students in the intermediate college course who attended class four days a week achieved significantly greater shorthand vocabulary knowledge and typewritten transcription rates than students attending class only three days a week. These students did not achieve differently on dictation speeds and mailable-letter production.[142]

Research Conclusions

Shorthand Accuracy

1. Students' degree of mastery of shorthand notes by the end of the theory course establishes limitations on achievement in future shorthand courses.

2. Since the major portion of symbol mastery takes place during the first semester, emphasis should be placed on thorough knowledge of shorthand theory during the first semester.

3. More emphasis should be given to shorthand principles and to the construction of difficult or uncommon shorthand outlines.

4. Because accurate outlines contribute to both building dictation skill and accurate transcription, writing correct outlines should continue to be stressed throughout the shorthand program.

5. Shorthand dictation achievement is significantly related to shorthand transcription ability.

6. The type of shorthand error increasing most with increases of speed is proportion errors; such errors frequently cause difficulties in transcription.

7. One of the most frequent errors in writing shorthand is confusion of *o* and *oo*. Other common errors are in the use of the past tense and confusion of left and right *s*.

8. Students frequently substitute long *i* for the shorthand sound of *e*, which may indicate they are writing by spelling rather than by sound.

9. Many omissions in students' transcripts are due to totally illegible outlines.

10. There is no conclusive evidence that context alone is the major factor in transcription, but context may enable a student to transcribe a sentence correctly even though some shorthand outlines are omitted or illegible.

11. The use of the shorthand transcript does not seem to make a significant difference in the achievement of students in beginning Gregg shorthand.

12. Emphasis on thought units in beginning shorthand appears to be more beneficial to students of high ability than to students of low ability.

Reading

1. A significant relationship exists between the ability to read shorthand and the ability to take shorthand dictation. Reading shorthand serves as an effective mediator to writing shorthand.

2. Emphasis on reading rates does not appear to affect end-of-course grades in shorthand.

3. The ability to read shorthand symbols in context has a significant effect on students' ability to transcribe shorthand notes taken during dictation.

Homework

1. Students who use an extensive reading method of homework

practice attain approximately the same level of competency as those who use an intensive writing method of practice.

2. Differences in reading rates attained by the practice of copying homework only and the combination of plates and printed material for homework are not significant.

3. The combination of plate and printed material produces greater word-list ability to write familiar words than copying plates only. However, it does not affect the students' ability to write and to take and transcribe dictation on familiar material when compared to copying plates only.

4. Beginning shorthand students doing their homework by the self-dictation method from the textbook achieve a better knowledge of shorthand theory than students who write homework from recorded dictation with texts open.

5. Self-dictation in which students write from print into shorthand appears to result in significantly better performance than do traditional homework procedures, especially when the print expands shorthand vocabulary.

6. The achievement of students using programmed homework materials is significantly better than the achievement of students using traditional homework procedures.

7. Research findings disagree on the specific values derived from the use of nontraditional shorthand homework assignments, but indicate that such practices may have considerable merit, especially in beginning shorthand.

Shorthand Dictation Materials

1. Brief-form derivatives are frequently written incorrectly by students and perhaps should receive greater instructional emphasis.

2. Familiarity of vocabulary appears to be highly significant in determining the difficulty of shorthand dictation material.

3. Syllabic intensity is not an accurate predictor of the percentage of high-frequency words within published dictation materials.

4. Syllabic intensity, when used as the sole measure, is a poor predictor of the difficulty of shorthand dictation materials. Factors such as percentage of most commonly used words, percentage of brief forms, outline length, and familiarity of vocabulary should be considered when determining copy difficulty.

5. Multiple regression equations for predicting shorthand outline errors do not predict transcription errors with comparable efficiency.

6. Errors increase as the number of shorthand strokes per word increases, as the number of syllables per word increases, and as the use of the words decreases.

7. Changes in student performance on dictation takes of the same syllabic intensity given at the same rate may be reflecting differences in the difficulty of the takes rather than changes in students' shorthand proficiency.

8. There is widespread disagreement in research findings regarding the use of controlled versus uncontrolled materials for shorthand dictation.

9. Variations in dictation rates may be attributed to differences in ability of the dictators and to the types and difficulty of the dictation.

10. The syllabic intensity of business correspondence is approximately 1.6. Consequently some of the dictation materials currently in use overrate students' dictation speed by approximately 18 percent.

11. The vocabulary distribution of many published takes is significantly different from that of contemporary business communications.

Building Shorthand Dictation/Recording Skills

1. Either vocabulary-controlled material or textbook material may be used to develop skill in recording dictation in beginning shorthand classes.

2. The speed-building practice pattern used to develop dictation skills does not affect the level of achievement in writing shorthand from dictation on speed takes.

3. There are no significant differences in the achievement of students taught by the micromolar behavioristic approach (fast cue-response) and those taught by the traditional method of skill building.

4. The use of the shorthand preview is more effective with students taking dictation at low rates, such as 60 wam than it is with students attempting to develop higher rates.

5. Early introduction of new-matter dictation neither increases nor hinders students' ability to take and transcribe new-matter dictation.

6. Early introduction of writing does not necessarily impede the students' shorthand progress and may even contribute to the attainment of higher shorthand standards.

7. Writing shorthand from a printed transcript is not detrimental to the student's progress if the student has first copied the same material from shorthand plates; in intermediate and advanced shorthand, copying from print and self-dictating material may produce significantly improved shorthand achievement.

8. Writing the homework practice twice may be more beneficial to some students than copying the shorthand plates only once.

9. There is a difference in dictation skill of approximately 20 wam between three-minute and five-minute takes.
10. As the length of the dictation period and the rate of dictation increases, transcription accuracy decreases.

Individualized Instruction

1. The evidence regarding the contribution of individualized instructional techniques to the improvement of shorthand learning and achievement is inconclusive. Some studies have reported improved student progress through the use of individualized procedures; others have reported better achievement using traditional procedures; still others have found no significant differences.
2. Students can effectively learn shorthand theory and achieve in early dictation practice through programmed instruction.
3. No significant difference has been found in achievement on theory quizzes, dictation rates, transcription rate, and vocabulary between students using programmed shorthand materials and those using traditional materials.
4. Isolated areas of shorthand (punctuation rules and homework) can be effectively learned in a programmed approach.
5. Programmed materials for reviewing punctuation in intermediate and advanced shorthand classes may be more effective with some students than the conventional methods.
6. Multiple-channel tape dictation does not produce significantly greater recording skills than does live dictation practice.
7. There is no conclusive evidence that the use of shorthand laboratories or taped instruction improves shorthand achievement.
8. Most students prefer a combination of taped instruction and teacher instruction to solely taped or teacher instruction.

Transcription

1. Early introduction of typewritten transcription does not appear to significantly affect shorthand students' dictation-speed development or transcription rates.
2. Poor proportion and inability to read shorthand notes are frequent causes of transcription errors.
3. Students' competency in shorthand transcription increases with competency in shorthand accuracy.
4. The accuracy with which shorthand notes taken from dictation are transcribed decreases when the transcription is deferred.
5. Context alone does not appear to be the major factor in transcription; correctly written shorthand outlines are as important as context in producing mailable transcripts.

6. Students using selected short transcription drills in beginning shorthand appear to be more skilled in recording dictation of unpreviewed material and to transcribe at higher rates with greater accuracy on three-minute dictation takes than students not using such drills.

7. Even after two years of shorthand instruction, some students can neither transcribe takes dictated at 80 wam with 95 percent accuracy, nor produce mailable transcripts.

8. Over 60 percent of the students' transcription time is devoted to nontyping activities such as erasing and correcting errors, deciphering shorthand notes, and dealing with spelling and punctuation problems.

9. Shorthand problems causing hesitations in transcribing are inability to read the notes, deciphering incorrectly written shorthand outlines, and reading shorthand for context and meaning. Transcribers writing accurate shorthand outlines are more efficient and faster transcribers than those using time deciphering incorrectly written outlines.

10. The average second-year shorthand student transcribes at the rate of 14 wam.

11. Transcribers type at approximately half their straight-copy rate during the time they are actually striking the keys.

12. Teachers should devote more time to transcription in order to meet the ultimate objective of the shorthand program— the mailable transcript.

Shorthand and Language Arts

1. A knowledge of English factors is no indication that students will be able to apply that knowledge in practical situations. Such knowledge is not necessarily transferred to the production of mailable transcription unless it is reinforced in a particular setting.

2. Shorthand students can be expected to perform significantly better than nonshorthand students in the language arts skills of punctuation, spelling, and vocabulary. They do not perform significantly better in the language arts skills of capitalization and word usage.

3. The most frequently recurring errors in transcription are related to language arts skills and typing.

Prognosis

1. No single device can be used effectively to predict success in shorthand. Several items used together, however, may indicate students who are likely to encounter difficulty in learning shorthand.

2. A number of factors, such as phonetic understanding, spelling, grade point average, English grades, symbol retention, and visual stimuli, may be helpful to some extent in predicting success in beginning shorthand.

3. The four verbal subtests of the Turse test may predict short-hand success better than the three mechanics-of-shorthand subtests.

4. The general score on the ACE may be as good a predictor of shorthand success as a shorthand aptitude test.

5. The use of grade point average plus scores on the Turse test increases the accuracy with which students may be counseled regarding their probable success or failure in shorthand.

6. The use of all six subtests of the revised edition of the Byers *First-Year Shorthand Aptitude Tests* to predict shorthand achieve-ment appears to be no more effective for prediction than the three selected subtests of Phonetic Perception, Observation Aptitude, and Disarranged Syllables.

7. There appears to be little relationship between formal knowl-edge of phonics and shorthand achievement measured by the number of correctly written words transcribed in longhand from shorthand plates.

Miscellaneous

1. Achievement in the construction and transcription of discon-nected outlines is higher when more class time is devoted to reading and writing activities.

2. Students attending shorthand classes that meet three, four, or five days a week appear to attain approximately the same degree of shorthand competency.

Research References

1. Joe M. Pullis, "The Relationship Between Competency in Shorthand Accuracy and Achievement in Shorthand Dicta-tion," doctoral dissertation, North Texas State University, Denton, 1966.

2. Joe M. Pullis, "Methods of Teaching Shorthand: A Research Analysis," independent study, Louisiana Tech University, Ruston, 1969.

3. Leo G. Goetz, "The Relationship Between Symbol Mastery and Selected Dictation Speeds in Gregg Shorthand," doctoral dissertation, University of North Dakota, Grand Forks, 1966.

4. William J. Karaim, "A Comparison of the Writing Practices of Two Diverse Achievement Groups of Shorthand Students When Writing From Dictation," doctoral dissertation, Uni-versity of North Dakota, Grand Forks, 1968.

407

5. Alfred Lloyd Patrick, "An Error Analysis of Selected Brief Forms and Principles in Shorthand Notes of Beginning Gregg Diamond Jubilee Shorthand Students," doctoral dissertation, University of Tennessee, Knoxville, 1965.

6. Barbara Joy Minnick, "An Evaluation of Systematic Repetition of Brief Forms Through Specially Constructed Dictation Materials for Gregg Shorthand Diamond Jubilee Series," doctoral dissertation, University of Tennessee, Knoxville, 1967.

7. Evelyn R. Hallman, "An Evaluation of Systematic Repetition of Principles Through Specially Constructed Dictation Material for Gregg Shorthand, Diamond Jubilee Series," doctoral dissertation, University of Tennessee, Knoxville, 1971.

8. William F. Fermenick, "An Analysis of the Relationship Between Applications of Some Principles of Gregg Shorthand Simplified and Errors in Transcription," master's thesis, Mankato State University, Mankato, MN, 1959.

9. Romayne Reed Cook, "Transcription Achievement of Eight Shorthand Classes in Milwaukee, Wisconsin," master's thesis, University of Wisconsin, Madison, 1966.

10. Berle Haggeblade, "Factors Affecting Achievement in Shorthand," doctoral dissertation, University of California, Los Angeles, 1965.

11. Richard C. Klaseus, "An Analysis of Some of the Factors That Contribute to the Difficulty of Transcription Materials in Gregg Shorthand—Diamond Jubilee Series," master's thesis, Mankato State University, Mankato, MN, 1964.

12. Neil R. Dortch, "A Study to Determine the Relationship Between Shorthand Outlines Constructed According to Theory and the Accuracy of the Transcript," doctoral dissertation, University of Wisconsin, Madison, 1976.

13. Jean T. Ellingson, "An Analysis of Errors Made in Shorthand Outlines and the Transcript to Determine Critical Nature of Errors," master's thesis, Mankato State University, Mankato, MN, 1964.

14. Milton Karle Howard, "The Relationship Between Knowledge of Principles and Transcription Errors in Writing Diamond Jubilee Gregg Shorthand as Compared with Gregg Shorthand Simplified at the Two-Year College Level," doctoral dissertation, New York University, New York, 1968.

15. Norma Crewdson, "A Comparison of the Effect on Accuracy in Transcription from Outlines or Context," master's thesis, University of Minnesota, Minneapolis, 1963.

16. Barbara Gallenberg, "A Study Showing the Relationship Between the Writing of Theoretically Correct Shorthand

Outlines to the Transcription Process," master's thesis, University of Wisconsin, Madison, 1975.

17. Joe M. Pullis, "The Relationship Between the Accuracy of Shorthand Notes and the Correctness of Transcripts Resulting from Nondeferred and Deferred Transcription," independent study, Louisiana Tech University, Ruston, 1971.

18. David Peters, "Critical Nature of Certain Types of Errors Found in Shorthand Outlines," master's thesis, Mankato State University, Mankato, MN, 1966.

19. Jean Alderfer Hooven, "The Effects of Intensive Practice on a Target Vocabulary in First-Year Gregg Shorthand," doctoral dissertation, Temple University, Philadelphia, PA, 1977.

20. Klaseus, op. cit.

21. Crewdson, op. cit.

22. Ruth Gaffga, "On-the-Job Shorthand Versus Shorthand Learned in School," *Business Education World*, November 1967, pp. 34–35.

23. Allan Doerr, "An Analytical Study of Selected Factors of Gregg Shorthand, Diamond Jubilee Series, to Evaluate the Degree of Difficulty Students Have in Adopting These Selected Factors," doctoral dissertation, New York University, New York, 1968.

24. Carolyn Schloemer, "A Study to Compare the Achievement Attained in Two Methods of Teaching Gregg Shorthand— The Theory Approach Versus the Non-Theory Approach," master's thesis, University of Wisconsin, Madison, 1964.

25. Joe M. Pullis, "Methods of Teaching Shorthand: A Research Analysis," independent study, Louisiana Tech University, Ruston, 1969.

26. Dorinda Ann Clippinger, "A Comparison of Two Shorthand Theory Methods," doctoral dissertation, Indiana University, Bloomington, 1978.

27. Frances Lipova, "An Experiment to Determine the Value of Stressing Thought-Units During the First Semester of Shorthand," master's thesis, Ohio State University, Columbus, 1960.

28. Shirley Barber, "The Effectiveness of Tachistoscope Training in Collegiate Elementary Shorthand," doctoral dissertation, University of Northern Colorado, Greeley, 1961.

29. Aileen S. Githens, "A Comparative Analysis of Teaching Shorthand With and Without Student Transcripts," master's thesis, Ball State University, Muncie, IN, 1969.

30. Israel H. Young, "An Analytical Study of the Effect of Choice-Making on the Speed of Writing Symbol Combina-

tions in Gregg and Pitman Shorthand," doctoral dissertation, New York University, New York, 1964.

31. Jane L. Manwaring, "The Effect of Doubling the Time Spent in Presenting Each Lesson of Gregg Shorthand Theory," doctoral dissertation, University of Northern Colorado, Greeley, 1965.

32. Joe M. Pullis, "The Relationship Between Fluency in Reading Shorthand Plates and Achievement in Shorthand Dictation," independent study, Louisiana Tech University, Ruston, 1972.

33. Donald L. Beringson, "The Relationship Between Oral Reading Ability From Shorthand Plate Material and the Ability to Take Dictation," doctoral dissertation, University of North Dakota, Grand Forks, 1971.

34. Delores J. Osborne, "Methods of Teaching Shorthand Symbol Reading and the Effect of Shorthand Reading Skill on Recording Dictation," doctoral dissertation, University of Northern Colorado, Greeley, 1970.

35. Diane Jensen, "The Effect of Grading Oral Reading Activities on Terminal Achievement in Beginning Century 21 Shorthand," master's thesis, Brigham Young University, Provo, UT, 1976.

36. Jean M. Prueher, "The Effect of Setting Daily Reading Goals on Success in First-Semester Shorthand," master's thesis, Wisconsin State University, Eau Claire, 1969.

37. Ronald L. Toulouse, "The Reading Approach Versus the Writing Approach to Shorthand Homework," doctoral dissertation, Georgia State University, Atlanta, 1971.

38. Boyd Eugene Arnold, "The Effect of Combining Shorthand Plates and Printed Material as Out-of-Class Writing Assignments in First-Semester College Gregg Shorthand," doctoral dissertation, Pennsylvania State University, University Park, 1974.

39. Myrtle Ione Hayes, "Shorthand Homework Practice Under Attention-Focusing and Vocabulary-Expanding Conditions," doctoral dissertation, University of Northern Colorado, Greeley, 1971.

40. Darvel J. Gregory, "A Comparative Study of Two Methods of Writing Shorthand Homework," master's thesis, Utah State University, Logan, 1968.

41. Robert N. Hanson, "Visual Stimulus Versus Combined Audio-Visual Stimuli for Out-of-Class Practice in First-Semester College Gregg Shorthand," doctoral dissertation, University of North Dakota, Grand Forks, 1966.

42. William G. Perry, "The Effect of Selected Homework Procedures on the Achievement of Second-Semester High

School Shorthand Students," doctoral dissertation, University of North Dakota, Grand Forks, 1975.

43. Joyce J. Stutte, "Programmed Gregg Shorthand Dictation ABC's," *Journal of Business Education,* March 1972, pp. 250–251.

44. Max L. Waters, "An Experimental Study of Programmed Shorthand Homework," doctoral dissertation, University of Northern Colorado, Greeley, 1963.

45. Barbara Elaine Pankhurst, "The Relationship Between Shorthand Achievement and Two Plans of Homework in Shorthand," doctoral dissertation, North Texas State University, Denton, 1972.

46. Rachel T. Jensen, "A Comparison of Two Homework Methods in Collegiate Shorthand; A Write-From-Dictation Homework Approach Versus the Traditional Read-and-Copy Homework Approach," master's thesis, Brigham Young University, Provo, UT, 1977.

47. Mildred C. Hillestad, "Factors That Contribute to the Difficulty of Shorthand Dictation Materials," doctoral dissertation, University of Minnesota, Minneapolis, 1960.

48. Elaine Uthe, "An Evaluation of the Difficulty Level of Shorthand Dictation Material," doctoral dissertation, University of Minnesota, Minneapolis, 1966.

49. William S. Henrie, "A Comparative Analysis of Difficulty Prediction Formulas for Shorthand Dictation Materials," doctoral dissertation, Utah State University, Logan, 1971.

50. Leonard R. Mickelson, "The Relationship Between an Index of Word Frequency and Transcription Errors at One Selected Speed Level of Shorthand Dictation," doctoral dissertation, University of North Dakota, Grand Forks, 1970.

51. Allen Wedell, "The Relationship of Syllabic Intensity, Word Frequency, and Stroke Intensity to the Difficulty of Shorthand Dictation Material," doctoral dissertation, University of North Dakota, Grand Forks, 1972.

52. Joe M. Pullis, "A Test of the Validation of a Triple Control (Percent High-Frequency Words, Average Word Length, and Overall Syllabic Intensity) as a Measure of Difficulty of Shorthand Dictation Material," independent study, Louisiana Tech University, Ruston, 1974.

53. Joe M. Pullis, "A Test of the Validity of Syllabic Intensity and Percent High-Frequency Words as a Measure of Difficulty of Published Shorthand Dictation Materials," independent study, Louisiana Tech University, Ruston, 1975.

54. Joe M. Pullis, "The Relationship Between Syllabic Intensity and Percentage of High-Frequency Words Within Published

Shorthand Dictation Texts," Louisiana Tech University, Ruston, 1977.

55. Ingeborg Antonie Nickerson, "A Measure of Difficulty of Shorthand Dictation Materials," doctoral dissertation, Louisiana Tech University, Ruston, 1977.

56. Gregg A. Condon, "Occurrences of Theory Principles of Gregg Shorthand, Diamond Jubilee Series, in a 5,000-Word List of High-Frequency Words," doctoral dissertation, Northern Illinois University, DeKalb, 1977.

57. Delma Jo Prince, "Using Word Frequency Lists for Accurate Transcription," *Balance Sheet,* September 1968, p. 18.

58. Pauline Crisp Rice, "The Effect of Controlled Vocabulary Materials During Theory Presentation in College-Level Beginning Shorthand," doctoral dissertation, University of Tennessee, Knoxville, 1975.

59. Nathan R. Larsen, "The Terminal Effect of Emphasizing the Most Frequently Occurring Words in Intermediate and Advanced Gregg Shorthand," master's thesis, Brigham Young University, Provo, UT, 1971.

60. Leona May Gallion, "A Comparison of Speed Dictation Development Materials and Methods in Beginning Shorthand," doctoral dissertation, University of Northern Colorado, Greeley, 1968.

61. Morris Mellinger, "Has the Syllabic Intensity Yardstick Lost Its Magic?" *Business Education World,* November 1965, pp. 9–11.

62. Devern Perry, "An Analytical Comparison of the Relative Word-Combination Frequencies of Business Correspondence with Phrase Frequencies of Selected Shorthand Textbooks," doctoral dissertation, University of North Dakota, Grand Forks, 1968.

63. Anthony A. Olinzock, "An Analysis of Business Dictation," doctoral dissertation, University of Pittsburgh, Pittsburgh, PA, 1976.

64. Rita Sloan, "An Application of the Micromolar Behavior Theory to the Instruction of Beginning Shorthand," doctoral dissertation, University of Minnesota, Minneapolis, 1967.

65. Marion L. Boss, "A Micromolar Behavioristic Approach to Dictation Skill Building in Beginning Shorthand," doctoral dissertation, University of Northern Colorado, Greeley, 1967.

66. Alberta R. Anderson, "A Comparison of Dictation Speed-Development Materials and Methods in Beginning Shorthand Using the Micromolar Approach," doctoral dissertation, University of Northern Colorado, Greeley, 1969.

67. Mark E. Langemo, "The Relative Effectiveness of Fast Cue-

Response Dictation Compared With Traditional Dictation in First-Semester Shorthand Instruction," doctoral dissertation, University of North Dakota, Grand Forks, 1972.

68. Catherine M. Pawelski, "An Experimental Study to Determine the Effectiveness of Fast-to-Slow Dictation in Building Speed in the Second Semester of Gregg Shorthand," master's thesis, The Catholic University of America, Washington, DC, 1966.

69. J. Lee Dye, "A Comparison of the Practice Patterns Used for the Development of Skills in Writing Shorthand Dictation," doctoral dissertation, Northern Illinois University, DeKalb, 1970.

70. Henry R. Stocker, "An Experimental Study in the Utilization of the DictaTutor as a Classroom and Homework Teaching Aid in Beginning Collegiate Shorthand," master's thesis, Utah State University, Logan, 1968.

71. Violet Boggess, "Results of Using Dictation Materials of Varying Difficulty for Speed Practice in Shorthand Classes," doctoral dissertation, Ohio State University, Columbus, 1970.

72. Harriet A. McIntosh, "The Effects of Repetitive Versus Nonrepetitive Dictation on Speed Achievement in Second-Semester High School Shorthand," doctoral dissertation, University of North Dakota, Grand Forks, 1970.

73. Sue Soellers, "The Effect of Preview Words on Errors in Shorthand Outlines and Transcription in Intermediate Shorthand," doctoral dissertation, University of New Mexico, Albuquerque, 1973.

74. Margaret A. McKenna, "A Study to Determine the Effect of the Early Introduction of New-Matter Dictation in the Teaching of Beginning Shorthand to College Students," doctoral dissertation, Michigan State University, East Lansing, 1965.

75. Bobbye Sorrels Pershing, "A Classroom Investigation of When to Begin New-Matter Dictation in Gregg Shorthand," doctoral dissertation, University of Oklahoma, Norman, 1966.

76. Jack Stanley Baird, "The Effectiveness of Introducing Regular Dictation of Unpracticed Material Before the Completion of Gregg Shorthand Theory," doctoral dissertation, Oregon State University, Corvallis, 1967.

77. William C. Ward, Jr., "An Investigation Indicating the Effect of Early Use of New-Matter Dictation on the Achievement of First-Year Shorthand Students," master's thesis, University of Utah, Salt Lake City, 1966.

78. Pershing, op. cit.

79. Baird, op. cit.

80. Ward, op. cit.

81. Rose Palmer, "A Comparison Between Two Groups of Shorthand Writers," doctoral dissertation, New York University, New York, 1963.

82. Joe M. Pullis, "Effect of Varying the Duration of Shorthand Dictation," *Delta Pi Epsilon Journal,* February 1970, pp. 17–20.

83. John A. Shank, "An Experimental Study Employing Auto-Instructional Materials for Learning Gregg Shorthand," doctoral dissertation, University of Pittsburgh, Pittsburgh, PA, 1972.

84. Annell Lacy Simcoe, "An Investigation of the Effectiveness of Gregg Shorthand IPM," *Business Education World,* November–December 1975, pp. 30–31.

85. Christine Gilmore, "A Comparison of a Traditional Approach and a Programmed Approach in Developing Shorthand Skill in Inner-City Schools," doctoral dissertation, University of Minnesota, Minneapolis, 1976.

86. Mary Alice Hardy, "A Comparison of Student Achievement Using Three Selected Teaching Methodologies in Intermediate and Advanced Collegiate Shorthand," master's thesis, Brigham Young University, Provo, UT, 1974.

87. Kathleen Suzanne Stringer Sigler, "The Development and Evaluation of a Video Taped Individualized Instruction Approach to Beginning Shorthand," Nova University, Fort Lauderdale, FL, 1977.

88. Helen W. Taylor, "Development and Evaluation of Programmed Materials for Theory Presentation in Beginning Shorthand Classes," doctoral dissertation, University of Tennessee, Knoxville, 1961.

89. Oleen Marjorie Henson, "The Development, Utilization and Effectiveness of Programmed Materials in Gregg Shorthand," doctoral dissertation, Temple University, Philadelphia, PA, 1964.

90. Ronald C. DeYoung, "An Experimental Investigation of the Outcomes of Learning Gregg Shorthand With Programmed Materials on the Collegiate Level," doctoral dissertation, Northern Illinois University, DeKalb, 1970.

91. Mary Margaret O'Connell, "An Experimental Study to Determine the Effectiveness of Programmed Gregg Shorthand Materials," doctoral dissertation, University of Wisconsin, Madison, 1967.

92. Henson, op. cit.

93. Waters, op. cit.

94. Carolyn Clark, "Development and Evaluation of Programmed Materials for a Beginning Junior College Course

in Gregg Shorthand, Diamond Jubilee Series," doctoral dissertation, University of California, Los Angeles, 1967.

95. Ruth Charlotte Moyer, "An Experiment to Determine the Effectiveness and Efficiency of Using Programmed Materials to Review Punctuation in Transcription Classes," Oklahoma State University, Stillwater, 1967.

96. Wilmert E. Perkins, "The Development and Evaluation of Programmed Punctuation Materials in Secondary School Transcription Classes," doctoral dissertation, University of California, Los Angeles, 1970.

97. Brenda G. Coleman, "The Effect of a Tape-Laboratory Instructional Approach Upon Achievement in Beginning Shorthand Classes," doctoral dissertation, Michigan State University, East Lansing, 1964.

98. Elise Douglas Palmer, "Development and Evaluation of Multiple-Channel Dictation Tapes in Beginning Shorthand Classes," doctoral dissertation, University of Tennessee, Knoxville, 1963.

99. Dorothy F. Laird, "A Study to Compare the Medial and Terminal Achievement of Academic Course Seniors Taught Shorthand by the Accelerated-Speed Tape Method With That of Academic Course Seniors Taught Shorthand by the Teacher-Dictation Method," doctoral dissertation, New York University, New York, 1971.

100. Ellen L. Lensing, "An Experiment to Determine Terminal Achievement in Second-Semester Shorthand Classes Taking Dictation from the Teacher and Classes Taking Dictation from a Range of Tape Recorded Material," doctoral dissertation, University of Wisconsin, Madison, 1961.

101. Suzie Hess, "The Comparative Performance of Students in Intermediate Collegiate Shorthand Taught by Contrasting Teaching Methods," doctoral dissertation, Indiana University, Bloomington, 1969.

102. Helen Tingey, "An Analysis of Teaching Intermediate Shorthand at Brigham Young University With Taped Instruction," master's thesis, Brigham Young University, Provo, UT, 1965.

103. Ted D. Stoddard, "An Experimental Study in the Utilization of Staff and Equipment for the Teaching of Intermediate Collegiate Shorthand," doctoral dissertation, Arizona State University, Tempe, 1967.

104. Linda C. Brent, "A Study to Determine the Effect of Early Introduction of Typewritten Transcription on Achievement in Beginning Shorthand," master's thesis, Northern Illinois University, DeKalb, 1970.

105. Donald F. Hampton, "The Effect on Achievement in First-Year Shorthand of Introducing Typewritten Transcription

Practice at Various Times During the Year," doctoral dissertation, Northern Illinois University, DeKalb, 1971.

106. John Frederick Keller, "Immediate Introduction to Typewritten Transcription Versus Deferred Introduction to Typewritten Transcription in First-Year Shorthand Classes," doctoral dissertation, University of North Dakota, Grand Forks, 1973.

107. Sister Mary Ivan Barras, "Transcription Achievement of Fourth-Semester Shorthand Students in Selected Catholic High Schools in the Midwest," master's thesis, University of Wisconsin, Madison, 1961.

108. Elizabeth Iannizzi, "Shorthand and Transcription Errors Among Elementary and Advanced High School Writers of Simplified and Diamond Jubilee Gregg Shorthand," doctoral dissertation, New York University, New York, 1967.

109. Alden Talbot, "An Evaluation of Vocational Shorthand Competency Attained in Utah High Schools," master's thesis, Utah State University, Logan, 1968.

110. Inez Frink, "A Comprehensive Analysis and Synthesis of Research Findings and Thought Pertaining to Shorthand and Transcription, 1946–1957," doctoral dissertation, Indiana University, Bloomington, 1961.

111. Barbara Fisher Kimbrel, "Equivalencies of Shorthand Takes of Differing Speeds, Durations, and Transcription Levels," doctoral dissertation, University of Florida, Gainesville, 1973.

112. Arnola Colson Bose, "An Experiment to Determine the Effects of Immediate Versus Delayed Knowledge of Results on Initial Learning and Retention of Selected Related Learnings in Transcription Classes," doctoral dissertation, Oklahoma State University, Stillwater, 1966.

113. Gertrude M. McGuire, "Pacing Transcription With Shorthand Skills: The Effect on Speed and Accuracy," doctoral dissertation, University of Tennessee, Knoxville, 1970.

114. Annice Mauldin Haney, "The Effect of Selected Shorthand Transcription Drills Upon Transcription Skill Development," doctoral dissertation, North Texas State University, Denton, 1976.

115. Donald D. Jester, "A Time Study of the Shorthand Transcription Process," doctoral dissertation, Northwestern University, Evanston, IL, 1959.

116. Jack E. Johnson, "The Effect of Beginning Shorthand on Learning in Selected Language Arts Skills," doctoral dissertation, University of North Dakota, Grand Forks, 1975.

117. Hazel Rose Bolan, "The Application of Knowledge of Se-

lected Grammatical and English Composition Factors in the Transcription of Shorthand Dictation," doctoral dissertation, Indiana University, Bloomington, 1967.

118. Frances A. Anderson, "Analysis of Spelling Errors in Transcripts in Advanced Shorthand Classes," master's thesis, Mankato State University, Mankato, MN, 1961.

119. Barbara Jeanne Vought, "A Study of Transcription Errors Made on Different Transcription Activities by Shorthand I and II Students of Peotone High School," master's thesis, Northern Illinois University, DeKalb, 1968.

120. Dorothy Swanson, "A Study of Nonshorthand Transcription Errors Made on Letters Transcribed by a Shorthand II Class at Moline Senior High School," master's thesis, Northern Illinois University, DeKalb, 1970.

121. Nancy Dupree, "The Effect of the Number of Punctuation Rules and Usages on Transcription Time and Punctuation Accuracy," master's thesis, University of Tennessee, Knoxville, 1968.

122. Sherry Barnes Spann, "A Study of the Relationship Between Selected Prognostic Factors and Achievement in First-Year Shorthand at the University Level," master's thesis, University of Tennessee, Knoxville, 1966.

123. Leonard J. Varah, "Effect of Academic Motivation and Other Selected Criteria on Achievement of First- and Second-Semester Shorthand Students," doctoral dissertation, Michigan State University, East Lansing, 1968.

124. Mary Wilkes Durso, "The Relationship of Receptive and Expressive Functions to Performance in Beginning Collegiate Shorthand," doctoral dissertation, Georgia State University, Atlanta, 1973.

125. Edward E. Byers, "Construction of Tests Predictive of Success in First-Year Shorthand," doctoral dissertation, Boston University, Boston, MA, 1958.

126. Kenneth W. Utley, "The Effect of Background Factors on Achievement in Second-Year Shorthand at Selected Universities," doctoral dissertation, Ohio State University, Columbus, 1970.

127. L. Michael Moskovis, "An Identification of Certain Similarities and Differences Between Successful and Unsuccessful College-Level Beginning Shorthand Students and Transcription Students," doctoral dissertation, Michigan State University, East Lansing, 1967.

128. Walter Pauk, "What's the Best Way to Predict Success in Shorthand?" *Business Education World,* April 1963, pp. 7–8, 33–34.

129. Mary Margaret O'Connell and Russell J. Hosler, "Predictors

of Success in Shorthand," *Journal of Business Education,* December 1968, pp. 96–98.

130. Evelyn June Rittenhouse, "A Study of Certain Factors Influencing Success in the Learning and Achievement of Shorthand," doctoral dissertation, Michigan State University, East Lansing, 1968.

131. Judith Johnson Lambrecht, "The Validation of a Revised Edition of the Byers First Year Shorthand Aptitude Tests," doctoral dissertation, University of Wisconsin, Madison, 1971.

132. James Lee Handorf and Aubrey Eugene Holderness, "Development of a Formula for Predicting Success in First-Year and Second-Year Shorthand," doctoral dissertation, University of Northern Colorado, Greeley, 1972.

133. Lorrine Barbara Skaff, "The Development and Validation of a Predictive Instrument to Measure Student Success in the First Semester of Gregg Shorthand," doctoral dissertation, Oregon State University, Corvallis, 1972.

134. Marguerite Patricia Mays Shane, "The Relationship of Personal Background Factors to Achievement in Beginning Shorthand in Urban High Schools in Missouri," doctoral dissertation, University of Nebraska, Lincoln, 1978.

135. Florence Nennick, "A Predictor Index for Use in Elementary Shorthand," doctoral dissertation, Temple University, Philadelphia, PA, 1974.

136. Cheryl Peat Hammers, "Predicting Success In Individualized and Traditional Beginning Shorthand Courses," doctoral dissertation, Texas Tech University, Lubbock, 1977.

137. Allen Ralph Ellington, "The Cloze Procedure and Selected Measures as a Means of Predicting Success in First-Year Shorthand," doctoral dissertation, University of Georgia, Athens, 1972.

138. Helen Elizabeth Foster, "A Study of Factors for Predicting Success in Beginning Gregg Shorthand," doctoral dissertation Northern Illinois University, DeKalb, 1977.

139. Marjorie Bell, "The Relationship of Knowledge of Phonics and Success in Beginning Shorthand," doctoral dissertation, University of Georgia, Athens, 1971.

140. Leland D. Skabo, "An Analytical Study to Determine the Relationship Between the Time Utilized for Selected Classroom Activities and Achievement in Shorthand Theory," doctoral dissertation, University of North Dakota, Grand Forks, 1968.

141. Linda Rees, "Comparative Shorthand Achievement of Students Attending Classes 5, 4, and 3 Days a Week," master's thesis, Brigham Young University, Provo, UT, 1969.

142. Mary Frances Hanrahan, "An Experimental Study Comparing Shorthand Achievement of Students Attending Class Three and Four Days a Week in Beginning and Intermediate Gregg Shorthand at the Collegiate Level," doctoral dissertation, Northern Illinois University, DeKalb, 1973.

INDEX

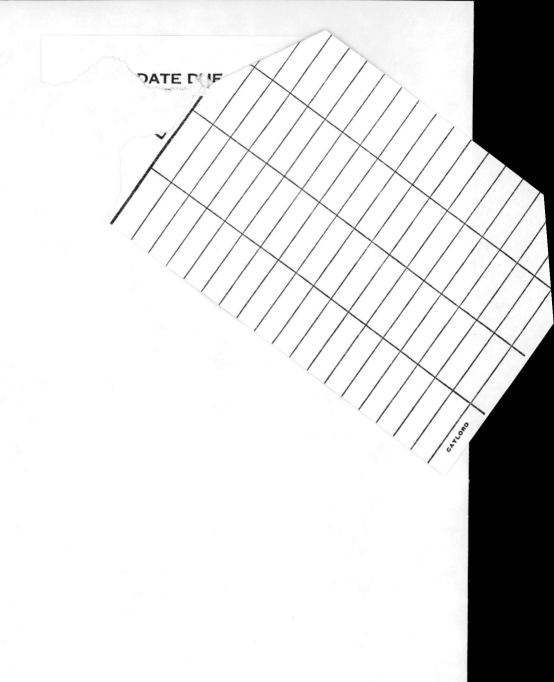

DATE DUE

GAYLORD